THE WINDFALL BATTLESHIPS

THE WINDFALL BATTLESHIPS

Agincourt, Canada, Erin, Eagle

and the Balkan & Latin-American Arms Races

AIDAN DODSON

PUBLISHING

To the memory of Dr Richard Osborne (1948–2021)

Frontispiece: View from the forecastle of *Almirante Latorre*, after her 1929–31 modernisation. *(Author's collection)*

Copyright © Aidan Dodson 2023
First published in Great Britain in 2023 by
Seaforth Publishing,
A division of Pen & Sword Books Ltd,
George House, Beevor Street, Barnsley S71 1HN

www.seaforthpublishing.com

British Library Cataloguing in Publication Data

A catalogue record for this book is available from the British Library

ISBN 978 1 3990 6322 7 (HARDBACK)
ISBN 978 1 3990 6324 1 (EPUB)
ISBN 978 1 3990 6325 8 (KINDLE)

All rights reserved. No part of this publication may be reproduced or transmitted in any form or by any means, electronic or mechanical, including photocopying, recording, or any information storage and retrieval system, without prior permission in writing of both the copyright owner and the above publisher.

The right of Aidan Dodson to be identified as the author of this work has been asserted by him in accordance with the Copyright, Designs and Patents Act 1988.

Pen & Sword Books Limited incorporates the imprints of After the Battle, Atlas, Archaeology, Aviation, Discovery, Family History, Fiction, History, Maritime, Military, Military Classics, Politics, Select, Transport, True Crime, Air World, Frontline Publishing, Leo Cooper, Remember When, Seaforth Publishing, The Praetorian Press, Wharncliffe Local History, Wharncliffe Transport, Wharncliffe True Crime and White Owl

Typeset in Caslon 11 on 13 and designed by Ian Hughes, www.mousematdesign.com

Printed and bound in Great Britain by CPI Group (UK) Ltd, Croydon, CR0 4YY

Contents

Preface   6
Introduction   8
Abbreviations and Conventions   10

1 August 1914 and Beyond   12
2 The Latin-American Connection   49
3 The Balkan Connection   96
4 With the Grand Fleet   142
5 Alternative Service: *Erin*, *Canada* and *Agincourt*   183
6 Alternative Service: *Eagle*   191
7 Ends and New Beginnings   213
8 The Ageing Queens of Latin America   229
9 Retrospect   255

Appendices: *Warships Under Construction for Foreign Customers*
   in August 1914   260
Notes   274
Bibliography   280
Index   283

Preface

THE GENESIS OF THIS BOOK CAME FROM my interest in the often-neglected ultimate fates of major warships. I was intrigued by references in the 'standard works' to HMS *Agincourt*'s alleged 'recommissioning for experimental purposes' in 1921 (glossed – as it turned out wholly inaccurately – in Richard Hough's seminal 1966 biography of the ship [see below], as 'like some offering to the vivisectionists').[1] There was also an allegation (again by Hough) that she had been 'brought back to Armstrongs where she was to be modernised by conversion to oil fuel only and the addition of much more protection [in order to] . . . make her a more saleable proposition . . . But no one was interested [and] the renovations were halted.'[2] In addition, Hough stated that, having been sold to the breakers, she had been 'taken into drydock towards the end of 1924, cut into halves, broken up after leaving dry dock'.[3] There were also a number references in various sources to her being earmarked for conversion to a 'mobile fleet base depot ship'.

The publication of David Murfin's article on the mobile fleet base project in the 2020 issue of the journal *Warship*[4] spurred me on to look further into the last years of the ship. Delvings into the archives yielded a proper timeline for the ship's last years, and a set of photographs and notes that documented her scrapping and verified her bisecting, albeit at a much later stage than implied in the published sources.

This led me back to looking into *Agincourt*'s earlier career, starting with Hough's aforementioned book, *The Big Battleship*.[5] This gives a still-good-in-parts overview of a chequered history that began with the initial ordering in the UK by Brazil, various changes of plan (with multiple keel-layings), sale to Turkey, and requisition by the Royal Navy in August 1914. However, Hough's book was published before access to many archival items was possible and thus has many problems as to detail – especially as regards the latter part of her career – and displays questionable attitudes towards non-British actors. Many of the issues surrounding her origins were resolved in a magisterial 1988 article by David Topliss in *Warship International*,[6] which covered the pre-Royal Navy history of not only *Agincourt*, but also the genesis of other battleships ordered by Brazil between 1906 and 1914. But *Agincourt*'s British service was still sketchy in the 'standard works', including the actual dates of the various modifications (particularly to her rig) that she underwent during the First World War.

All this came to engender a wider interest in the South-American dreadnought race leading up to 1914, which saw battleships ordered not only in the UK but also in the USA. These soon came to be coveted by Mediterranean naval powers desperate to bolster their battle fleets in the face of rivals, and the subjects of numerous attempts at purchase. Of these attempts, only one was successful, when the *Agincourt*-to-be was acquired by Turkey. She was intended to join a ship directly ordered in the UK a few years earlier. Both battleships were requisitioned in 1914, with two ships building for Chile also to be acquired by the British during the First World War. Yet another Turkish battleship still on the stocks would, however, come to be abandoned.

Since the full stories of these ships remain untold – with published accounts riddled with errors and misunderstandings, including the creation of non-existent ships – the present book aims to provide a comprehensive coverage of the careers of not only HMS *Agincourt*, but also HM Ships *Erin* and *Canada*, respectively commenced for Turkey and Chile. It will also outline the early career of HMS *Eagle*, begun as a battleship for Chile (a sister of *Canada*), but completed as a pioneering aircraft carrier that would serve the Royal Navy until sunk in 1942. A further aim is to place those histories within the contexts of the political and military rivalries of South America and the Balkans. It was these that both created the ships and influenced their careers. Furthermore, it provides more summary accounts of the careers of other ships built as parts of the same programmes. Some would go on to have long operational careers, while others were stillborn or died an early death as a consequence of the First World War.

In doing so, I have attempted to consult not only published sources, but also all key available archival materials in the UK, although it has not been possible to extend the latter aspect abroad. As a result, my thanks are owed to many people and institutions for information and access to material, including Ian Buxton (University of Newcastle), Andrew Choong Han Lin (National Maritime Museum), Selina Kendall (Cumbria Archive Service), Dirk Nottelmann, Sergey Trubitcyn, and the staffs of the Rare Books Room of Cambridge University Library, the Tyne & Wear Archives Service and the UK National Archives.

I am also very grateful to John Jordan and Ian Sturton for permission to use their excellent drawings, whose styles I have followed in my own to ensure a coherent 'look and feel'. Finally, I am indebted to Victoria Baylis-Jones, Andrew Choong Han Lin, Vanessa Foott, Anne and Dyan Hilton for proof-reading, and materially improving, the manuscript.

Introduction

THE BATTLESHIPS *AGINCOURT*, *ERIN* AND *CANADA* were all 'ones of a kind' in the Royal Navy's First World War Grand Fleet. Although all were built to designs by Josiah Perrett, Chief Naval Architect of the British Armstrong combine, and constructed either by their parent's shipyards or that of their rivals-cum-collaborators Vickers, each had been ordered by a foreign power, their acquisition by the Royal Navy due simply to their still being in the hands of their builders when the UK found itself faced with war in the summer of 1914. As such, they could be seen as 'windfalls' or 'gift horses' – useful additions to the navy, but not perhaps quite what their new owners would have ideally wanted when looked at in any detail.

All three were manifestations of the international rivalries which, although not on the scale of the so-called Anglo-German 'race' that followed the German Fleet Laws of 1898, directed much of the national budgets of impecunious South-American and Balkan states towards armaments, and in particular warships. Costs were exacerbated by the re-setting of battleship technology at the launch of HMS *Dreadnought* in 1906, and the further escalation of ship size, gun calibres and numbers over the following few short years. Thus, no sooner had a ship been ordered, a rival might order something 'better', requiring much heart (and purse) searching as to the best means of reaction. This situation is beautifully illustrated by the Brazilian battleship *Rio de Janeiro*, laid down no fewer than three times to ever-larger and more heavily-armed designs, before being sold incomplete to allow a completely new ship, with even bigger guns, to be built instead. Only the outbreak of the First World War broke this beggar-my-neighbour cycle of escalations.

Comparison of ships built for national service by a major naval power on one hand, and by its local yards for export on the other, is always instructive. The Royal Navy's Directorate of Naval Construction, and its predecessors and successors, was always faced with criticisms that its products had less 'bang for buck' than vessels built in the very same shipyards for foreign customers to private designs. But all warship design is a compromise between competing characteristics: superior performance in one area almost inevitably means a diminution in another. So, while *Agincourt* and *Canada* were faster than their Admiralty-designed contemporaries, they had thinner armour throughout (although better underwater protection than some, and *Agincourt*'s turret faceplates were the thickest in the fleet when commissioned). *Erin* seemed to combine all the offensive features of her British-specified contemporaries (indeed, with a superior secondary battery), on a much smaller displacement. But she was much more cramped internally, and difficult to dock owing to her great beam.

All these themes will be explored in this book, starting with the three ships acquired at the beginning of the First World War and the steps required to fit them for service with the Grand Fleet. The chapter will also provide an overview of other ships being built to foreign accounts at the outbreak of war: not just in the UK, but elsewhere as well. We will then step back in time to look at their backgrounds, including the ways in which their parent navies grew (or were planned to grow) during the opening years of the twentieth century – resulting in other 'windfalls' for the combatant navies of the First World War.

Focus will then switch back to the British service of *Agincourt*, *Erin* and *Canada*, taking them through their time with the Grand Fleet until the latter's dissolution in 1919. The divergent fates of the three ships will then be followed until the return of *Canada* to her original Chilean owners in 1920, and the disposal of *Agincourt* and *Erin* for scrap in the wake of the 1922 Washington Naval Treaty, which set to naught plans that might have given one or both of them additional leases of life. In parallel we will trace the story of *Canada*'s sister ship which, never finished as a battleship, played a crucial role in the development of British carrier aviation, and would have a long and distinguished career as HMS *Eagle*.

Even longer were the careers of the former *Canada* and the pairs of battleships actually completed for Brazil and Argentina, which will next be followed down to their final disposal during the 1950s. While never used in direct international conflict, many of them played a role in the social and political upheavals of their own nations. When sold for breaking-up in 1959, the former *Canada* was the penultimate vessel left to have fought at the Battle of Jutland – leaving just the cruiser HMS *Caroline*, now preserved as a museum. The stories and back-stories of *Agincourt*, *Erin*, *Canada* and *Eagle* thus embrace almost the whole of the twentieth-century battleship era, and take us down little-explored byways of international naval power, ranging from the Pacific to the Black Sea, and from the line of battle to mutiny and revolution.

Abbreviations and Conventions

Abbreviations

(2F)	Squadron Second Flagship (in tables)
A-H	Austria-Hungary (in tables & Index)
ARA	Armada de la República Argentina (prefix of Argentine naval ship names)
ARG	Argentina (in tables & Index)
AUS	Australia
BB	battleship (in tables & Index)
BCF	Battle Cruiser Force/Fleet
BCS	Battle Cruiser Squadron
BRA	Brazil (in tables & Index)
BS	Battle Squadron
BU	broken up
BUL	Bulgaria (in tables & Index)
CAN	Canada (in tables & Index)
CDS	coast defence ship (in tables & Index)
CHL	Chile (in tables & Index)
CHN	China (in tables & Index)
CL	light cruiser (in tables & Index)
CS	Cruiser Squadron
CUL	Cambridge University Library (in image credits)
DD	destroyer (in tables & Index)
DF	Destroyer Flotilla
DNC	Director of Naval Construction
EOC	Elswick Ordnance Company
(F)	Squadron Flagship (in tables)
FRA	France (in tables & Index)
GRC	Greece (in tables & Index)
HMS	His/Her Majesty's Ship (prefix of British naval ship names)
ITA	Italy (in tables & Index)
IWM	Imperial War Museum (in image credits)
JPN	Japan (in tables & Index)
LCS	Light Cruiser Squadron
LoC	US Library of Congress (in image credits)
MEX	Mex (in tables & Index)
NARA	US National Record & Archives Administration (in image credits)

NHHC	Naval History & Heritage Command (in image credits)
NLD	Netherlands (in tables & Index)
NMM	National Maritime Museum (in image credits)
NOR	Norway (in tables & Index)
NZ	New Zealand (in tables & Index)
PER	Peru (in tables & Index)
POL	Poland (in tables & Index)
PRT	Portugal (in tables & Index)
ROM	Romania (in tables & Index)
RUS	Russia (in tables & Index)
SMS	Seiner Majestät Schiff (prefix of German and Austro-Hungarian naval ship names)
SPA	Spain (in tables & Index)
SS	submarine (in tables & Index)
T&WA	Tyne and Wear Archives
TNA	United Kingdom National Archives
TUR	Turkey (in tables & Index)
USNA	United States National Archives
USS	United States Ship (prefix of US naval ship names)
VTE	Vertical Triple Expansion

Unless otherwise stated, years in parentheses denote a ship's launch; 'nl' indicates that the ship was never launched.

In quotations from archival documents, original spellings and typography have been retained.

In 1914, the Pound Sterling (£) was worth the equivalent of £137 at 2022 prices.

A number of drawings used in this book were kindly provided by Ian Sturton and John Jordan. The author has produced further drawings by adapting some of these, and also original drawings imitating the styles of these. Authorship of individual images is indicated on the drawings themselves as follows:

IAS	Ian Sturton
IAS/AMD	Adaptation of Ian Sturton drawing by the author
JJ	John Jordan
JJ/AMD	Adaptation of John Jordan drawing by the author
AMD	Original drawing by the author

CHAPTER 1

August 1914 and Beyond

IN THE SUMMER OF 1914 BRITISH shipyards had in hand, as well as myriad vessels for the Royal Navy, a healthy order book of ships for foreign navies. At J Samuel White's yard at Cowes, Isle of Wight, were four large destroyers for Chile. On the Clyde, John Brown at Clydebank had in hand two destroyers for Greece, with two more building for the same customer at the Fairfield yard at Govan. Beardmore at Dalmuir had orders for two submarines for Turkey (subcontracted from Vickers), and Yarrow at Scotstoun had two destroyers for Japan. Cammell Laird at Birkenhead were building two light cruisers for Greece. For Turkey, Sir W G Armstrong, Whitworth & Co on the Tyne were gathering material for two scout cruisers, and had sub-contracted four destroyers to Hawthorn Leslie on the same river. Armstrong also had a pair of coast defence vessels under construction for Norway, and at Vickers Ltd's Barrow yard were three river monitors, originally ordered by Brazil, but now up for sale. But much more significant were the four dreadnought battleships being built by Armstrong, and two more of the type being built by Vickers (who were also building a floating dock for Turkey).

Armstrong and Vickers had been at the vanguard of warship exports from the UK for many years, although Armstrong had produced three times the tonnage of her west-coast rival.[1] This was principally because Armstrong had begun its international shipbuilding business two decades before Vickers. Armstrong had been producing medium and heavy guns since 1859, when the Elswick Ordnance Company (EOC) had been established at the eponymous site on the north bank of the Tyne, and had begun to build ships in 1868 through an amalgamation with the Charles Mitchell's yard at Low Walker. During 1882–5, the Elswick complex was expanded to include a shipyard. The first ships built there were a continuation of a pioneering series of company-designed deck-protected cruisers, begun with the construction at Low Walker of the Chilean *Esmeralda* (i – see p 51) during 1881–4, but henceforth known as 'Elswick cruisers'. Intended for export, nearly thirty were built for navies around the world down to the beginning of the twentieth century (alongside a handful of Admiralty-designed vessels built under contract for the Royal Navy).

Battleships were added to the yard's repertoire with the laying-down of HMS *Victoria* in 1885, four export battleships (three for Japan, one for Chile) being laid down between 1894 and 1902. Armstrong products were usually both built and armed by the company's divisions (guns by EOC), although the combine did not include boiler-making and engine-building facilities, which were subcontracted to specialist firms on the Tyne and elsewhere.

Vickers were originally a steelmaker, expanding into the manufacture of armour plate, and into medium ordnance in 1888.[2] They entered the shipbuilding business in 1897 by buying the Naval Construction & Armaments Co yard at Barrow-in-Furness, in which they invested heavily. This included an expansion of the Vickers gun and gun-mounting manufacturing capabilities, and by the following year Vickers, Sons & Maxim were able to lay down two battleships, for one of which (HMS *Vengeance*) they were able to supply all metal, guns and machinery. The other ship, the Japanese *Mikasa*, was armed by the EOC, as required by the customer, who already had a large arsenal of Armstrong weapons. Vickers' capabilities were further enhanced in 1900 by the purchase of the rights to the Holland-type submarine. The concern was renamed simply Vickers Ltd in 1911.

Both Armstrong and Vickers (as well as the other major yards) had extensive design departments, and were able to produce both 'stock' designs (some of which, for smaller cruisers and torpedo craft, might actually be laid down on speculation for 'spot' sales – especially in South America: cf p 53), and those to meet the specific requirements of customers. The latter could result in the drafting of reams of designs to provide options or to address an iterative bidding process: a number of examples are given in this book. At the beginning of the twentieth century, Armstrong and Vickers had an advantage over their competitors for export orders in having a duopoly in the manufacture of heavy guns and mountings, meaning that they could effectively shut out other firms by quoting very high prices for these items. To short-circuit this, in 1905, John Brown, Cammell Laird and Fairfield jointly founded the Coventry Ordnance Works to provide a 'third force' for the provision of heavy and medium guns.

Armstrong and Vickers rapidly recognised that a degree of co-operation was more sensible than constant direct competition. A first manifestation of this was in 1902, when Chile ordered two battleships (p 54), and one was built by Armstrong and one by Vickers. Although of the same design, each yard provided guns and mountings of their own pattern (albeit able to use the same ammunition). The Armstrong ship had Humphreys & Tennant machinery, while the Vickers vessel's machinery was of in-house manufacture. The same approach was taken with the Japanese *Kashima* class battleships, laid down in 1904. Subsequently, however, such 'shared' projects had Vickers machinery and

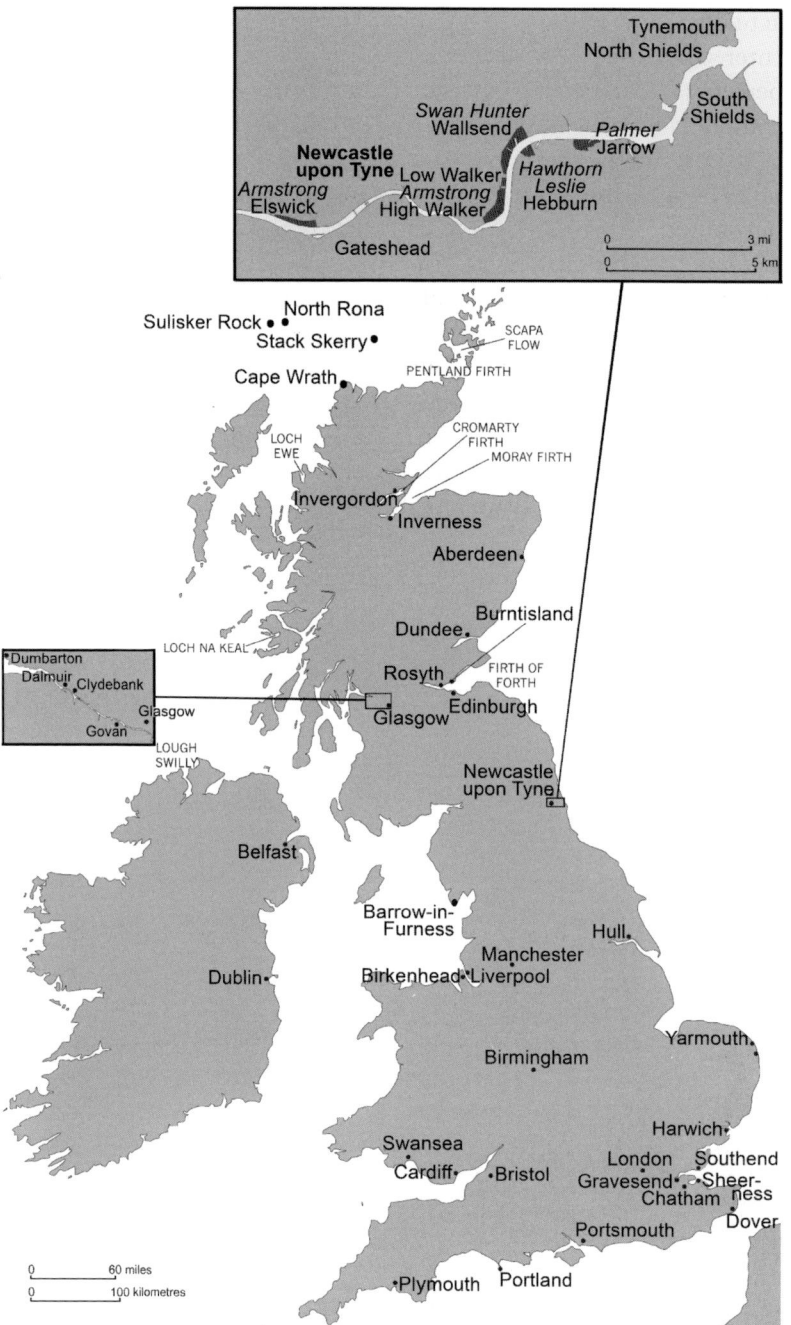

Map of the British Isles. *(Author)*

guns of one firm's design, even if a given mounting was actually built by the other. *Reşadiye* (later HMS *Erin*) is an excellent example of this, being built by Vickers to an Armstrong design, with guns and mountings of Vickers types. Yet only the after two turrets and their guns were actually made at Barrow, the other three being the work of Elswick. Inter-company agreements varied between customer, with a range of percentage transfer-payments depending on the country and components involved.[3]

The four battleships under construction on the Tyne in the summer of 1914 were the Turkish *Sultan Osman I*, originally ordered by Brazil but sold the previous year, the Chilean *Almirante Latorre* and *Almirante Cochrane*, and the Brazilian *Riachuelo*. The first two were completing afloat, *Cochrane* was a few months away from launch, and *Riachuelo* due to be laid down on 10 September. At Barrow, the Turkish *Reşadiye* was in the final stages of fitting-out: her last major component (a funnel) had been installed on 22 January 1914, and her first dock trial had run on 2 July. The keel of her sister, *Fatih Sultan Mehmed*, had been laid in June as Yard No 460, to be delivered in 36 months. As of July 1914, *Sultan Osman I* was contractually due for delivery in October, and *Reşadiye* in November.

Sultan Osman I fitting-out at High Walker in June 1914.
(The Engineer, 7 July 1914, p 67)

The Turkish Ships

Sultan Osman I

Sultan Osman I began her first sea trials on 7 July, although lacking two of her fourteen main guns, with a civilian crew and carrying a number of Ottoman technicians who had been standing by the ship during the final stages of fitting-out. These included a voyage to Devonport for docking, with her departure delayed by a short strike by her civilian stokers in a dispute over pay. She then returned north to run speed trials on the measured-mile off St Abb's Head, making 22.42kt at 40,126 shp.

The battleship then proceeded to the Forth, arriving on 18 July – just as the crisis following the assassination of Archduke Franz Ferdinand, heir to the Austro-Hungarian throne, on 28 June was moving towards the fatal Austro-Hungarian ultimatum to Serbia on 28 July. *Sultan Osman I* arrived back on the Tyne on 22 July and came alongside at Walker, being met by her prospective Captain, Hüseyin Rauf Orbay (1881–1964), who was understandably anxious to have the missing guns and gunsights installed and ammunition embarked. The main body of

Sultan Osman I on passage from the Tyne to Devonport in the second week of July 1914; note the lack of guns in '5' turret (CUL GBR/0012/MS Vickers Doc 2455)

The installation of the missing guns in '5' turret of *Sultan Osman I* on 1 August 1914. (Author's collection)

the Ottoman crew arrived aboard SS *Neshid Pasha* on the 27th, with the outstanding armament fitted on 1 August, and the ship's inclination experiment carried out. Formal handover was scheduled for 2 August, and commissioning the morning of the 3rd.

Ammunition was, however, still lacking, and on 31 July the First Lord of the Admiralty, Winston Churchill, wrote to King George V that: 'I have taken the responsibility of forbidding the departure of the Turkish battleship Osman (late Rio) with the Prime Minister's approval. If war comes she will be called - and shd Your Majesty approve - the Agincourt & will convey Sir Henry Jackson to reinforce, & at the regular date assume command, the Mediterranean.' In parallel, a letter was sent to Armstrong, requiring that they not 'permit the ship to a Foreign Power or to be commissioned as a public ship of a Foreign Government, or leave their jurisdiction'.

All this was a consequence of not only the spectre of the UK becoming involved in war, but concerns as to the likely orientation of the Ottoman government if hostilities did indeed break out. There were particular worries that *Sultan Osman* (and the other Turkish battleship, *Reşadiye*) might be taken to Germany by their Turkish crews. Accordingly, on the morning of 2 August 1914, a company of the Sherwood Foresters infantry regiment boarded *Sultan Osman I*. Those Turks already aboard were decanted to *Neshid Pasha* within the hour, for immediate repatriation alongside the rest of the crew.

As the legal formalities of acquiring the ship for the Royal Navy proceeded, the royal yacht *Victoria and Albert* (1899) was ordered on the afternoon of 3 August to pay off at Portsmouth. She was to provide the nucleus of the crew of what was now indeed becoming HMS *Agincourt* (taking the name of a newly-cancelled battleship: see p 27), including her Captain, Douglas Nicholson (for details of him and other ships' captains, see pp 180–2). An advance party from the yacht arrived on Tyneside early on the 4th, and took over their new ship from her army guardians.

A meeting that same day with yard personnel noted a number of issues. Of the guns just hurriedly installed in '5' turret, one had a flaw and one was of a different type and could only be hand-loaded; although both needed to be replaced, the ship was not to be delayed. Only two of her outfit of six 21in torpedoes were aboard, and they lacked their warheads. Also missing were two 18in torpedoes, and there was no prospect of making up this deficiency for a month. Clothing and food was being ordered, while six to seven days were needed to replace Turkish shipboard signage. Action was in hand to replace the Turkish-style 'squat' heads, with temporary arrangements for some officers' installations that could not immediately be replaced by those of a 'Western' pattern. The next day it was estimated that work would complete on 11 August, with everything to be done on the Tyne.

On 5 August, the Treasury was formally informed 'that the sum of £690,000 will be paid forthwith to Messrs Armstrong Whitworth, being the amount of advances paid by the Turkish Government to that firm in respect of the ship "Osman I," now acquired for His Majesty's Government and renamed "Agincourt"'.

Agincourt commissioned at 09:00 on 7 August 1914, with additional personnel progressively drafted from various sources, including detention

Sultan Osman I as completed. (Author's collection)

barracks. A final pre-departure modification was proposed by the Captain on the 7th: the removal of a massive (82-ton) boat-carrying flying deck over the midships turrets. This was undertaken by a floating crane on the 9th, anticipating the Admiralty agreement that was forthcoming on the 10th; the forward derrick was also removed (although it would be replaced and removed again more than once during the ship's career). A scheme was rapidly worked out to re-stow the displaced boats onto the upper deck, slightly reducing the overall numbers.

In military terms, *Agincourt* was very different from any ship currently in UK service. Designed for South American waters, her nominal endurance was double that of many contemporaries, but her coal stowage was assessed as poorly designed (cf similar remarks regarding *Reşadiye*, p 23), with bulkheads pierced on the lower deck, including by two ammunition passages. Her main guns (EOC Pattern W, taken into British service as Mk XIII) were very similar to the British Mk X, fitted in *Dreadnought* (1906), and the *Lord Nelson* (1906), *Bellerophon* (1907), *Invincible* (1907) and *Indefatigable* (1909–11) classes. She was therefore fully compatible with her new fleet-mates (although British battleships had long since shifted to the 13.5in gun, and 15in guns were now imminent). Unlike British vessels, however, *Agincourt*'s main mountings had fixed loading angles. Rather than being given conventional British letter-designations,[4] the seven turrets were simply numbered from forward to aft.[5]

Her 6in (EOC Pattern QQ[?]; UK Mk XIII) weapons were heavier than those of UK types, with a muzzle-velocity intermediate between the Mk VII (fitted in the *Iron Duke* class) and the Mk XII (*Queen Elizabeth* and *Revenge* classes). In possessing a tertiary 3in battery, *Agincourt* was unique among British dreadnoughts, such a feature having been last seen in the *King Edward VII* class (1903–4). However, such guns had continued to feature in German service. This was because German doctrine regarded secondary guns as for use against other capital ships, not flotilla craft, as was British practice: *Agincourt*'s guns (EOC Pattern ZZ1, UK designation '3in QF 23cwt Mk I') were similarly intended as anti-torpedo-boat guns.

Agincourt had two beam and one stern torpedo tubes of a 27.7ft-long Elswick 21in side-loading type, which was also fitted in *Reşadiye* and the ships building for Chile. Since they were too short to carry the standard 22.3ft British Mark II torpedo, when taken over for UK service they were given torpedoes built by Whitehead's Weymouth works for overseas customers, cut-down in length by removing a section behind the warhead. *Agincourt*'s first outfit comprised eight Mk II examples from a Japanese order, and two Turkish-ordered Mk IIIs for her stern tube.

Ships laid down for the Royal Navy at the same time as *Agincourt*, in 1911 (*King George V* class), had side protection ranging in thickness from 8in to 12in; in *Agincourt* the range was from 4in to 9in. Barbettes in the *King George V*s were 3–10in; in *Agincourt* they were 3–9in; decks were also thinner in *Agincourt*. However, *Agincourt*'s turrets had 12in faces, an inch greater than contemporary Royal Navy designs, although exceeded in new 15in-gunned ships. Below water, *Agincourt* only had armoured bulkheads abreast the magazines; in the *King George V*s, these extended to the engine (but not boiler) rooms. Indeed, *Agincourt*'s protection (see pp 173, 259) was much more akin to that of the battlecruisers *Lion*, *Princess Royal*, *Queen Mary* and *Tiger* (1910–13). The relatively light protection contributed to an extra knot of speed over the UK-standard 21kt for battleships.

On 17 August, *Agincourt* was ordered to sail as soon as possible for gunnery and torpedo trials in Loch Ewe. She was technically ready for sea on 22 August, but it took another two days to complete ammunitioning and provisioning. She finally cast off at 04:45 on the 25th, dropping the pilot and contractor's staff at 07:00 at the mouth of the Tyne. She arrived at Scapa Flow at 08:35 on the 26th, in company with a number of other ships. There, she became part of the 4th Battle Squadron, alongside *Dreadnought* (flag), *Bellerophon* and *Temeraire* (1907). She stayed in the Flow until 19:15 on the 28th, when she left for initial gunnery trials. As carried out between 08:00 and 18:00 the next day, these involved firing-off fifty-six rounds of 12in (from '1', '3', '4', '6' and '7' turrets), eighty of 6in and six of practice 3in. A number of defects were revealed. The following day was spent testing the ship's sights and swinging the compass, with the last day of August occupied with practice with the aiming rifles.

The first two days of September 1914 were spent on gunnery drills, until fog required the ship to lie stopped off North Rona from the afternoon of the 2nd until it began to lift at 07:00 the next morning. *Agincourt* anchored in Loch Ewe at 06:05 on the 4th and coaled, before undertaking further firings on the 6th. Weighing anchor at 04:36 that morning, between 11:00 and 18:35 she fired her 12in guns at Stack Skerry, with further firings by them and the ship's 6in guns between 11:00 and 13:00 on 7 September, during which the Grand Fleet hove into view. A total of seventy-four 12in and seventy-three 6in shells had been expended by the time the new battleship took up a position in the wake of her squadron-mate *Bellerophon* at 13:42.

Reşadiye

On 17 September 1914, *Agincourt* was joined in the 4th BS by HMS *Erin* – until the previous month known as the Imperial Ottoman

August 1914 and Beyond

Erin (ex-Reşadiye) on trials, before the removal of her torpedo nets between 4 and 7 September 1914. (Author's collection)

battleship *Reşadiye*. She had been taken over by the Admiralty on 31 July, to ensure that no Turkish sailors came aboard (although her crew was actually still in Turkey; they left on 4 August and were recalled on the 7th). On 5 August the results of her inclining experiment were forwarded by Vickers to the Admiralty, and on 21 August she was ordered commissioned as HMS *Erin*. Accommodation arrangements differed significantly from Royal Navy practice, and thus *Erin* required the same kinds of sanitary and related modifications undertaken in *Agincourt*. Other changes prior to commissioning included the removal of the mainmast, with searchlights removed from the foremast to the aft superstructure soon afterwards.

Her Captain, the Hon Victor Stanley (lately in charge of the Royal Naval College, Dartmouth), and crew came aboard at 08:00 on 23 August. At 08:15 the ship began to be moved through the locks out of the shipyard basin, and at 12:00 was secured outside. At 13:10, a collier came alongside and coaling commenced, which was finished at 01:10 the next day after 500 tons had been taken aboard. At 12:15 on the 24th, *Erin* proceeded to sea, starting to adjust compasses at 14:15. At 16:00, the pilot was dropped and course set for Liverpool. Engine trials took place that night, a full-power trial completing at 03:45 on the 25th. Forty-five minutes later, the Mersey pilot was picked up, and at 06:45 the battleship was anchored off Liverpool. At 12:35, the anchor was weighed and she proceeded into the Gladstone Dock, opened the previous year, for her first docking, while also preparing to embark ammunition.

Erin remained in dock until 30 August. The dock was flooded at 16:00, allowing her to exit at 17:40, and at 20:00 she secured to a buoy in the river off Birkenhead. The next day she acted as venue for a Court of Enquiry into a collision in thick fog between the newly-converted armed merchant cruiser (ex-Cunarder) *Aquitania* (1913) and the Leyland liner *Canadian* (1900) on 22 August off the Irish coast, which had crushed *Aquitania*'s stem. Over the following few days ammunition was loaded aboard *Erin*, and her 6in and 13.5in gun crews drilled at anchor.

On 3 September, it was reported that the ship's anti-torpedo nets were non-standard, difficult to unship, and that two booms had already been damaged by lighters alongside. Furthermore, having replaced them, Vickers only had one spare left. Since nets were not being fitted to new construction, the First Sea Lord was asked to approve their removal on the 4th. Nets had been deleted by the time she slipped her mooring at 08:30 on the 7th and undertook torpedo, gun trials and machinery trials in the Mersey estuary. Various issues were identified, including some design defects, and problems with 'Q' turret prevented its planned firings from being completed. The ship temporarily anchored at the mouth of the Mersey, before returning upriver at 01:00 on the morning of the 8th. Between 03:00 and 15:00 she lay anchored off New Brighton, but at 19:10 she was at sea, heading for Loch Ewe and gunnery trials.

At 12:22 on 10 September, *Erin* anchored in Loch Ewe, and the next day was occupied by the drilling of gun, magazine, shell-room and submerged tubes' crews. At 09:30 on the 12th, she headed to sea for fire-control and rangefinding exercises using a trawler as target; at 15:27 she anchored back in the loch. In the late afternoon of the 13th, the 1st, 2nd and 4th BS (including *Agincourt*) arrived, and *Erin* was visited by Admiral Jellicoe. The next morning, the battleship was back at sea for subcalibre firings,[6] and then, after a short stop back in the loch, undertook overnight gun and searchlight drills, anchoring back at 07:56 on the 15th. The fleet remained at Loch Ewe until the 17th. At 16:00, Winston Churchill and Jellicoe came to visit, and at 17:20 *Erin* weighed anchor with the rest of the fleet and put to sea, now part of the 4th BS, and the 2nd Div, of the Grand Fleet.[7]

Erin had much in common with British 13.5in ships, although 7 per cent shorter than the *King George V*s, and 3.3 per cent wider on the same tonnage; her greater beam prevented the ship from being docked at Devonport, Malta or Gibraltar (Chatham could not take any dreadnought). Her Vickers Mk A 45-calibre guns (UK Mk VI) had marginally less muzzle velocity than the standard Royal Navy Mk V weapon. As originally planned, the guns would also have been of a different external shape from the Mk V weapon, but having requested an Admiralty evaluation of the latter, the Turks had requested that the Mk A conform to the Mk V's external form. In the event this aided bringing *Erin* speedily into British service, as it allowed Mk Vs to be substituted for two missing guns, although they had to use non-standard charges to match the muzzle velocity of the original guns.

The presence of a 6in secondary battery was a key way in which *Erin* differed from the contemporary *King George V*, which had 4in only. A heavier secondary outfit had only been instituted in the *Iron Duke* class. As compared with the latter, *Erin* benefitted from the fact that her forecastle deck was carried all the way to 'X' barbette, meaning that the 6in battery was sited much further aft than in the short-forecastle *Iron Duke*s. It was therefore considerably dryer than in the *Iron Duke*s (and also in the later *Queen Elizabeth*s).

The secondary guns were Vickers Mk O (UK Mk XVI), very similar to the Mk VII, but with a higher muzzle velocity: indeed, they had the highest m/v of any gun in Royal Navy service using anything other than a supercharge. *Erin* had the same Elswick type of torpedo tubes as *Agincourt*, and received ten shortened ex-Japanese Weymouth Mk IIs.

She was much more akin to British battleship practice than *Agincourt* in protection (see pp 173, 259), although with a number of shortfalls. These included a relatively shallow main belt, thinner barbette and battery armour, all 6in shells and some of their propellant stowed directly below the middle deck, and poorer subdivision. A particular concern (shared with *Agincourt*) was the presence of ammunition passages extending the length of the machinery spaces. On the plus side, unlike the *King George V*s and the *Iron Duke*s, she had an armoured bulkhead abreast the whole of the citadel below the waterline. Fuel stowage was, however, only two-thirds that of her British contemporaries, and difficult to access. As CinC Grand Fleet remarked to DNC:

> The Erin is I fear going to be a trouble to me. She only has 1000 tons of coal that is available for steaming. The rest is athwart Engine Rooms & can't be trimmed forward for real steaming. The nominal 2000 tons is a fraud. I am telling her to use oil whenever possible to help the coal out.[8]

The Ottoman reaction and the fate of the 1914 Turkish programme
The Turkish response to the takeover of the two battleships was distinctly negative, although all monies paid were to be reimbursed by the British government, and on 9 August 1914 the Ottoman Grand Vizier agreed to sell the ships. However, the arrival of the German battlecruiser *Goeben* and light cruiser *Breslau* (both 1911) in Turkish

waters on the 10th, and the Turkish refusal to enforce their neutrality by interning the ships and their crews, led to a negative shift in the British position. The situation was now judged such that it would be politically impossible to pay any lump sum to the Ottoman government for the duration of the war. Furthermore, when £113,000-worth of Ottoman Treasury Bills issued to fund *Reşadiye* (see p 112) became due for payment on 14 September, the Turks refused to pay. They also threatened to suspend payments against the battleship, cruisers, destroyers and submarines ordered in April 1914 (p 118) if guarantees of non-requisition were not given. Although the British government finally gave such assurances in late October, a week later the UK was at war with Turkey.

It has often been stated that the requisitioning of the battleships was a key factor in Turkey allying with Germany at the beginning of November 1914, but the Ottoman War Minister, Enver Pasha (1881–1922), had already offered an alliance with Germany a week prior to the takeovers. However, the loss of the battleships certainly undermined the positions of pro-British elements in Turkey. It provided a lever for the Germans, which they employed by transferring *Goeben* and *Breslau* on their arrival in Turkish waters as 'replacements' for *Sultan Osman I* and *Reşadiye*. This 'transfer', complete with officers and men, placed the Ottoman navy under German command, and led directly to the Turco-German bombardment of Russian ports on 28 October, and provoked Allied declarations of war early in November.

In the Turkish public reaction to the takeovers, much was made of the notion that *Reşadiye* (in particular) had been paid for by public subscription, making the 'seizure' a particularly heinous act. However, the actual situation was rather different. Donations from private individuals in support of the navy had, since July 1909, been funnelled through the Ottoman Navy League (Donanma Cemiyeti). This had been set up in the wake of the 1908 revolution to promote the improvement of the navy, both through membership fees and one-off donations. Membership came both from within the Ottoman Empire and the wider Islamic world.

In reality, only a tiny proportion of the purchase price of *Reşadiye* (and still less *Sultan Osman I*) had come from such gifts.[9] Indeed, of the £1.8 million price of *Reşadiye*, all payments made to Vickers and her partners in the supply of the ship had come from bonds and international loans (cf p 112, below) – and these had added up to only 36 per cent of the price at the point at which the Admiralty had acquired the two battleships. On 30 August 1915, £6957 9s 5d (£6957.47) was paid to British bondholders affected by the takeover of the two Turkish battleships.[10]

Comparison between the Turkish scouts and the *Centaur* class light cruisers that were built on the slips vacated by them. The Turkish vessels were essentially modernised versions of the 1903-launched *Hamidiye* (p 102), a vessel very well-regarded by the Ottoman navy, while the British pair were the latest iteration of the series of vessels begun with the *Arethusa* class in 1912. *(Author)*

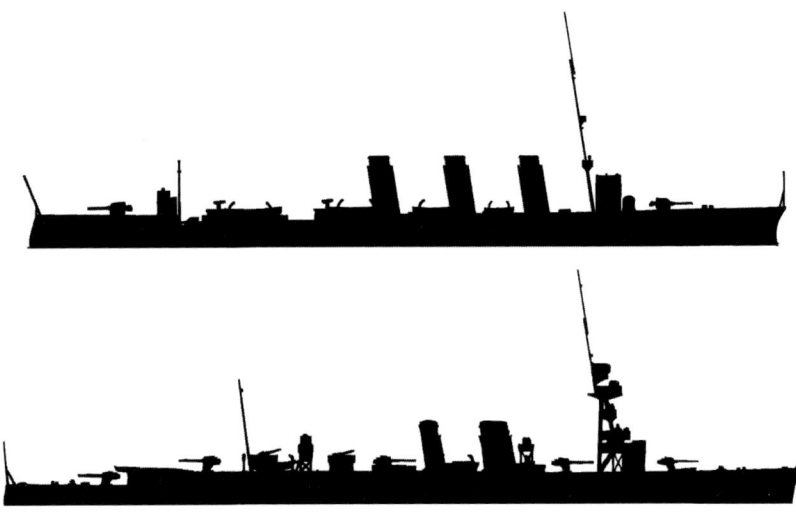

	Turkish ships	*Centaur* class
Displacement:	3550 tons	3828 tons
Length:	400ft (pp), 423ft (oa)	420ft (pp), 446.5ft (oa)
Beam:	41ft	41ft
Draught:	13.5ft	13.5ft
Boilers:	Eleven Yarrow (coal/oil)	Six Yarrow (oil)
Bunkerage:	700 tons coal 250 tons oil	823 tons oil
Turbines:	Three-shaft Parsons	Four-shaft Parsons
Power:	24,000 shp	28,000 shp
Speed:	27kt	28kt
Main belt:	–	1.5–3–2in
Armour deck:	1.25in (flats) 2.5in (slopes)	–
Conning tower:	6in	3in
Armament:	Two 6in/50 Six 4in/50 Four 3pdr Two 3in AA Two 21in TT (deck)	Five 6in/45 Two 3pdr Two 21in TT (submerged)

The other Turkish vessels

Although the battleships had been taken over, and the Turkish acceptance commission in the UK withdrawn in protest (which the British contractors informed the Turks would delay the delivery of other vessels by six weeks), there was still hope that the other ships on order for the Ottoman navy might yet be delivered. Indeed, as noted above, the British government had been prepared to guarantee that no more Turkish ships would be taken over for British service. The UK firms involved were especially concerned at the capital they had already tied up in the work in question, that not yet been paid for by the customer.

Accordingly, as soon as war broke out between the UK and Turkey on 5 November 1914, Vickers enquired whether the Admiralty might wish to take over the whole Ottoman programme, comprising *Fatih*, the two scout cruisers, four destroyers, two submarines and the floating dock. The Admiralty response was that it very much depended on delivery schedules, which included 21 months for *Fatih* and October 1915 for the submarines.

In the end, the Admiralty decided not to take over the order for the battleship, such material as had yet been erected on the slip (valued at £21,000, plus £13,200 put into the machinery) being cleared away around the end of 1914.[11] The £0.7 million that had been paid by the customer towards her construction (and the rest of the April 1914 package) had been repaid to the Turks on 1 August.

The barely-begun Turkish scout cruisers were also not proceeded with, although some of the material being gathered for them was reassigned to the new light cruisers of the *Centaur* class ordered by the Admiralty soon after the outbreak of war. However, while built on the slips allocated to the Turkish vessels, the two new British ships were of a completely different design from them, and no significant components or machinery were reallocated.[12]

On the other hand, the contracts for the four Turkish destroyers at Hawthorn Leslie were taken over, and the ships laid down between the end of 1914 and the summer of 1915. They were armed with five 4in guns and four (designed for six) 21in torpedo tubes. Originally to be named *Napier*, *Narborough*, *Offa* and *Ogre*, in February 1915 they became *Talisman*, *Termagant*, *Trident* and *Turbulent*, respectively. All completed during the first half of 1916, with *Turbulent*, only 19 days in commission, being lost in collision with the battleship SMS *Westfalen* (1908) early in the morning of 1 June 1916 during the Battle of Jutland. *Termagant* reduced to care & maintenance at Portsmouth in October 1919, and

The Turkish-ordered destroyers *Talisman* and *Termagant* at the Hawthorn Leslie shipyard, Hebburn, on 5 November 1915, respectively two and four months prior to completion. Moored outboard is the destroyer leader *Marksman*, to be commissioned 12 days later, with the new monitor *General Wolfe*, built at the nearby Palmer's yard, in the background (Tyne & Wear Archives & Museums 4471/3)

August 1914 and Beyond

HMS/M *E25*, built from material being gathered for a Turkish submarine at Dalmuir. (Author's collection)

Trident and *Talisman* did so at the Nore (the naval anchorage off Sheerness) in March 1920.

Similarly, such material gathered by Beardmore for the Turkish submarines (hull: valued at £8000; machinery: £15,500) was used to build vessels of the very similar standard official design – HMS/M *E25* and *E26*, ordered in November 1914. They took the same yard numbers as the Turkish vessels, being regarded as 'already building' by the Admiralty.[13]

The South American Ships

There was never any likelihood that the material so far gathered for the Brazilian *Riachuelo* would ever be taken forward after the outbreak of war (although work was not formally suspended until January 1915: see p 77). It was initially assumed that the war would be short (even if not necessarily 'over by Christmas'). This had already resulted in the cancellation of the latest of the Admiralty's own battleships, the *Queen Elizabeth* class *Agincourt* (whose name was rapidly reallocated to the former *Sultan Osman I*), and the *Revenge* class *Resistance*, *Renown* and *Repulse*. The Brazilian ship was thus never laid down, construction being suspended on 14 January, and formally stopped on 15 May.

Almirante Latorre

In contrast, both the Chilian battleships were well advanced, albeit suspended on the outbreak of war in August 1914. However, there was no plan to precipitously take over the two vessels. First, they were many months from completion, and second, Chile was not only an unequivocally friendly power, but also an important source of nitrates, used in both agriculture and munitions. Nevertheless, on 16 August 1914, the following note was sent to the Third Sea Lord:

> An early report is to be furnished on the "Almirante Latorre" and "Almirante Cochrane" now building at Elswick, stating the fighting value of these ships compared with the nearest similarity of design in the British navy.
>
> There is no suggestion at present considering their purchase but in view of possible eventualities involving their acceleration it is desirable that the question of ammunition supply and torpedo outfit should be closely investigated and reported upon.
>
> The matter is to be kept very confidential.

The ships were of similar configuration to *Erin* and the British *Orion*, *King George V* and *Iron Duke* classes, with ten big guns in twin turrets on the centreline. While they were of a calibre, 14in, that had not hitherto been used by the Royal Navy,[14] the Elswick Pattern A (UK Mk I) had a similar muzzle velocity to the 13.5in and 15in guns in UK service. The Chilean ships' ten guns also offered a 2 per cent heavier broadside than the eight 15in of the *Queen Elizabeth* class. Secondary guns were Elswick Pattern TT (UK Mk XVII, modified to use the same charges as UK Mk VII guns). Magazine space was some 60 per cent greater, and shell-room space 17 per cent greater, than in an *Iron Duke*. Torpedo tubes were of the same pattern as in *Agincourt* and *Erin*, and as a result, when taken over for British service, special short torpedoes were required. These were the unique Royal Gun Factory Mark II*** VB, of which only a single batch seems to have been manufactured.

The Chilean battleships' protection (see pp 174, 259) was much more akin to that of *Agincourt* than *Erin*. Furthermore, owing to an increase in draught during construction the 9in main belt (3in thinner than in the contemporary *Iron Duke*) was submerged at full load, restricting their effective side armour to a 7in upper belt. Other armour thicknesses were more comparable to UK practice, although there was no longitudinal internal armoured bulkhead abreast the engine rooms.

Almirante Latorre fitting out in late 1914 (Jane's Fighting Ships 1914, 3rd edition, p 441)

The Admiralty also felt that there were too many watertight doors in the coal bunkers. Like *Agincourt*, *Latorre* and *Cochrane* were much longer than their contemporaries, being 6 per cent longer than an *Iron Duke*. They were also 1.75kt faster, with 27 per cent more designed power.

By the end of August, it was clear that the war was not likely to end in the immediate future, and the Admiralty accordingly began to look into taking over overseas orders that had not yet been requisitioned but held the prospect of being completed in time to take part in hostilities. Negotiations were thus opened with Chile for the purchase of ships being built for her in British yards. An initial offer valued *Latorre* and *Cochrane* together at just over £2 million, but the eventual agreement covered just *Latorre* and the four destroyers, acquired together for £2,036,162. Approved by the Cabinet on 5 September 1914, the agreement took effect on the 9th.

Armstrong were advised immediately:

> I am to inform you that arrangements are being made transfer to H.M. Government the Chilean Battleship "Almirante Latorre" under construction at your works. A further communication will be made to you in due course as to the details of the transfer on the financial side. In the meantime it is desired that all possible steps may be taken to complete the ship for service at the earliest possible date, working full overtime and day and night shifts as necessary.

The terms under which *Latorre* was acquired were enshrined in a memorandum of 10 October 1914, with a revised version issued on the 26th.[15] This stated:

> That the instalments which have already been paid by the Chilean Government shall forthwith be repaid through Messrs. Sir W. G. Armstrong, Whitworth & Co., Ltd., together with interest at 5% over the periods comprised between the dates of payment and repayment.

> That all out of pocket expenses incurred to date by the Chilean Government in connection with the contract, duly vouched for, shall be repaid forthwith, through Sir W. G. Armstrong, Whitworth & Co., Ltd.

> That the further expenses involved in the completion of the ship for service including the cost of any improvements upon the original design deemed necessary by the Admiralty shall be

defrayed by the Admiralty dealing direct with Sir W. G. Armstrong, Whitworth & Co., Ltd.

If the war is over before the ship is completed she shall be delivered on completion to Chile if the Chilean Government so desire on the basis of the original contract, and so that the Chilean Government shall have not lost or gained by the ship having been taken over.

If the ship is commissioned as arranged above and employed in the war she shall be transferred to Chile after the war, if the Chilean Government so desire, at a price based upon the original contract, either in good repair or with an allowance for the cost of repair.

If the ship should be sunk or irreparably damaged in the war Great Britain would, if the Chilean Government so desire, cede to Chile a battleship of approximately equal power at an agreed price, provided that the safety of Great Britain and her naval superiority were not endangered thereby.

If at the conclusion of the war the Chilean Government should order the construction in the United Kingdom of a vessel to replace the "ALMIRANTE LATORRE" and the cost per ton be greater than the cost per ton at which the contract price of the "ALMIRANTE LATORRE" works out, the British Government will make good the difference, provided that, in the judgment of the Admiralty, the enhanced cost is due to dearer materials or dearer labour.

The "ALMIRANTE COCHRANE" remains entirely at the disposal of the Chilean Government. However, should circumstances prove the acquisition of this vessel to be of essential importance to the British Government, and should the Chilean Government find that they are not in urgent need of it, the latter would be prepared to consider the question in the same friendly spirit as in other similar cases.

The December 1914 Navy List showed the addition of HMS *Canada*, as *Latorre* had now been renamed. The choice of name was presumably to reinforce Canadian morale, as battlecruisers already existed named for the Dominions of Australia and New Zealand, with India represented by the new battleship *Emperor of India*. A similar intent regarding Ireland doubtless lay behind the decision to give the name *Erin* to the former *Reşadiye*. All countries had been honoured by members of the *King Edward VII* class, but these ships were all now trumped in political importance by dreadnoughts.

As *Latorre* was much less advanced in fitting-out than the all-but-complete ex-Turkish battleships, it was possible to undertake more modifications to meet normal Royal Navy practice when completing her. The conning and torpedo-control towers had not yet been ordered, although their communication tubes were in place, while no work had been done on the masts, bridges and fire-control arrangements.

Accordingly, it was decided to fit the ship as far as possible with items of the types and designs intended for the new *Revenge* class (including modifications planned for its now-cancelled latest ships, *Resistance*, *Renown* and *Repulse*). Thus, *Latorre*'s planned large bridge, with an integral charthouse, was superseded by a much-simplified structure, with a higher tripod mast, the intention being that the ship should generally be run from the conning tower (see drawing on pp 91 and 92).[16] The conning and torpedo-control towers to be used were diverted from items already being procured for the first *Revenge*s, although 115 tons of additional supporting armour had to be provided from scratch. Instructions were given to Armstrong to implement the various changes on 17 September 1914. Lieutenant-Commander (T) Alfred Watts was appointed to the ship on 4 March 1915 to oversee her completion.

The foremast was placed 3ft further aft than originally planned (to allow access to the new conning tower), and although the original steel pole was to be used, the supporting struts would be differently arranged. New platforms were added, a lower one for one of the two 14in directors that were to be installed in the ship, and an upper one for the spotting tower, with a 9ft rangefinder. The unique tandem main masts and aft admiral's bridge and compass platform (see p 92) were to be replaced by a single stump-mast, with a topmast for wireless telegraphy purposes, but no control positions. The funnels were to be reduced in height by 10ft to minimise interference with the spotting and director towers on the foremast, since *Canada*'s forefunnel was much closer to this than the single funnel of the *Revenge* class. Although there were concerns that this reduction might adversely affect the generation of maximum power, this was assessed as being negligible. Indeed, as it turned out (p 32), *Canada*'s problem would be *too much* boiler power. A searchlight platform was to be added aft of the second funnel, and the twin 24in searchlights originally planned replaced by single 38in units.

As completed, all turrets were given 15ft rangefinders, as fitted in the *Queen Elizabeth* class. A Dreyer Mk IV fire-control table was installed, and three 6in control hoods added on each side: one on the forecastle, and one each on the forward and after shelter decks. The actual 6in directors were on the compass platform. With two directors, one at the masthead and one in an armoured shield atop the conning tower, *Canada* had as good a set of fire-control gear for her main battery as the new 15in-gunned classes.

Special trains arrived at Walker at 07:30 and 08:45 on 10 August 1915, and at 09:00 the ship was commissioned by Captain William Nicholson. On the 20th, *Canada* slipped her mooring at the shipyard at 08:35 and entered the recently-arrived floating dock (later *AFD4*) at Jarrow Slake at 10:25. She remained there until the 29th, when she was towed back to Walker, where the battleship was moored in the stream. The embarkation of ammunition began on 2 September, and on the 30th she departed at 18:30, arriving at Rosyth at 11:36 the next morning.

Canada remained at Rosyth until 14 October 1915, leaving at 16:02. While making for Scapa Flow, at 20:15 she began to work up to full power, and beginning at 22:55 the ship carried out her first full-power trials. These produced unexpected results: with all boilers on line, rather than something around her designed 37,000 shp, no less than 55,410 shp was generated – a figure some 50 per cent higher than anticipated. In the process, the seals of the first stage of the high-pressure (HP) turbines began to fail, causing significant damage.

This was owing to a peculiarity of the requirements laid down by the Chileans, which was that the ship should have 'spare' boiler power to allow for defects (see pp 92–3). This fact had seemingly not been made known to the Royal Navy crew, who simply fired all the boilers according to UK practice, with these unfortunate results. As a result, while some patching-up of steam leaks was done in July and November 1916, *Canada* could not henceforth be pushed beyond 21kt. However, as this was the British fleet speed, it was not a major problem. Indeed, although parts had been manufactured, repairs had not been carried out before the battleship was re-engined at the end of the 1920s (p 232).

Canada soon after her arrival at Scapa Flow in October 1915; her then squadron-mate *Erin* is visible over her stern.
(NMM N16795)

Speed was eased to 17kt at 02:00 on the 15th, and the ship moored at berth A4 in Scapa Flow at 16:52. *Canada* had been allocated to the 4th Battle Squadron in September 1915, to join her fellow 'windfalls' *Agincourt* and *Erin*, currently together with *Benbow* (flag), *Emperor of India*, *Queen Elizabeth*, *Temeraire*, *Bellerophon* and *Dreadnought* – a short-lived eclectic mix of the oldest and newest, fastest and slowest, modern battleships in the fleet.

Agincourt, *Erin* and *Canada* respectively cost the British government £2.72 million, £2.4 million and £2.5 million. This compared with between £1.9 million and £2.1 million that had been paid for the ships of the *Orion* (1910), *King George V* (1911) and *Iron Duke* (1912) classes, and the £2.7 million that would be paid for most of the *Queen Elizabeth*s (1913).[17]

Almirante Cochrane

When suspended in 1914, *Cochrane* was still on the slip, but well advanced and only a few months from launching (see below). However, little work had been done on manufacturing her main guns and mountings.[18] Although some 45 per cent of the materials for the latter had been procured, only 8 per cent of the work had been done, with the first mounting a year away from completion. Three guns had been completed, but were diverted to France for potential use as railway guns, while some forgings had been made.[19]

During 1917, with the increasing importance of aviation at sea, a review of hulls with potential for conversion to aircraft carriers had been carried out. HMS *Argus*, purchased in September 1916, was already in hand for conversion from an incomplete Italian liner, and plans were in place for the first purpose-built carrier, *Hermes* (see p 193). As a large hull, reasonably advanced in construction, *Cochrane* was identified as a candidate for completion in advance of *Hermes*. These investigations were initially carried out indirectly via Armstrong personnel, 'as [it was] deemed better not to create suspicion in view of [the] presence of Chilean Officers and the present uncertainty of events'.[20] It was noted that:

> [a]s regards construction the vessel is very well on, practically the whole of the steelwork being complete. The upper and forecastle decks are complete and riveted – except in the vicinity of [the] Engine Room where plates are loose for shipping machinery.
>
> The Boilers are on board and uptakes complete to forecastle deck. The Boiler Rooms may be said to be complete. The funnel are in Yard but not erected. A large amount of auxiliary machinery is on board.

> The watertesting is practically complete.
> No wood decks yet laid.
> Fitting out store rooms not yet started.
> Cabin Furniture well in hand but nothing on board.
> No Joiner work at all on board.
> No sheet iron work started.
> Masts complete but not on board.
> "Q" and "X" Barbette supports riveted.
> "A" "F" [sic] "Y" not riveted.
> No barbette armour in place but is in Yard available.
>   (No backing to this armour)
> No side armour in place but is in Yard available.
> The backing to this armour is about complete.
> The Conning Tower and Tube armour not yet delivered.
> No battery armour in place but all available.
> Armoured Ammunition hoists are in ships complete.
> Transverse armour bulkheads are in place and riveted.
> The boats, with the exception of the Vedette Boats, are being made by the Firm are well in hand[.]
> [T]he piping to the pumping and flooding arrangements &c is well in hand and the pumps (50 ton) are in place.
> The rudder is finished but not yet shipped.
> The steering gear (Screw & Hand, by Bow McLachnan) is in place.
> The Capstan Gear has completed shop trials but is not yet delivered.
> The Electric Generating machinery has been appropriated for other services.
> The ring main is about ¾ complete but very little other Electrical work has been done.
> The machinery is practically complete – so far as [the firm's] information goes.
> [...]
> The weight on ship at present is over 9000 tons, while the estimated weight of Hull is 10350 tons.
> As will be seen [the] vessel is practically ready for launching – practically all the valves are in place.
> Firm desire to have steam on boilers before launch.

A formal proposal to turn the ship into a carrier was made on 23 January 1918 and the decision to purchase and convert was made on the 25th, subject to satisfactory agreement with Chile. Accordingly, that day a letter was sent to the Foreign Office:

> Their Lordships would be much obliged if immediate steps could be taken to bring this proposal before the Chilean Government, and they trust that every endeavour may be made to induce that Government to agree to satisfactory arrangements being completed for the purchase of the vessel.[21]

However, on 29 January it was requested that the letter be returned or destroyed. This was because the details of the October 1914 memorandum for the purchase of *Latorre* had been noticed in the interim: 'It appears that negotiations with regard to this ship were included in the negotiations of October 1914 between the 1st Lord and the Chilean Ambassador, and I am asking the 1st Lord to take the matter up where it was then left.' Discussions over the next few days considered the best way ahead, with the result that direct negotiations between the Admiralty and the Chilean Ambassador took place in parallel with the dispatch of a formal letter (dated 5 February) from the Foreign Office to the Chilean government requesting approval and terms – all with the pre-knowledge that Chile was favourable towards the proposal.

On 13 February 1918, the First Sea Lord made the following submission:[22]

> The approval of the War Cabinet is desired to the acquisition of the Battleship "Almirante Cochrane", which is now building at Elswick for the Chilean Government.
>
> Should the acquisition be sanctioned, it is proposed to convert the vessel into a seaplane-carrier for which she is admirably adapted, as she could accommodate a large number of machines. About 9,000 tons of steel are already built in the ship, the boilers are on board, and from 1,600 to 1,800 tons of additional plate would be required for the conversion, which would take about 9 months to carry out.
>
> She would, therefore, be available as a seaplane-carrier in the autumn of this year, whereas the seaplane-carrier "Hermes" could not possibly be completed before the summer of 1919. It will be seen that by adapting the "Almirante Cochrane" as proposed, the provision of a large seaplane-carrier will be expedited by at least 9 months.
>
> In the autumn of 1914, when the purchase of the "Almirante Latorre" (now H.M.S. "Canada") from the Chilean Government was negotiated, the possibility our acquiring the "Almirante Cochrane" was foreshadowed.
>
> The Chilean Authorities have been approached and the

Chilean Minister states that his Government are willing to transfer the ship on terms similar to those agreed in 1914 with respect to the "Almirante Latorre". He adds that his Government ask that, in consideration of their agreeing to sell the "Almirante Cochrane", that the British Government will see their way to supply the Chilean Government with some aeroplanes (of which some at least should be up-to-date machines) during the next 12 or 18 months, and he points out that for this consideration to be of value the aeroplanes must be supplied during the war as subsequently they would be easily procurable elsewhere. The Chilean Government do not, however, make the transfer of the "Almirante Cochrane" conditional upon compliance with this request.

The Admiralty propose to investigate what could be done in the direction of meeting the wishes of the Chilean Government in this respect, bearing in mind that shortly after the "Almirante Latorre" was acquired, 6 submarines which we had ordered in the United States were transferred to Chile at the request of the Government of that Country.

The total cost of acquiring and completing the "Almirante Cochrane" would be approximately £3,000,000, of which about £500,000 represents the estimated cost of completing and adapting the ship as a seaplane-carrier.

This was approved at the War Cabinet meeting of 20 February 1918,[23] with a letter of thanks to the Chilean government sent the same day. *Cochrane* was formally purchased by the UK for £1.3 million on the 28th.

The provision of aircraft to Chile was strongly supported by the Admiralty, and the 'handing over to Chile of 50 Aeroplanes of a recent type as a free gift, in compensation for loss involved in the transfer of the "Almirante Cochrane" to the British Government' was approved by the Treasury on 25 April.[24] The same day, the Air Ministry proposed to allocate forty DH6 training aircraft for immediate delivery, and ten Avro 504s within three months. However, the reaction of the Chilean ambassador was decidedly negative: he stated that Chile had adequate numbers of trainers, and was looking for good fighting aircraft, 'although naturally not any of the latest type'.[25] They were hoping for 'six squadrons, composed of 6 bombing and fighting machines, 5 double-engine machines and 9 scouts, and . . . would be prepared that the matter should stand over, if necessary, for a year or 18 months, if this would make it easier to meet their desire that fighting machines should be transferred'. The Admiralty view to the Air Ministry was that '[in] view of the very great assistance and consideration shewn by the Chilean

Government in connection with the transfer of the "ALMIRANTE COCHRANE", their Lordships would be glad if it were possible to give favourable consideration to the wishes of the Chilean Government'.[26]

On 15 May, it was proposed that six Sopwith Camel fighters, three Airco DH9 bombers and three Sopwith Baby seaplanes be handed over immediately, with all to be delivered by 1 July 1919. In practice, three Babies and twelve Bristol M.1C monoplane fighters (plus one for spares)[27] were sent before the end of the war, with their Vickers machine guns included in the delivery.[28] Six Short 184 seaplanes arrived in Chile in 1919 (Navy), twenty-seven Avro 504s in 1920, and twenty DH9s in 1921, together with a Felixstowe F2A flying boat and eight SE5A fighters.[29] All but twenty-three of Avro 504s were supplied as part of the '*Cochrane* deal'. Flight Lieutenant Arthur Huston of the RAF was sent to Chile at the end of 1918 to act as Chief Instructor for the new force, with the rank of Major,[30] remaining until September 1919. As such, he made the first flight of one of the Babies in July 1919.[31]

The apparent substitution of double the number of Bristol M.1s for the Camels is interesting. The Bristol aircraft had originated in the middle of 1916, flying for the first time on 14 July. Its configuration went against a prejudice in the British service against monoplanes; indeed, in 1912, they had been banned for five months after a crash in September of that year. Although cleared by a Monoplane Committee in 1913, there remained an unofficial preference for biplanes, and this seems likely to have been a factor in the type's limited production and deployment.

The main substantive objections were the downward vision from the cockpit, but this was not regarded as serious by pilots, and was offset by unlimited views upwards – at a time when all kinds of stratagems were being employed to enhance such views from biplanes. The M.1 also had a fine performance, judged equal or better than the later Royal Aircraft Factory SE5 and Sopwith Snipe. Nevertheless, although 125 were finally put on contract in August 1917, the aircraft were only ever issued to squadrons in Macedonia and Mesopotamia, with two or three sent to Palestine – and just one to France for evaluation.

This lack of official enthusiasm for the M.1 was doubtless why it was selected for gifting to Chile in 1918, and probably why double the number were supplied as compared to the originally-intended Camels. They formed the Primera Compañía de Aviación at El Bosque, on the southern outskirts of Santiago. One of them, still carrying its British markings and serial (C4899), made the first aerial crossing of the Andes, from El Bosque to Mendoza in Argentina, 185km away, on 12 December 1918. The pilot was Lieutenant Dagoberto Godoy Fuentealba (1893–1960).

Six of the M.1s were deployed to Arica in the north of Chile in August 1920, following Chile's mobilisation the previous month in the face of a border dispute with Bolivia.[32] The aircraft returned to their normal base in April 1921, except for one destroyed in a crash in November 1920.

In the interim, the design for the conversion of the battleship to an aircraft carrier had been fleshed out, with drawings approved by the Board on 14 February 1918. An early concern was the intention to retain the mixed firing capabilities of the boilers, Director of Air Services writing on 5 February 1918 that '[t]he coaling of this ship is viewed with apprehension. It has been regarded as a first principle that a modern carrier should be free of coal dust. It is not quite apparent how the coaling can be satisfactorily carried out.' In *Campania* (see p 191) it had been necessary to disembark all aircraft before coaling began, making the evolution even more time-consuming than normal and imposing significant operational limitations. Nevertheless, on the 8th it was confirmed that '[a]rrangements will be made so that coal only, coal and oil, and oil only, can be used at will without change of fittings for an output of 37,000 shp normal, on coal or oil [and] overload 55,000 shp using coal and oil'.

Armstrong were informed of the way ahead and given an instruction to proceed on 11 March. The ship was allocated to Chatham for storing purposes on the 19th and renamed *Eagle* on the 23rd, the Liverpool establishment that had hitherto borne the name being renamed *Eaglet*.

Cruisers and Destroyers

As already noted, the Turkish destroyers and submarines were taken over by the Admiralty in November 1914. Of the Greek light cruisers *Antinavarchos Kountouriotis* and *Lambros Katsonis* at Cammell Laird, the former had only been laid down on 27 March 1914, and her sister would not join her on the ways until 7 October. Given the early expectation of a short war, and their early stage of construction, they were not for the time being taken over. It was not until after *Kountouriotis* had been launched on 18 January 1915 that they, and the four destroyers also building for Greece (see below), were acquired for the Royal Navy. The cruisers became HM Ships *Birkenhead* (*Kountouriotis*) and *Chester* (*Katsonis*).

Both were very similar to the existing British 'Town' group of cruisers, built since 1909, differing from the latest of the type (the *Birmingham* class) in carrying ten 5.5in/50, rather than nine 6in/45 guns. These were to match the calibre of the secondary guns of a Greek battleship on order in France (p 133). These weapons would prove to be well-liked in British service, and would be used for the secondary batteries of the large light cruiser (later aircraft carrier) *Furious*, the battlecruisers of the *Hood* class, and the aircraft carrier *Hermes*. The pair received directors and tripod foremasts in July 1917 (*Birkenhead*) and May 1918 (*Chester*).

Birkenhead was completed in May 1915 and *Chester* was launched in December 1915, being completed in May 1916, just in time for the Battle of Jutland, at which she was badly damaged. Serving with the 3rd LCS of the Grand Fleet throughout their wartime careers, they reduced to reserve in 1919, *Birkenhead* at Portsmouth in April (flagship) and *Chester* at the Nore.

The four Chilean destroyers being built by Samuel White at Cowes were part of a six-ship order, two sisters having already been delivered (p 95, below). Designed for the punishing waters off the Chilean coast, they were of exceptionally large size for their day, and ideally suited for British service as flotilla leaders. *Almirante Simpson* and *Almirante Goñi* were acquired on the outbreak of war, and commissioned respectively as HMS *Faulknor* on 25 August 1914 and HMS *Broke* in October. The other two, less advanced, vessels were acquired at the same time as *Latorre*, *Almirante Williams* commissioning as HMS *Botha* in March 1915 and *Almirante Riveros* as HMS *Tipperary* in May 1915. They retained their original armaments of six 4in guns and four 21in TT until 1918, being redeployed from the Grand Fleet to the Dover Patrol at the end of 1916 (less *Tipperary*, sunk at Jutland). They then swapped four 4in guns for two of 4.7in calibre, having been increasingly outranged by German opponents. The three survivors were reduced to reserve in 1919, by November being in care & maintenance at the Nore (*Botha*), Portsmouth (*Broke*) and Devonport (*Faulknor*).

HMS *Chester*, laid down as the Greek *Lambros Katsonis*, as completed; a tripod foremast would later be fitted (see p 204) (NHHC NH 50159)

HMS *Broke*, formerly the Chilean *Almirante Goñi*; when re-sold to Chile, she became *Almirante Uribe*. (Author's collection)

Two destroyers for Greece, *Kriti* and *Lesvos*, were on the stocks at John Brown at Clydebank, and two sisters, *Chios* and *Samos*, at Fairfield, Govan. They were very similar to the Royal Navy's 'M' class, armed with three 4in guns and four 21in TT, and were renamed in the same name series. *Kriti* commissioned as HMS *Medea* in May 1915, *Lesvos* as *Medusa* in May 1915, *Chios* as *Melampus* in June 1915 and *Samos* as *Melpomene* in August 1915. All spent their war service with the Harwich Force, *Medusa* being lost in March 1916 following a collision. The others were laid up in the spring of 1919.

In contrast to the other ships building in the UK for overseas customers, the two destroyers for Japan had been ordered by a country with its own warship-building industry. However, Japan was still keen to ensure that it had access to the very latest technology, and as a result had made what proved to be its last major overseas purchases between 1910 and 1913. First, the battlecruiser *Kongo* (1912) had been ordered from Vickers, with technology transfer to allow her three sisters, *Hiei*,

HMS *Melampus* had been laid down as the Greek *Chios*. (Author's collection)

Kirishima and *Haruna* (1912–13), to be built in Japan. Second, a submarine had been ordered from a French specialist yard, and third, contracts were placed for two destroyers, from Yarrow on the Clyde.

This yard had been at the cutting-edge of destroyer development from the invention of the type in the 1890s and, following problems with the domestically-designed and built *Umikaze* class (1910), *Urakaze* and *Kawakaze* were ordered under the Japanese 1911 Estimates. Powered by Brown-Curtis turbines, they were the first oil-only ships intended for the Japanese navy, and were originally intended to have diesel cruising motors (an issue with the *Umikaze* class had been their very poor endurance), with Föttinger hydraulic transmissions.[33] However, although the ships were laid down in October 1913, the Föttinger couplings had yet to be delivered from Germany before the outbreak of the First World War. Accordingly, the space reserved for the diesels was replaced by an additional oil tank. Works congestion meant that neither vessel was launched until 1915, and although finished in October that year, *Urakaze* was then laid up and did not enter Japanese service until 1919. *Kawakaze* was sold by Japan to Italy on 3 July 1916, as *Intrepido*, but was renamed *Audace* just before her launch in September, and was completed in March 1917. An eponymous replacement for *Kawakaze* was laid down at Yokosuka Naval Yard in February 1917, and completed in November 1918.

Of the two Norwegian coast defence ships, *Nidaros* had been launched by Armstrong on 9 June 1914, while *Bjørgvin* took to the water on 8 August. Displacing 4807 tons, they were to be armed with a pair of 9.45in/50 and four 5.9in/50 guns. By November it was recognised that they would be ideal for coastal bombardment duties, alongside the new monitors now being planned (cf pp 138–9, below). Accordingly, arrangements were made to reimburse the Norwegians the payments already made to Armstrong, and on 9 January the latter were ordered to complete the ships for the Royal Navy, with guns relined to 9.2in and 6in calibres.[34] They were renamed *Gorgon* and *Glatton* on 8 April 1915,

The Yarrow-built Japanese destroyer *Urakaze* at Wuhan during 1930–3. (Author's collection)

but construction was suspended in May to allow resources to be diverted to the large light cruisers *Courageous* and *Furious*, also being built by Armstrong. Work was resumed in September 1917 to a revised design, with *Gorgon* to be given priority, and work on refitting the old battleship *Illustrious* as an ammunition store-ship could be deferred/simplified to free up the requisite resources. However, it was not until 1 May 1918 that *Gorgon* finally commissioned, *Glatton* following on 31 August – only to be lost following an internal explosion at Dover on 16 September.

As well as the takeover of the great *Sultan Osman I* and *Reşadiye*, 3 August 1914 had also seen the beginning of the acquisition of two much smaller vessels for service under the White Ensign. These were two submarines that had been ordered in the USA for Chile in 1911, as *Iquique* and *Antofagasta*, but were now laid up at Seattle, WA. This was due to disputes between Chile and the shipyard, Seattle Construction and Drydock Company. With war looming, the head of the shipyard, J V Paterson, while visiting the Union Club in Victoria BC, Canada, 90 miles north of Seattle, made it known that the boats might be available for sale (at a price that represented a 50 per cent premium over the value of the Chilean contract – and without the knowledge of the Chileans).

The Premier of British Columbia, Sir Richard McBride (1870–1917), conferred with the Canadian and British governments. While it was agreed that the purchase was desirable, it was clear that there would be insufficient time for a conventional purchase before the outbreak of war. Consequent US neutrality would prevent delivery. Accordingly, McBride decided to use the province's own funds to buy the boats for $1.1 million (£0.23 million), with a cheque to be handed over when they reached Canadian waters.

HMS *Glatton*, the former Norwegian *Bjørgvin*, during her brief service life, ended by internal explosion at Dover on 16 December 1918.
(IWM SP 2595)

The submarines left Seattle at 22:00 on 3 August, being met at daybreak a few miles off Victoria. There, they underwent an inspection that lasted four hours, the cheque was handed over, the White Ensign was hoisted, and the boats made their way to Esquimalt Dockyard, 7 miles to the west. Their acquisition by the Canadian navy from British Columbia was authorised by an Order in Council on 7 August, and the province reimbursed the purchase price (with a $40,000 commission to Paterson).

They were initially renamed *No 1* (ex-*Iquique*) and *No 2* (ex-*Antofagasta*). In October 1914, however, owing to their similarity in size to the 'C' class submarines launched for the Royal Navy between 1906 and 1910, they became *CC1* and *CC2*. Considerable criticisms were levelled both at the boats themselves (which had numerous design shortcomings) and the way in which they were acquired, but a Royal Commission inquiry concluded that, on balance, the move had been justified.

They initially operated from Esquimalt, but on 21 June 1917 they left for the east coast. Heavy-weather damage required them to undergo repairs at San Francisco and at various other stopping points on their onward journey (under tow) via the Panama Canal to Halifax, NS, where they arrived on 17 October 1917. Although the intention had been for them to be sent to operate in the Mediterranean, their condition was such that they required long refits. After these they were to be used primarily for anti-submarine training. With the transfer of HMS/M *H14* and *H15* to Canada in February 1919, as *CH14* and *CH15*, *CC1* and *CC2* became surplus to requirements and were offered for sale in 1920, finally being disposed of in 1925.

Chile finally got submarines in 1917. Soon after the outbreak of war, Charles M Schwab (1862–1939), of the US shipbuilder Bethlehem Steel, had offered to build twenty 'H' class submarines for the Royal Navy.[35] All were begun during November at the Fore River (Quincy, MA), and Union Iron Works (San Francisco) yards. However, it soon became apparent that the US government's interpretation of its neutrality laws would lead to a prohibition of the export of complete submarines. As a result, it was agreed between Bethlehem and the Admiralty that the components of the San Francisco boats, and two of those at Fore River, should be transported to the Canadian Vickers yard at Montreal, and be assembled as *H1–H10*. Since the yard could only manage ten boats at once, construction of the remaining ten Fore River vessels (*H11–H20*) continued at Quincy, with the delivery schedule left open, dependent on any future relaxation of the US government position.

The first boat was laid down at Montreal in January 1915 and all had been delivered by the summer. However, the ten at Fore River were impounded under the control of Commandant Boston Navy Yard once they had completed their trials. In September 1916, as there seemed little prospect of their being released for UK service in the near future, the UK offered to transfer five of the boats to Chile as part-payment for ships taken over in 1914. This was agreed, with the addition of a sixth boat on the Chileans' own account: all vessels were to be delivered by 8 June 1917, whether or not the war was still in progress. The US authorities acquiesced, subject to the proviso that the Chileans could not sell any of the boats on to a belligerent power. Released from US navy custody in January 1917, *H13* (to be the Chilean *H1*), *H16* (*H2*), *H17* (*H3*), *H18* (*H4*), *H19* (*H5*) and *H20* (*H6*)[36] were then overhauled at the Fore River yard before being handed over to their new owners. The Chilean cruiser *Chacabuco* (1898) brought crews, and the boats were formally transferred on 7 March 1917.

Meanwhile in Europe . . .

Of other nations that were soon to be combatants, German yards were building a battleship for Greece, two cruisers for Russia, four destroyers for Argentina, four torpedo boats for the Netherlands, and five submarines for Austria-Hungary and one for Norway. In France there was also a Greek battleship, plus four destroyers for Argentina, and two submarines for Greece and one for Japan. Italy, who would join the conflict in 1915, was building four destroyers for Romania and one for Portugal, plus a submarine for each of Germany and Russia. The USA, which would not join the war until 1917, was completing two battleships for Argentina.

Although each of these countries had all previously exported warships, none had produced the sheer volume for foreign customers that had come out of British yards. French yards had, however, produced significant vessels, especially the Forges et Chantiers de la Mediterranée at La Seyne, which had constructed ironclads for Germany, battleships for Spain, Chile and Russia between the 1880s and the early 1900s, as well as cruisers and numerous torpedo vessels.

France
Of the ships building in French yards, the Greek battleship *Vasilèfs Konstantinos*, at the St Nazaire yard of Penhoët (p 133), was, like *Fatih*, barely begun. She thus had no value in reinforcing the French fleet during the foreseen short war. In addition, the call-up to the army of all Frenchmen aged between 21 and 48 stripped the shipyards of crucial workers. However, although work was stopped, as the ship was intended

for a country not seen as a potential enemy, the slip was not immediately cleared, and it ultimately fell to Greece in 1916 to request that no further work be carried out. In contrast, four Argentine destroyers (p 85), at Nantes, were essentially complete. Indeed, all had run trials in 1912, but had failed to achieve required speeds at operational loads, Argentina accordingly refusing to accept them. The ships remained laid up while discussions continued, and although it appeared in the summer of 1914 that acceptance might be possible, war supervened. All were formally requisitioned by France on 9 August 1914, and added to the French navy list on the 17th. However, their American armament (of 4in guns and 21in torpedo tubes – to match the battleships building in the USA) needed to be replaced with French guns before the vessels could join the fleet. It was thus not until September that *Opinâtre* (ex-*Rioja*), *Aventurier* (ex-*Mendoza*) and *Intrépide* (ex-*Salta*) entered service, joined by *Teméraire* (ex-*San Juan*) in November.

Two unnamed submarines of 457 (surface)/670 (submerged) tons were on order for Greece at the Schneider yard at Chalon-sur-Saône, being taken over by France on 3 August 1915 while still on the slip, and named *Amazone* and *Antigone* on the 14th. Launched in August and October 1916, they were completed in June 1917. Two more boats of the same design had been ordered by Japan in 1912. One (*No 14*) was launched in November 1913 and one (*No 15*) in April 1914. The latter was delivered to the Japanese in 1917, but *No 14* was taken over by France along with her Greek sisters in August 1915. A week later the boat was transferred to Toulon via the river Rhône; renamed *Armide*, she commissioned for trials on the 20th. However, it was not until 6 June 1916 that she was fully commissioned. A modified replacement was built in Japan, which was completed in 1920.

Germany
The largest of the ships in hand in German yards in August 1914 was the 19,500-ton Greek battleship *Salamis* (pp 130–1), which was launched by AG Vulcan at Hamburg in November 1914. However, all work then ceased owing to the fact that her armament, and much of her armour, was still with their manufacturers in the USA – beyond the British blockade. Making up the deficit from German sources was not practicable and the ship thus remained laid up at Hamburg throughout the war (see pp 137–8).

Although armament was also lacking for two 4300-ton cruisers building for Russia by Friedrich Schichau at Danzig (*Muravev-Amurskiy* and *Admiral Nevelskoi*), this was not a problem, as the ships had simple hand-worked pedestal guns and German weapons could easily be substituted.[37] Following Germany's declaration of war on Russia on 1

August, *Muravev-Amurskiy*, the more advanced vessel (already launched in April 1914), was provisionally requisitioned on 5 August 1914. However, it was not until the 27th that a first payment was made by the German navy to the yard and the ship formally taken over. Even then, it was not until November that a price was agreed, to also apply to the less-advanced *Nevelskoi*, whose purchase had been authorised on 17 September; she was launched in November.

Muravev-Amurskiy commissioned in December as SMS *Pillau*, armed with 5.9in/45 guns in place of the intended Russian 5.1in/55 weapons. She also differed from the original design in having greatly heightened funnels. *Nevelskoi* was more extensively modified, with many standard German navy fittings, before entering service as SMS *Elbing* in September 1915.

Work in hand for Russia also contributed two further light cruisers to the German navy.[38] AG Vulcan was manufacturing the four turbines for the Russian cruiser *Svetlana*, building at the Russo-Baltic yard in Reval (Talinn), and in August 1914 it offered to use them to build a pair of large destroyers. This offer was rejected by the German navy, but further discussions resulted in the construction of the cruiser-minelayers *Brummer* and *Bremse* (1915–16) with the ex-Russian engines. They were laid down in April 1915, and completed in the summer of 1916, becoming two of the German navy's most active vessels.

Four 1100-ton destroyers on the stocks for Argentina, ordered from Germania at Kiel in April 1913 (p 85) were taken over on 6 August 1914. Launched over the next three months, they commissioned

SMS *Elbing*, laid down as the Russian *Admiral Nevelskoi*, on trials in 1915. The inset shows the ship as designed, and shows much modification was needed to meet the requirements of a new owner. (*Dirk Nottelmann collection*)

One of the German G101 class, originally laid down for Argentina. (NHHC NH 92717)

between March and June 1915 as *G101* (ex-*Santiago*), *G102* (ex-*San Luis*), *G103* (ex-*Santa Fé*) and *G104* (ex-*Tucuman*). Designed for American 4in guns and 21in torpedoes like the Argentine ships acquired by France, they entered service with 3.5in guns and 20in tubes; the former were replaced by 4.1in weapons in 1916.

Much smaller were four 335-ton vessels for the Netherlands, being built by Vulcan at Stettin under the names *Z1* to *Z4*. Taken over on the slips on 10 August 1914, they became *V105* to *V108* in German service in early 1915. As four more (*Z5* to *Z8*) were already building in Dutch yards, replacements for the German-built ships were laid down in the Netherlands in 1914 and 1916, but not completed until 1919–20.

German firms were also providing important material for destroyers building in Russia. Schichau had in 1913 obtained orders for nine destroyers of the *Gogland* class, to be assembled at their new Mühlgraben Shipyard at Riga. The first four were still on the stocks in August 1914.[39] The German yard thus had material and machinery in hand that could not be delivered, and accordingly offered to build nine vessels for the German navy from this. However, the offer was declined owing to the quoted delivery time (18 months) and a feeling that, at 1350 tons, the ships would be too large to fit German operational conceptions – the latest *G37*, *S49* and *V49* classes displaced only 800 to 850 tons.

Similarly, turbines and stem and stern castings were being made by Vulcan for the Russian *Orfey* class destroyers *Lieutenant Ilin*, *Kapitan Konon-Zotov*, *Gavriil* and *Mikhail* (1914–16) building at St Petersburg and Reval. However, in this case Vulcan and Blohm & Voss were prepared to offer a six-month delivery schedule. Admiral von Tirpitz,

SMS *B97*, built around material ordered for a Russian destroyer. (Author's collection)

State Secretary at the Reich Naval Office (RMA) accordingly waived concerns about the vessels' size (in this case 1370 tons) to immediately order *B97*, *B98*, *V99* and *V100* from the two yards. All four were completed during the first half of 1915, with two more (*B109* and *B110*) ordered in October 1914, to be built from scratch by Blohm & Voss. Two further orders (*B111* and *B112*) followed in January 1915, although an offer by the yard to build four additional vessels was rejected owing its impact on cruiser-building at the Blohm and Voss yard. These orders, together with the four ex-Argentine boats, allowed the formation of a complete flotilla (the II.) of destroyers that were a third larger than anything else currently in the German fleet. They were also the German navy's first all-oil fired destroyers.

The final major warships under construction in German yards for foreign customers were five submarines at Germania. Four, of 775/915 tons, had been begun in 1913 for Austria-Hungary, and were to have become their *U7* to *U10*. As it was assumed that it would not be possible for them to be delivered to the Adriatic under war conditions (something that was soon to be disproved by wartime operations), payments were refunded by the German navy, and the boats became respectively their own *U66* to *U70*. The fifth boat was the last of a series of four 270/335 ton boats (*A2* to *A5*) built for Norway by Germania from 1912; while the first three had all been delivered by the outbreak of the war, *A5* was not quite ready, was taken over on 5 August 1914, and commissioned as *U0* on the 14th; she was renamed *UA* two weeks later.

CHAPTER 2

The Latin-American Connection

UNTIL THE 1870S, BRAZIL HAD BEEN the premier maritime power of South America, having provided the naval component of the Triple Alliance (comprising Argentina, Brazil and Uruguay) that had fought against Paraguay during 1865–70. However, British yards laid down the first major Argentine and Chilean warships during that decade, the 3500–4200-ton central battery ships *Almirante Brown* (Argentina, launched 1880) and *Almirante Cochrane* and *Blanco Encalada* (ex-*Valparaiso*, Chile, 1874–5). Brazil ordered a turret ship of over twice this size in 1873 (*Independencia*, 1874), but she was delayed by problems at her launch.[1] As a result, she was still running trials in February 1878

The Argentine central battery ship *Almirante Brown*, launched in 1880, and shown as rebuilt 1897–8. (NHHC NH 60513)

HMS *Neptune*, launched in 1874 as the Brazilian *Independencia*, but acquired by the Royal Navy in February 1878, while still in the hands of her builders. Under normal circumstances, she would have long since been completed and delivered to Brazil, but when her launch was first attempted on 16 July 1874 she refused to move, and a second attempt on 30 July left her half-way down the slip. By the time the ship was successfully put afloat on 10 September, she had suffered significant hull damage, and repairs severely delayed her fitting-out, meaning that sea trials had only begun at the very end of 1877. (Author's collection)

when she was purchased by the UK (along with other capital ships under construction in the UK for foreign customers – see p 96) during a Russian war scare. *Independencia* would serve as HMS *Neptune* until the beginning of the twentieth century.

Both the Argentine and Brazilian navies bought further major ships, mainly from UK yards, during the 1880s. These included the Brazilian battleship *Riachuelo* (1882), and a lighter-draught version, *Aquidabā* (1885). *Riachuelo* made a major impression on the US Navy, and later served as a model for the first US capital ships, *Maine* (1890) and *Texas* (1892).

In parallel, rivalries between Argentina, Chile and Brazil were growing, particularly between the first two, where boundary disputes

The Brazilian battleship *Riachuelo*, as completed with a full rig in 1884; for her final configuration, 20 years later, see p 60 (NHHC NH 74107)

The Latin-American Connection

The Brazilian battleship *Aquidabã* as built, in US waters in 1892; she would go on to have the unfortunate distinction of being sunk twice. (NHHC NH 59872)

(going back to poor delineations of responsibility during Spanish imperial rule, particularly in Patagonia) made relations increasingly poisonous. Chile had been victorious in the War of the Pacific during 1879–83 against Peru and Bolivia, during which she had captured the small turret ship *Huáscar* (1865); the rest of the Peruvian fleet was lost by capture, accident or scuttling. Before the war was over, in 1881 Chile had ordered the pioneering 10in-gunned deck-protected cruiser *Esmeralda* (1883) from Armstrong. Then, in 1887, she had contracted with La Seyne for building of the battleship *Capitan Prat* (1890) and the protected cruisers *Presidente Errazuriz* and *Presidente Pinto* (1890).

These ships formed part of a formal programme to create a balanced fleet, which also included the torpedo-gunboats *Almirante Lynch* and *Almirante Condell*, launched by Laird in the UK in 1890. The navy was on the side of the winning faction in the 1891 Chilean revolution, the

The Chilean battleship *Capitan Prat* as built. (*Engineering* 4 January 1895)

naval CinC, Jorge Montt (1845–1922) being President from 1891 to 1896. However, during the conflict the central battery ship *Blanco Encalada* was sunk by a torpedo from *Lynch*: it was the first such sinking of a major warship in history.[2]

Argentina countered with the Laird-built coastal/riverine battleships *Independencia* and *Libertad* (1890–1) and the Armstrong 'stock' protected cruisers *Veinticinco de Mayo* (1890) and *Nueve de Julio* (1892). Strained relations between Chile and the USA soon after the Chilean revolution were accompanied by Argentine intimations that they might support the USA if matters came to war; this further stoked the naval race. Each country therefore acquired a further Armstrong protected cruiser – *Blanco Encalada* (ii, Chile, 1893) and *Buenos Aires* (Argentina, 1895, a former 'stock' ship). Chile then ordered an armoured cruiser from the same yard, *Esmeralda* (ii, 1896), financed in part by selling the original *Esmeralda* to Japan in late 1894. Chile also bought a protected cruiser from Armstrong that had originally been ordered by Brazil (*Ministro Zenteno* [1896]).

In parallel,[3] an Argentine naval commission was dispatched to Europe, fortified by a growing economy. This lead to the purchase of the Italian armoured cruiser *Giuseppe Garibaldi* (i) in 1895, which joined the Argentine fleet as ARA *Garibaldi* at the end of 1896. In March of that year, Chile had ordered a further armoured cruiser (*General O'Higgins* [1897]), and on 25 April, Argentina concluded a preliminary agreement to buy *Garibaldi*'s sister *Varese* (i), which became ARA *San Martin* in June 1898. Two more ships of the same class were bought from the Italian navy by Argentina in the summer of 1897 (*Giuseppe Garibaldi* [iii] and *Varese* [ii]), which joined the fleet as ARA *Pueyrredón* and *General Belgrano* in September and November 1898.

In May 1898, tensions between Chile and Argentina had reached such a pitch that they agreed to submit their underlying south-Andean boundary disputes to the UK for adjudication. In addition, it was agreed

The Argentine coastal battleship *Libertad* soon after completion; she would survive as a coastguard stationship until 1968. (Author's collection)

The Argentine armoured cruiser *Garibaldi*, whose acquisition from Italy in 1895 stoked the Latin-American naval race. (Author's collection)

that a further dispute left over from the War of the Pacific (regarding the Puna de Atacama area) would in effect be determined by the US ambassador to Argentina. A symbolic seaborne meeting between the countries' presidents also helped reduce tensions.

However, while the Puna de Atacama dispute was soon resolved, the Andean adjudication was not to be completed until 1902; the naval race thus continued. In 1901, Chile purchased an already-complete protected cruiser (*Chacabuco* [1898], built on speculation by Armstrong), and made enquiries about acquiring from the USA the three *Indiana* class (1893) battleships. In reply, Argentina signed a letter of intent with Ansaldo in May 1901 for the building of a pair of 14,480-ton battleships, to be named *Maipu* and *Chacabuco*.[4] Based on the Italian navy's *Regina*

The Chilean armoured cruiser *General O'Higgins*, ordered in the UK in 1896. (Author's collection)

Bernardino Rivadavia, the fifth Argentine armoured cruiser, launched in Italy in October 1902. (Author's collection)

Margherita class (1901), they would have had four 12in, six 8in, twelve 6in and sixteen 3in guns.

Argentina also took over a Spanish contract at the yard for a ship of the *Garibaldi* class, to have been named *Pedro de Aragon* by the Spaniards, and now to be *Rivadavia*. However, the contract was then cancelled without any work having been undertaken, and on 23 December 1901 the Argentines made fresh firm orders for a pair of new-build *Garibaldi*s. These were laid down as *Mitra* and *Roca* in March 1902, but launched as *Bernardino Rivadavia* and *Mariano Moreno* in October. In reply, Chile authorised in late 1901 a pair of vessels (*Constitucion* and *Libertad*, one to be built by Armstrong, one by Vickers) classified as battleships, but essentially intended to be *Garibaldi*-killers.

However, these beggar-my-neighbour programmes were brought to an end by the British, fearing for their own regional interests in the event of hostilities between the two powers. Linked with the UK's final adjudication of the Andean boundary dispute, three 'Pacts of May' were signed in 1902. The third dealt with the naval race, and led to a naval limitation treaty of 9 January 1903. For the next five years, each country could only buy new ships if the other had been given 18 months' notice. Ships under construction were to be sold as soon as possible, while *Garibaldi* and *Pueyrredón*, along with the Chilean *Capitan Prat*, would be placed in reserve for the duration of the treaty. The treaty put *Constitucion*, *Libertad*, *Rivadavia* and *Moreno*, all either afloat or about to be launched, under British control until such time as they were sold.

THE LATIN-AMERICAN CONNECTION

Launched in January 1903 as *Constitucion*, the Chilean-Argentine naval treaty signed three days earlier required the Chilean battleship's sale. In December she became HMS *Swiftsure*, shown here outbound for the Mediterranean in April 1909. (Author's collection)

The two modified *Regina Margherita*s were cancelled, and any materials gathered or ordered for them (including guns) absorbed into Italy's own battleship programme.

Constitucion and *Libertad* were offered to Japan in October 1902, but they were not at that time interested. However, by the autumn of 1903 deteriorating Russo-Japanese relations resulted in a more positive response, but insufficient funds were available. Russia had also become interested, and to avoid *Constitucion* and *Libertad* being potentially used against their Japanese allies, the British decided to buy the two ships themselves. They were formally purchased on 4 December 1903, by which time the ships had already run trials (*Libertad* completing hers of the 5th). On 19 December, the Japanese managed to set an emergency budget, which included funds to obtain *Constitucion* and *Libertad* from the British. However, the latter refused to sell-on, citing the terms under which the UK Parliament had acquiesced to the acquisition. The vessels accordingly joined the British fleet as *Swiftsure* (ex-*Constitucion*) and *Triumph* (ex-*Libertad*) on completion in 1904, the latter leaving Barrow for Chatham on 14 June 1904.

However, the British did offer their good offices to Japan over acquiring *Rivadavia* and *Moreno* (also of interest to the Russians). The two cruisers were purchased for Japan on 30 December 1903, and formally transferred to their new owners on 7 January 1904 as *Kasuga* and *Nisshin*.

The Windfall Battleships

Map of the Americas. *(Author)*

Brazil

The 1907 Naval Programme

In contrast to her neighbours, it was not until the beginning of the twentieth century that Brazilian thoughts and resources were directed towards a significant modernisation and expansion of the fleet.[5] Following the overthrow of the monarchy in 1888, the navy had been at loggerheads with the dominant army, revolting in both 1891 and 1893–4. The latter conflict – the Revolta da Armada – ended in failure, with the battleship *Aquidabã* sunk in shallow water by the newly-purchased government torpedo-gunboat *Gustavo Sampaio* (1892),[6] although subsequently salved and repaired.

While Brazil had in 1885 laid down an ambitious locally-built 4000-ton protected cruiser, *Almirante Tamandaré* (1890), the conflicts of the early 1890s left navy verging on the moribund as the nineteenth century ended. Four 3500-ton protected cruisers had been ordered from Armstrong during the 1890s (one un-named; *Barosso*; *Amazonas*; and *Almirante Abreu*), but only *Barosso* (1896) ever entered Brazilian service. The first ship was sold to Chile (see p 52, above), owing to Brazil's inability to pay further instalments of her purchase-price, and the last two were acquired by the USA in March 1898 (as *New Orleans* and *Albany*), as the Spanish-American War loomed. *Amazonas* had already been commissioned with a Brazilian crew in the UK, and was transferred at Gravesend, a US crew having been ferried across by USS *San Francisco* on 18 March 1898. *Abreu* was not completed for the USA until 1900, long after the war had ended. The La Seyne-built (but Armstrong-armed) coast defence ships, *Marshal Deodoro* (1898) and *Marshal Floriano* (1899), entered service during 1900–1, but there was little coherence between the vessels available to Brazilian navy, with many obsolescent at best. In addition, the provision and training of manpower was wholly inadequate.

However, a movement towards a renewal of the fleet had begun in 1895, especially as Argentina and Chile developed their own navies during the decade, including fast armoured cruisers that Brazil had nothing to match. This culminated in the April 1904 publication of a report by the Navy Minister Admiral Juilio César de Noronha (1845–1923). This proposed the construction of three 12,500–13,000-ton battleships, three 9200–9700-ton armoured cruisers and six 400-ton destroyers, plus minor vessels. The equal numbers of battleships and armoured cruisers reflected contemporary Japanese force plans,[7] as well as the numbers of the latter available to Argentina and Chile, and underlined the aim to give Brazil a proper balanced fleet.

Informal discussions had already taken place with Armstrong. By

Brazil was the only Latin-American state to attempt to build a major warship in its own yards during the late nineteenth century, but the resulting 1890-launched protected cruiser *Almirante Tamandaré* was not wholly satisfactory, and spent much of her career as a stationary headquarters ship. Built with three masts, the aft pair of masts were replaced with a single new one in 1894. (Author's collection)

The coast defence ship *Marshal Deodoro*, launched at La Seyne in 1898, and sold to Mexico in 1924 as *Anáhuac*, the receipts being used to buy the submarine *Humaytá* (1927). (NHHC NH 101480)

November 1903 they had prepared designs for: a battleship (Design 364) based on the Chilean *Constitucion* (later UK *Swiftsure*) class; an 'armourclad' (365 – perhaps intended as an improvement on the *Deodoro* class); a coast defence ship (354), derived from the Norwegian *Tordenskjold* (1897) and *Eidsvold* (1900) classes; and an armoured cruiser (352). The following summer, a pair of larger (9700–10,250-ton) armoured cruiser designs (405, 406) were also prepared, each armed with a dozen 7.5in guns. These may have been influenced by interest in the design of the newly-designed Italian *Pisa* class (1907–8). There also seem to have been contacts with John Brown, Fairfield and Germania over scoping potential designs.

Soon afterwards, in October 1904, the Brazilian Congress passed a bill providing for the construction of twenty-eight warships. These included three 13,000-ton battleships and three 9700-ton armoured cruisers, together with six 400-ton destroyers, six 130-ton and six 50-ton torpedo boats, three submarines, a collier and a training ship. The formal decree was issued on 14 December 1904, allowing official

The Latin-American Connection

procurement action to be initiated, with invitations to tender issued before the end of the year; bids were due in February 1905.

Although eleven tenders were submitted, it was clear from the outset that orders for the new programme would go to British yards, the bids for the big ships – the battleships and armoured cruisers – being submitted jointly by Armstrong and Vickers. There was considerable negotiation over technical details, amid suggestions within Brazil that something along the lines of an improved *King Edward VII* (with four 12in and four 10in guns – as per *Kashima* [1905], constructed by Armstrong for Japan) should be built. Eventually, Admiral Noronha signed a contract on 23 July 1906 with Armstrong for three battleships, armed with twelve 10in guns.

This was just two days after the third Pan-American Conference had opened in Rio de Janeiro. The USA, which had been concerned since the spring at the impact of the Brazilian programme on the balance of power in South America, made an approach to Brazil in September to try to persuade them to cancel the order. The Brazilians demurred, remarking that, given that the US navy was rapidly expanding, the approach was both hypocritical and imperialistic.

The ships were to conform to Armstrong's Design 439A (p 62), the work of their chief naval architect, Josiah Perrett. Born in 1848 in Plymouth, he was trained at the Royal School of Naval Architecture at South Kensington, before working at the Torquay experimental tank with the Froudes from 1871 to 1883. In 1886 he joined Armstrong as principal assistant to Philip Watts, and became chief naval architect when the latter moved to the Admiralty as Director of Naval Construction (DNC) in 1903. He had been responsible for the final design of the Chilean *Constitucion* and *Libertad* (*Triumph* and *Swiftsure*), and had recently designed the aforementioned Japanese battleship *Kashima*. Down to his retirement in 1916, he would have responsibility for all designs produced by Armstrong, and thus the future *Agincourt*, *Erin*, *Canada* and *Eagle*. He would die in Newton Abbott, Devon, in 1918.

The planned ships were to be of 13,000 tons, and carried their dozen guns in twin turrets, one forward, one aft, and two on each beam. A 9in belt was provided, with reciprocating engines to give a speed of 19kt. Two vessels (to be *Minas Geraes*[8] and *Rio de Janeiro*) were to be built by Armstrong, while the third ship (*São Paulo*), and the machinery for all three vessels,[9] was subcontracted to Vickers. They were laid down in November 1906, as Elswick 791 and 792, and Barrow 347 (to be delivered in 24, 29 and 26 months, respectively). Regarding the armoured cruisers, a Vickers design (172A) was put forward, with eight 10in guns (in two twin and four single turrets), but no order was placed.

Josiah Perrett (1848–1918), designer of all Armstrong's dreadnought battleships. (Author's collection)

Having been torpedoed and sunk in shallow water in 1894, *Aquidabā* was salved and refitted, and then reconstructed by Vulcan at Stettin during 1897–8, when she received two heavy military masts, as shown here. (Author's collection)

This was ultimately due to the catastrophic loss from internal explosion of the battleship *Aquidabā* on 21 January 1905 (shortly before the bids were received). This tragic event cost 223 lives, including three admirals and several other senior officers. These included people closely involved in the formulation of the 1904 programme. The disaster also reduced the Brazilian battle fleet to just *Riachuelo*, plus the two *Marshal Deodoro* class, underlining the dire need for new ships.

Following March 1906's presidential election, a new Navy Minister, Admiral Alexandrino Faria de Alencar (1848–1926), instituted a review of the programme in the light of current developments in naval technology. In particular, the launch of HMS *Dreadnought* in February

Riachuelo at New York while in US waters for the Jamestown Exposition Naval Review in June 1907. She had been rebuilt during 1893–5, with her fore and mizzen masts replaced by heavy military ones, which were then removed in 1904. (Detroit Publishing Co via LoC)

The Latin-American Connection

1906 highlighted the likely trajectory of future battleship development. Consequently, it appeared that although the new Brazilian ships would be, like her, 'all big gun' vessels (albeit with 10in, rather than 12in, guns), they were now too small, too slow and too weakly protected. A stormy debate in the Senate was followed by the submission on a new naval plan on 8 November 1906, which proposed increasing the size of the battleships to 18,000 tons each. A decree of 24 November replaced the 1904 programme with a revised one. As finalised in early 1907, this provided for a smaller number of larger ships within the same funding. There would now be three 19,250-ton battleships, three 3150-ton scout cruisers, ten 560-ton destroyers, three submarines, a minelayer and a submarine support ship. Accordingly, work on the battleships was suspended soon after laying-down in November 1906, and in January 1907 the material erected on the slips began to be dismantled, while new designs were prepared.

The Brazilian Dreadnoughts

Perrett had begun to work on new designs as soon as the direction of travel in Brazil had become apparent, and a new contract was signed by Admiral Alencar on 20 February 1907. The revised design (494A) was 4500 tons larger, with the 10in guns replaced by 12in/45 weapons, backed up by twenty-two 4.7in/50 weapons. The arrangement of the ship was entirely new, with superimposed turrets fore and aft, and the remaining two wing turrets arranged en-echelon (but with no provision for the cross-deck firing found in the later British *Neptune/Colossus* class and the German *Kaiser* class – not to mention various late nineteenth-century turret ships). In place of the 'traditional' upperworks of the

São Paulo fitting out at Barrow alongside HMS *Vanguard* in early 1910. *(Author's collection)*

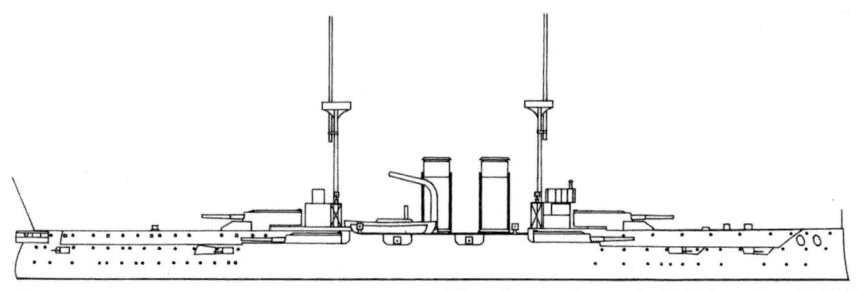

Minas Geraes class as first laid down Nov 06 (439A)
14,564 tons; 428 x 78 x 24.1ft; 14,000ihp = 19kt
Ten 10in/50, twelve 12pdr, eight 3pdr guns; five 18in TT
Main belt 9in

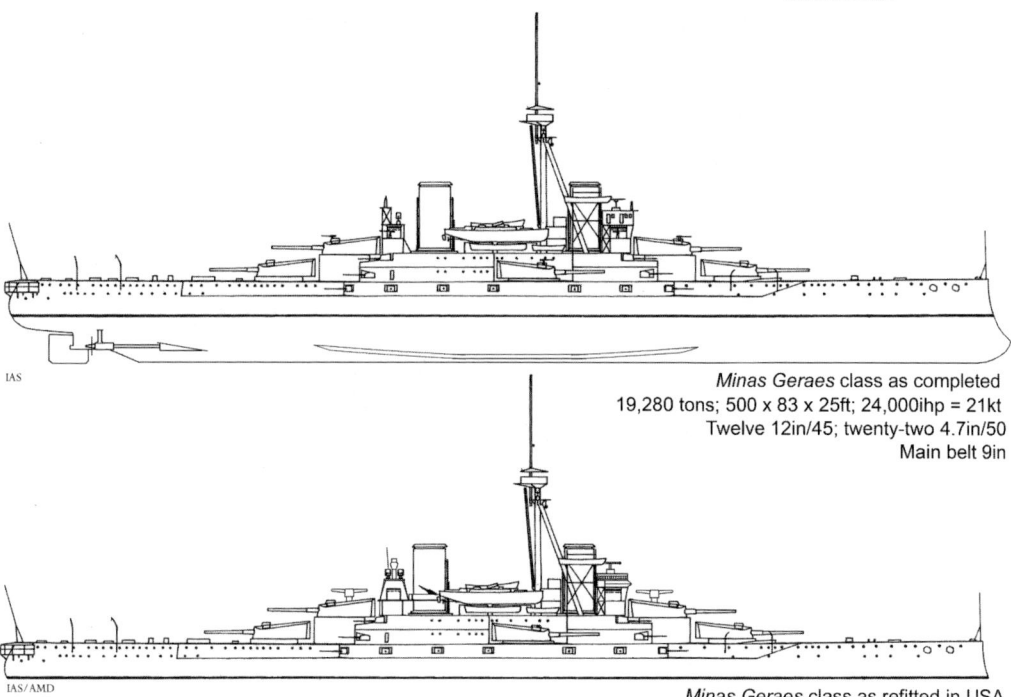

Minas Geraes class as completed
19,280 tons; 500 x 83 x 25ft; 24,000ihp = 21kt
Twelve 12in/45; twenty-two 4.7in/50
Main belt 9in

Minas Geraes class as refitted in USA

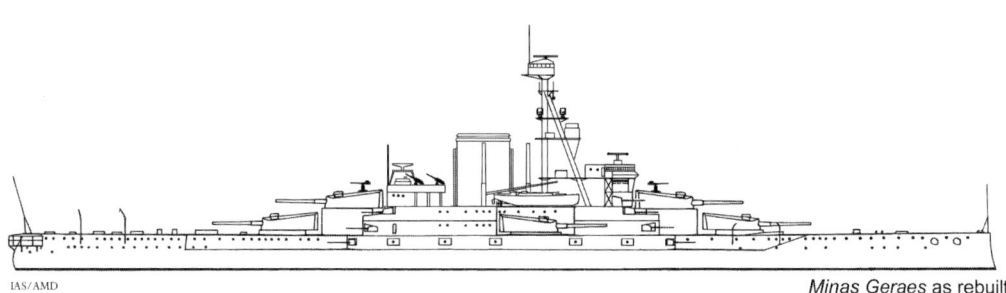

Minas Geraes as rebuilt

The launch of *Minas Geraes* at Elswick on 10 September 1908, and fitting-out at Walker in late 1909. *(Author's collection)*

original design, the superstructure was very similar to that of *Dreadnought*, including the combined tripod mast-cum-boat derrick directly behind the forefunnel. One area which remained little changed was the machinery, which continued to use reciprocating engines (albeit now uprated to give 21kt), rather than *Dreadnought*'s turbines. This was doubtless a matter of risk-reduction, as well as recognising the likely issues with maintaining such new technology in Brazil.

The building programme was amended so that *Rio de Janeiro* would now be laid down after the launch of *Minas Geraes*, using the same slip. Thus, the keel of *Minas Geraes* was re-laid on 17 April 1907, and that of *São Paulo* on 24 September. Work was delayed by strikes, *Minas Geraes* not being launched until 10 September 1908, and *São Paulo* on 20 April 1909.

In the meantime, further orders had been placed in the UK for smaller vessels of the programme, the scout cruisers *Bahia* and *Rio Grande do Sul* being laid down by Armstrong in August 1907 (a proposed sister, *Ceara*, was cancelled in 1909). They were essentially a slightly larger, more heavily-gunned, turbine-powered version of the *Adventure* class, laid down for the Royal Navy in 1904. Launched in 1909, they were completed in 1910. Yarrow received an order for ten destroyers of the *Pará* class.

Nevertheless, financial difficulties were looming in Brazil – but at the same time relations with Argentina were in a bad way, with the latter planning a major naval programme of her own. In an attempt at combining economy with conciliation, feelers were put out in early September 1908 towards the cancellation of the third Brazilian

The scout cruiser *Bahia*, launched in 1909; reconstructed during 1925–6, she would be lost in a freak accident in 1945, with very heavy casualties. (*Brazilian Navy*)

The destroyer *Amazonas*, built by Yarrow at Scotstoun, and launched in 1908; she is shown here on 7 September 1923 at Porto Alegre. (*Brazilian Navy*)

battleship. Armstrong's reaction was that, while financing terms could be stretched out, under the existing contract they were expecting the go-ahead to lay down *Rio de Janeiro* in the very near future, as the slipway was just about to be vacated by the launch of *Minas Geraes*. Negotiations resulted in a postponement of *Rio de Janeiro* in exchange for financial concessions, but by the summer of 1909 Brazil's financial woes were worsening. Fresh negotiations were begun, crossing with a wholly contradictory direct agreement between the Brazilian minister and Armstrong to both accelerate the completion of *Minas Geraes* and to lay down *Rio de Janeiro* as soon as the former was complete. Against this background, the summer of 1909 saw rumours of a potential sale of the first two ships to Turkey, funded by a French loan. In the end, the Brazilians decided not to sell.[10]

To support the new battleships, an invitation to tender was issued in 1909 for a floating dock with a 22,000-ton lifting capacity. Vickers' bid of £190,000 was successful in October 1909, and the dock was begun at Barrow under the yard number 400. Launched in three sections on 7, 8 and 9 June 1910, the dock – now named *Affonso Penna* – left in tow

The floating dock *Affonso Penna*, designed specifically for the Brazilian dreadnoughts, en route to Rio de Janeiro in July 1910. *(CUL GBR/0012/MS/Vickers Doc 2336)*

Minas Geraes with her mast lowered to pass under the Tyne bridges on 16 August 1909. *(Author's collection)*

for Rio de Janeiro on 5 July. She would dock *Minas Geraes* for the first time on 23 December 1910.

However, an area not fully addressed in the implementation of the programme was the manning of the new ships, especially the matter of training. Non-commissioned technical specialists were lacking across the whole Brazilian navy, with an 80 per cent overall shortfall in 1909, some specialisms being without any available trained personnel. This of course massively undermined the efficiency of the new ships.

The handover of *Minas Geraes* occurred on 5 January 1910, the ship sailing for the Americas on 5 February, and commissioning at Rio de Janeiro on 18 April. *São Paulo* commissioned at Barrow on 12 July and sailed from Greenock on 16 September, arriving at Rio via Cherbourg

São Paulo on her sea trials. *(CUL GBR/0012/MS/Vickers Doc 2283)*

(where she embarked the Brazilian president) and Lisbon (where she was caught up in the Portuguese revolution) on 25 October. With the two new battleships now in service, the old *Riachuelo* was finally retired; she was sold for scrap in 1914, arriving at Bo'ness in the tow of two Dutch tugs for breaking-up on 14 May 1914.

Also in Brazilian waters in 1910 were the new scout cruisers *Bahia* (left the Tyne 16 April 1910) and *Rio Grande do Sul* (handed over 19 July 1910) and the first of the ten *Pará* class destroyers. Thus, much of the 1904/07 programme had been achieved, with only the submarines and their tender, and three river monitors, still to be put under contract. The submarines and tender were ordered from Fiat-San Giorgio at La Spezia as *F1*, *F3* and *F5*, and *Ceara*, in 1912, the monitor contracts going to Vickers at the same time. However, while the submarines joined the fleet in July 1914, followed by their tender in 1917, the monitors were caught up in the financial crisis that would contribute towards the sale of *Rio de Janeiro* at the end of 1913 (pp 74–5), and were similarly put on the market. Although Romania showed some interest, this came to nothing, and the vessels, *Javary*, *Solimões* and *Madiera*, were still laid up at Barrow in August 1914. Then, they were purchased from Vickers by the Admiralty, and became HM Ships *Severn*, *Humber* and *Mersey*, respectively.[11]

Soon after *São Paulo*'s arrival, she, her sister *Bahia* and the old *Deodoro*, plus four smaller vessels, became involved in the naval mutiny known as the Revolt of the Lash (Revolta da Chibata). On 16 November

The Brazilian submarines *F1*, *F3* and *F5* commissioning at La Spezia on 17 July 1914. *(Author's collection)*

THE WINDFALL BATTLESHIPS

View from the quarterdeck of *Minas Geraes*. (Bain News Service via LoC)

1910, a sailor received 250 lashes for injuring a shipmate. This became the catalyst for a long-simmering revolt that broke out on 22 November, based on demands for improved pay and conditions, and the abolition of corporal punishment. Having been seized by their crews, the battleships fired their secondary batteries at military installations around Rio de Janeiro. Although an amnesty bill was already passing through Congress, an attack by vessels led by *Rio Grande do Sul* was planned for the morning of the 25th. However, this was cancelled and once the amnesty bill had passed, the mutineers stood down on 26 November. A result of the mutiny was a distrust of the navy, and even discussion of the battleships being put up for sale, Turkey once again showing interest. However, it was decided to keep the ships, but for the time being the breechblocks of the battleships' guns were removed and stored ashore.[12]

The Third Dreadnought

Back at Elswick, work had begun on the *Rio de Janeiro* three days after *Minas Geraes* had been handed over, and by 16 March 1910 almost the whole keel was in place. It is not clear how far her design was intended to deviate from that of the original pair. A series of designs had been prepared for fitting turbines, all based on the installation in HMS *Superb*, laid down by Armstrong in 1907 and engined by Wallsend Slipway, but with the existing *Minas Geraes* boiler-room layout left unchanged. However, it is unknown which option had been chosen. All would have required the relocation of the magazines and shell rooms that had been placed between the two engine rooms, along the centreline, in the original pair, as the turbine-fit would have required the full width of the hull. As a result, the ship would certainly have had to be lengthened.

However, by the time that *Rio de Janeiro* had finally been laid down, the design was some three years old, and the era of the 'super-dreadnought' had begun with the start of the first of the UK's 13.5in-armed *Orion* class at the end of November 1909. In addition, Argentina had now ordered a pair of battleships in the USA, which would be laid down in the summer of 1910 (see pp 78–83). While nominally possessing the same main armament as the Brazilian ships, the guns were more powerful and capable of cross-deck fire (giving two more guns on the broadside), while the Argentine secondary batteries were much more powerful. Accordingly, on 7 May 1910, the head of the newly-established Brazilian Naval Commission in the UK, Admiral Duarte Huet de Bacellar Pinto Guedes (1836–1921), instructed Armstrong to cease work and prepare a completely new design.

Within a few days, three options had been identified, with two formal designs, one with ten (643) and one with twelve (645) 14in guns, submitted to the Brazilians; the latter was selected for further consideration. As well as providing larger guns, the new design allowed cross-deck firing by the en-echelon wing turrets, and was refined as Design 653. Discussions held in both the UK and Brazil resulted in the signature of a new contract on 10 October 1910. However, the latest laying-down of *Rio de Janeiro* was delayed by a strike and lockout that lasted until 15 December. In addition, in the wake of the Revolt of the Lash, approval was temporarily withheld by the Brazilian authorities, which contributed to Argentina limiting their battleship procurement to two vessels for the time being (p 85).

As soon as the ship had been laid down, Russia showed interest in her. This was against the background of Turkish naval expansion, and concerns that the Ottomans might try to acquire not only the new Brazilian ship, but one or more of the Argentine battleships building in the USA.[13] The true characteristics of *Rio de Janeiro* were, however,

Minas Geraes coaling. *(Bain News Service via LoC)*

difficult to ascertain, the only available published data estimating her at 32,000 tons with twelve 14in guns, for completion in the autumn of 1912. Nevertheless, the Russians were concerned that the *Sevastopol* class battleships due to be completed in 1914 for the Baltic Fleet would not be fully effective for some time after this, and if they could get *Rio de Janeiro* it would allow a partial filling of the capability gap between them and the Germans in the Baltic.

Acquiring the ship would also lessen the need to acquire additional cruisers, which could only be achieved in the short term by buying vessels of 'off the shelf' designs (*Dresden* or *Kolberg* class) from Germany. As a result, enquiries were made regarding the possibility of purchase, but on 8 June 1911 the Russian agent in the UK reported that the ship was not for sale, also providing the news that the ship's design was now being revised as compared to previous reports, although no details were available. This fact contributed to Russia dropping any plans to make further investigations into purchases, attention being focussed on the implementation of their big 1911 naval programme.

These changes to the design were the result of the appointment, in November, of a new Brazilian Navy Minister, Admiral Margues Leao. In accordance with the revised contract, he had to reapprove the order

The Latin-American Connection

(subject to any changes being cost-neutral), and in doing so he had reopened the matter of the calibre of the main armament. While in Germany earlier in 1910, he had been persuaded by Kaiser Wilhelm II that an increase to 14in was unnecessary. This was both on the basis that the German navy was perfectly happy with 12in guns for its battleships (although it would jump to 15in within two years), and that possessing guns of a uniform calibre would aid the three Brazilian battleships in operating and fighting together.

Right and overleaf: Armstrong designs for *Rio de Janeiro*.

Apr/May 1910

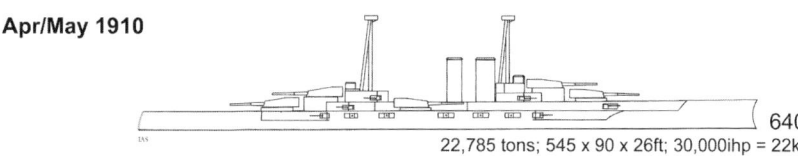

640
22,785 tons; 545 x 90 x 26ft; 30,000ihp = 22kt
Twelve 12in/50, twenty-two 4.7in/50 guns; three 21in TT
Main belt 12in

May 1910

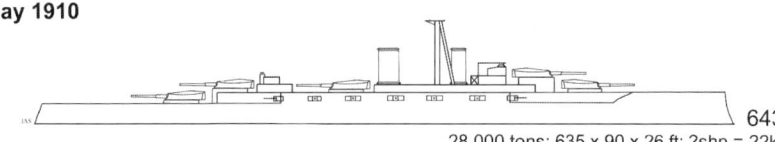

643
28,000 tons; 635 x 90 x 26 ft; ?shp = 22kt
Ten 14in/45, fourteen 6in/50, eight 3pdr guns; three 21in TT
Main belt 12in

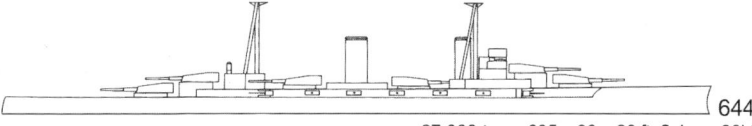

644
27,000 tons; 635 x 90 x 26 ft; ?shp = 22kt
Twelve 12in/50, fourteen 6in/50, eight 3pdr guns; three 21in TT
Main belt 12in

645
30,000 tons; 655 x 92 x 26 ft; ?shp = 22kt
Twelve 14in/45, fourteen 6in/50, eight 3pdr guns; three 21in TT
Main belt 12in

September 1910

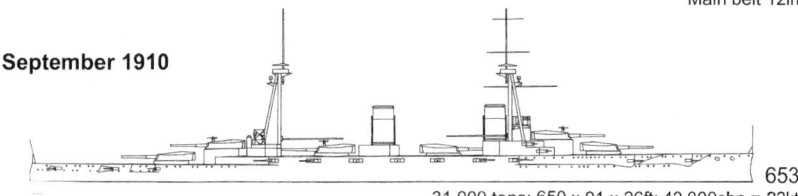

653
31,000 tons; 650 x 91 x 26ft; 42,000shp = 22kt
Twelve 14in/45, fourteen 6in, fourteen 4in, eight 3pdr guns; three 21 TT
Main belt 12in

January 1911

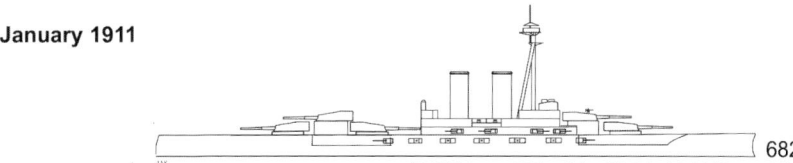

682
19.350 tons; 500 x 84 x26.5 ft; 23,400ihp = 22kt
Ten 12in/45, twenty-two 4.7in, eight 3pdr guns; three 21in TT
Main belt 9in

The Windfall Battleships

January 1911

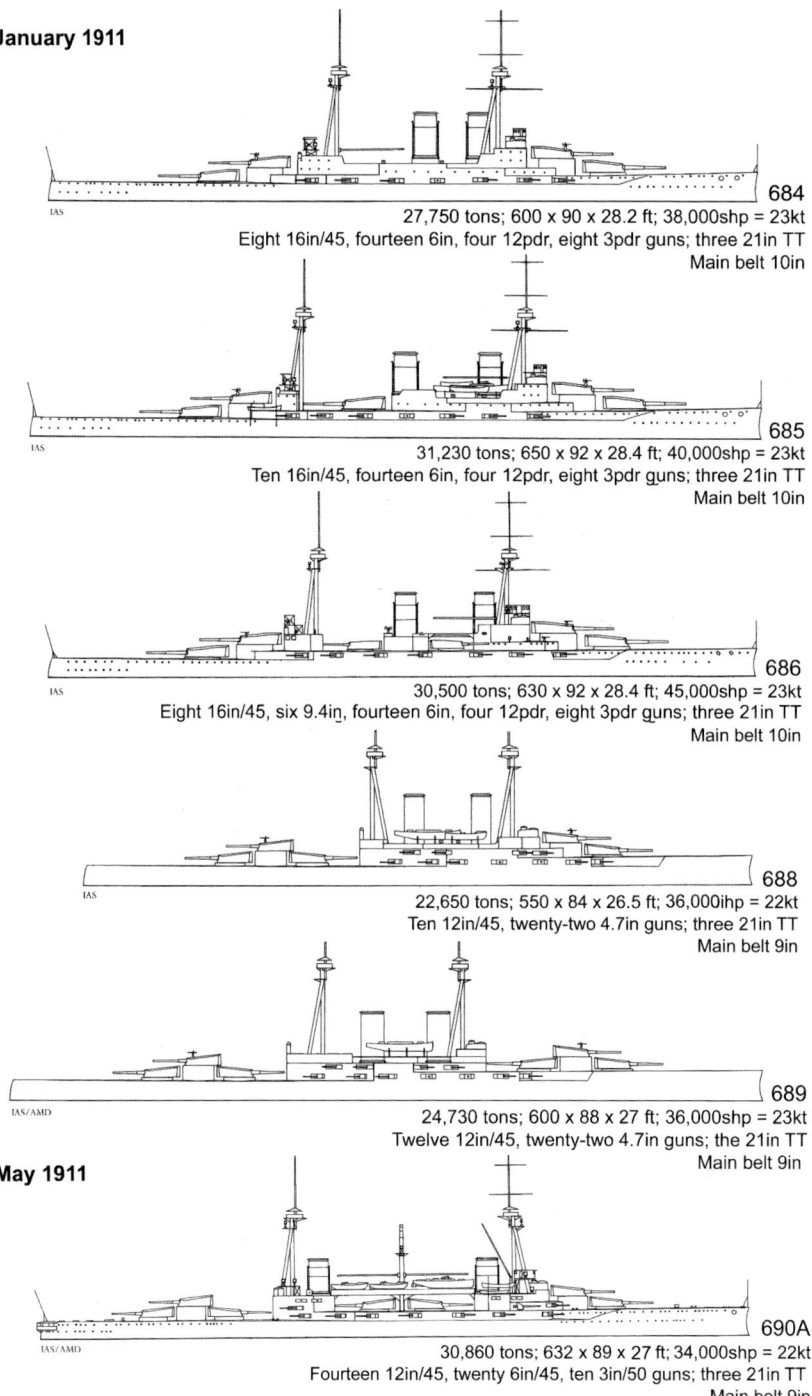

684
27,750 tons; 600 x 90 x 28.2 ft; 38,000shp = 23kt
Eight 16in/45, fourteen 6in, four 12pdr, eight 3pdr guns; three 21in TT
Main belt 10in

685
31,230 tons; 650 x 92 x 28.4 ft; 40,000shp = 23kt
Ten 16in/45, fourteen 6in, four 12pdr, eight 3pdr guns; three 21in TT
Main belt 10in

686
30,500 tons; 630 x 92 x 28.4 ft; 45,000shp = 23kt
Eight 16in/45, six 9.4in, fourteen 6in, four 12pdr, eight 3pdr guns; three 21in TT
Main belt 10in

688
22,650 tons; 550 x 84 x 26.5 ft; 36,000ihp = 22kt
Ten 12in/45, twenty-two 4.7in guns; three 21in TT
Main belt 9in

689
24,730 tons; 600 x 88 x 27 ft; 36,000shp = 23kt
Twelve 12in/45, twenty-two 4.7in guns; the 21in TT
Main belt 9in

May 1911

690A
30,860 tons; 632 x 89 x 27 ft; 34,000shp = 22kt
Fourteen 12in/45, twenty 6in/45, ten 3in/50 guns; three 21in TT
Main belt 9in

THE LATIN-AMERICAN CONNECTION

As a result, a series of 12in-armed designs (682, 683, 687–690) were submitted to Admiral Bacellar on 27 February 1911 – together with five armed with 16in guns (684–686). One of the latter, Design 686, was most unusual in having, at the request of Bacellar (who still favoured a larger-calibre main gun), an intermediate battery of six 9.4in guns installed amidships. Plans and models were prepared for final negotiations in Brazil, but before Armstrong's chief designer, Eustace Tennyson-D'Eyncourt (1868–1951), arrived there it had become clear that the Minister had won the argument and that a 12in-gunned ship was required.

The contract required that the new order be of at least equal value to the one for the 14in-gunned ship, which was of course more than the

Summary of the principal characteristics for the various designs submitted for *Rio de Janeiro*.

Design No	640	641	643	644	645	653
	Apr/May 10	Apr/May 10	11 May 10	11 May 10	11 May 10	May 11
Length (pp)	545	590	600	600	620	650
Length (oa)			635	635	655	690
Beam	90	90	90	90	92	92
Draught	26	26	26	26	26	26
Displacement	22,785	25,600	28,000	27,000	30,000	31,000
Armament	12 x 12in/50	10 x 14in	10 x 14in/45	12 x 12in/50	12 x 14in/45	12 x 14/45
	22 x 4.7in	16 x 6in	14 x 6in/50	14 x 6in/50	14 x 6in/50	14 x 6in/50
						14 x 4
	3 x 21in TT	3 x 21in TT	3 x 21in TT	3 x 21in TT	3 x 21in TT	3 x 21in TT
Engines	VTE	VTE				Tu
IHP/SHP	30,000	30,000	?	?	?	42,000
Speed (kt)	22	?	22	22	22	22
Main Belt	12in	12in	12in	12in	12in	12in

Design No	682	683	684	684A	685	685A
	Jan 11	Jan 11	Jan 11	Jan 11	Jan 11	Jan 11
Length (pp)	500	526	600	620	650	670
Length (oa)	536	556	640	666	690	710
Beam	84	85	90	92	92	92
Draught	26.5	26.5	28.2	28.2	28.3	28.3
Displacement	19,350	19,600	27,750	29,000	31,230	32,300
Armament	10 x 12/45	10 x 12in/50	8 x 16in/45	8 x 16in/45	10 x 16in/45	10 x 16in/45
	22 x 4.7in	22 x 4.7	14 x 6in	14 x 6in	14 x 6in	14 x 6in
			4 x 12pdr	4 x 12pdr	4 x 12pdr	4 x 12pdr
			8 x 3pdr	8 x 3pdr	8 x 3pdr	8 x 3pdr
	3 x 21in TT	3 x 21in TT	3 x 21in TT	3 x 21in TT	3 x 21in TT	3 x 21in TT
Engines	VTE	VTE				
IHP/SHP	23,400	23,400	40,000	38,000	40,000	41,000
Speed (kt)	22	22	23	23	23	23
Main Belt	9in	10in	10in	10in	10in	10in

Design No	686	687	688	689	690	690A
	Jan 11	Jan 11	Jan 11	Jan 11	Jan 11	May 11
Length (pp)	630	500	550	600	625	632
Length (oa)	670	540	590	640	665	668
Beam	92	86	87	88	89	89
Draught	28.3	26	26.5	27	27	27
Displacement	30,500	20,500	22,650	24,730	26,750	27,850
Armament	8 x 16in/45	10 x 12in/45	10 x 12in/45	12 x 12in/45	14 x 12in/45	14 x 12in/45
	6 x 9.4in/51.7					
	14 x 6in	22 x 4.7in	22 x 4.7in	22 x 4.7in	22 x 4.7in	20 x 6in/45
	4 x 12pdr					10 x 12pdr/50
	8 x 3pdr	8 x 3pdr	8 x 3pdr	8 x 3pdr	8 x 3pdr	4 x 3pdr
	3 x 21in TT	3 x 21in TT	3 x 21in TT	3 x 21in TT	3 x 21in TT	3 x 21in TT
Engines	VTE	VTE	VTE	Tu	VTE	Tu
IHP/SHP	45,000	28,000	36,000	36,000	36,000	34,000
Speed (kt)	23	21.5	23	23	23	22
Main Belt	10in				9in	9in

price of a repeat *Minas Geraes*. This meant that any new design had to be a very clear step-up from the earlier ship. The latter only had a ten-gun broadside, so options such as Design 689, with twelve guns on the centreline, were certainly more powerful in military terms. However, *on paper* there appeared to be no improvement, and this fact contributed to the final decision, which was to go with the fourteen-gun Design 690.

Last-minute discussions included increasing the secondary gun-calibre from 4.7in to 6in, and thickening the upper belt from 8in to 9in, but on 3 June 1911 the final contract for *Rio de Janeiro* was signed. She was laid down again on 14 September 1911, construction proceeding a background of considerable secrecy. Indeed, it was reported that key elements of the ship's plans were kept in the possession of Armstrong Chairman Sir Andrew Noble.[14] To allow her to be docked, an additional 159.5ft section was ordered from Vickers in mid-1913 to lengthen the floating dock *Affonso Penna* from 548ft to 715ft, and to increase its lifting capacity by 50 per cent, to 30,000 tons. It is unclear whether his section (Vickers Job 447) had actually been laid down before *Rio de Janeiro* was sold to Turkey, but material had certainly been gathered, and the contract survived to be taken over by the Admiralty towards the end of the First World War. The dock was thus completed with two 75ft extensions at each end to make a 309.5ft structure (Works No 1518B) capable of taking two 300ft ships abreast. Launched on 1 May 1919 from berths 7–9 at Barrow, it left in tow on the 12th, probably for the Gareloch, where most of its remaining life was spent. Never used by the Royal Navy, it was sold to A Fletcher in November 1920 for £50,000, and then for scrap in 1927, arriving at Troon prior to 5 January 1928.[15]

Eustace Tennyson d'Eyncourt (1868–1951), Armstrong's chief designer, and then Director of Naval Construction at the Admiralty from 1912 to 1924. *(Bain News Service, via LoC)*

However, long before *Rio de Janeiro*'s launch on 22 January 1913 (by Admiral Bacellar's wife), it had become clear that the Brazilians had backed the wrong calibre-horse. Even before her final laying-down, on 17 April 1911 the USA had begun the 14in-armed *Texas*, followed by her sister *New York* on 11 September. Worse, on 27 November, Armstrong themselves had laid the keel of a 14in-gunned ship for Chile, with a sister to follow. Argentina was also talking of a third battleship with bigger guns – perhaps of up to 16in calibre. Even the Germans were giving up their 12in policy, with designs for ships with 13.7in and 15.7in guns presented to the Kaiser in September 1911 and January 1912. These would result in the 15in-armed *Bayern* class battleships, ordered under the 1913 programme, and the 13.7in-armed *Mackensen* class battlecruisers. The British had already gone to 15in guns in the *Queen Elizabeth* class laid down in 1912–13.

Worse still, the Brazilian economy was again doing badly. Accordingly, striving to make required savings, Alencar (now again Navy Minister) embraced the capability issue by announcing in the summer

THE LATIN-AMERICAN CONNECTION

The waterfront at Elswick in January 1914, showing *Sultan Osman I*, the cruiser HMS *Birmingham*, and *Almirante Latorre* at various stages of fitting-out. (Author's collection)

that *Rio de Janeiro* would be sold, since 'the design of the ship did not harmonize with the organization of the fleet'. It was also hinted that *Minas Geraes* and *São Paulo* might also be disposed of. Thus, by 4 September 1913, Brazil's bankers, Rothschilds – who had throughout played a crucial role in Brazil's battleship programme – had been instructed to attempt to sell *Rio de Janeiro*, with a reserve price understood to be £2.75 million. Armstrong countered with a proposal to replace the seven 12in turrets with single 15in mountings to resolve the 'capability' issue, but nothing came of this. The key Brazilian requirement was immediate cash, and a delay in any recycling of that cash by making any replacement order. Accordingly, during the coming weeks, interest was reported from Italy, France, Greece and Turkey, as means of boosting their fleets of capital ships.

Russia had previously been interested in the ship (cf pp 69–70), but was not a bidder now that *Rio de Janeiro* was finally for sale: it was judged that the costs of making the ship compatible with Russian standards would be too high.[16] The Brazilian decision to sell had also coincided with a diplomatic clash between Russia and Germany over the arrival of a German military mission in Turkey. In this context, a bidding war with the latter over the battleship would have not been productive in light of Russia's relationship with the UK.[17]

Italy was reported at the time to be the likely purchaser, although there actually appear to be no documents in the Italian archives to

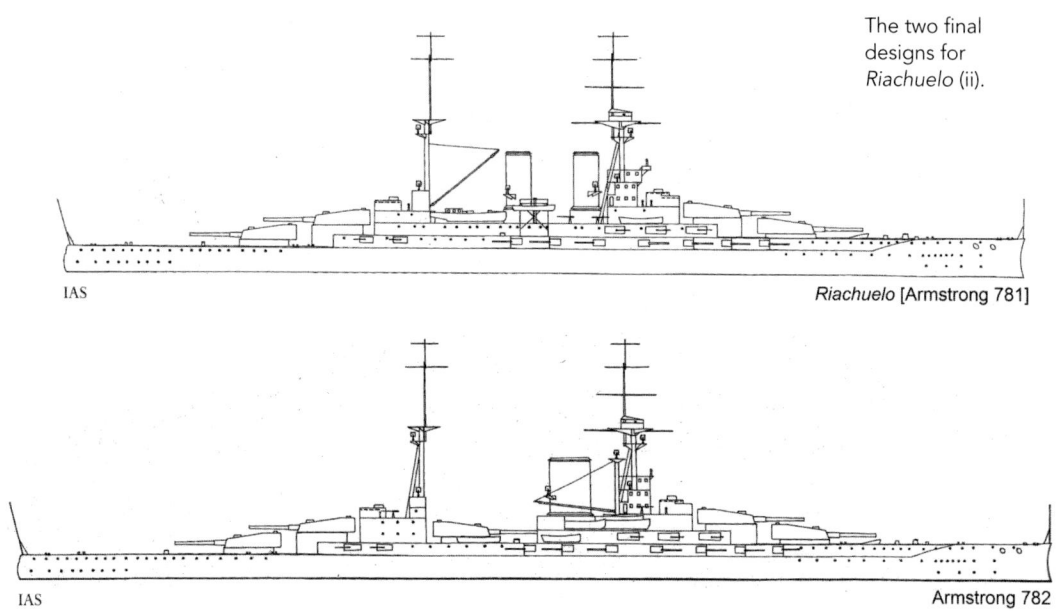

The two final designs for *Riachuelo* (ii).

Riachuelo [Armstrong 781]

Armstrong 782

Design No	Vickers 670	Vickers 671	Vickers 672	Vickers 677	Vickers 688	Vickers 689
	3 Dec 13	3 Dec 13	3 Dec 13	Jan 14	Mar 14	Mar 14
Length (pp)	605	625	605	570	575	625
Beam	94	95	94	94	94	96
Draught	28.5	28.5	28.5	27	28	28
Displacement	28,950	30,500	28,560	26,000	27,000	30,000
Armament	8 x 16in/40 10 x 6in/50 8 x 6pdr 8 x 3pdr 4 x 3in AA 6 x 21in TT	10 x 15in/45 10 x 6in/50 8 x 6pdr 8 x 3pdr 4 x 3in AA 6 x 21in TT	8 x 15in/45 10 x 6in/50 8 x 6pdr 8 x 3pdr 4 x 3in AA 6 x 21in TT	8 x 16in/40 10 x 6in/50 8 x 6pdr 8 x 3pdr 4 x 3in AA 4 x 21in TT	8 x 15in/45 14 x 6in/50 10 x 4.7in/50 4 x 3pdr 2 x 3in AA 3 x 18in TT	10 x 15in/45 14 x 6in/50 10 x 4.7in/50 4 x 3pdr 2 x 3in AA 3 x 18in TT
SHP	60,000	60,000	60,000	?	35,000	37,000
Speed (kt)	25	24.5	25	22	22	22.5
Main Belt	12	12	12	12	12	12
Barbettes	10	10	10	10	10	10

Design No	Armstrong 781	Armstrong 782	Armstrong 783	Armstrong 784	Armstrong 785	Armstrong 786	Armstrong 787	Armstrong 788
	25 Feb 14	25 Feb 14	25 Feb 14	25 Feb 14	25 Feb 14	25 Feb 14	25 Feb 14	25 Feb 14
Length (pp)	620	670	620	670	600	660	600	660
Length (oa)	660	710	660	710	640	700	640	700
Beam	94	96	94	96	93	95	93	95
Draught	28	28	28	28	28	28	28	28
Displacement	30,500	34,500	30,750	34,250	28,000	32,500	28,050	32,250
Armament	8 x 15in/42 14 x 6in/50 10 x 4in/50 4 x 3pdr 3 x 3in AA 2 x 21in TT	10 x 15in/42 14 x 6in/50 10 x 4in/50 4 x 3pdr 3 x 3in AA 2 x 21in TT	8 x 15in/42 14 x 6in/50 10 x 4in/50 4 x 3pdr 3 x 3in AA 2 x 21in TT	10 x 15in/42 14 x 6in/50 10 x 4in/50 4 x 3pdr 3 x 3in AA 2 x 21in TT	8 x 15in/42 14 x 6in/50 10 x 4in/50 4 x 3pdr 3 x 3in AA 2 x 21in TT	10 x 15in/42 14 x 6in/50 10 x 4in/50 4 x 3pdr 3 x 3in AA 2 x 21in TT	8 x 15in/42 14 x 6in/50 10 x 4in/50 4 x 3pdr 3 x 3in AA 2 x 21in TT	10 x 15in/42 14 x 6in/50 10 x 4in/50 4 x 3pdr 3 x 3in AA 2 x 21in TT
SHP	?	?	?	?	?	?	?	?
Speed (kt)	22.5	22.5	?	24	22	22.5	23.5	24
Main Belt	13.5	13.5	13.5	13.5	13.5	13.5	13.5	13.5
Barbettes	13	13	13	13	13	13	13	13

Designs for *Riachuelo*

suggest serious interest.[18] In any case, France then intervened with the British government to delay any sale to give themselves a chance to bid – apparently on behalf of Greece. The underlying priority for the French, however, was to avoid Italy acquiring *Rio de Janeiro* and upsetting the dreadnought balance between her and France (both had four ships due for completion by 1914). In fact, Italy seems to have dropped out of the race of its own volition on 27 November 1913, leaving the field to the two Balkan nations – with Turkey the eventual winner (see next chapter).

Having disposed of *Rio de Janeiro*, and despite the ongoing financial crisis, Brazil requested fresh designs from both Armstrong and Vickers. The latter provided six (670–672, 677, 688, 689) between December 1913 and March 1914, and the former eight (781–788) in February 1914. Both offered options with eight and ten 15in guns, Vickers also having an eight-16in design (670); displacements ranged from 26,000 tons to 34,250 tons. Options also included both 'fast' oil-fired vessels (following the concept of the *Queen Elizabeth* class [Vickers 670–672, Armstrong 784, 788]) and 'slower' (but still faster than the UK-standard 21kt) mixed-firing designs.

In the end, Armstrong's Design 781 was selected. It was a 30,500-tonner, with eight 15in/42, fourteen 6in/50, ten 4in/50, three 3in AA, four 3pdr and two 21in TT, and of 22.5kt speed. Armour included a belt of up to 13.5in thickness, and barbettes and conning tower up to 13in. All were somewhat thicker than the contemporary British *Revenge* class, reversing the trend of earlier Armstrong export battleships. Ordered on 14 May 1914, only some material had been gathered for the laying-down of what had now been named *Riachuelo* on 10 September when this was postponed by the outbreak of the First World War. Work was suspended on 14 January 1915 and formally stopped on 13 May 1915, bringing an end to the convoluted story of the Brazilian battleship programme.

Argentina

In parallel with the first phases of the Brazilian battleship programme, in 1906 Vickers and John Brown offered Argentina designs for similar ships.[19] Vickers began with the 10in-armed Design 192 (very similar to the original *Minas Geraes* concept), followed in May by the 14,000-ton, eight-12in-armed Design 211, and Design 214, with four 12in and twelve 9.2in guns. Both were based on HMS *Lord Nelson*, launched in 1906. The same month John Brown put forward two designs of similar size. Further designs were proposed in 1907, the 19,000-ton Vickers Design 265 having eight 12in and eight 10in, and Design 282 a dozen

The Windfall Battleships

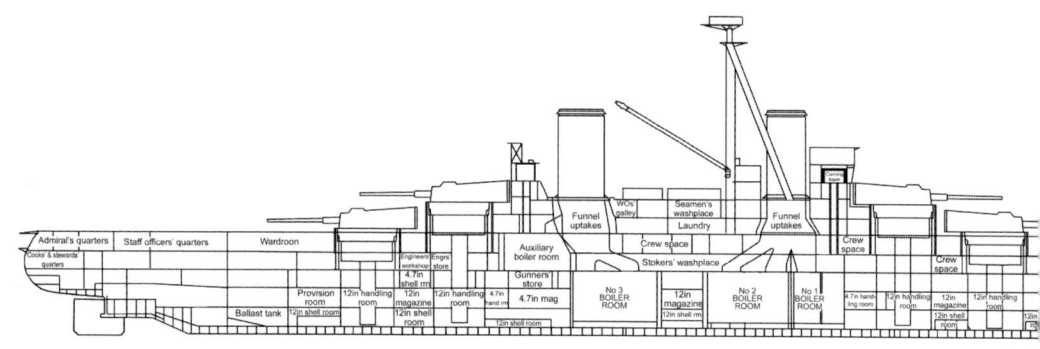

Displacement: 19,105 (*São Paulo*)/19,280 (*Minas Geraes*) (normal), 21,370 (full load) tons.
Dimensions: 500 (pp), 543 (oa) x 83 x 24.7 (normal), 27.25 (full load) feet.
Machinery: Eighteen Babcock & Wilcox boilers; two shafts; VTE; 23,400ihp = 21kt.
Armament: Twelve 12in/45, twenty-two 4.7in/50, eight 3pdr, four 75mm guns.
Complement: 850.

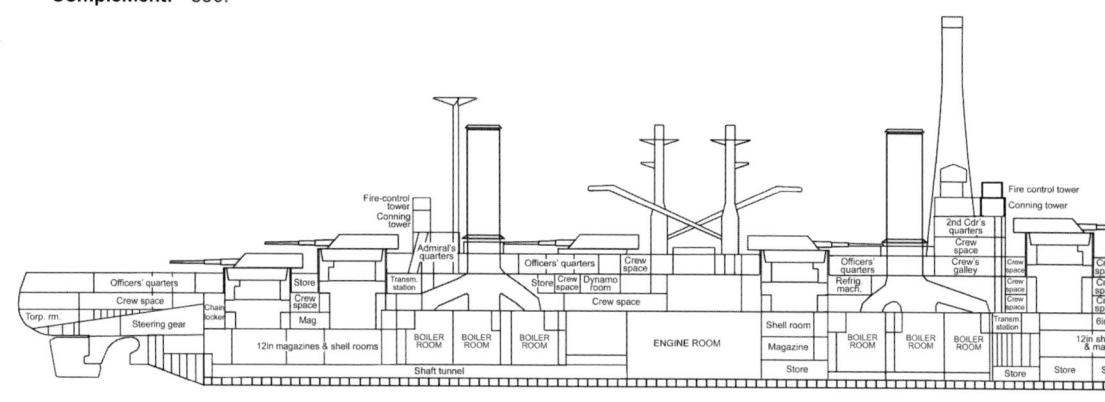

Displacement: 28,000 (normal), 30,600 (full load) tons.
Dimensions: 557.8 (pp), 604 (oa) x 95.5 x 27.8 feet.
Machinery: Eighteen Babcock & Wilcox boilers; three shafts; Curtis turbines; 39,500shp = 22kt.
Armament: Twelve 12in/50, twelve 6in/50, twelve 4in/50 guns; two 21 in TT.
Complement: 1080.

12in. Design 312 was put forward in 1908, carrying triple turrets fore and aft, for a total of fourteen 12in weapons.

By this time the Brazilian battleship programme had led Argentina to decide against renewing her naval treaty with Chile, meaning that the ships paid off as a result could be recommissioned and new ships ordered from the summer of 1907 onwards without advance notification. As far as the challenge presented by the Brazilian programme itself was concerned, September 1907 saw a £7.2 million naval bill being planned by the Argentine cabinet, subject to obtaining a necessary international financial loan. In June 1908, a plan was devised by Foreign Minister

The Latin-American Connection

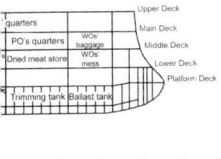

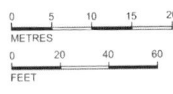

© Aidan Dodson 2021

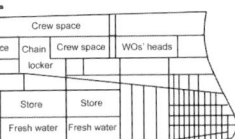

Estanislao Zeballos (1854–1923) proposing that Brazil be requested to transfer one of the new battleships to Argentina to preserve the naval balance – and that if they refused, Rio de Janeiro should be occupied by the Argentine army. This was swiftly leaked to the media, and Zeballos was forced to resign.

The desirability of Argentina building ships in reply to the Brazilian pair was much debated. There was much press sabre-rattling against Brazil, which insisted in response that the new ships were simply required to replace obsolete tonnage. This led in August 1908 to the passage of a bill by the Argentine Chamber of Deputies authorising the acquisition of three battleships. Three months later, the bill was defeated in the Senate. As a consequence, the government made a formal offer to purchase one of the Brazilian battleships; this was rejected by Brazil. The bill was reintroduced and passed by the Senate on 17 December 1908, authorising a sum equivalent to £14 million.

Concerned at the implications of a South-American naval race, the USA exhorted the parties to pull back, but renewed border disputes between Argentina, Brazil and Uruguay over jurisdictions in the River Plate provided ammunition for those urging the building of Argentine battleships. A battleship procurement office had already been established at the Argentine legation in London, and in October 1908, expressions of interest were invited. The requirement was for two (three, should Brazil continue with *Rio de Janeiro*) ships of 20,000 tons, with 12in guns, an 'adequate' secondary battery of 6in guns, 9in armour and 20.5kt speed – i.e. to at least match the *Minas Geraes* class (for whose armour, see p 259). Four 650-ton scouts and six 350-ton destroyers were also desired.

Thirty-eight firms made submissions, with a total of 144 separate tenders. Fifteen shipyards, from the United States, Great Britain, Germany, France and Italy, made proposals for the supply of the battleships, individual options numbering sixty-seven in all. Yards included: Germania (Kiel); Blohm & Voss (Hamburg); Armstrong; Vickers; John Brown; Cramp (Philadelphia); Newport News; Fore River (Quincy MA); New York Shipbuilding (Camden NJ); Ansaldo (Genoa); and La Seyne. All yards were given strong diplomatic support by their governments, in the case of the USA enhanced by the inauguration of President William Taft (1857–1930) in March 1909.

American aid to its yards went as far as sharing various US official specifications with the Argentine authorities, including those for the building and engining of USS *North Dakota* (the first US turbine-powered battleship) and USS *Perkins* and *Sterett* (destroyers being built by Fore River). Data was also provided for the manufacture of 12in Mk V, 8in Mk VI, 7in Mk II, 6in Mk VII Mod 1, 5in, 4in and 3in guns, mountings and sights. US navy systems were allowed to be used in bids submitted by US firms, and the manufacture of torpedo tubes for the ships was to be allowed at the Washington Navy Yard. US bankers were also prevailed upon to offer a £2 million loan to Argentina in support of the programme, and adjustments made to US customs duties on Argentine goods. A range of other external pressures on the procurement programme existed, including a pro-Italian Vice President of Argentina, and the Ministry of War arguing for German weapons to align with new army artillery recently ordered from Krupp. The influential newspaper *La Prensa* supported a US solution and opposed the procurement office, which was seen as pro-British.

As noted earlier, Armstrong and Vickers had already provided Argentina with a number of designs, their armaments ranging from eight to fourteen 12in guns, in either twin turrets or a mixture of twins and newly-developed triples.[20] Germania's offering looked rather like the *Nassau* class, laid down in 1907, but with the main guns superimposed fore and aft, and placed en-echelon amidships. This of course mirrored the Brazilian ships, but with cross-deck firing possible, and this layout was from the outset preferred by the Argentines.

Ansaldo's proposals[21] included a wide range of variations on a 21,000-ton, 577ft baseline design (A). These included the arrangement of the six twin 12in turrets (all on the centreline or with the midships pair en-echelon), the mounting of the sixteen 6in secondary guns (in single casemates or twin turrets), propulsion (reciprocating, turbine or combined), and speed (20.5–21.5kt). There were also more ambitious schemes. The 21,630-ton Design B had five turrets in a unusual layout, mounting either fifteen 12in or ten 14in guns, while the 21,400-ton Design C sacrificed one turret (giving twelve 12in or eight 14in) for 25kt speed. Other 'fast' (22–23kt) designs (F, G, H, L, M, O) were of 18,000 tons, with four triple 12in turrets (either on the centreline or en-echelon) and the secondary batteries reduced to 4.7in calibre and the tertiary guns to 3in. All featured a 9in belt, as did the 23,100-ton Design D. This had six turrets, each with either three 12in or two 14in guns, paired abreast on the forecastle and amidships, and superimposed aft. Versions of a number of these designs had also been submitted to Russia during the first phase of the competition for the design of what became the *Sevastopol* class, laid down in 1909.[22]

Ansaldo were judged to have produced the best technical options, including the typically Italian placement of the engines amidships, between separated groups of boiler rooms.[23] There were, however, concerns at delivery schedules, given the reliance of the Italian big-gun industry on Vickers and Armstrong,[24] who were, of course, also in competition for the order. The French offers were least well-regarded. However, financially, the Fore River offer appeared the best value (and

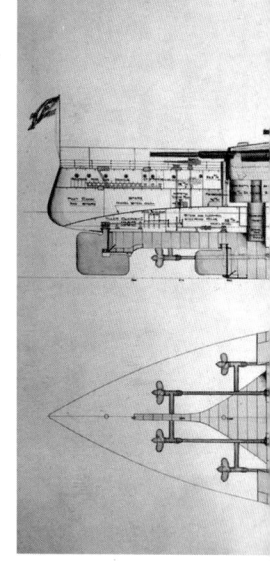

The Latin-American Connection

offered a good delivery schedule), followed by Ansaldo, the French and UK yards and then the German ones.

The requirement was then revised by the Argentine authorities, both in light of the proposals received and of the more detailed information now available regarding the *Minas Geraes* class, which ruled out some less-capable proposals. In October 1909, revised bids were invited, much to the disgust of the firms involved, as material from a number of the previous submissions was included in the data provided to guide the new round of tendering. This was seen by them as a gross breach of commercial confidentiality, permitting proprietary (and national) data to circulate around competitors.[25] The new invitation formally required the battleships to have a dozen guns of each of the 12in, 6in and 4in calibres, at least a 10in belt and a speed in excess of 22kt. At the same time, the scout/destroyer requirement was increased to twelve vessels (four of 100 tons, five of 530 tons and four of 1000 tons).

Ansaldo thickened the armour of their previous proposals that otherwise met the requirement to 10in, and increased speeds to 24kt, while other bidders were also revising their designs to accord with the revised Argentine requirements. These featured US-style cage masts, as well as the Italian-style machinery layout.[26] A further thickening of the belt armour to 12in at the waterline abreast the midships-placed machinery was also implemented in some designs. As a result, the final round of designs were visually all very similar, although with many detail differences (e g, the placement of the mast[s], and numbers of shafts [Vickers Design 428 had four shafts; Fall River offered three]). The final

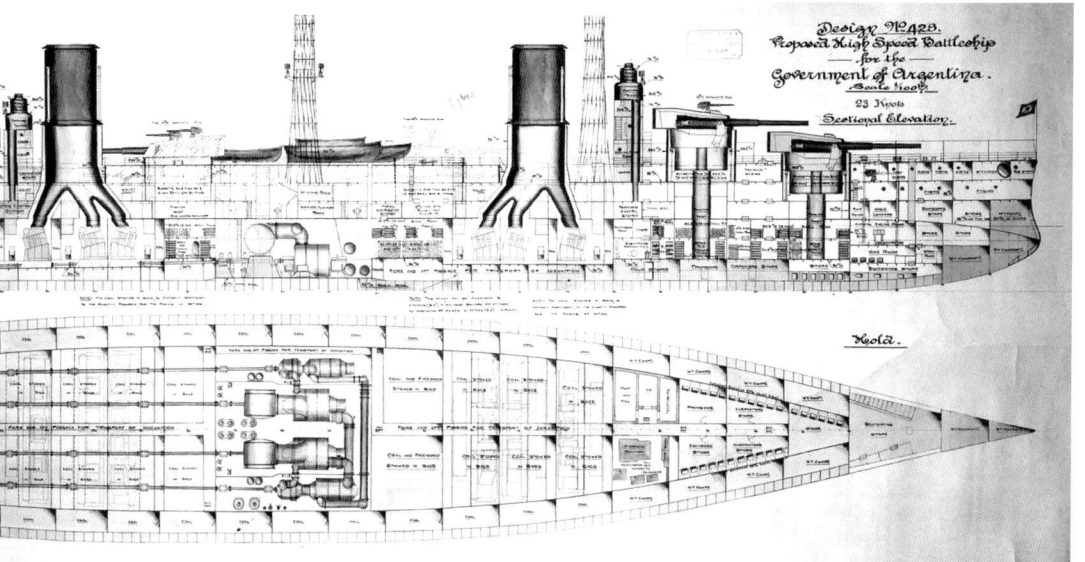

Vickers' Design 428 for the Argentine battleship order. *(NMM)*

The Windfall Battleships

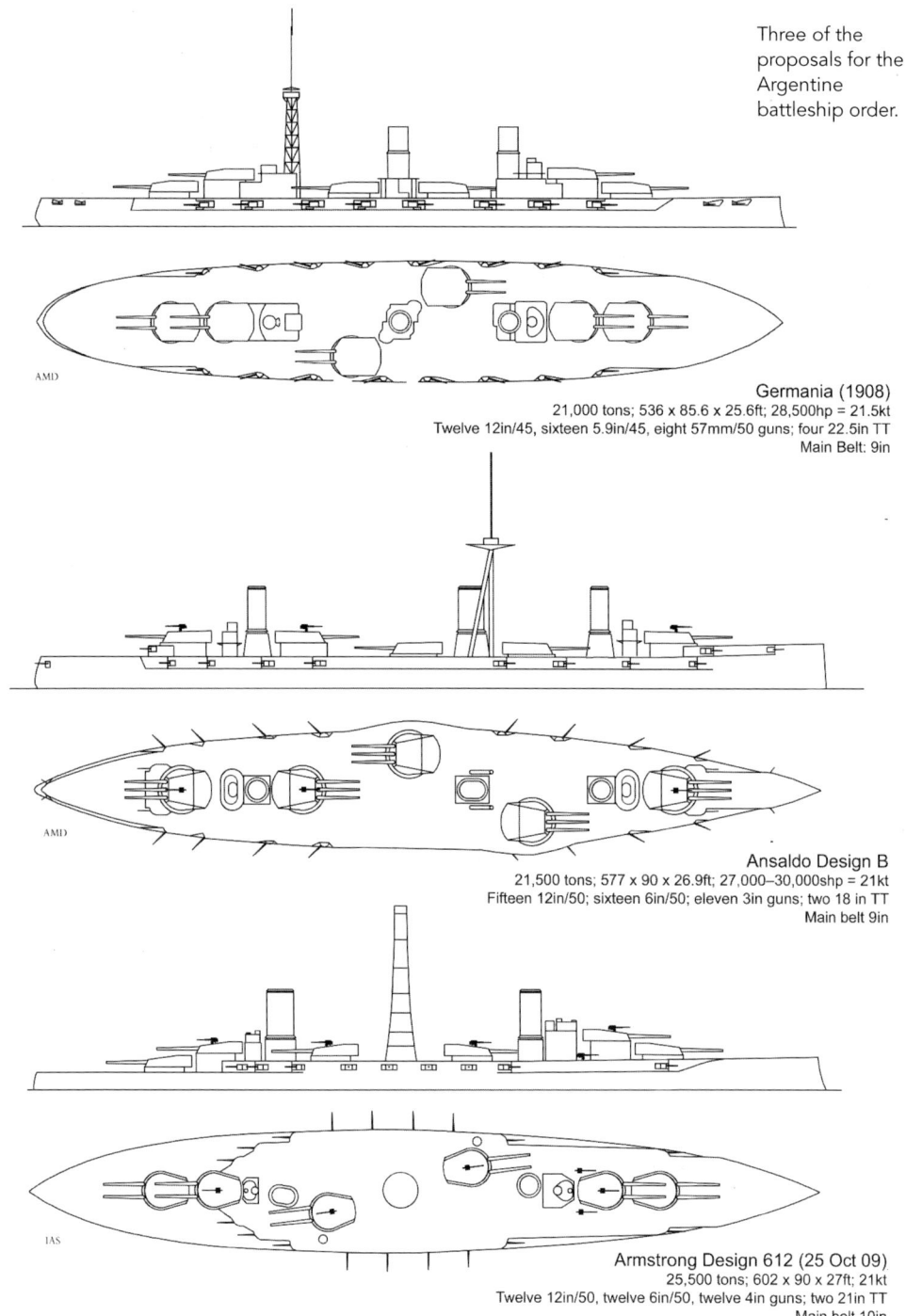

Three of the proposals for the Argentine battleship order.

Germania (1908)
21,000 tons; 536 x 85.6 x 25.6ft; 28,500hp = 21.5kt
Twelve 12in/45, sixteen 5.9in/45, eight 57mm/50 guns; four 22.5in TT
Main Belt: 9in

Ansaldo Design B
21,500 tons; 577 x 90 x 26.9ft; 27,000–30,000shp = 21kt
Fifteen 12in/50; sixteen 6in/50; eleven 3in guns; two 18 in TT
Main belt 9in

Armstrong Design 612 (25 Oct 09)
25,500 tons; 602 x 90 x 27ft; 21kt
Twelve 12in/50, twelve 6in/50, twelve 4in guns; two 21in TT
Main belt 10in

The Latin-American Connection

	Fore River	Vickers / Armstrong			La Seyne			Blohm & Voss		Ansaldo
Displacement (tons)	27,940	29,060	28,040	27,540	27,810	25,170	26,900	25,930	24,900	25,600
Speed (knots)	22.5	24	22.75	22	22	22	22	22.5	22	22
Main belt (inches, max)	12	12	12	12	10	10	12	12	12	10
Price per ship (£M)	2.19	2.50075	2.45075	2,42375	2.36275	2.2	2.358	2.304	2.2	2,2
Delivery (months)	24 & 27	-	-	33	-	29	27	30	-	24 & 28
Price per ton (£)	78.03	86.30	87.30	86.70	84.80	87.40	87.60	88.90	88.30	83.90

The final adjudication of Argentine dreadnought competition.

adjudication was carried out between the Fore River design, three options from Vickers and Armstrong, three from La Seyne, two from Blohm & Voss, and one from Ansaldo. All but two of the La Seyne designs and Ansaldo's had 12in belts amidships, speeds varying from 22kt to 24kt and displacements from 24,000 tons (Blohm & Voss) to 29,060 tons (Vickers/Armstrong, with 24kt speed). Delivery offers were 24/27 months (first ship/second ship) from Fore River, 24/28 months (first ship/second ship, Ansaldo), 27–29 months (La Seyne), 30 months (Blohm & Voss), and 33 months (Vickers/Armstrong). The cheapest offer was from Fall River, at £2.19 million per ship (£78.08 per ton); the highest were the three Vickers/Armstrong designs (£2.424–£2.501 million per ship, £86.30–£86.70 per ton).

The Fore River price and delivery schedule were clearly the most attractive, and despite a British attempt to give Armstrong and Vickers a chance to lower their prices, US diplomatic action smoothed the award of a contract for both ships to Fore River on 21 January 1910. Ansaldo felt particularly aggrieved at the result, given their original top-placing. This was further deepened when the UK, Germany and France received destroyer orders as part-compensation for their lack of success in the battleship competition (see below), but Italy got nothing.

Compared with *Minas Geraes* and *São Paulo*, the new Argentine battleships were some 9000 tons larger and 60ft longer. They had 16,000hp more power (provided by turbines, rather than reciprocating engines), 1.5kt more speed, and 40 per cent greater endurance.[27] In armament, the Argentine ships again had a significant edge. While the main batteries comprised a dozen 12in in both cases, spilt between axial and wing mountings, the Argentine vessels had 50- rather than 45-calibre weapons, with the midships guns capable of some cross-deck firing, increasing the potential broadside from ten to twelve guns. The Argentine secondary batteries were also heavier, with a dozen 6in, in broadside batteries, and a dozen 4in guns, six in embrasures fore and aft, two on the forecastle deck, two adjacent to the wing turrets, and two on top of the superimposed 12in turrets, although the turret-top guns seem not usually to have been mounted. Against this, the Brazilian battleships had twenty-two 4.7in weapons; the Argentine ships also had torpedo tubes, which the Brazilians lacked. Finally, the Argentine armour was thicker, 25 per cent more so on the waterline amidships.

The Argentine vessels' US origin was made clear by their cage masts forward, but other aspects of their design recalled European-designed vessels. The en-echelon arrangement of the midships turrets was never used by the US navy (although wing turrets had been a feature of a battleship design offered to the US navy by Fore River in 1906),[28] but were employed in some UK and German ships. The placement of the engine rooms amidships, between the boiler rooms, had, as already noted, long been a feature of Italian designs. The triple shafts had, however, been standard in German big ships since the 1890s.[29]

As noted above, the twelve destroyers that formed part of the programme were divided between Britain, France, and Germany. The German four-ship order was divided between Germania's 995-ton *Catamarca* class (*Catamarca* and *Jujuy*) and Schichau's 875-ton *La Plata*s

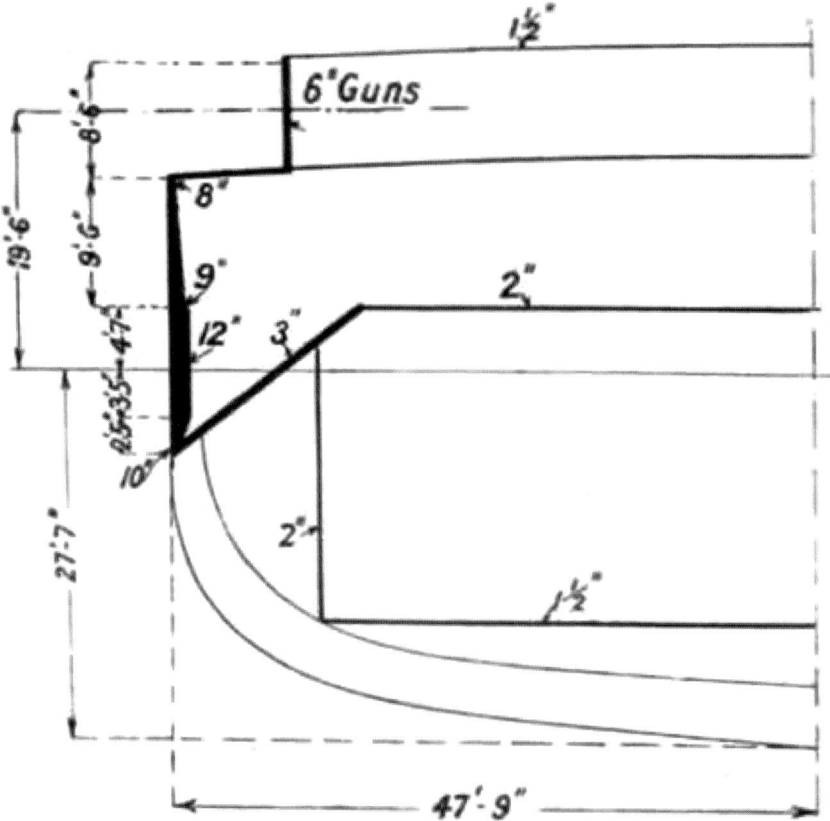

The midships armour scheme of the *Rivadavia* class; see p 259 for full scheme. (The Engineer, 1 December 1911, p 555)

(*La Plata* and *Córdoba*). Launched in 1910–11, they joined the Argentine fleet in the summer of 1912. The UK orders all went to Cammell Laird for the 980-ton *San Luis* class, launched in 1911. However, all four were sold to Greece in October 1912 (see pp 128–9, below), having proved disappointing on trials. The French-built 940-ton *Mendoza* class (*Mendoza*, *Rioja*, *Salta* and *San Juan*) were ordered from the Ateliers et Chantiers de Bretagne at Nantes, with two of the hulls subcontracted to the firm of Dyle et Bacalan at Bordeaux. Although launched in 1911, they also failed to reach their acceptance speeds, and were still the subject of negotiations when taken over by the French navy at the beginning of the war (p 45). Likewise overtaken by the war were four 1116-ton vessels ordered from Germania in April 1913 to replace the boats sold to Greece (*Santiago*, *San Luis*, *Santa Fé* and *Tucuman*). All were still on the stocks in August 1914, and were launched later that year, commissioning into the German navy in 1915 (p 47). These ships were designed with auxiliary diesels for cruising, but these were never installed. The takeover of these vessels meant that of sixteen destroyers ordered by Argentina between 1910 and 1914, only four ever joined the Argentine fleet.

Although the battleship contract had gone to Fore River, to speed delivery one ship was subcontracted to New York Shipbuilding, Camden NJ. The contract also contained an option for a third ship, but lobbying for this was undermined by the Brazilian Revolt of the Lash (pp 67–8, above), which demonstrated the flawed state of the Brazilian navy. Nevertheless, the third Argentine ship (to be named *Roca*) was ultimately authorised in October 1912, contingent on the completion of *Rio de Janeiro* by Brazil – which of course never happened. Whether such a ship should be a full sister of the current pair, or be of an enhanced design, was a moot point. Options discussed during 1912/13 included fourteen 12in or 14in guns (2 x 3 + 4 x 2, with the foremost and aftermost turrets triples; the midships turrets could have been either en-echelon or on the centreline). In case an armament of 14in guns might be contemplated, Fore River had been provided with some of the contract plans of the battleships USS *New York* and *Texas* and their 14in Mk I guns by the US authorities in October 1910, as well as the hull specifications of both *Texas* and the 12in-gunned *Arkansas*.

But even before the sale of *Rio de Janeiro*, the implications of the Revolt of the Lash had led to renewed calls from within Argentina for the country's existing ships to be sold. In December 1912 a New York yacht broker released a circular concerning a possible sale of the ships. These became more concrete after the disposal of *Rio de Janeiro*, although there was a complication in that the USA did not wish their naval technology in the ships to fall into the hands of certain powers. The contract with Fall River gave the US navy first refusal in the event

Rivadavia fitting out on the Weymouth Fore River at Quincy, on 2 December 1912. *(Bain News Service, via LoC)*

of any sales, but they did not want the ships, which were incompatible with the latest trends in US battleship design (e.g. 'all or nothing' protection and 14in guns). The US authorities accordingly tried to discourage any thoughts of sale.

THE LATIN-AMERICAN CONNECTION

As noted elsewhere (pp 94, 116, 117–18, 133–4), a number of nations expressed interest in purchase, but all three bills introduced into the Argentine Congress in May 1914 requiring the ships be sold failed. The ordering of *Riachuelo* that same month might have revived the idea of a third Argentine ship, but the onset of the First World War shortly afterwards reset the situation for the foreseeable future.

The Argentine ships took the names of the armoured cruisers that had been sold to Japan in 1904, *Rivadavia* being laid down at Quincy on 25 May 1910. *Moreno* followed suit at Camden on 9 July. They were launched on 26 August and 23 September 1911, respectively. *Rivadavia*'s initial sea trials were scheduled for late August 1913, off the coast of Maine, but turbine defects delayed these until mid-September. On

Rivadavia on sea trials in late 1914. (Bain News Service, via LoC)

16 September, she made 22.567kt, but during the 30-hour trial that began the next day, damage to one turbine meant that the ship had to divert to Boston. Engine problems continued, and in July 1914 a turbine was dropped from a crane while being reinstalled and had to be taken out again for further repairs.

When the First World War broke out, Germany expressed concerns to the US government that the ships might be handed over to the UK by Argentina on delivery; conversely, the UK were worried that they might fall into the hands of the Germans. *Rivadavia* was formally commissioned into the Argentine navy on 27 August 1914 in Boston harbour, finally completing in December 1914 – 59 months from date of contract and well over double the 24-month delivery timescale that had contributed towards the original Fall River success in the competition. She sailed from New York on 23 December and arrived at Buenos Aires, via Barbados, on 19 February 1915. There, she was visited by 47,000 people over three days, and then joined the Training Division. In this, she served alongside the cruisers *Garibaldi* and *Nueve de Julio*,

Moreno in dry dock at New York Navy Yard in October 1914. *(Author's collection)*

the destroyers *Catamarca* and *Jujuy*, and the old turret ship *La Plata* (1874), complemented in 1916 by the cruiser *Belgrano*, the coast defence ship *Libertad* and the destroyer *Córdoba*.

Moreno began her trials in October 1914, but also suffered from engine trouble, a complete turbine failing on 2 November. This required her to sail to the Fore River yard, which built the machinery for both ships, for repairs. She was handed over on 20 February 1915 and commissioned on the 26th, just in time to participate in an international naval review at Hampton Roads to mark the opening of the Panama Canal. On a run out to the Delaware River, she sank a barge in a collision and then ran aground on 26 March 1915. Refloated, she grounded again on 15 April, finally arriving in Argentine waters in on 26 May. In October, the battleship sailed with the active fleet to Puerto Madryn.

Chile

The ability of Chile to react to her neighbours' naval programmes was constrained by economic issues following on from the Valparaíso earthquake of 1906 and falls in the nitrate market in 1907. However, there remained issues with Argentina, and also Peru. The latter had ordered the 3100-ton cruisers *Almirante Grau* and *Coronel Bolognesi* from Vickers in 1905, and aspired to acquire three light battleships, three armoured cruisers and six destroyers. However, only the armoured cruiser *Dupuy de Lôme* (1890) and the destroyer *Actée* (1909), plus the submarines *Ferre* and *Palacios*, were ever purchased, from France (see p 94).

The Chilean Congress passed a bill on 6 July 1910 that provided funds for two battleships, six destroyers and two submarines. The resulting request for proposals required that the ships have British-manufactured guns, armour and machinery, implying that orders would go to British yards. Nevertheless, the battleship USS *Delaware* (1909) visited Chile in February 1911, primarily to return the body of the recently-deceased Chilean ambassador to the USA, but also implicitly to promote US materiel. During February–April 1911 Germany had sent the battlecruiser *Von der Tann* to Argentine and Brazilian waters, once again with a hope of demonstrating the capability of her owner's equipment. Indeed, US yards put forward proposals for both 12in and 14in-gunned ships for Chile, with guns to come from Armstrong in the UK or Bethlehem in the USA, and armour from Bethlehem.[30]

However, the order for the first battleship went to Armstrong in November 1911. Five designs by Perrett had been submitted to Chile on 4 April 1911, all with ten main guns, of 12in (Designs 666 and 695) or 14in/45[31] (669, 670 and 696) calibre, and secondary batteries of twenty 4.7in (666, 695, 696), eight 6in + twelve 4.7in (669), or fourteen 6in (670) guns. Four 21in submerged torpedo tubes were also included (see opposite for drawings of the principal designs).

The 27,400-ton Design 696 was chosen, and laid down as *Valparaiso* (Elswick Job 845) on 1 May 1912. The 14in gun had been selected to give a clear advantage over the Brazilian and Argentine battleships, its shells being some 60 per cent heavier than the 12in munitions of her potential opponents. Even if the Argentine vessels were successful in achieving cross-deck firing of their midships turrets, the Chilean ship would have a broadside over 35 per cent heavier.

The armour protection (see pp 174, 259) was explicitly designed to protect the vessel from the 12in guns of the Argentine ships, which were regarded as the most likely opponents. These fired a fairly light shell at a high muzzle velocity, and this fact underpinned the protection scheme, based on the assumption (shared with most other navies) that battle ranges would probably be short. In this context, the side armour, comprising a 9in waterline belt, together with 7in and 4.5in upper belts, was regarded as wholly adequate. It was only after the First World War demonstrated that ranges could be far greater than hitherto generally anticipated that the Chilean ship's protection could be seen as less appropriate. Soon after construction began, the secondary battery was changed to sixteen 6in/50. This reflected the increasing size of contemporary torpedo craft, as was the case with the shift from 4in to 6in secondary batteries in the UK's *Iron Duke* class and *Tiger*. The alteration increased the Chilean ship's displacement by 600 tons and added £154,000 to the cost. While improving capability, the changed weights increased the immersion of the main belt, which would now be submerged at full load, and reduced top speed by 0.25kt. A need to add 213 tons of ballast forward led to a 1ft trim by the bow.

Other changes worked into what was now Design 696A modified the rig, swapping the positions of the foremast and forefunnel, and deleting the tripod mainmast in favour of an unusual arrangement of two stump masts, placed abreast at the forward end of the aft superstructure. This latter feature was intended to provide additional flexibility for signalling in connection with the admiral's bridge mounted on the aft superstructure. The change to the forward rig reflected the (re)discovery by the Royal Navy that the placement of the foremast abaft the forefunnel, while enabling the boat-derrick to be rigged from it, meant that the control top could became unusable owing to smoke interference.[32]

Dreadnought had been fitted with a single mast behind the forefunnel, but the following *Bellerophon* and *St Vincent* classes had two tripod masts, one in front of each funnel, with *Neptune*'s mainmast

THE LATIN-AMERICAN CONNECTION

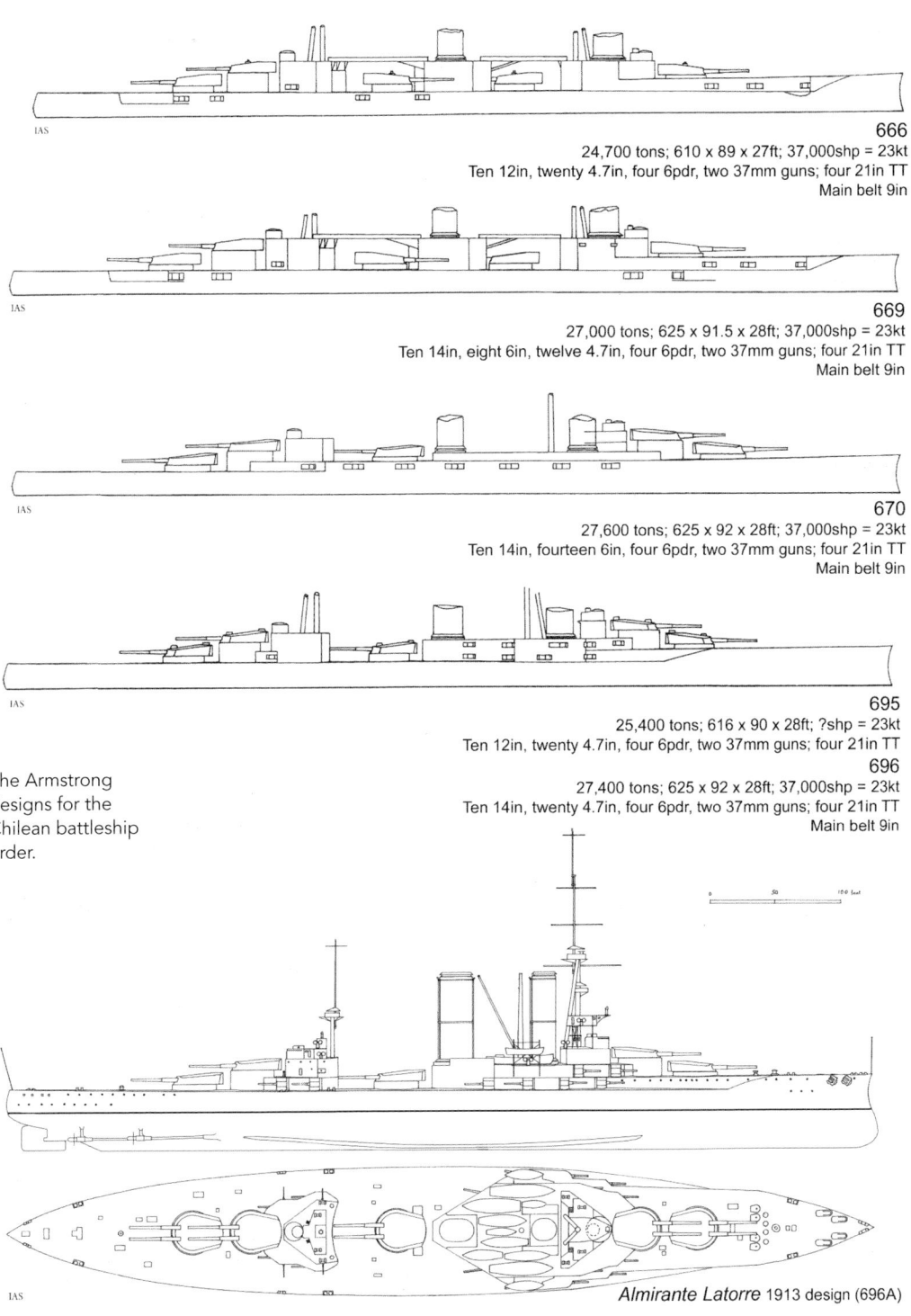

666
24,700 tons; 610 x 89 x 27ft; 37,000shp = 23kt
Ten 12in, twenty 4.7in, four 6pdr, two 37mm guns; four 21in TT
Main belt 9in

669
27,000 tons; 625 x 91.5 x 28ft; 37,000shp = 23kt
Ten 14in, eight 6in, twelve 4.7in, four 6pdr, two 37mm guns; four 21in TT
Main belt 9in

670
27,600 tons; 625 x 92 x 28ft; 37,000shp = 23kt
Ten 14in, fourteen 6in, four 6pdr, two 37mm guns; four 21in TT
Main belt 9in

695
25,400 tons; 616 x 90 x 28ft; ?shp = 23kt
Ten 12in, twenty 4.7in, four 6pdr, two 37mm guns; four 21in TT

696
27,400 tons; 625 x 92 x 28ft; 37,000shp = 23kt
Ten 14in, twenty 4.7in, four 6pdr, two 37mm guns; four 21in TT
Main belt 9in

The Armstrong designs for the Chilean battleship order.

Almirante Latorre 1913 design (696A)

Artist's impression of *Almirante Latorre* and *Almirante Cochrane* as designed, including large bridges fore and aft, and unique twin mainmasts; see also drawing on p 91. (J de Lacy, Illustrated London News, 13 December 1913)

moved aft to the rear superstructure. However, the *Colossus* and the immediately following *Orion* and *King George V* classes were designed to revert to the *Dreadnought* arrangement, which was also applied to the *Lion* class battlecruisers. These ships completed from mid-1911 onwards, and although the *Orion*s were broadly satisfactory, the *Colossus* class were much less so, and *Lion*'s trials were disastrous, her control top being completely untenable.

As a result, *Lion* and her nearly-complete sister *Princess Royal* had their forward superstructures and uptakes rebuilt, to transpose the positions of the forefunnel and the foremast. The *King George V*s were similarly altered while fitting-out, the change also being made to ships under construction for foreign customers. Experience with *Neptune* (and also the battlecruiser *Indefatigable*) had also shown that the control top on the mainmast was unusable owing to smoke, resulting in the deletion of the aft tripod from the Chilean battleship, and also from the Turkish *Reşadiye* (pp 111, 115).

The 22.75kt speed was still significantly higher than most contemporary battleships. This probably reflected Chilean experience of the importance of swiftness during the War of the Pacific and the Chilean Civil War of 1891, and subsequently manifested in the then-exceptional 18.25kt speeds of the battleship *Capitan Prat* (launched in 1890) and cruiser *Esmeralda* (1883). To guarantee this, the originally-proposed eighteen boilers in three compartments were increased to twenty-one in four boiler rooms in the final design, raising the nominal installed power from 31,000 shp to 37,000 shp. However, the total capacity of the boiler outfit was well in excess of that required to generate this power, providing ample redundancy and allowing full speed to be achieved even if a number of boilers were off-line owing to defects or for planned maintenance. Indeed, it was planned that full speed could be maintained with half the maximum steam-pressure available. As already noted (p 32), this would cause problems for the first ship in Royal Navy service – but would be useful when the second ship of the class was appropriated for a very different role (see p 208).

The ship was equipped to carry 3300 tons of coal and 520 tons of oil, to give a maximum range of 4400 miles at 10kt. The engines were interesting in having Brown-Curtis HP turbines (built by John Brown itself, at Clydebank) on the outer shafts and Parsons LP ones (manufactured by Wallsend Slipway) on the inner. Funnels were heightened during construction to meet a new Chilean requirement that full speed be possible without forced draught. They would then be cut down again (albeit not to their original height) when taken over by the UK (p 31). Work on the ship was delayed by the late delivery of armour, but (having briefly been renamed *Libertad*), she was launched as

The launch of *Almirante Latorre* on 27 November 1913, and the ship alongside the fitting-out wharf at Elswick. *(Author's collection)*

Almirante Latorre (after the eponymous officer who had died on 9 July 1912) on 27 November 1913, by Olga Budge de Edwards, the wife of the Chilean ambassador to the UK.

Financial issues prevented an immediate parallel contract for the second battleship, and US Secretary of State Philander Knox (1853–1921) attempted to tempt the Chileans to at least fit the second ship with US systems. This included an invitation to send a commission to inspect ordnance factories in the US and a proof-firing of the new US 14in/45 Mk I gun, in case the Chileans could be persuaded to substitute this for the Armstrong weapons in the second ship.

US hopes were briefly raised with a war scare between Chile and Peru during October–November 1911, which came soon after Peru had agreed to buy the French armoured cruiser *Dupuy de Lôme* (plus a destroyer and two submarines) in July 1911. The cruiser was to be refitted ready for delivery in the spring of 1912. This would have (on paper) greatly enhanced Peruvian maritime capabilities, the ship being double the size of the Peruvians' existing pair of scout cruisers. She was, indeed, nearly the same size as the Chilean battleship *Capitan Prat*, as well as faster and better armoured, albeit less well-armed. As a result, the Chileans made an enquiry in Washington whether they might be able to acquire one of the battleships under construction for the US Navy, to ensure clear superiority over the Peruvians' new acquisition.

This was rapidly rebuffed by the US authorities, but the Fore River yard attempted to get Argentine agreement to sell one of their two ships, and were promised the second Chilean battleship order if they could offer one ready in time to meet *Comandante Elias Aguirre* (ex-*Dupuy de Lôme*). As it was, the war scare soon fizzled out,[33] and when the second Chilean battleship was ordered in June 1912 (for £2.425 million, part-funded by a 4.5 per cent bond issue), both hull and guns were to be built by Armstrong, as a full sister of *Almirante Latorre*.[34] Originally to be *Santiago*, the name was changed to *Almirante Cochrane* at the time of ordering. She was laid down on 24 February 1913 (Elswick Job 858), on the slip vacated a month earlier by *Rio de Janeiro*. By the summer of 1914 the hull and machinery were nearly finished, and some armour was in place (see pp 33–4, above). Russia made an offer for *Almirante Cochrane* during May/June 1914, but this was rejected by Chile.

Although disappointed over the matter of the battleship order, Bethlehem did receive a £500,000 contract for Chilean coastal artillery, while another US firm, Electric Boat, obtained the orders for the two submarines of the Chilean programme, for a total of $818,000 (£168,000). The half-sisters *Iquique* and *Antofagasta* were of 313/379 tons, with *Antofagasta* 13ft longer. Both carried five 18in torpedo tubes, with the surfaced speed to be 13kt. Subcontracted to the west-coast

The undelivered Chilean submarines *Iquique* and *Antofagasta* were laid up at Seattle in 1914. They would subsequently be acquired by Canada as *CC1* and *CC2*, shown here off Vancouver, around 1916; *CC1* is in the foreground. (Government of Canada)

Seattle Construction and Drydock yard, to ease delivery, the boats were launched in June and December 1913, respectively. However, they were rejected by the Chileans on the grounds of excessive weight and inadequate endurance, compared to what was specified in the contract. Payments were stopped and the boats laid up at Seattle to await their fate (see p 43).

The six 1500-ton Chilean destroyers were ordered from White of Cowes in 1911, which prompted an expansion of the yard including the installation of an 80-ton hammerhead crane in 1912. They were considerably larger than contemporary boats (50 per cent bigger than their Argentine contemporaries), in view of seakeeping requirements for Pacific operation. The first two, *Almirante Condell* and *Almirante Lynch*, were launched in 1912–13, and joined the Chilean fleet in 1913–14, but the others, *Almirante Simpson*, *Almirante Goñi*, *Almirante Williams* and *Almirante Riveros*, were, as already noted (pp 39–40), still in shipyard hands in August 1914, and were taken over by the Royal Navy.

Chapter 3

The Balkan Connection

IN THE WAKE OF THE 1904 Entente Cordiale with France, and the increasing perceived threat from the growing German navy, the British had begun to diversify their approach to maintaining their interests in the Mediterranean.[1] In 1908 a British mission had been sent to Turkey to help reorganise the Ottoman navy, with a similar one sent to Greece in 1911. The Ottoman navy was much the bigger of the two, but that of Greece was, at the beginning of the twentieth century, the more efficient.

The Ottoman Empire

The years of stagnation
The Ottoman navy had been of some consequence down to the 1870s, numerically the third fleet in the world. It included a number of modern broadside and central battery ironclads, mainly built in the UK, France or Austria during the 1860s – although a shortage of funds had meant that the 10,700-ton *Fatih* had been sold on the stocks to Prussia in February 1867, to become their *König Wilhelm*.[2] Another ship was ordered from Constantinople Dockyard in 1871 (*Nüsretiye*, later *Hamidiye* [ii]), with four further ships ordered in the UK between 1871 and 1874. While the 9000-ton *Mesudiye* was delivered at the end of 1875, her sister *Hamidiye* (i – ex-*Mahmoudiye*, renamed in 1876), and the 4800-ton 'rams' *Peyk-i Şeref* and *Büruç-u Zafer*, were still in their builders' hands when war broke out between Turkey and Russia in April 1877. Accordingly detained to meet British neutrality regulations, they were then purchased for the Royal Navy in February 1878, along with the Brazilian *Independencia* (p 50), to bolster UK forces in case Britain was dragged into the Russo-Ottoman conflict. *Hamidiye* became HMS *Superb*, *Peyk-i Şeref* became *Belleisle* and *Büruç-u Zafer* became *Orion*.

The war actually ended a month later, the Empire's defeat (which lost her many Balkan dominions) having a lasting effect on the fleet, most of which was now laid up. Contributing to this decision was the navy's role in the overthrow of Sultan Abdulaziz in 1876, and an enduring suspicion of it on the part of his second successor, Abdul Hamid II, who came to the throne after the ephemeral reign of his brother Murad V. During the 1880s, the ironclad corvettes *İclaliye* and

The Ottoman Empire. (Author)

The Balkan Connection

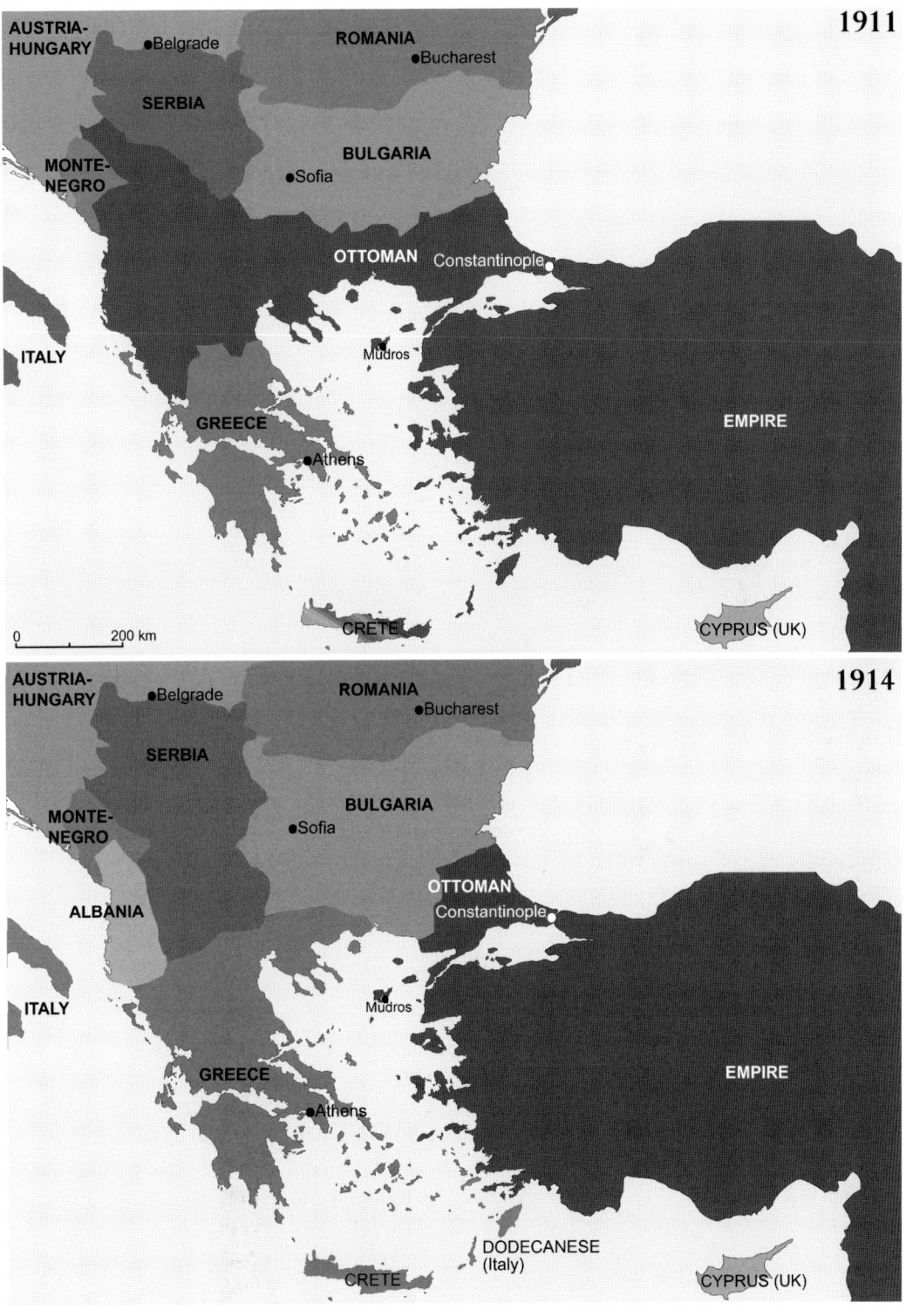

The Windfall Battleships

Mukaddeme-i Hayir were initially kept in full commission as stationships at Crete and Tripoli, but the rest of the fleet was kept moored off the Golden Horn. All were stripped to their lower masts, with only one-third complements, and were joined by *İclaliye* in 1886. Although nominally at 14 days' notice for completing with stores, fuel and personnel, in 1883 the British naval attaché estimated that it would take six months to get the five ships that were in a reasonable condition to sea. During 1886–97, some ships were indeed made ready for service at times of crisis, but never actually sailed. The only big ships to sail from the Golden Horn were *Feth-i Bülend* in 1889, to escort the German imperial yacht, and *Osmaniye* for gunnery trials around 1886.

The latter was to test the replacement of the ancient upper-deck muzzle-loading guns with slightly less-antique army coast defence Krupp breech-loaders, and had mixed results. During 1890–4, *Osmaniye* and *Aziziye* were cut down fore and aft and fitted with two single 9.4in/35 guns on land-service mountings, in barbettes of wood covered in 0.5in plating. Eight 5.9in/25 and five 4.1in/25 weapons were fitted on the old gun deck and in a superstructure battery; *Osmaniye* was also reboilered. Light military masts were fitted, giving the ships a modern appearance that belied their deep flaws as fighting ships. *Mahmoudiye* was in hand for similar modifications in 1900, with the hope that new 8.2in weapons could be fitted, although old 9.4in were probably actually

The Golden Horn at Constantinople in the late 1880s/early 1890s, showing, from the left: *Mesudiye*, with *Avnillah* or *Muin-i Zafer* behind; *Asar-i Tevfik*; *Muin-i Zafer* or *Avnillah*; members of the *Osmaniye* class, with *Feth-i Bülend* or *Mukaddeme-i Hayir* behind. (NHHC NH 93934)

THE BALKAN CONNECTION

fitted as in her sisters. It was reported in 1906 that at least *Aziziye* had had her 9.4in guns replaced by an 8.2in forward and a 5.9in aft. The other ship of the class, *Orhaniye*, had been much less extensively altered during 1892–4, retaining her full rig and simply having her gun-deck armament removed and three sponsons added on each beam for new guns at upper-deck level.

Right and above right: *Hamidiye* completing, and *Osmaniye and Aziziye* rebuilding, at Constantinople Dockyard at the beginning of the 1890s. *(Abdullah Frères via LoC)*

Osmaniye as rebuilt, in the mid-1890s.

Hamidiye in 1897. (Abdullah Frères via LoC)

While the *Osmaniye*s were rebuilding, Constantinople Dockyard was finally completing *Hamidiye* (ii) – the central battery ironclad ordered back in 1871, laid down in 1874 and launched in 1885. She would run trials without armament in 1893, and when she finally entered service it was as a stationary training ship, armed with four 10in muzzle-loaders and ten 5.9in breech-loaders.

The yard also had on the stocks a battleship and three cruisers. The 8100-ton battleship *Abdül Kadir* had been laid down in 1892, to be armed with four 11in and six 5.9in Krupp guns. However, work had proceeded slowly, and in the event she was never launched, eventually being cleared from the slip in 1909. The cruisers *Feyza-i Bahri* and *Saıye* (1612 tons, six 5.9in/45) had been laid down in 1891, followed by *Hüdavendiagar* (4050 tons, two 8.2in, six 5.9in) in 1893, but work stopped in 1897; a projected sister, *Selimiye*, was cancelled in 1902. Although there were thoughts of restarting work on *Hüdavendiagar* to a revised design in 1902, these came to nought, and all three vessels were cleared from the slips during 1905–9.

By the end of the nineteenth century, the navy was thus moribund, and when it was attempted to mobilise the fleet for the Greco-Ottoman War of March–May 1897, most proved unfit for operational service. Four (out of a planned six) ironclads and five supporting vessels managed to sail into the Sea of Marmora on 22 March, to anchor at Chanak, while after the ceasefire (29 May), four ironclads (*Osmaniye*, *Orhaniye*, *Necm-i Şevket* and *Hifz-ur Rahman*) and three smaller vessels made a short cruise in the Aegean during 2–3 August.

These extremely limited deployments underlined the poor state of the materiel, *Hamidiye* suffering major boiler failures. Significant machinery defects manifested themselves in *Mesudiye*, and armament

Part of the hull of the abortive battleship *Abdül Kadir* on the slip at Constantinople, with, inset, a sketch plan of the ship issued in 1904; the slip was cleared in 1909. (Author's collection; Flottes de Combat 1904)

problems were experienced across the fleet. These included the discovery that the breechblocks of *Aziziye*'s 9.4in guns had been left ashore.

Reconstructions

In the wake of this debacle, plans were laid for modernisation of the navy and its infrastructure by foreign companies. However, these were hindered by intrigue, double-dealing and unrealistic expectations. Eventually, contracts were let with a range of firms, in some cases in connection with foreign claims for compensation for damage to property caused during the Armenian massacres of 1894–7.

First, in November 1898, Ansaldo bid for the reconstruction of *Mesudiye* and *Asar-i Tevfik*, with guns to be supplied by Vickers. The ships arrived at Genoa for survey on 28 January 1899, contracts being agreed in the autumn. The work on *Mesudiye* was to be carried out by Ansaldo themselves, and on *Asar-i Tevfik* by Germania at Kiel. Germania also received a contract on 11 August 1900 to refit *Orhaniye*, *Aziziye*, *Mahmudiye*, *Osmaniye*, *Avnillah*, *Muin-i Zafer*, *Feth-i Bülend* and *Mukaddeme-i Hayir*, despite having bid a price 17 per cent higher than

Armstrong for this work. The last four were to be reconstructed with new engines and boilers, as well as new guns (with profiles resembling that of the rebuilt *Mesudiye* – see below), but in the other ships, work was to be restricted to rearmament and general overhaul. Ansaldo had made proposals for the full reconstruction of these vessels as well, but it was recognised that this would not represent value for money.

Although frustrated over the capital-ship modernisations, Armstrong eventually received a contract to build the cruiser *Abdül Hamid* (*Hamidiye* [iii] from 1908) in the spring of 1900, although negotiations continued until July 1901. Even then she was not laid down until November 1902, owing to the non-payment of the first instalment of her price and delays in deciding between cylindrical and watertube boilers. Armed with two 6in and eight 4.7in guns, she was launched in September 1903, and was commissioned in April 1904.

A very similar cruiser was ordered from Cramp in the USA in May 1900, in exchange for the waiving of US claims over damage to American property caused during the Armenian massacres. *Abdül Mecidiye* was laid down in November 1901, launched in July 1903 and commissioned with the abbreviated name *Mecidiye* in November of that year. While *Hamidiye* was a great success, *Mecidiye* suffered from stability problems (cf p 122) which constrained her high-seas employment.

The cruiser *Mecediye* completing at the Cramp shipyard in Philadelphia in the autumn of 1903. (NHHC NH 48569)

THE BALKAN CONNECTION

Mesudiye before 1894, and unrecognisable after her 1898–1903 reconstruction. (NHHC NH 94224/author's collection)

The Ansaldo reconstruction contract was delayed by problems in financing the work, *Mesudiye* being laid up only partly complete following a failure to pay the third instalment of her price. A March 1901 agreement linked a resumption of work to ordering two *Akhisar* class torpedo boats from Ansaldo. A December 1902 amendment reduced the follow-on reconstruction programme to *Avnillah*, *Muin-i Zafer* and *Feth–i Bülend* only, with the work to be carried out by Ansaldo and Armstrong at Constantinople Dockyard.

Mesudiye herself finally completed trials in March 1904, after the most comprehensive reconstruction of an early ironclad in any navy. Her single-shaft single-expansion machinery was replaced by a completely new two-shaft VTE installation, with watertube boilers.[3] A new superstructure was erected, housing fourteen 3in guns, with single

The Italian cruiser *Libia*, seized on the stocks in 1912 when she was being built as the Turkish *Drama*, seen at Shanghai in 1925. (Author's collection)

9.2in/40 mountings fore and aft. The gun deck was re-equipped with a dozen 6in/45 BL guns, directly replacing the old 10in ML weapons, but the old iron armour was left untouched.

With *Mesudiye* finished, discussions began for the construction of a sister for the Armstrong-built *Hamidiye* by Ansaldo. Ordered as *Drama* in April 1904, a contract was not agreed until August 1907, the ship still being on the stocks when seized by Italy in September 1912 at the outbreak of the Italo-Ottoman War (qv).

Asar-i Tevfik had arrived at Kiel on 29 May 1900, and was dismantled pending confirmation from the Ottoman authorities of the way ahead. Nothing happened until the beginning of 1904, when a new agreement provided for carrying out the work at a reduced price and the building by Germania of the two torpedo-cruisers of the *Peyk-i Şevket* class. Work on *Asar-i Tevfik* resumed in April, when Germania's parent firm, Krupp, received a highly profitable artillery order from the Ottoman army to offset the mounting losses against the navy contracts.

Ansaldo's original plans for *Asar-i Tevfik* had envisaged work along the lines of *Mesudiye*, with 9.2in guns fore and aft. However, the work carried out at Kiel was rather more modest, the old single engine being kept, although now supplied with steam by watertube boilers. As in *Mesudiye*, her old gun-deck muzzle-loaders (six 8.7in) were directly replaced by breech-loaders (in this case by 4.7in/40), but no substantive new superstructure was erected, apart from that supporting a new bridge

Asar-i Tevfik, as built, and in 1910 after her 1900–7 rebuilding. (NHHC NH 48570; author's collection)

and conning tower. Three 5.9in/40 and two 57mm guns were grouped around the bridge, four more 57mm behind bulwarks further aft, and a 4.7in weapon on the quarterdeck. *Asar-i Tevfik* finally sailed for home on 19 November 1906.

The torpedo-cruisers had eventually been laid down in February 1906, with *Peyk-i Şevket* launched four days after the departure of *Asar-i Tevfik*. Her sister, *Berk-i Satvet*, took to the water on 1 December, the two ships reaching Constantinople on 13 November 1907.

Muin-i Zafer before 1894. *(NHHC NH 94226)*

Feth-i Bülend completing her 1903–7 reconstruction at Constantinople; originally, she was very similar to *Muin-i Zafer*, and the latter's 1903–6 rebuilding was along the same lines as that of *Feth-i Bülend*, and her sister *Avnillah* (cf p 106). *(Author's collection)*

Ansaldo successfully rebuilt *Avnillah*, *Muin-i Zafer* and *Feth-i Bülend* at Constantinople between 1903 and 1906–7, to a scheme along the lines of that finally applied to *Asar-i Tevfik*. Boilers were replaced by watertube units and 5.9in/40s directly replaced muzzle-loaders in the batteries (four 9in in *Avnillah* and *Muin-i Zafer*, 8.7in in *Feth-i Bülend*). Six 3in were also added (all on the upper deck in *Feth-i Bülend*, four of them in the batteries of the other two). The completion of the truncated reconstruction programme meant that the Ottoman navy had five armoured warships able to go to sea, but still of only marginal capability.

The last significant vessels to be acquired by the Ottoman navy before the 1908 'Young Turk' revolution were ordered from French yards, as a diplomatic offset for the aforementioned German army guns. Under a contract signed on 22 January 1906, four destroyers of the *Samsun* class, four torpedo boats of the *Demirhisar* class and nine gunboats of the *Taşköprü* class were to be built, all completing during 1907–8.

Revolution and renewal

The revolution of 1908 forced Sultan Abdul Hamid II to restore the constitution that had been granted in 1876, but suspended two years later in the wake of the Russo-Turkish War of 1877–8. In 1909, the reactionary sultan was himself deposed and replaced by his half-brother Mehmed V. Among the early reforms of the new regime was to begin the revival of the Ottoman navy, a British Naval Mission being appointed to help in its reorganisation in December 1908.

In 1909, the Ottoman authorities, having lost out to Greece in bidding for an incomplete armoured cruiser in Italy (which would become *Georgios Averof*, pp 126–7), began to enquire after the purchase of second-hand battleships. At the suggestion of the head of the British Naval Mission, the Turks proposed to buy HM Ships *Triumph* and *Swiftsure* which, as originally ordered for Chile, were non-standard in the Royal Navy (pp 54–5). However, the British authorities were only prepared to grudgingly offer two of the much older *Royal Sovereign* class (1891–2). Disappointed, in December, the Ottoman Grand Vizier proposed to the German military attaché that Turkey purchase an armoured cruiser and three destroyers from Germany.[4]

The attaché consulted with the British Naval Mission, who agreed with him that the acquisition of additional big ships was incompatible with the current state of Ottoman naval training. This view was communicated to Berlin, with a further note that the transfer of a modern capital ship to Turkey would expose its details to British inspection. However, Admiral Tirpitz was happy to aid the sale of destroyers, by allowing (on 10 January 1910) the Schichau company to sell four vessels currently being built for the German navy (as *S165–S168*), with replacements to be laid down immediately. The vessels were formally sold in March.

The armoured cruiser issue was complicated on 24 March 1910 by an off-the-cuff offer of the brand-new *Blücher* to the Ottoman ambassador by the State Secretary at the German Foreign Office. There was some support for *Blücher*'s disposal and replacement, given that the completion of the British *Invincible* class had made her obsolescent on completion. On the other hand, there was a shortage of large cruisers for service with the German fleet, with *Scharnhorst* and *Gneisenau* scheduled to go to the Far East in the near future. It was eventually agreed by the German authorities that, if such a deal were to be made,

SMS *Blücher* as built. *(Author's collection)*

it would have to be for a price no less than that of a replacement ship: 44 million Marks (£2.15 million).

In response, the Turks expressed a formal a wish to buy *Blücher*, but at a lower price, also stating the unacceptability of a German idea that any deal should include a condition that future naval orders should be placed with German yards. On 8 April Kaiser Wilhelm II announced his willingness to sell *Blücher* for 44 million Marks, but with the proviso that she have German officers.

This was distinctly unattractive to the Ottomans, who then made a direct approach to the Blohm & Voss yard at Hamburg, which had two battlecruisers under construction for the German navy (*Moltke* [launched 7 April 1910] and H [to be *Goeben*, laid down 7 December 1909]). Blohm & Voss were happy to sell, provided that the German authorities

SMS *Moltke* visiting Hampton Roads, USA, in June 1912. *(Harris & Ewing, via LoC)*

were also happy with the resulting delay that would arise from needing to lay down a replacement ship. To speed delivery to the Turks, Blohm & Voss were prepared to send *Moltke* without the two 11in turrets that had yet to be installed, as even the resulting six 11in guns would match the four 9.2in and eight 7.5in guns of the newly-acquired Greek *Averof*. The remaining guns would be installed at Constantinople.

However, all further discussion was ended by Tirpitz on 15 July 1910, who was not prepared to part with any of the big cruisers (in part owing to the difficulties that would follow in the Reichstag), but would be prepared to sell the four *Brandenburg* class battleships, launched in 1891, for 10 million Marks each. Each was armed with six 11in guns, and had all been extensively refitted between 1901 and 1905. Two had compound armour throughout, but two had significant parts of their protection in the newer nickel-steel; it was the latter pair that the Turks chose to purchase.

A contract for the sale of *Kurfürst Friedrich Wilhelm* (to be *Barbaros Hayreddin*) and *Weißenburg* (*Turgut Reis*) to the Ottoman Navy League (p 24, above) was signed on 5 August 1910 and the ships left Wilhelmshaven with German crews, supplemented by twenty-four Ottoman officers and thirty-eight seamen on the 14th. Half the purchase price (18 million Marks for the ships, 9 million Marks for ammunition) came from the personal accounts of the former Sultan Abdul Hamid II. The rest allegedly came from the League but, in fact, the balance had been paid in the form of Ottoman Treasury Bills issued by Deutsche

Turgut Reis soon after her arrival in Turkish waters. *(Bernd Langensiepen collection, via Dirk Nottelmann)*

Bank, which had become part of the Turkish national debt, although packaged in such a way as to give the impression nationally and internationally that funds for the battleships (and the destroyers) had indeed been contributed by the League.

The battleships arrived at Çanakkale on 29 August 1910, being welcomed by the cruiser *Hamidiye*. The battleships were formally transferred to the Ottoman navy and commissioned on 1 September. They then sailed to Constantinople, escorted by the German-built destroyers *Muavenet-i Millye* (ex-*S165*), *Yadigar-i Millet* (ex-*S166*), *Nümune-Hamiyet* (ex-*S167*) and *Gayret-i Vetaniye* (ex-*S168*), all of which had commissioned on 17 August. To crew the new vessels, personnel had to be obtained by diluting the complements of other ships with raw conscripts or reducing ships to care and maintenance. Inexperience with the German equipment soon led to chronic condenser problems in the battleships, which reduced their maximum speeds by up to half for some time.

New battleships

During 1909–10, Vickers and Armstrong made a number of proposals to Turkey for the building of capital ships. These included 15,000–19,200-ton battleships (six or eight 12in or eight 13.5in/14in guns), and 11,950–12,650-ton armoured cruisers (eight 9.2in or six 12in, from Vickers).[5] While the British Naval Mission remained of the opinion that Turkey would be best served by flotilla craft, the Turks themselves still wished to create a battle fleet. Two vessels were thus formally projected in 1910. There were aspirations to build them at Constantinople (16,200 tons; six 12in, six 9.2in, twelve 4in guns) but, more realistically, negotiations were begun with Armstrong in the summer of 1910. These concerned both the possibility of buying the incomplete *Rio de Janeiro* (and even the now-in-Brazil *Minas Geraes*), and acquiring a brand-new ship. Josiah Perrett accordingly produced a series of designs,[6] as did Vickers.[7]

The Naval Mission had now grudgingly recommended something around 16,000 tons, reflecting the size of the Armstrong and Vickers proposals received to date, but a new series of designs submitted from March 1911 were of 18,800 tons upwards. Armstrong began with Design 699, with the number of main guns increased to ten, by replacing of two of the twin turrets by triple mountings. Design 700 reverted to eight guns (13.5in), with its 6in secondary battery in turrets rather than broadside batteries; this was also a feature of Design 698A, which had five twin 12in main turrets on 20,600 tons (see p 146).

Vickers opened with Design 514, very similar to Armstrong 699; Vickers 512 and 519 placed the ten 12in guns in twin turrets, while 517 fitted eight 13.5in into the same hull. Deliberations extended into the summer of 1911, the order being placed on 8 June and a contract finally agreed on 27 July for a vessel of Armstrong Design 698B, some 2500 tons bigger than anything hitherto envisaged, with ten 13.5in guns, and costing £1.8 million. She was to complete 22 months from 14 June 1911.

Inevitably, discussions regarding the ship's specifications continued, and on 1 August it was agreed that the displacement should be increased by a further 1400 tons to 23,000 tons, the length to 525ft, the beam to 91.25ft and the draught to 28.5ft. Armour thicknesses and arrangements were adjusted, power increased from 25,000 shp to 26,500 shp, bunkerage enlarged, and more pumping capacity installed. All this added £71,400 to the cost of the ship, and at least three weeks to the delivery schedule, placing the ship's completion in May 1913.

The final Design 689C was ready in September 1911 and featured ten 13.5in/50, sixteen 6in/50in and ten 6pdr/50 guns, the latter primarily intended for use in subcalibre firing of the main guns. However, six pedestals were fitted to allow some to be used as part of the regular armament; two holding rings were provided to allow them to be carried by the ship's boats. Two Vickers machine guns, capable of taking 7.65mm Mauser ammunition, were also part of the outfit, with boat mountings and adjustable tripods. There were also two naval landing limbers to take two machine guns and their adjustable tripods, and two 3in landing guns with landing carriages and limbers.

Two heavy tripod masts were to be fitted, fore and aft, the forward

The originally-planned silhouette of Reşadiye (see also p 146). (Author)

example placed behind the forefunnel in accordance with current British practice (cf p 92). Unlike contemporary ships, however, the forecastle deck was carried aft to 'X' turret, securing better command for the secondary battery, as well as more accommodation space for the crew.

It had originally been hoped to buy two ships together. However, of the ten-year £4.5 million credit voted by the Ottoman Parliament in May 1911, £1.35 million had already been committed, meaning that two battleships were unaffordable. As a result, just one ship was to be ordered for the time being. There were suggestions that the remaining credit be used to order the hull of the second ship, with the armament and armour to be added to the contract when additional credits could be obtained, but this was a non-starter in practical terms.

The actual contract was let on a consortium of Armstrong, John Brown and Vickers; an agreement dated 8 August 1911 between the three companies defined their responsibilities and shares of the ultimate contract price of £1,867,900. Vickers were to build the hull for £529,000 and the machinery for £221,275, with armour production (£371,550) to be divided as equally as possible between the three firms. The armament (£609,500) was split between Armstrong (to build 'X' and 'Y' turrets) and Vickers ('A', 'B' and 'Q').

These arrangements (and the original Ottoman aspiration to order two ships together) caused much confusion in contemporary newspapers and specialist periodicals; this was perpetuated in later works. These have stated as fact that the Turks ordered *two* battleships in August 1911, one from Armstrong (*'Reshad-i-Hamiss'*) and one from Vickers (*Mehmed Reşad V*, soon to become *Reşadiye*). These sources also allege that the *'Reshad-i-Hamiss'* was suspended soon after laying-down in 1912, and subsequently cancelled in the wake of the Balkan Wars. However, Armstrong records show quite clearly that only one ship was ordered in 1911 – the one to be built by Vickers (but to Perrett's Armstrong design). It should be noted that the name of the alleged 'Armstrong ship' was simply a doubling of the name of the Vickers one, in two different languages: 'Hamiss' (more correctly *hâmis*) is the Osmanli (Ottoman court language) writing of the Turkish 'Reshad' (*reşat*) – an epithet of Sultan Mehmed V, for whom the ship was named.

The funding of *Reşadiye* was complex.[8] As in the case of the German battleships and destroyers, it was claimed that funds raised by the Naval League paid for the new battleship, with that assertion later extended to embrace the acquisition of *Sultan Osman I* at the end of 1913. However, when *Reşadiye* was ordered, the League had no available funds, and Ottoman Treasury Bills had to once again to be used, special 'Rechadieh Bills' being issued, some £0.9 million-worth being placed, directly or indirectly, with various international financiers. Vickers also agreed to take £0.32 million Rechadieh Bills towards the cost of the ship, as well as loaning the National Bank of Turkey £0.04 million. The company was thus lending money to itself to build the ship, since it might lead to 'profitable business in Turkey, the Balkan States, Greece etc'. Some other sources may have been tapped – but there is no evidence that anything came from the League. However, the myth of League funding was brought forward in July 1913 when the question of the maturity of the Rechadieh Bills raised the issue of whether *Reşadiye* might be offered for sale – not to mention after the ship was taken over by the UK in August 1914 (p 24).

The ship was laid down on 1 August 1911 as Barrow Job 425, and in January 1912 the UK Admiralty nominated British officers to supervise construction on behalf of the Turks. There was, however, some dispute as to their terms of reference, and it required UK Foreign Office intervention before it was agreed that the UK supervisors would undertake any tests necessary to ensure that armour and other materials were in accordance with specifications. Work was suspended a few months before launch following the outbreak of the First Balkan War between the Ottoman Empire and a coalition of Bulgaria, Serbia and Greece on 18 October 1912. The Empire had already suffered the loss of Libya (and the cruiser *Drama*, seized on the stocks) during the Italo-Ottoman War that began on 29 September 1911 and was ended by the Treaty of Lausanne/Ouchy of 18 October 1912 – the day that the new conflict began. The Treaty of London, which ended that war on 30 May 1912, deprived the Empire of almost all its European possessions, although some territory was recovered when the Second Balkan War was ended by the Treaties of Bucharest and Constantinople in August and October 1913.

A number of Turkish ships were lost during the Italo-Ottoman War, most notably *Avnillah*, torpedoed by the armoured cruiser *Giuseppe Garibaldi* at Beirut on 24 January 1912. The Balkan Wars saw most of the Ottoman fleet in poor condition, with its armoured core comprising *Mesudiye*, *Âsâr-ı Tevfik* and the two ex-German ships, supported by the cruisers *Hamidiye* and *Mecidiye*, plus the eight French- and German-built destroyers.

Avnillah lying sunk at Beirut, having been torpedoed by *Giuseppe Garibaldi* on 24 January 1912. *(NHHC NH 42779 & NH 85070)*

On 16 December, the major units of the Ottoman and Greek fleets engaged for the first time off the Dardanelles at the Battle of Elli, with the Turks withdrawing after being hit a number of times. The forces met again at the Battle of Lemnos on 18 January 1913, with a similar result, the two ex-German battleships being hit numerous times, in exchange for just two hits on the Greek flagship *Georgios Averof*. A final inconclusive action took place on 11 April 1913. The majority of naval activities comprised duties in support of the army, including escorting transports and carrying out bombardments. In addition, the cruiser *Hamidiye* carried out raiding operations that took her as far as the Red Sea and the Adriatic between January and September 1913.

In the wake of the outbreak of the Italian war, an extensive construction programme was formulated in early 1912, which envisaged five more battleships, four scout cruisers, twenty destroyers, six submarines, two minelayers, a repair ship and a training ship, plus a new dock big enough to handle the battleships. The Naval Mission suggested some adjustments, with more cruisers, and perhaps substituting battlecruisers for two of the battleships.

The British Admiralty had become concerned in late 1912 that *Reşadiye* might be put up for sale by the Turks owing to the financial pressures of the Balkan Wars, and that, if this proved to be so, she should not pass into foreign hands. They thus intimated to the Ottomans that, if so, the Royal Navy should be given first refusal. The response was that there was no intention to sell, and work restarted in May 1913, as the First Balkan War came to an end.

By the time that work resumed, the design had been altered, primarily as a result of experience with smoke interference with the control tops in British capital ships (p 92). Thus, the positions of the

The launch of *Reşadiye* at Barrow in August 1913. *(Author's collection)*

The Balkan Connection

Reşadiye fitting out at Barrow in the spring of 1914. Clearly visible is the pole mainmast that was removed as soon as the ship was taken over by the British. *(Author's collection)*

forefunnel and foremast were transposed, and the mainmast reduced from a tripod to a pole. The foremast retained its forward-facing support legs, which combined with the now closely-grouped funnels to give the ship a distinctive appearance. The ship was launched as *Reşadiye* on 3 August 1913 by Naile Hanoum, daughter of the Turkish ambassador Tevfik Pasha (later the last Ottoman grand vizier), the hull weighing 9000 tons at the time of launch.

The same month, a meeting took place in Hamburg between Turkish and Brazilian representatives, concerning a possible purchase of *São Paulo* in the context of influencing the progress of the peace talks that were to end the Second Balkan War. However, as the war was still formally in progress, the Brazilians were not prepared to compromise their neutrality by discussing such a sale.[9]

Russia was particularly concerned at the expansion of the Ottoman navy,[10] as it would challenge their long-standing domination of the Black Sea. While only the previous year (1910) it had completed the battleships *Ioann Zlatoust* and *Sviatoi Evstafi* (1906), their principal armament comprised only four 12in and four 8in, with a 16kt speed. The first Black Sea dreadnought, *Imperatritsa Mariya* (1913), was laid down on 30 October 1911, but she and her sisters, *Imperatritsa Ekaterina II* (later *Velekaya* – 1914) and *Imperator Aleksandr III* (1914) would not be ready until the summer of 1915 at best,[11] leaving a significant capability gap once *Reşadiye* was ready (originally to be April 1913, but now delayed by her suspension).

The existence of the South American battleships under construction in the UK and USA presented both a threat and an opportunity for the Russians. They might be subject to purchase by Turkey, thus exacerbating their problem – or they might be subject to purchase by Russia, as a quick means of strengthening the Black Sea Fleet in the face of the arrival of *Reşadiye*. In July 1913 it had thus been suggested within the Russian Foreign Ministry that Russia should form a Mediterranean squadron, built around the acquisition of *Rio de Janeiro*, and perhaps Argentine or Chilian vessels,[12] but when *Rio de Janeiro* actually came on the market in September, her acquisition was turned down on technical grounds (p 75, above). The idea would, however, be revived in 1914.

From the other side of the Black Sea, during October 1912, Turkey had made approaches to Argentina over the possible acquisition of *Rivadavia* and *Moreno*. In late November it was believed that they might be sold to the Ottoman navy for a total of £5 million. This came to nothing, but in October 1913 it was reported that Italy might sell the two *Pisa* class armoured cruisers (sisters of the Greek *Averof*) to Turkey, along with the cruiser *Libia* – the seized Turkish *Drama*.

In the meantime, *Rio de Janeiro* had actually come on the market, and by late November 1913 only Greece and Turkey were left in the running to buy her. It is likely that there had been discussions between Turkey and Armstrong in conjunction with their negotiations for a new shipyard at Gölçük (see p 118, below), but the key issue for both potential purchasers was finance. As described below (p 132), Greece's bid ran into difficulties, and before they could be resolved, the French Périer Bank provided a loan to the Turks (nominally 'for the purpose of paying the overdue salaries of some of her officials') that allowed them to buy *Rio de Janeiro* for £1.2 million (3,387,485 gold lira) on 29 December; she was renamed *Sultan Osman I*. The price covered work and materials to date on the ship, with at least this much again required to complete her. Italy unsuccessfully attempted to persuade the Turks to

Sultan Osman I fitting out at Elswick in the spring of 1914. (Author's collection)

swap the battleship for the two *Pisa* class armoured cruisers, plus the chance of buying two submarines at advantageous prices.

The French loan came in the form of the purchase of Ottoman Treasury Bills, with a real interest of 20 per cent, but, as with the case of *Reşadiye*, it was claimed that the purchase of the battleship was being funded by the Ottoman Navy League.[13] To this end, in December 1913 Ottoman civil servants had been required by emergency legislation to donate that month's salaries to the League. This raised £0.64 million, but this represented only 20 per cent of the price of the ship, and it seems unlikely that any of the money found its way to the League, Armstrong or the Brazilians.

There was continued Turkish interest in second-hand ships, including the Italian armoured cruiser *San Marco*. The Russians also understood that Turkey was interested in one of the Chilean battleships on the Tyne. Attempts were made by Russia to put pressure on the UK to prevent any such sale, and also to hinder the impending order for a sister to *Reşadiye* (see below), but the UK government claimed that there was no legal scope for its interference in commercial transactions.

Beginning in January 1914, Russia also made enquiries concerning the purchase of the Argentine and Chilean vessels, with Imperial approval for the activity being given on 20 February. Extant treaties would have made it impossible for the ships to pass through to the Black Sea; they would therefore have formed the core of a Russian Mediterranean squadron, rather as had been mooted by the Foreign Ministry the previous year (p 116).¹⁴ Thus, during February–March, Russia carried out discussions with the Argentine authorities and their contractors in Buenos Aires and Washington DC, but with the result that Argentina confirmed she had no desire to sell. During April–May Russian attention therefore shifted to Chile, but the latter's officials were also intractable, pointing out that Chile required her own ships to balance those (still) being acquired by Argentina (and already possessed by Brazil). A request for British aid in the negotiations merely resulted in the UK Foreign Office confirming the Chilean unwillingness to dispose of their ships to anyone. Against this background, a fourth ship was added to the Black Sea fleet construction programme. However, *Imperator Nikolai I*, laid down in January 1915, would never be completed.

Meanwhile, Turkish plans for naval expansion were suffering from ongoing funding crises. Attempts were made in February 1914 to float a loan in New York to pay for more (as well as existing) ships, and on its failure, a Paris loan in April secured £25 million. The British then proposed to package the £0.95 million owing on *Reşadiye* and the £0.78 million on *Sultan Osman I* as a fresh loan, although this did not happen.

A month before the purchase of *Rio de Janeiro*, Armstrong had been given authority to construct a new shipyard at Gölçük, the right to be prime contractor for all future Turkish naval shipbuilding and an interest in Constantinople Dockyard, which would be owned along with the Gölçük by an overarching body, the Imperial Ottoman Docks, Arsenals and Naval Construction Company. On 29 April 1914, this concession was complemented by a large order from a consortium led by Armstrong and Vickers, known as the 'Eastern Construction Committee'. This comprised the long-desired sister of *Reşadiye*, to be named *Fatih Sultan Mehmid* (to be built by Vickers),¹⁵ plus two scout cruisers (Armstrong),¹⁶ four destroyers (subcontracted by Armstrong to Hawthorn Leslie),¹⁷ two submarines (subcontracted by Vickers to Beardmore, but with their machinery to be manufactured and installed by Vickers) and a floating dock (Vickers Job 456; to be assembled at La Seyne owing to lack of space).

This whole package was worth £4 million, with a credit of £61,600 granted to Vickers on 15 May 1914 (£56,600 as the first instalment on *Fatih*, £25,000 for the submarines), and £63,000 to Armstrong (for the cruisers); a further £49,900 would be released for the first instalment on the destroyers once they were on subcontract (which occurred on 29 May, at a total cost of £520,000).

For political balance, the Ottomans also ordered from France six destroyers (based on the Russian *Izyaslav* class [1915], to be laid down in July 1914, with six more to follow) and two submarines. Four further destroyers (of the *Indomito* class [1912–13]) were ordered from Italy. No work was done on any of these ships.

The Balkan Connection

Fatih was to be a modified version of *Reşadiye* (Armstrong Design 691). Full details do not seem to survive, but the 6pdrs were to be replaced by six 3in 'anti-balloon' guns and mountings, while 13.5in and 6in fire control was to be via the 'latest pattern Vickers "Follow-the-Pointer" electric fire control system', with nine full 9ft Barr & Stroud rangefinders replacing the four 9ft and two 6ft examples planned for *Reşadiye*. The new ship was be fitted for the Pollen Clock fire-control computer and rangefinders in 'B' and 'X' turrets, with just Pollen rangefinders in 'A', 'Q' and 'Y'. In addition, consideration was being given to giving *Fatih* a single rudder, rather than the twin set being fitted in *Reşadiye*. This proposal was in line with what Armstrong were providing

Top: *Sultan Osman I* passing through the Swing Bridge at Newcastle on her way from Elswick to High Walker in June 1914 for the final stages of fitting-out. Bottom: the Swing and High Level Bridges in 2022, showing the limited vertical and lateral clearances presented by them. Accordingly, no big ship would be built at Elswick after *Almirante Cochrane*. (Author's collection; Dyan Hilton)

in the Chilean ships, and was also being installed in the latest British *Revenge* class, in contrast to immediately-preceding classes.

As in *Reşadiye*, turret production was to be split, with the final decision being that Elswick would make 'A' and 'B' mountings, and Vickers 'Q', 'X' and 'Y'; firm orders were placed in May 1914. *Fatih*'s 6in guns were to be made by Vickers at Erith, while turbine forgings and shafting was split 50:50 between Vickers and John Brown.

In June 1914, *Sultan Osman I* proceeded downriver from Elswick to Walker to complete fitting-out. As was the case with other big ships built at Elswick, the depth of the river was such that there was a limit to how much weight could be built into vessels at the upstream yard. The journey was complicated by the presence of the Tyne bridges, which required masts, and especially the high tripods of modern capital ships, to be lowered to fit (see also p 66). There was also a need to squeeze through the swing bridge (with only around a few feet of clearance on either side of the ship), all of which had led to the decision in 1910 to build the yard at High Walker. *Almirante Cochrane* was thus the last large ship to be laid down at Elswick (in February 1913).

Also in June 1914, the ongoing situation with Greece led to a request by Turkey that *Reşadiye* proceed immediately to the Bosphorus. However, although sea trials were scheduled for July, fitting-out was not sufficiently finished to allow an early departure. Completion was expected in the third week of August.

The eve of the war
The presence of Armstrong/Vickers personnel in the docks and harbours enterprise meant that they had an intimate knowledge of the state of many Turkish warships just prior to the outbreak of hostilities. The following is an extract from a report on Ottoman warships submitted by Armstrong and Vickers to the First Lord on 17 November 1914.[18]

> "MESSUDIEH" [*Mesudiye*]
> Docked about eight months ago. Engines, boilers and hull in good condition. New training gear fitted to the 12 – 6-inch Guns and these with all the smaller guns are in good condition. The two 9.2-inch guns are still in England under repair,[19] and in their turrets have been fitted dummy guns made of wood and canvas.
>
> "BARBAROSSE" [*Barbaros Hayreddin*]
> Docked three months ago. Engines, boilers and hull in good condition: all guns in working order with exception of one 4.1-inch gun in the starboard casemate which is still under

repair in the Arsenal. The centre turret of this ship with its gearing was considerably damaged by shell fire during the last war, and one of the 11-inch guns has its outer jacket split where struck by a shell but the gun is still considered serviceable and the turret and gearing has been repaired. New training Gear was fitted to all the 4.1-inch Guns and a new fire control station was fitted in the lower tween decks. The voice pipes, however, connected to the same are only two inches diameter and they evidently causing trouble as an attempt is now being made to fit three inch pipes, but as suitable copper pipes can not be found in Turkey it is improbable that the change can be effected.

The aft torpedo tube with all its apparatus has been removed and the torpedo room converted into a ward room. During the late War the armour belt was pierced in many places by 6-inch shells and these holes have been plugged with forged iron plugs and covered on the outside by ¾-inch thick plates recessed into armour and secured by screwed rivets.

The fire mains are not in good condition, and the water-tight doors through the vessel are in doubtful condition. The vessel, otherwise, can be considered as a serviceable fighting unit.

"Tourgood Reiss" [*Turgut Reis*]

Sister ship to "Barbarosse". Docked four months ago. Hull, engines and boilers in good condition. All guns in place and in good condition with the exception of one 4.1-inch gun in the starboard casemate which is still under repair in the Arsenal. Also in this vessel the aft torpedo tube and fittings have been permanently removed. New training Gear was fitted to all the 4.1-inch Guns and a new fire control station was fitted in the lower tween decks. The voice pipes, however, connected to the same are only two inches diameter and they evidently causing trouble as an attempt is now being made to fit three inch pipes, but as suitable copper pipes can not be found in Turkey it is improbable that the change can be effected. The fire mains are in poor condition as also all the water-tight doors throughout the ship. Except for the foregoing the vessel can be considered a useful fighting unit.

"Hamidieh" [*Hamidiye*]

Cruiser 3,830 tons. Docked 2½ months ago. Rudder stock twisted and rudder bent; also some keel-plates damaged, but these do not affect vessel's seaworthiness. Hull, engines and boilers in first class condition. New training gear fitted to all guns, but they are controlled from the bridge, as when the vessel was built. A wireless cabin has been erected on the deck and the masts have been prepared for wireless fittings, but so far as we know the wireless apparatus has not been installed. She is a good serviceable boat and her speed should be the same as when new.

"Medjidieh" [*Mecediye*]

Cruiser 3,250 tons. Docked two weeks ago. Hull externally in good condition. Tank below boilers in poor condition. Boilers (Niclausse) have had very extensive repairs just now, but they are still unreliable. Engines have been thoroughly overhauled but they are a poor job. The vessel is top-heavy and is always listed to one side or the other, which is probably the reason that the two torpedo openings through the shell on the main deck forward have been closed up with rivetted plates, so abolishing the two torpedoes.

All her guns have been fitted with new training gear and all are in place and in good condition. The fire control is as originally fitted, viz., from the bridge and tops. A wireless cabin has been prepared and new top masts have been fitted adapted for wireless, but no wireless installation has been fitted so far. Taking her altogether she is a poor boat, and her instability must adversely affect her fighting capacity, and neither her engines or boilers can be relied on for long periods of service.

"Muin – i – Zaffer" [*Muin-i Zafer*]

Coast defence iron-clad. Docked about ten months ago. Hull and guns in good condition, but practically incapable of steaming as one of the main condensors is split from top to bottom and repairs will take at least one month or more.

"Peik-i-Sefket" [*Peyk-i Şevket*]

(Torpedo gunboat built at Germania Works, Kiel)

This vessel was docked one month ago, and is in very good condition throughout, having had a thorough overhaul. All guns and torpedo tubes are complete in place and new range finding apparatus has been fitted on the bridge. This vessel has no wireless but a wireless cabin has been constructed on deck, and new top masts fitted ready to receive the wireless gear but no wireless apparatus has yet been fitted.

This vessel's speed should be the same as when new and she can be the same as when new and she can be considered an efficient fighting unit.

"Pelenk-i-Deria" [*Peleng-i Derya*, torpedo gunboat]
Had just been sent to the Arsenal two weeks ago for an overhaul, which however has not been started, so the ship could probably be taken to sea again. She is said to be in a very poor condition. She has no wireless.

Four German Destroyers
Built at Schichau. "Yadikar Millet", "Numun-i-Hamiet", "Gairet Watanie" and "Mauvenet Millet" [*Yadigar-i Millet, Nümune-Hamiyet, Gayret-i Vetaniye, Muavenet-i Millye*]. All in bad condition. Two of these vessels are under extensive repair including new coal bunkers, part renewal of decks, new boiler tubes &c. These repairs will take at least one month if not more. The turbines of these boats were removed some time ago by the Turks for overhaul, but report says they have lost considerably in speed, and since the Germans have been in charge they have been over-hauling the turbines. The results are unknown.

Torpedo Boats
"Hamid Abad"   "Sultan Hissar"
"Sivri Hissar"   "Timur Hissar"
[*Hamidabad, Sultanhisar, Sivrihisar, Demirhisar*]
No wireless in any of these boats. All these torpedo boats have been overhauled and may be considered as efficient as when new. Two of the vessels were in dock a fortnight ago for hull repairs which would occupy say one week, so that all four boats are now probably at sea.

"Berkefshn" [*Berkefşan*]
This boat has been under extensive repairs for the past three months. Hull, engines, boilers, guns and torpedo fittings are all in good condition and she can be considered equal to new. She has no wireless. She will probably not be ready for sea before the end of the month.

"Younous" [*Yunus*]
Torpedo Boat. Just finished extensive overhaul including renewal of 50% of the vessel's shell plating. She can be considered equal to new.

"Samsoun" [*Samsun*]
Torpedo Boat. Same as "Younous", in good condition.

Aftermath

The Turks dissolved the Imperial Ottoman Docks, Arsenals and Naval Construction Company in February 1915. Although nothing could be done for the duration of the war, Vickers and Armstrong took careful note of the legal options that might be available when peace was restored. These were: to accept cancellation and claim damages; or to argue that such agreements were not annulled by war but merely suspended. The latter would allow a claim for full performance or an indemnity on this basis, not just a recovery of sunk costs (an approach that was supported by the British government). In the event, it would not be until the end of the 1920s that the commercial issues surrounding the events of 1914–15 were resolved.

The Ottoman Empire signed the Armistice of Mudros on 30 October 1918, bringing its participation in the First World War to a close. However, while Turkish forces withdrew from advanced positions and Allied occupations began – including of Constantinople itself – the dictated Treaty of Sèvres of 10 August 1920 was rejected by the Ottoman parliament. The Turkish War of Liberation of 1919 to 1923 then resulted in the old imperial regime being replaced by the new Ankara-based Turkish Republic.

New negotiations were begun in November 1922 towards a new peace treaty which, although confirming the loss of the empire, was far less punitive than that of Sèvres, and finally concluded with the signature of the Treaty of Lausanne on 24 July 1923. Article 58 of the Treaty included a clause that 'Turkey also agrees not to claim from the British Government or its nationals the repayment of the sums paid for the warships ordered in England by the Ottoman Government which were requisitioned by the British Government in 1914, and renounces all claims in the matter'. This dealt with the matter of the requisition of *Reşadiye* and *Sultan Osman I*, but three other issues remained open.

One concerned ammunition for *Reşadiye* that had been ordered on 31 March 1913, and for which a £95,000 down-payment had been made, and which had been deducted from the amount paid by the British government to Vickers when it had taken over the contract. Turkey argued that this contract was not covered by Article 58, and that they were due the refund of the £95,000 and damages for the non-performance of the contract. A second concerned money paid towards the building of *Fatih*, which had never been taken over by the British government, and thus was definitely not covered by Article 58. Finally, in the other direction, Vickers and Armstrong disputed the validity of the cancellation of the Docks and Arsenal Concession of 1913, and sought reimbursement for the costs they had incurred to date, in particular the manufacture of components for the floating dock.

On 27 February 1925, it was reported to the Vickers Board that the

Hon Gideon Murray had been sent to Ankara as delegate under terms of the Treaty of Lausanne to enter into negotiations regarding Vickers and Armstrongs' claims, but that as no agreement had been reached, the claims were going to arbitration, as provided for by the Treaty. This, however, proved abortive, the British and Turkish experts taking completely incompatible positions, with the whole matter referred to Swiss mediation.

With matters dragging on, and doing serious damage to the now-merged Vickers-Armstrong's chances of successfully bidding for Turkish work, on 8 May 1929, the company's Board considered a scheme to resolve outstanding issues. Under this, an allowance of £250,000 would be made (less any sum awarded under the Ottoman Dock Contract) in full settlement of the company's liabilities towards Turkey. On 11 December 1929, the Chairman reported to the Board that he had been in discussions with the Turkish Ambassador and made an offer of £150,000 cash (or £200,000 credit against any new contracts), in full and final settlement of all outstanding questions. The cash offer was accepted under an agreement of 23 December 1929, finally drawing a line under Vickers and Armstrong's Turkish naval adventure.

Greece

At the beginning of the twentieth century, the core of the Greek navy comprised three 4885-ton French-built battleships of the *Hydra* class, launched during 1889–90, and armed with three 10.8in guns. There were also two old ironclads, *Vasilèfs Georgios* (1867) and *Vasilissa Olga* (1869), in use as training ships, as was the cruiser *Navarchos Miaoulis* (1877). Various torpedo boats and gunboats existed, none built later than 1885.

Plans from 1905 envisaged three new battleships, but the first new construction comprised eight destroyers launched during 1906–7, half by AG Vulcan in Germany (the *Niki* class) and half from Yarrow in the UK (the *Thyella* class). In 1909, a *Pisa* class armoured cruiser, on the stocks at the Orlando yard at Livorno, was put up for sale. She had been laid down on speculation in 1907, with the expectation/hope that the Italian navy would buy her (as they had her two earlier sisters),[20] but this had not occurred and the ship had been suspended pending finding another customer.[21] Although some sources suggest that Brazil showed interest in the ship, and indeed paid some money to the shipyard, this cannot be verified, and seems unlikely in the context of Brazil's known construction programme (p 61, above).

Two definite potential customers for the cruiser were Turkey and Greece. The latter was successful in paying the required £250,000

The Greek battleship *Hydra* as built, and her sisters *Psara* and *Spetsai*, the latter pair shown after their 1897–1900 refits. *(NHHC NH 94217; author's collection)*

deposit, from a legacy left by the businessman Georgios Averof (1815–99) for enhancing the Greek navy. The ship was thus acquired in October 1909, and launched in March 1910, under the name of her benefactor.

The Greek armoured cruiser *Georgios Averof* early in her long career; she still survives as a museum near Athens. (*Author's collection*)

She commissioned in May 1911. Her modern four 9.2in/45 and eight 7.5in/45 guns[22] transformed the Greek navy's capabilities, and, as already noted, spurred the Ottoman navy into a programme of expansion. Also in 1909, two submarines, *Delfin* and *Xifias*, were ordered from Schneider in France and delivered in 1912.

In the spring of 1911, a British Naval Mission arrived in Athens. In the summer of 1911, the order of *Reşadiye* (and the alleged second vessel) by the Ottomans made a decision on future Greek naval programmes urgent. Prime Minister Eleftherios Venizelos (1864–1936) favoured a coast-defence navy along the lines of those of Sweden and Denmark, with big-ship additions limited to a pair of armoured cruisers along the lines of the existing *Georgios Averof*, coupled with a programme of disposals of old ships. The British Naval Mission recommended the immediate ordering of a single armoured cruiser, four destroyers and four torpedo boats, alongside upgrading Salamis Dockyard.

However, a committee of Greek naval officers, convened in early 1912, put forward a rather more ambitious programme, which was approved in March 1912. This provided for a 13,000-ton armoured ship (its size limited by the existing floating dock at Piraeus), two destroyers, six torpedo boats, two submarines and a depot ship. Twenty-three international firms expressed an interest in fulfilling the requirements. Armstrong's offerings included Design 735, with eight 12in, along with the six 14in-armed Designs 737, 738, 741[23] and 743, while Vickers put forward the nine-10in gunned Design 509.[24]

Although the majority of bidders were British, with half the Board on Naval Construction members also British, the outcome was not the expected walkover by Armstrong or Vickers. Not only was there real competition from other British firms, but also the UK-built *Thyella* class destroyers were felt to be inferior to the German *Niki* class. Furthermore, the French bidders presented a united front, in contrast to the British.

This all led to deadlock within the Board on Naval Construction, a decision being put off pending the result of upcoming elections. In the interim, lobbying got underway from both the British Minister in Athens, and from Kaiser Wilhelm II himself, who regularly holidayed in Corfu – and was the brother of the Greek Crown Princess Sofia. As a result, Venizelos promised the Germans the armoured ship and four torpedo boats, plus possibly the destroyers. However, this could only follow a new round of bids for the armoured ship.

New battleships
A dozen fresh bids were received, from Vulcan, Orlando, Germania, Palmers, Cramp, Vickers, Beardmore, Armstrong, Fairfield, Penhoët and Thames Iron Works. A number gave alternative armament suppliers: Vulcan offered both Bethlehem and Škoda options; Orlando, Bethlehem and Vickers; and Palmers, Bethlehem and Coventry Ordnance Works.[25] The three lowest acceptable bids were £1.09 million for Vulcan/Bethlehem, £1.16 million from Orlando and £1.22 million from Vickers; accordingly, the contracts were awarded to Vulcan and Bethlehem on 30 July 1912. Vulcan had already received (on 29 June) a contract for two destroyers and six torpedo boats (the latter with Bethlehem guns). The torpedo boats would form the *Aigli* class, delivered in 1913, while quick delivery of the destroyers was achieved by diverting two vessels (*V5* and *V6*) already under construction for the German navy (as had been done with the earlier Turkish order); they became *Nea Genea* and *Kervanos*. New vessels were laid down for the German authorities, who were keen to do all they could to facilitate Vulcan's prospects.

Orders for two submarines went, however, to Schneider, although both were overtaken by the outbreak of the First World War and completed for French service. A French yard was on the verge of a signing a contract to refit the old *Hydra* class, but this was frustrated by the beginning of the First Balkan War.

On 19 September 1912, just before this conflict began, four destroyers were acquired from Argentina for £0.15 million each. Lying at the Cammell Laird yard in the UK (p 85), they already had Argentine crews aboard and, already flying the Greek flag these took the ships (*San Luis* [to be *Aetos*], *Santa Fé* [*Ierax*], *Santiago del Estero* [*Panthir*] and

Four destroyers ordered by Argentina from Cammell Laird at Birkenhead had proved disappointing on trials, and thus when Greece was seeking ships for the First Balkan War their owner was happy to sell them. This is the former *Santiago del Estero*, in the Mersey awaiting to sail for the Mediterranean to become the Greek *Panthir*. She was rebuilt during 1925–7, and would remain in service until 1945. (Author's collection)

Tucumán [*Leon*]) to Algiers, where Greek sailors came aboard, and then to Palermo, where they were formally taken over by their new commanding officers. *Nea Genea* and *Kervanos* also made it to the Mediterranean in time to take part in the war. Two further flotilla craft were acquired by salving the Turkish torpedo boats *Tokad* and *Antalya* (both 1904), scuttled at Preveze on 5 November 1911 during the Italo-Ottoman War; they became the Greek *Totoi* and *Nikopolis*. On 10 October, it was reported that the Chinese cruiser *Chao Ho*, building by Armstrong (see p 137), had been sold to Greece for £300,000, but this did not go through. Alleged interest in the ship from Turkey also came to nothing.

As ordered from Vulcan, the armoured ship was to carry a main battery of six 14in guns, of the same type installed in USS *New York*. However, as such a ship would be badly outgunned by *Reşadiye*, only a few weeks after the ship had been ordered there were calls to modify the design to increase its capabilities. Initially, an increase to 16,500 tons was contemplated, but after the outbreak of the First Balkan War, further enlargement was demanded, a 19,500-ton version being the subject of a contract amendment dated 23 December 1912, with a final price of £1.693 million, in spite of attempts by Venizelos to cancel the change.

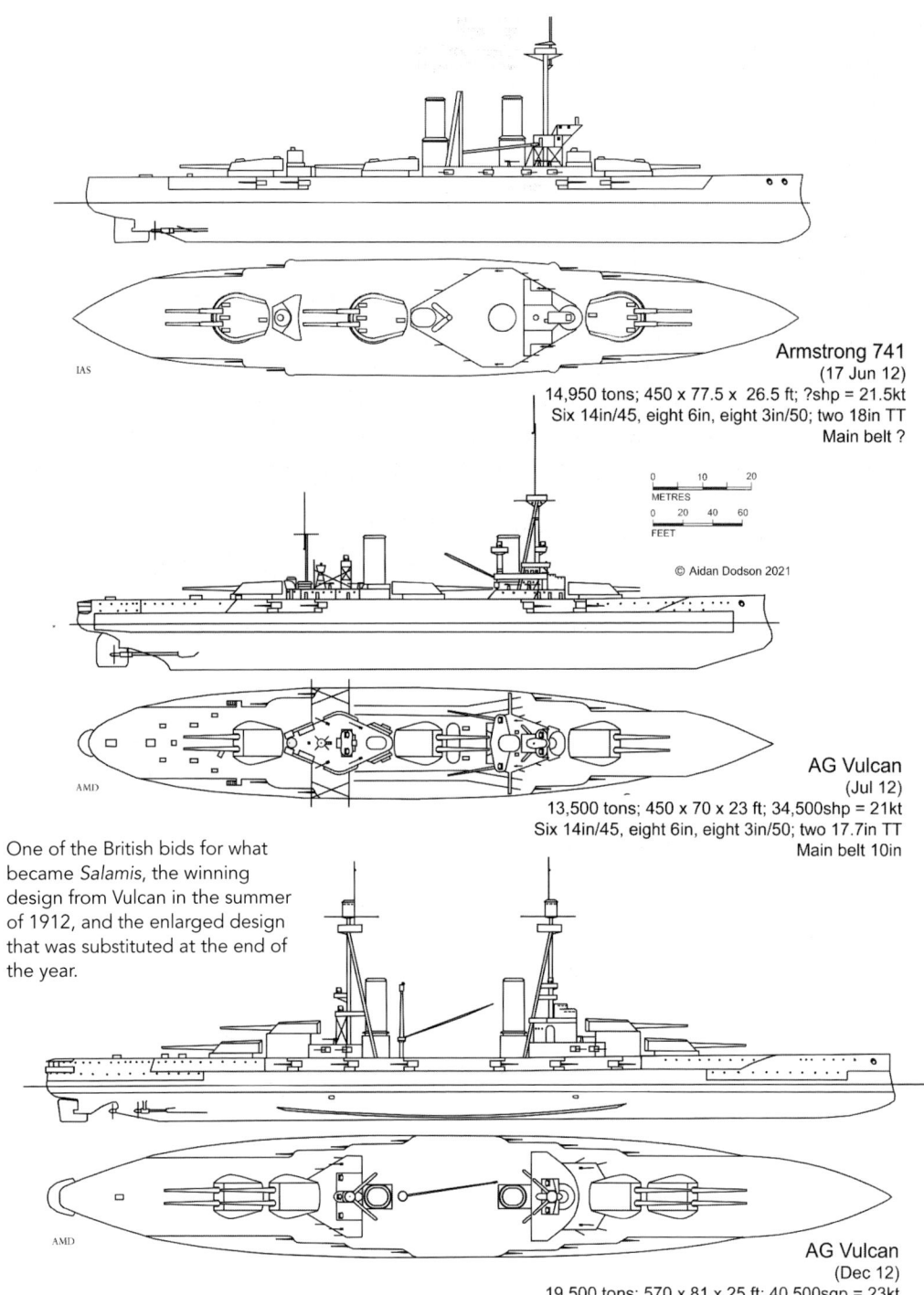

Armstrong 741
(17 Jun 12)
14,950 tons; 450 x 77.5 x 26.5 ft; ?shp = 21.5kt
Six 14in/45, eight 6in, eight 3in/50; two 18in TT
Main belt ?

AG Vulcan
(Jul 12)
13,500 tons; 450 x 70 x 23 ft; 34,500shp = 21kt
Six 14in/45, eight 6in, eight 3in/50; two 17.7in TT
Main belt 10in

One of the British bids for what became *Salamis*, the winning design from Vulcan in the summer of 1912, and the enlarged design that was substituted at the end of the year.

AG Vulcan
(Dec 12)
19,500 tons; 570 x 81 x 25 ft; 40,500sgp = 23kt
Eight 14in/45, twelve 6in/50, twelve 3in/50 guns; three 20in TT
Main belt 10in

THE BALKAN CONNECTION

Artist's impression of the final design of *Salamis*. (Journal of the United States Artillery 45 [1916])

As re-cast as a fully-fledged battleship with eight 14in guns in July 1913, the ship, initially to be named *Salamis*, was nevertheless still inferior in firepower to *Reşadiye*.

To help make up for this, on 21 October 1913 the Greek Chargé d'Affaires in Berlin was instructed by the new Greek King Konstantinos I (brother-in-law of Kaiser Wilhelm II) to contact the German State Secretary at the Reich Naval Office, Admiral Alfred von Tirpitz, and 'beg him to ask His Majesty the Emperor if he would allow us to enter into talks with the Weser shipyards for the purchase of the incomplete battleship "Ersatz Weissenburg"'. This vessel had been launched in June 1913, when she had been named *Markgraf*.

The following day, Tirpitz minuted to the Kaiser:

> In this regard ... even if it may be very desirable to get an order of this kind for German shipyards, a sale of this nature would be unlawful [on the basis of the German Fleet Laws].
> I am deeply convinced that any attempt to overcome the legal difficulties within the Reichstag would compromise and greatly endanger Your Majesty's naval policy.

He further noted that the sale of *Markgraf* (or a new-build of the same design) would lead to her technical secrets becoming known to the British via their naval mission to Greece.[26] The Kaiser agreed to all of Tirpitz's points and the Greek request was rapidly turned down.

The availability of *Rio de Janeiro* offered another opportunity to the Greeks to acquire a battleship, and on 27 November 1913 they offered cost-price, plus £50,000, while attempting to raise a £1 million deposit with French help. Unfortunately, impolitic comments by the Greek king combined with a French ministerial crisis to delay the process, allowing the Turks to make the purchase (ironically with the aid of a French private bank, p 116).

Greece's failure to secure the former *Rio de Janeiro* meant that *Salamis* would be faced by a second Turkish foe. However, in this case her guns would outrange those of the now-*Sultan Osman I* by some 4000 yards, and fire a broadside of around the same weight, despite the disparity in the number of guns. As a result, an approach was reportedly made to Chile immediately afterwards to acquire *Latorre* for a figure of £2.9 million, and also to Brazil for one or both of their existing battleships. New York Shipbuilding proposed around the same time that it might be possible for them to acquire five old US battleships, with three to be sold on to Greece, if a new ship were ordered at the same time. The old ships on potential offer (the *Kearsage* and *Illinois* classes) were, however, not found to be attractive to the Greek navy.

Greece's displeasure at the Ottoman purchase of *Rio de Janeiro* with French money was considerable. It was then offset by a French governmental offer to facilitate the financing and construction of new battleships of the *Bretagne* class in French yards. With ten 13.4in guns and twenty-two 5.5in, each would have been a close equivalent of the *Reşadiye* and any sisters. It was initially hoped to up-arm them with 14in Bethlehem guns, for homogeneity with *Salamis*, but it was soon agreed to keep the original French armament to avoid delays. On the other hand, the French offered to enhance the machinery to increase the new ship's speed to something closer to *Salamis*'s 23kt, rather than the 'standard' *Bretagne*'s 20–20.5kt.

The French battleship *Bretagne*, as completed. *Vasilèfs Konstantinos*, begun in July 1914, was to be a version of her class, with more powerful machinery. (*NHHC NH 55630*)

Although British hopes of getting any further Greek battleship contract(s) are indicated by the existence of Armstrong Design 779 of late 1913 (18,500 tons, six 15in guns – very much an enlarged version of 741),[27] and three by John Brown (26,000–28,200 tons, eight 15in),[28] a contract was signed on 22 April 1914 for the construction by Penhoët at St Nazaire of a ship of the *Bretagne* class (with the addition of a dozen 3in guns), to be named *Vasilèfs Konstantinos*. Work began on 12 June 1914, with the formal ceremonial laying down on 9 July 1914. However, all work ceased on 3 August, on the outbreak of the First World War, and in March 1916 the Greek authorities requested the cancellation of the contract.

In February 1914, there were reports of Greek orders for four light cruisers, two in Germany and two in the UK. In reality, only the latter pair were placed on contract (with plans for a third), together with four destroyers. Rather than the established export-players, such as Armstrong, Vickers and Yarrow, the contracts went to the relatively-new 'Coventry Syndicate', of the John Brown, Cammell Laird and Fairfield shipyards, plus their jointly-owned Coventry Ordnance Works. Cammell Laird at Birkenhead were to build the cruisers, to a modified version of the Royal Navy's *Chatham/Birmingham* design. The principal difference was the fitting of 5.5in, rather than 6in, main guns, to match the secondary battery of the French-built battleship. The first cruiser, *Antinavarchos Kountouriotis*, was laid down in March 1914, while the second, *Lambros Katsonis*, followed in October – by which time the UK was at war. Although continued on the Greek account until after the launch of *Antinavarchos Kountouriotis* in January 1915, contracts were then taken over by the Admiralty and the ships ultimately commissioned for the Grand Fleet (p 38).

The destroyer contracts went to the Clydeside yards in June 1914: John Brown took *Kriti* and *Lesvos*, and Fairfield received *Samos* and *Chios*. As in the cases of the two cruisers, they were all still on the stocks at the beginning of the First World War, and would end up being completed for the Royal Navy (p 40).

Plugging the gap
Even with two dreadnoughts on order, Greece still faced a capability gap between the autumn of 1914, when Turkey would have available *Reşadiye* and *Sultan Osman I* (not to mention *Barbaros Hayreddin* and *Turgut Reis*), and the 28 March 1915 contractual delivery date of *Salamis* (to be renamed *Vasilèfs Giorgios* to match the new French-built ship), and the late-1916 one of *Vasilèfs Konstantinos*. A further attempt at buying *Almirante Latorre* was rebuffed by the Chilean authorities, as was an offer to buy *Moreno* from Argentina (at a 50 per cent premium over her

Two unsuccessful attempts were made by Greece to acquire ships of the German *König* class, *Markgraf* in October 1913, and *Kronprinz* (shown here) in April 1914. (Author's collection)

construction cost [£3.5 million]) while she was actually on passage from the USA to Argentina. An offer to buy *Markgraf*'s sister, *Kronprinz*, in April 1914 also came to nothing, as did feelers towards acquiring the Japanese *Kongo*.

Against the background of the imminent upsetting of the Balkan balance of power by the delivery of *Reşadiye* and *Sultan Osman I*, US President Woodrow Wilson proposed to enhance Greek capabilities and tide them over the capability gap by offering (subject to Congressional approval) two of the newest US predreadnoughts. The vessels involved were the twins *Mississippi* and *Idaho*, launched in 1905 and armed with 12in, 8in and 7in guns. They were, however, smaller and a knot slower than both the parallel *Connecticut* class and the preceding *Virginia* class, making it difficult for them to tactically combine with the rest of the US battle line. Their disposal was thus not wholly an altruistic move, especially as the ships would be sold for a sum in excess of their probable market value.

Passage of the requisite amendment to the Naval Appropriations Bill, then going through Congress, was less than smooth, while the Ottoman ambassador in Washington DC argued that the sale would give the Greeks a short-term advantage that might result in an attack on Turkey. The Turks accordingly offered to pay even more than the Greeks for the two ships if released to them. Germany also attempted to dissuade the USA from the proposed sale. Winston Churchill was prepared to sell Greece two British predreadnoughts instead, but the offer never made it to the Greek authorities. Nevertheless, Congress passed the amendment on 30 June:

> The President may, in his discretion, direct the sale, in such manner, at such price not less than the original cost price and upon such terms as he may deem proper, of the two battleships

Idaho and Mississippi. All moneys received from the sale of said vessels shall be deposited by the Secretary of the Navy in the Treasury. After said sale, in addition to the two battleships herein before authorized, the President is hereby authorized to have constructed a first-class battleship carrying as heavy armor and as powerful armament as any vessel of its class, to have the highest practicable speed and the greatest desirable radius of action, and to cost, exclusive of armor and armament, not to exceed $7,800,000.

The 'the two battleships herein before authorized' were to become *New Mexico* (1917) and *Mississippi* (ii, 1917), while the ship to be paid for by the money received from the sale of the older ships became *Idaho* (ii, 1917). Each ship carried a dozen 14in guns, and accordingly, in exchange

The former USS *Mississippi* after having been handed over to Greece as *Kilkis* at Newport News on 21 July 1914. (NHHC NH 77442)

The Windfall Battleships

for two ships of marginal utility at best, the USA now received an additional vessel of overwhelmingly greater power.

The ships were formally sold for $11.5 million (£2.3 million) to Fred J Gauntlett on 8 July 1914. The ex-*Mississippi* (renamed *Kilkis*) steamed from Pensacola (where she was being used as an aviation support ship) to Newport News to decommission on 21 July and be transferred to the Greek navy the same day. She arrived at Phaleron Bay on 24 August. The ex-*Idaho* (*Lemnos*) was already in the Mediterranean on a midshipmen-training cruise, but put in at Villefranche in France on 17 July, where her crew transferred to the battleship USS *Maine* (1901); she was formally handed over to her new owners on the 30th.

The Chinese cruiser *Fei Hung* on the slip at Camden NJ, prior to her launch in 9 May 1912, and as commissioned into the Greek navy as *Helle* in the summer of 1914. On 15 August 1940 she would be sunk by an Italian submarine, over two months before Italy's invasion of Greece. (*Author's collection*)

A further immediate-term addition to the fleet had been achieved a few weeks earlier. In 1910, China ordered three essentially identical training cruisers, from Armstrong (*Chao Ho* [1911]), Vickers (*Ying Swei* [1911]) and New York Shipbuilding (*Fei Hung* [1912]; all had Armstrong guns). It had been originally planned that the British-built pair sail for China at the end of 1911. This would have allowed them to proceed in company with the Chinese flagship-cruiser *Hai Chi* (1898), which was in Europe for King George V's coronation review. However, following the Chinese Revolution of 1911–12, funds were initially unavailable, and the three ships were put up for sale. As previously seen (p 137), Greece attempted to buy *Chao Ho* in October 1912. At length, funding was found by China for the two British-built ships, and they sailed for the Far East in March and May 1913. However, funds were still lacking for *Fei Hung*, and in May 1914 Greece was successful in securing her as *Helle*, for £0.24 million. While no means comparable to the light cruisers being built in the UK for Greece, she represented a useful addition to the fleet.

Other negotiations for new warships were underway when they terminated as a result of the beginning of the First World War. Four more submarines were desired, with Germania prepared, with the blessing of the German navy, to offer the nearly-complete *U33–U37*, although possibly linked with the Greeks also ordering four destroyers from Schichau. The French were, however, also making efforts to secure the submarine order for themselves, but everything was overtaken by outbreak of war.

Eclipse
As already described, the Greek vessels under construction in the UK were taken over for British service in 1915, while work on *Vasilèfs Konstantinos* had ceased in August 1914. This just left *Salamis/Vasilèfs Giorgios* at Hamburg, with the hull structurally complete and with boilers and some other machinery installed. However, the ship lacked the two superimposed main barbettes, side armour, conning tower and parts of her armour deck, not to mention her turrets and main and secondary guns. The vast majority of the latter items were still awaited from the USA, with just 17 per cent of the armour delivered to date, and none of the armament.

The Greeks had made progress payments amounting to the equivalent of £450,000 up to July 1914, just over a quarter of the total purchase price, and work initially continued until November, when the ship was launched (as *Vasilèfs Giorgios*). However, since no further payments were received from Greece, no further work was done apart from housing over the openings in the deck of the ship, which work had been completed by the end of December 1914. The unfinished ship then remained at Hamburg in a state of preservation throughout the First World War.[29] No serious consideration was given to acquiring and completing the vessel for German service, in particular since the production of the missing armament and armour would have taken at least two years.

At the outbreak of war, the guns and their mountings were nearly complete at the Bethlehem plant, the first gun having been proof-fired in March 1914.[30] However, it was clear from the beginning of the war that these items, as well as the outstanding armour, would not be allowed through the British blockade of Germany. Accordingly, in November 1914, the president of the Bethlehem Steel Corporation, Charles Schwab, having secured an order for twenty 'H' class submarines from the Royal Navy (see p 43), offered the complete armament of the Greek battleship to the Admiralty, together with their ammunition. A contract was signed on 10 November 1914, the weapons being shipped across the Atlantic in the Cunard cargo-passenger liners *Ausonia* and *Transylvania* in February 1915.

The 14in guns, designated 14in BL Mk II* in UK service, and their mountings, were rather different from those of British design. In particular, the mountings were electrically, rather than hydraulically, powered, and differently arranged. The guns themselves were of all-steel, rather than the British wire-wound, construction, and were designed for a different propellant. Each of the twin turrets was installed in an *Abercrombie* class monitor, designed specifically to carry them. All were

The monitor HMS *Abercrombie*, armed with a 14in turret intended for *Salamis*; she is shown at Imbros in 1915. (NHHC NH 63153)

laid down in December 1914, launched in April 1915 and commissioned during May–June.

As no spare guns had been ordered by Greece, the British acquired four similar guns from the US Navy (US Mk I Mod 4, which became the UK Mk IV and V), and had two more made in the UK at the Royal Gun Factory at Woolwich (Mk II), using British constructional principles (wire-wound, as against the American all-steel). Of the twelve 6in guns (designated 6in QF Mk IV), eight were used in coast-defence batteries at Scapa Flow, and the rest in defensively-armed merchant ships.

Salamis/Vasilèfs Giorgios was still at Hamburg at the end of the First World War. Regardless of her actual naming on launch, she was still, and would continue to be, generally referred to by her original name. This may have been in part owing to the travails of the Greek monarchy during and following the war, culminating in its decade-long abolition in 1924 with the overthrow of King Giorgios II.

That the Greek authorities had early thoughts of getting the ship completed is suggested by a 1919 Armstrong proposal to Greece to supply three single 15in/45 and twelve 4in/50 weapons, with *Salamis* the only obvious recipient.[31] However, it was only in 1920 that formal action regarding the unfinished battleship began.[32] In October 1920, the Allied Conference of Ambassadors determined that, since the ship was being built to a foreign order, she did not fall under the provisions of Article 186 of the Treaty of Versailles, which required that all warships under construction in Germany be destroyed.[33] There were thus no Treaty-based objections to her being completed (albeit without guns and armour), and that a decision on the future of the ship was wholly a matter between the Greek government and AG Vulcan.

Directly after this decision, the Greek government wrote to the shipyard stating its desire to cancel the contract on the basis that the ship was now obsolete, and requesting terms. The ensuing negotiations proved unsuccessful, and in July 1923, the Greek government brought an action before the Greco-German Mixed Arbitral Tribunal (established under Article 304 of the Treaty of Versailles) that the contract be declared null and void, both owing to the obsolescence of the ship and as under Article 192 of the Treaty of Versailles (which forbade the manufacture of arms, munitions or naval war material in German territory for export to foreign countries), AG Vulcan would be frustrated from fulfilling its obligations under the contract. Interestingly, Bethlehem refused permission for the British Admiralty to confirm that the guns and mountings had been sold to them, presumably to evade liability for contributing to the impossibility of completing *Salamis* as designed.

In August 1925, the tribunal declared the Greek claim was invalid, as Article 192 did not prohibit the export of an unarmed and

The unfinished hulk of *Salamis* at Hamburg during the 1920s. *(NARA 68155073)*

unarmoured vessel and that Greece's claims regarding the obsolescence were overstated and insufficient grounds for voiding the contract. Greece had in the meantime not helped her case by, following a failure to reach a naval limitation agreement with Turkey in 1924, making an enquiry to Vulcan about completing the ship as a counter to the potential refitting of the battlecruiser *Yavuz* (ex-*Goeben*).

An attempt by Greece to harness a new German law prohibiting the export of war materials (including ships fitted for war purposes) in support of their case was frustrated when the new law, as passed in July 1927 (and agreed with the Allied Conference of Ambassadors), specifically excluded foreign contracts for ships let prior to 1 August 1914 (the only one extant being that for *Salamis*). However, the question of whether Versailles Articles 190 (forbidding Germany to construct warships other than to replace her own vessels allowed under the Treaty) and 192 might prohibit the delivery remained without authoritative determination – and with the dissolution of the Allied Commissions of Control at the end of January 1927, the mechanism for obtaining such a decision became unclear.

In anticipation of a favourable outcome to the dispute, AG Vulcan made it known that when completing *Salamis*, arming and armouring would probably be carried out in a British yard, with Beardmore at Dalmuir a leading candidate. However, Greece then brought the matter before the Council of the League of Nations in September 1927 in an attempt to get the outstanding Versailles Articles interpreted by the International Court of Justice.

In 1928, concerns at the impending recommissioning of *Yavuz*, whose refit had just begun (she recommissioned in 1930), meant that Greece changed tack again to consider responding positively to an offer from Vulcan to reach a compromise. One option put forward was to complete and modernise *Salamis*, and also supply a 20,000-tonne floating dock, with the costs being met from German reparations payments due to Greece for 1928–31. The Greek Minister of Marine argued strongly for such a solution, studies being commissioned that indicated that a modernised *Salamis* would be a match for *Yavuz*. Others argued against, further suggesting that *Kilkis* and *Lemnos* should be kept, rather than disposed of as was currently being planned.

In May 1929, rumours were circulating that a deal had been reached, with a Dutch newspaper alleging in August that work was actually restarting on the ship. But the final decision went against completing *Salamis*, particularly in view of treaties signed in 1928 and 1930 that resolved many of the difficulties between Greece and Turkey.[34] In any case, the international financial crash of 1929 meant that funds were simply no longer available for the work. Against this background, a final ruling by the Tribunal on 23 April 1932 produced a pragmatic solution that annulled the contract and gave ownership of the ship to AG Vulcan, who would both retain the money already paid and also receive the equivalent of a further £30,000 from the Greeks. Having taken ownership, the shipyard lost little time in selling the hulk for scrap. So ended the Balkan battleship race.

Romania

Of the powers on the western side of the Black Sea, Romania possessed only a handful of small and obsolete ships at the end of the nineteenth century. However, she aspired to a navy of some size, an 1899 programme envisioning six coastal battleships, four 300-ton destroyers and a dozen 80-ton torpedo boats, plus vessels for use on the Danube. Only some of the latter were built. An ambitious 1912 programme comprised six 3500-ton cruisers, twelve 1500-ton destroyers and a submarine, with a supplement that called for a 13,000-ton battleship as well. Only four ships had actually been ordered before the outbreak of the First World War – the large destroyers *Vijelie*, *Vârtej*, *Vifor* and *Viscol*, ordered from the Pattison yard at Naples in 1913.

When Italy joined the conflict in May 1915, they were respectively 50, 20, 60 and 0 per cent complete, and were taken over for the Italian navy. *Vijelie*, *Vârtej* and *Vifor* each completed during the war as *Sparviero* (July 1917), *Nibbio* (May 1918) and *Aquila* (February 1917), but the fourth ship was not finished, as *Falco*, until January 1920. Two were re-purchased by Romania on 1 July 1920, *Sparviero* (ex-*Vijelie*) becoming *Mărăști* and *Nibbio* (ex-*Vârtej*) becoming *Mărășești*. Both would remain in service until the beginning of the 1960s. The other two ships remained in the Italian navy until January 1939, when they were transferred to Nationalist Spain.

Bulgaria

Romania's southern neighbour began the twentieth century with an even smaller navy. This was enhanced by the acquisition of six 97-ton torpedo boats from Schneider in France, with final assembly taking place at Varna. *Drski*, *Smeli*, *Hrabri*, *Shumni*, *Letyashti* and *Strogi* were all completed during 1908–9. During this same time, Russia offered some old ships to the Bulgarian navy, but these were declined, and there were no attempts to expand the navy prior to the First World War.

CHAPTER 4

With the Grand Fleet

1914

As we have already seen, *Agincourt* had physically become a member of the Grand Fleet's 4th Battle Squadron on 7 September 1914, while *Erin* had followed suit ten days later (for an overview of the battle fleet's organisation between 1914 and 1919, see pp 176–9). During the intervening period, *Agincourt* had been at sea with the fleet, and now the two ex-Ottoman ships sailed together from Loch Ewe on 17 September on a voyage that would take them to Scapa Flow a week later. On passage, both ships tested and exercised their armaments. On the 18th, *Agincourt* fired off thirty 12in and twenty-eight 6in shells against a towed target, while *Erin* undertook range-keeping exercises in conjunction with *Temeraire*. The two 'newcomers' detached from the fleet to exercise together between 08:00 and 22:25 on the 23rd, *Agincourt* towing a target for *Erin*. Scapa Flow was reached the following morning, *Agincourt* anchoring at 07:40 and *Erin* two hours later.

The stop was a short one, as on the evening of the next day the 4th BS and the fleet flagship *Iron Duke* (tactically part of the formation) put to sea, not returning until midday on the 29th. The ships were back at sea on the evening of 2 October, and on the 5th *Agincourt* and *Erin* separated from the main fleet to undertake target practice together. On the 6th, *Erin* towed the target for a 12in day shoot, and a 6in night firing, by *Agincourt*, which expended thirty 12in, seventy-two 6in and thirty-four 3in rounds. The next day, the two ships split up to undertake separate shoots against stationary targets, coming back together on the afternoon of the 11th to rejoin their squadron, anchoring back at Scapa the next morning.

Erin and *Agincourt*, as new (and non-standard) ships, required intensive working-up, and as such again exercised together at the beginning of a sweep by the 1st and 4th BS that began on the morning of 16 October. This included ranging and deflection exercises and night firings of their secondary batteries. Work-up was hampered for *Agincourt* by her not having been fitted with subcalibre guns, which took some time to remedy. On the 20th, with the rest of the 4th BS (*Temeraire, Bellerophon, Iron Duke* and *Dreadnought*), the pair narrowly missed intercepting the German minelayer *Berlin* between Rockall Bank and the Hebrides: a week later one of her mines would sink the battleship *Audacious* off the north-west coast of Ireland.

At this time, concerns at the security of Scapa Flow against submarine attack had led to a decision to temporarily move the fleet to the west coast, the 1st and 4th BS going to Lough Swilly. They arrived on 22 October, anchoring off Rathmullan, remaining there until 3 November, when the ships put to sea to cruise between the Hebrides, Faroe and Shetland Islands, carrying out exercises when possible; the latter included *Erin* firing her 13.5in guns against Bills Rocks on 5 November, and on the 7th her towing a target for *Dreadnought*. The 4th BS arrived back at its normal moorings in Scapa Flow on the morning of the 9th, having been preceded by the 1st BS on the 7th, and the 2nd BS on the 8th.

During the first half of November, the battlecruisers *Princess Royal*, *Invincible* and *Inflexible* were detached to the Atlantic to counter potential movements of the German East Asiatic Squadron, and would not return until the New Year. As *Tiger* was not yet fully worked-up, and amid worries that the new German *Derfflinger* was armed with 14in guns (rather than her actual 12in), FO Battlecruisers, David Beatty, requested that either the 2nd CS (*Shannon*, *Cochrane*, *Natal* and *Achilles*) or *Agincourt* be temporarily transferred to the battlecruiser force. However, Admiral John Jellicoe, CinC Grand Fleet, rejected both proposals, on the basis that 'the 2nd Cruiser Squadron is the only Cruiser Squadron [in] the Battle Fleet and ... the "AGINCOURT'S" comparatively low speed and rather poor radius of action makes her unsuitable. Her oil fuel installation is practically of very little use.'[1]

On 17 November, *Erin* carried out torpedo exercises in the Flow, and after an overnight sortie on the 20/21st, the 4th BS sailed in the late afternoon of the 21st for a deployment with the whole Grand Fleet (1st, 2nd, 3rd and 4th BS; the 1st BCS; the 2nd and 3rd CS; the 2nd LCS; and the 2nd and 4th DF) that would last until the morning of the 27th. Just before departure, *Erin*'s Captain '[a]dmonished Mr Albert G. Baggs, Chief Gunner for neglect of duty in not having satisfied himself of the actual amount of ammunition in the magazines since the original embarkation of ammunition Aug 27th to Sept 2nd 1914'.

In December, the 4th BS was reinforced by the new *Benbow* and *Emperor of India*, which became flagship (relieving *Dreadnought*) and 2nd flag, respectively. On 3 December, work began on painting *Agincourt*'s superstructure a lighter shade of grey than her hull, giving her for a while a unique appearance. She and *Erin* sailed with the Grand Fleet in the early afternoon of 16 December in support of the 2nd BS and the British battlecruisers. These had skirmished with the German High Seas Fleet in the wake of the German battlecruiser bombardments

Agincourt in the winter of 1914/15, sporting an unusual paint scheme. *(Andrew Choong Han Li collection)*

of Hartlepool, Scarborough and Whitby the previous day. However, by the time the fleet was in the appropriate location on the 17th, the Germans had returned to port, and the Grand Fleet headed for home, taking the opportunity of its concentration (including the Harwich Force) to carry out battle practice. The 2nd BS was detached at 17:00 on the 17th, but the 1st and 4th BS remained, together with the 1st BCS and 1st LCS, at sea off the Orkneys during the 18th for exercises. That evening the battleships set a course for Scapa Flow, while the battlecruisers and most cruisers made for Cromarty. The battle squadrons were back at Scapa on the morning of the 19th, with *Agincourt* at berth A3 and *Erin* at A4.

The 2nd and 4th BS were back at sea on 23 December, heading west to carry out shoots against the remote Sulisker Rock (Sula Sgeir) on the 24th, and then back through the Pentland Firth to participate in a sweep by the fleet through the southern North Sea. By the early afternoon of the 25th, 200 miles east of the Forth estuary, the two squadrons had met up with the 1st BS, 6th CS and 2nd DF from Scapa, the 3rd BS, 3rd CS, 1st BCS and 1st LCS from Rosyth, and the 1st and 2nd CS and 4th DF from Cromarty. It had now become routine for the dreadnought battle squadrons (1st, 2nd and 4th) to be rotated from Scapa to the Cromarty Firth, for both strategic and practical reasons. The latter included the ability to undergo maintenance at Invergordon, whence floating dock *AFD5* (as it was later known) had been brought from Portsmouth in September 1914. This dock could take battleships, and was supplemented in the autumn of 1916 by a smaller example (a requisitioned Dutch order, returned in 1920) for light cruisers and destroyers.

Having come together, the fleet then headed northwards, but a rising sea required a turn southwards during the evening. The weather worsened, and the destroyers had to be detached the next morning to their bases, a south-easterly gale then forcing a cancellation of the sweep, the Rosyth- and Cromarty-based elements being directed back to their

WITH THE GRAND FLEET

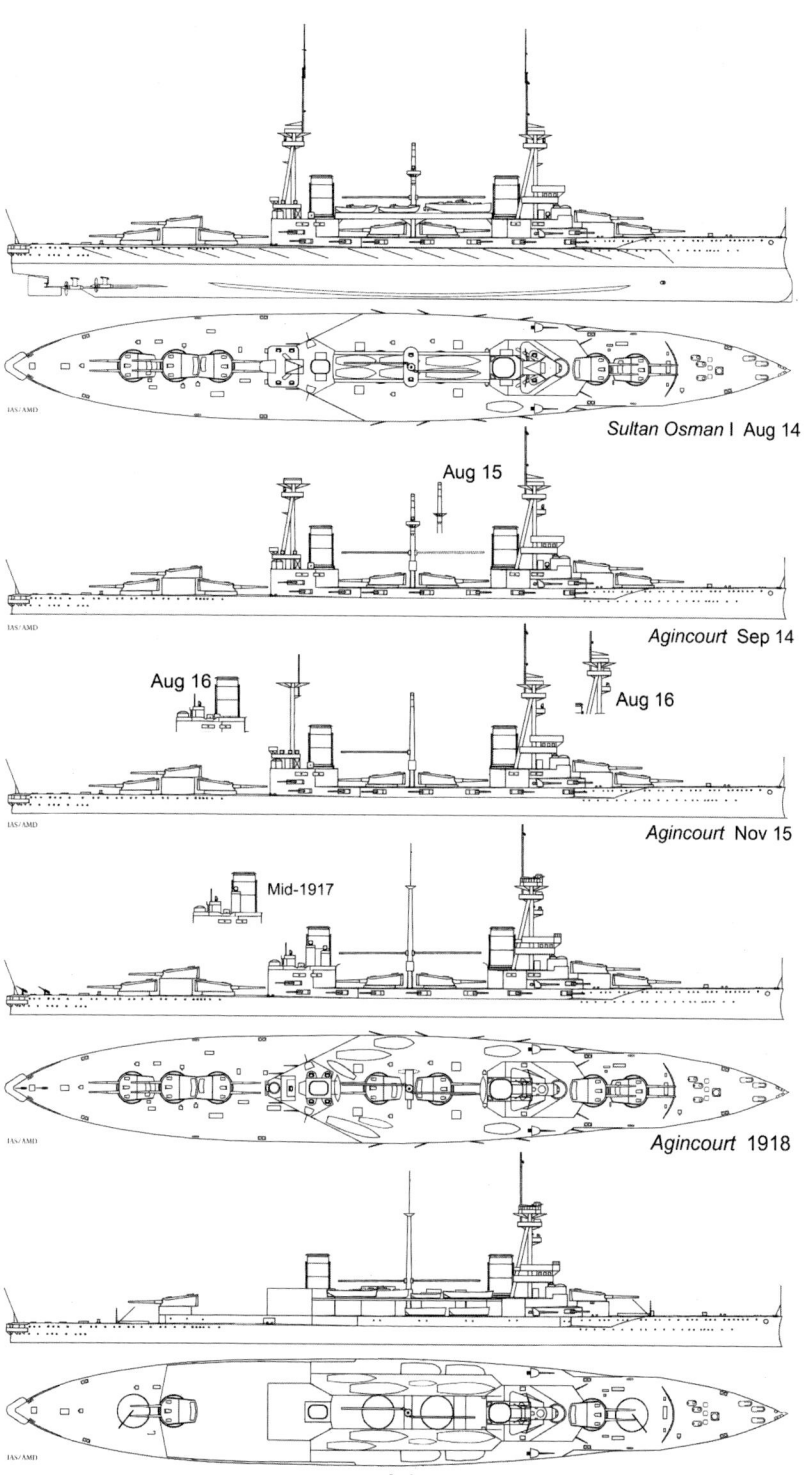

Sultan Osman I Aug 14

Agincourt Sep 14

Agincourt Nov 15

Agincourt 1918

Agincourt project as mobile fleet base 8 Dec 21

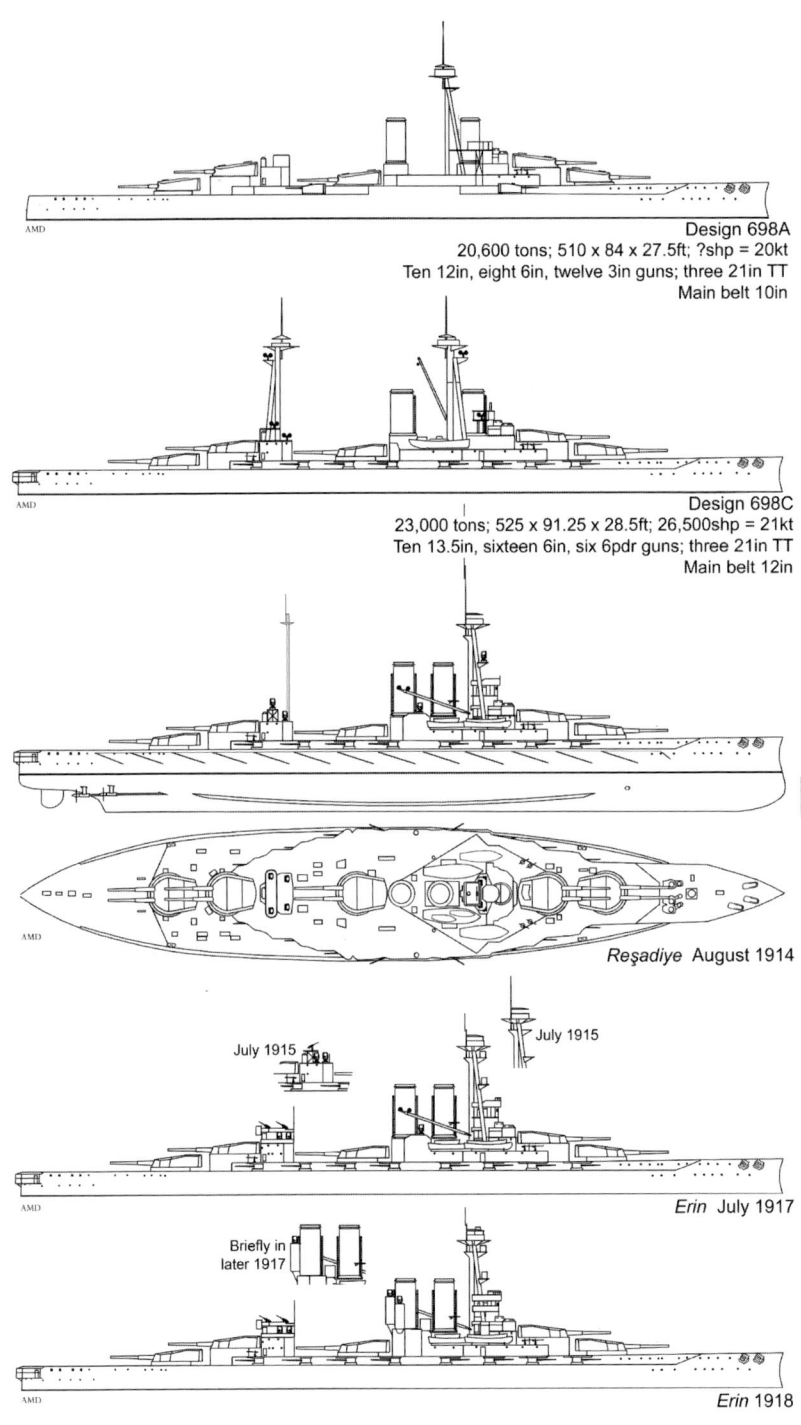

Design 698A
20,600 tons; 510 x 84 x 27.5ft; ?shp = 20kt
Ten 12in, eight 6in, twelve 3in guns; three 21in TT
Main belt 10in

Design 698C
23,000 tons; 525 x 91.25 x 28.5ft; 26,500shp = 21kt
Ten 13.5in, sixteen 6in, six 6pdr guns; three 21in TT
Main belt 12in

Reşadiye August 1914

Erin July 1917

Erin 1918

normal anchorages. Conditions in the Pentland Firth were very difficult for the remaining ships as they headed for Scapa, with funnel smoke forced ahead of the vessels by the following wind.

As the leading squadron (the 2nd BS) entered harbour in the dark on the morning of 27 December, *Conqueror* rammed *Monarch* in the stern, and although the 1st BS entered safely, the 4th BS, with the fleet flagship *Iron Duke*, sailed westward through the Pentland Firth until the (very late northerly) dawn. Reversing course in the weather conditions was not easy, and it was not until an hour before midday that the 4th BS was safely anchored in Scapa Flow, and even then two anchors were employed and steam kept up until 13:00.

More firings by the 4th BS took place on 11 January 1915, both against Sulisker Rock and floating targets, *Agincourt* and *Erin* firing both their main and secondary batteries. The former ship in particular undertook many gunnery-related exercises within Scapa Flow during the months of December to January.

Agincourt had commissioned with personnel that ranged from the crew of the Royal Yacht to individuals taken directly from the detention barracks (cf pp 17, 18). This kind of eclectic mix of whatever officers and men could be conjured up from such sources, leavened by reserves, had also been used for commissioning other ships that were only ready after the outbreak of war. This was because all 'spare' personnel had been funnelled to ships that had commissioned for the July 1914 test mobilisation. Accordingly, as part of a review of the future of the navy's older pre-dreadnought battleships, a note to the First Sea Lord in December 1914 commented: 'I consider further that the complements of "Benbow", "Emperor of India", "Agincourt", and "Erin" ought to be improved as far as possible by exchanging reserve men for active service ratings as opportunity offers from the older cruisers in Cruiser Forces "E", "I" and "G"[2] and from older battleships.'[3]

1915

The first major deployment of the new year began on the evening of 23 January 1915, when the fleet sailed in response to information from wireless intercepts that indicated a German sortie to the Dogger Bank. It was to provide support to the 1st and 2nd BCS and 1st LCS from Rosyth, plus the Harwich Force, when the latter engaged the German Scouting Force at what became the Battle of Dogger Bank. The main fleet never came near to participation, and was back at Scapa on the morning of the 26th.

Between 31 January and 2 February, divers were employed repairing damage to one of *Erin*'s submerged torpedo tubes. On 18 February, the ship was honoured by a visit by the new FO 4th BS, Admiral Sir Doveton Sturdee (fresh from his victory at the Battle of the Falkland Islands), and his deputy, Rear Admiral Alexander Duff. On 2 March, *Erin* and *Agincourt* together undertook subcalibre firings in the Flow, and on the 7th sortied with the fleet for a cruise in the northern North Sea. This included various battle exercises, from which most ships (including the 4th BS) returned on the morning of 10 March, although the 2nd BS and 7th CS remained at sea for another 24 hours.

On the 16th, the fleet sailed again, for the northern and central North Sea, carrying out a strategic exercise early in the morning of the 18th, although a second exercise was cancelled owing to concerns over the possible presence of German submarines, exacerbated by exceptionally clear conditions. These were realised when the periscope and a torpedo-track of *U29* was sighted, but the submarine was rapidly rammed and sunk by *Dreadnought*. Along with her crew, she took with her Kapitänleutnant Otto Weddigen who, while commanding *U9*, had sunk the cruisers *Cressy*, *Abukir* and *Hogue* on 22 September 1914 and *Hawke* on 15 October. The fleet continued east through the Pentland Firth in case of the presence of further submarines, after which the ships turned to head for port. The 4th BS moored in the Cromarty Firth on the morning of the 19th, and remained there until the 29th, when they sailed to join the rest of the fleet for a North Sea sweep. This was, however, cancelled, and the ships returned to Cromarty, where they remained until 11 April, bad weather preventing a number of planned deployments. However, on the evening of that day the 4th BS, together with the 1st CS, headed to sea, to join the rest of the battle fleet plus the Battle Cruiser Fleet (BCF) and the 3rd BS for a day's exercises in the central North Sea. The 4th BS now returned to Scapa Flow, mooring on the evening of the 14th.

During the afternoon of 17 April 1915, *Erin* and *Agincourt* undertook subcalibre firings in the Flow, and after a few hours' rest, sailed that night with the fleet for a sweep into the southern North Sea, rendezvousing with the BCF, 3rd BS and 3rd CS at 16:00 on the 18th. During the night, these latter forces were detached, the battle fleet sailing northwards to the east of the Shetlands, where target practice was carried out throughout the 19th and into the following morning. *Erin* fired thirty rounds of 13.5in, while *Agincourt* loosed off thirty-five 12in shells, together with a hundred 6in and ten 3in rounds.

Back at Scapa on the morning of 21 April, the ships were at sea with the fleet once more around midnight, to undertake a sweep towards the Danish coast. At 08:00 on the 22nd, the 1st, 2nd and 4th BS with two ships detached from the 6th BS, plus cruisers and destroyers, were 200 miles west of Stavanger, and were joined by the Rosyth-based forces at 16:00. These were detached during the night, and the battle fleet was back at Scapa (including the 4th BS) and Cromarty on the morning of the 23rd.

May was punctuated by *Agincourt* and *Erin* making short runs for exercises both within and outside the harbour, and participating in full fleet sweeps into the central North Sea from the 17th to the 19th and the 29th to the 31st, the latter as far as the Dogger Bank. On the evening of 11 June, the 4th BS, together with the 2nd BS and supporting vessels, headed northward from Scapa Flow, primarily for gunnery practice and large-scale tactical exercises with the rest of the battle fleet. Passing through the Pentland Firth, firings were carried out the next day north-west of the Shetlands against targets towed by colliers, before the force was joined by the 1st BS and 7th CS from Cromarty that afternoon. Night firings were then carried out, joined by the newly-arrived BCF; the entire Grand Fleet exercised together on the 13th. Ships then returned to their bases, the 4th BS arriving back at Scapa on the evening of 14 June.

At 11:53 on 28 June, *Erin* sailed for docking and refit at Portsmouth. The ship moored at the latter's No 9 buoy at 01:00 on the 28th, and at 13:00 was in C Lock, and 20 minutes later in No 3 Basin. There, the 240-ton crane removed the guns from 'Q' turret. On 1 July, 308 shipwrights, 41 boilermakers, 3 apprentices, 54 labourers, 117 electricians, 60 hydraulic party and 6 chargemen are recorded as working on the ship. Modifications included the addition of a platform below the foretop, wired to carry a main-battery director (not fitted until the summer of 1916), moving the searchlights on the platform on the aft superstructure down to the superstructure itself, and installing a single 3in AA in their place. On the 2nd, the battleship shifted her berth to D Lock, where she remained until undocked at 08:00 on the 12th; she then moored at North Ship Jetty. At 17:00 the next day, *Erin* was at No 4 buoy, and at 21:25 put to sea. Two hours after midnight on the 17th, she was at Scapa Flow's C5 berth.

While *Erin* was at Portsmouth, *Agincourt* had been present when King George V visited Scapa on 7 July, and was then part of a cruise (including exercises) by the battle fleet to the area of the Shetlands from 11 to 14 July. However, the afternoon following *Erin*'s return, *Agincourt* herself sailed for Portsmouth to refit. She arrived at 22:36 on 20 July, and entered dry dock at 11:30 on the 24th. The ship was in dock until 18:00 on 5 August, when she proceeded to the North Railway Jetty, where she commenced ammunitioning at 20:00. Work undertaken at Portsmouth included the removal of the searchlights mounted on the derrick standard, and the reinstatement of the forward derrick. The 24in signalling searchlight was moved further down the foremast from the platform below the foretop. This platform was, as in *Erin*, wired for a main-battery director (again, not to be installed for some time). *Agincourt*'s voyage back to Scapa Flow began at 22:00 on 7 August, but as the ship neared the Orkneys she ran into thick fog, and it was not until 36 hours after passing Cape Wrath – only 60 miles distant – that the battleship was finally able to enter the Flow, at 19:34 on the 12th. The ship had made a number of attempts at entry, but had ultimately been forced to cruise westward until conditions had cleared sufficiently.

While *Agincourt* had been away, her squadron, including *Erin*, had sailed for Cromarty on the evening of 3 August, arriving early the next morning. *Agincourt* left Scapa at 15:00 on the 19th to join them, arriving that evening. *Erin* fired three rounds from each of her 13.5in guns the next day. The squadron left for Scapa around midday on the 24th, reaching the Orkneys later in the afternoon. The use of large peacetime-type towed targets in the Moray Firth, operating out of Cromarty, had been reintroduced in August, it having been recognised that firings against small targets and rocks had not been satisfactory. Given the danger of submarines, only two big ships could be on the range at a time, with a strong anti-submarine screen to seaward.

On the afternoon of 31 August, *Agincourt* undertook torpedo-firing practice within Scapa Flow, before sailing with the battle fleet on the evening of 2 September for a sweep of northern waters. Exercises and

Agincourt and *Erin* at sea with the 4th BS in September 1915. (Author's collection)

Agincourt at sea with a member of the *Iron Duke* class, and two of the *Bellerophon/St Vincent* class. It is unclear whether this photograph was taken before or after her transfer from the 4th to the 1st BS in October 1915, as both squadrons had ships of these classes at this time. (NHHC NH 2712)

night firings were undertaken during the cruise, which ended on the 5th. *Erin* undertook torpedo practice at Scapa on 10 September, with subcalibre, aiming-rifle and high-angle exercises on the 14th. On the 24th, the 4th BS went to sea for a day of tactical and rangefinder exercises, and on 13 October went out with the full battle fleet to cruise in the northern North Sea.

The fleet's return to Scapa Flow on 15 August coincided with the arrival of *Canada*, which was the catalyst for a significant reorganisation of the Grand Fleet's battle squadrons. On commissioning, *Canada* had been placed alongside her fellow windfalls in the 4th BS, replacing *Queen Elizabeth*, which now became part of the reconstituted 5th BS. The latter, with the newly-arrived *Barham* and *Warspite* from the 2nd BS, was now to become the 'fast wing' of the battle fleet. However, the union of *Agincourt*, *Erin* and *Canada* would be short-lived: on 24 October *Agincourt* went to the 1st BS, swapping places with *Superb*, and *Erin* went to the 2nd BS, as a replacement for *Warspite*. Tactically, this latter move made a lot of sense, as it meant that the 2nd BS returned to being an all-13.5in formation, which otherwise comprised the surviving three *King George V*s and the four *Orion* class. *Erin* was thus implicitly an ultimate replacement for *Audacious*, whose loss over a year earlier had not initially been admitted.

The 1st BS retained its previous calibre balance, all-12in, with the exception of its 13.5in-gunned flagship, *Marlborough*. The 4th BS remained a very mixed bag, with ships carrying 12in, 13.5in and now unique 14in weapons, exacerbated in May 1916 by the addition of the new 15in-gunned *Royal Oak*, replacing *Dreadnought*. This formation would endure until the following summer.

The newly-configured 2nd BS went to sea on 25 October 1915 for rangefinding and fire-control exercises, while *Canada* left at 08:03 for rangefinding practice with her squadron-mate *Temeraire*. On completion, she did not return to her normal berth, but moored at the Scapa North Shore at 12:46. She stayed there the next day, carrying out

The Windfall Battleships

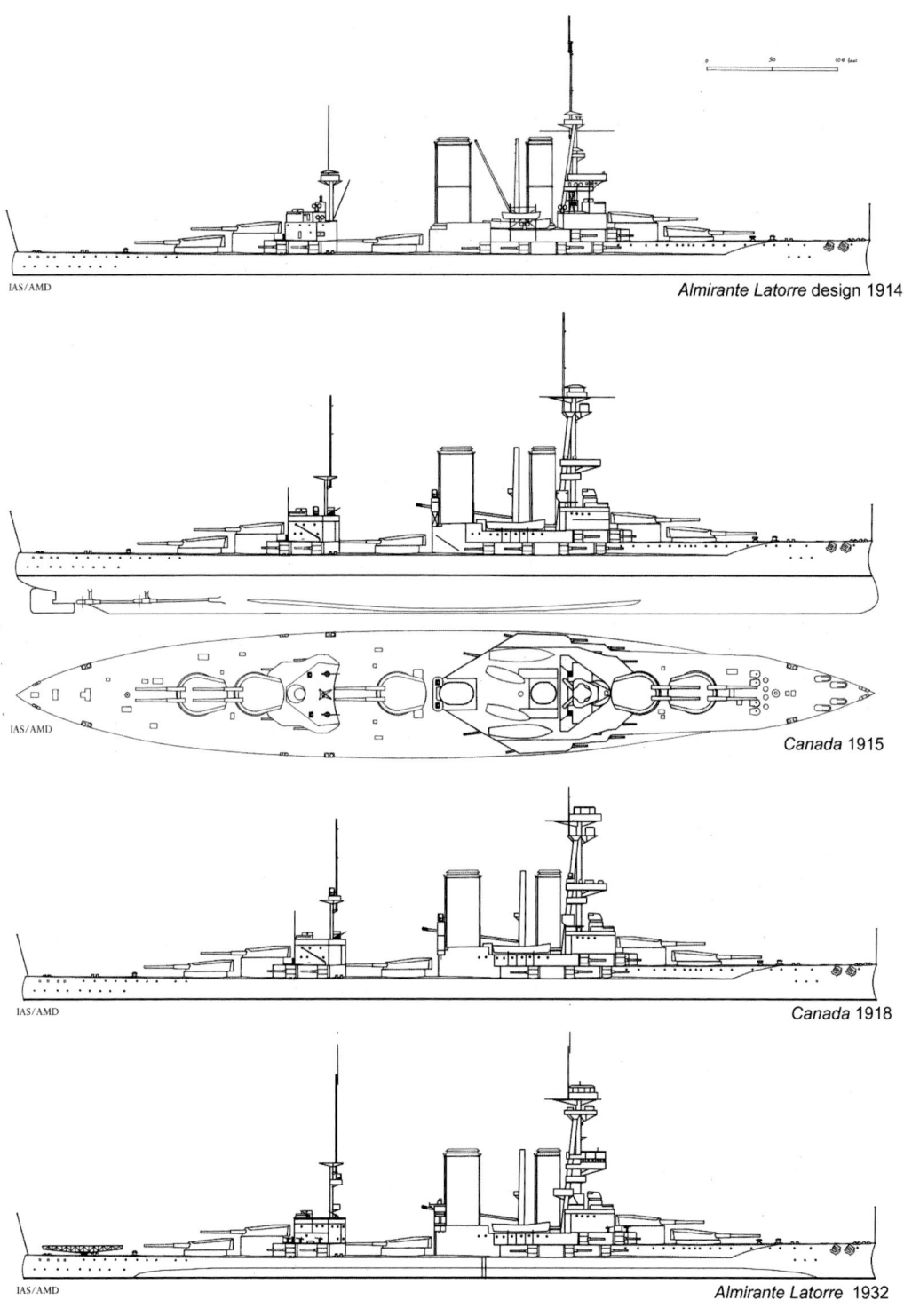

Almirante Latorre design 1914

Canada 1915

Canada 1918

Almirante Latorre 1932

turning trials with *Iron Duke*, together with more rangefinding exercises, subcalibre and torpedo-firing practice. Mooring at 17:00, she finally returned to the main anchorage, in berth A4, on the morning of the 28th. *Erin* had joined *Canada* at the North Shore the previous morning, and came back shortly before her. *Canada*, as part of her work-up, carried out further rangefinding, subcalibre and torpedo-firing exercises during the first two weeks of November, transferring to Cromarty on the 12th, steaming in the wake of the new 5th BS flagship *Barham*.

In the meantime, *Agincourt* had sailed to Cromarty on 25 October, staying until 16 November, to undergo a refit at Invergordon. Modifications included the removal of the struts from the mainmast reducing it to a pole (as had originally been proposed by the Captain on 4 March); the control top and the searchlight below were also taken out, as was (again) the forward derrick. As in other ships, the aft top had proved useless in view of its placement directly above the smoke-plume of the aft funnel. At 11:00 on the 16th, she began an all-turret firing, followed on the range by *Canada* for an all-calibre shoot. This was completed at 14:30, after which *Canada*, *Agincourt* and *Barham* sailed in company to Scapa Flow, arriving in the early evening. *Erin* was also at Cromarty, for 13.5in half-charge firing, from 15 to 30 October.

The full battle fleet, with the 1st, 2nd, 4th and 5th BS, plus the 1st, 2nd and 7th CS, the 1st LCS and two flotillas of destroyers, sailed on 2 November to cruise west of the Orkneys, which included tactical exercises and subcalibre firings. At the end of the deployment, *Agincourt* went with the 1st BS to Cromarty, arriving at midday on the 5th, while the remaining battleships went to Scapa, *Erin* and *Canada* arriving soon after 08:00.

Canada continued her round of working-up exercises during the last week of November and into December, mainly based on the Scapa North Shore, although putting to sea with her squadron for a morning of rangefinder work on 23 November 1915. *Agincourt*, *Erin* and *Canada*

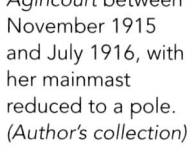

Agincourt between November 1915 and July 1916, with her mainmast reduced to a pole. (Author's collection)

were at sea with the fleet from 1 to 4 December, exercising to the west of the Orkneys. Although *Agincourt* and *Canada* returned to Scapa, *Erin*'s squadron pushed on to Cromarty, where she remained until the 17th, when the 2nd BS headed for Scapa. *Canada* and the 4th BS arrived at Cromarty the same day, remaining in the Cromarty Firth until 10 January 1916, with *Canada* going to sea for a firing on 20 December, where she witnessed the destruction in the Firth of the cruiser *Natal* by internal explosion on 30 December.

1916

In January 1916, *Canada*'s captain submitted a paper to the Third Sea Lord critiquing various issues with her bridgework conning tower and the positioning of searchlights. This seems to have been in light of the fact that the ship had been fitted with essentially *Revenge*-class bridgework, and was intended to inform potential modifications in these ships, the first of which (*Revenge*) was due to join the fleet in March.

On the 4th BS's departure from Cromarty, its place there was taken by *Agincourt* and the 1st BS. *Agincourt*'s Captain Nicholson then left the ship, to be replaced by Henry Doughty, from the monitor *Abercrombie*, who would remain with her until April 1917. *Agincourt* carried out a seven-turret firing on the 14th, and remained in the Cromarty Firth until 6 February 1916.

Back at Scapa, *Canada* continued her exercises, and while carrying out torpedo-firing exercises early in the afternoon of 27 January, the side door of the aft starboard tube burst open, flooding the aft torpedo flat. Watertight doors were closed, and the ship anchored at 14:00 to allow divers to place a plug over the tube. Exercises continued, however, with a 14in firing at sea on the 31st, a 6in one on 2 February, and of both calibres on the 5th. *Erin* had a rather more successful firing of two torpedo tubes on 1 February, proceeding to Cromarty with the 2nd BS on the 7th, following the return of *Agincourt* and the 1st BS.

Bad weather had hindered high-seas operations during January, but on 10 February 1916 British sloops were attacked by German destroyers near the Dogger Bank, and overnight the BCF was dispatched from

The three aftermost turrets of *Agincourt*, officially designated '5', '6' and '7'. There is no archival support for their alleged naming after the seven days of the week. (Author's collection)

Rosyth, with the 5th LCS from Harwich; the battle fleet put to sea from Scapa and Cromarty around 06:00 on the 11th. By 10:30 it was clear that the raiding force had only comprised destroyers and that they had returned to base. The fleet therefore returned to base. The Cromarty ships (including *Erin*) initially put into Scapa on the 12th, but they were back off Invergordon on the 14th.

The fleet was back at sea on the morning of 26 February, for a sweep and exercises in the northern North Sea; it had been intended to probe the Heligoland Bight in conjunction with the Harwich Force, but weather conditions were unsuitable. Tactical exercises were held that afternoon, with the BCF joining at 08:00 on the 27th, allowing further exercises to be carried out, including deploying the fleet from its cruising to battle order. *Canada* was back at her Scapa mooring at 08:09 on the 28th, followed by *Agincourt* at 08:30; *Erin* anchored at Cromarty at midday.

A few days later *Erin* shifted to Invergordon for docking. She entered the floating dock on 2 March, remaining there until 16:25 on the 11th. The ship sailed to Scapa on the 13th, but was back at Cromarty on the 16th, returning to Scapa the next day with the new *Malaya* and *Valiant*, carrying out a full-calibre firing en route. Shortly before these ships departed Cromarty, *Canada* arrived there with the 4th BS, which stayed from 17 March to 15 April.

On 24 March, the Harwich Force had sailed for an attack on the German airship base at Tondern, covered by the BCF. Collisions between British ships involved in the operation led to a decision to put the battle fleet to sea in case of need. It sailed at first light on the 26th, but both Scapa and Cromarty were beset with heavy snowstorms, followed by a gale – accompanied by very poor visibility. By 16:30, with the weather even heavier, the fleet was sent back to its bases, *Agincourt* and *Erin* arriving at Scapa at 07:30 and 08:30 on the 27th, respectively, by which time *Canada* was already back at Cromarty. The fleet returned to sea on the afternoon of 29 March for another northern North Sea cruise, with exercises undertaken on the 30th and ships back at their usual ports on the 31st; the destroyers had to proceed independently owing to the ongoing bad weather.

Agincourt arrived at Invergordon for docking on 17 April. In dock from the 19th to the 29th, she arrived back at Scapa at 17:00 on 2 May. During her time away, both *Erin* and *Canada* had been involved in exercises and trials at Scapa, and also in a fleet deployment on 21 April. This was a sweep towards the Horns Reef that was intended to discourage any shifting of German ships from the North Sea to the Baltic, where the Russians were re-laying minefields in the wake of the break-up of winter ice.

This deployment included both the battle fleet and the BCF, with the 3rd BS and 3rd CS from Rosyth also at sea in case of need. Fog descended in the afternoon of 22 April, the battlecruisers *Australia* and *New Zealand* colliding around 18:00, and by 22:00 all ships were enveloped in dense fog. Turning away from the Danish coast, the battleship *Neptune* and three destroyers were involved in collisions overnight, and the next morning the operation was abandoned. *Canada* and *Erin* moored at Scapa around 05:00 on the 24th to coal, before proceeding to sea again that evening to make another southern sweep.

This deployment was in response to signals intelligence that the German fleet had sailed and that an objective was Yarmouth. Actually, the first target of the German battlecruisers was Lowestoft, the follow-up attack on Yarmouth being hindered by fog and also by an attack on the German light cruisers and destroyers by the Harwich Force. In the event, the German forces withdrew, as did the Harwich Force and the Grand Fleet, the latter's progress having been held up by heavy weather. Ships were back at Scapa by 07:00 on the morning of the 26th. A consequence of the raid was that the 3rd BS was moved from Rosyth to Sheerness and no longer regarded as part of the Grand Fleet organisation.

The fleet again put to sea early in the morning of 3 May to support an attack by carrier-borne aircraft on the Tondern airship sheds, which proved largely abortive, although it indirectly resulted in the destruction of an airship by British cruisers. The fleet withdrew on the 4th, its progress hampered by fog, but was back at Scapa soon after midday on the 5th.

The 1st BS, including *Agincourt*, was at Cromarty from 7 to 16 May, *Erin* sailing there with the 2nd BS on the 17th. The 2nd BS was still there on 30 May, when the order came to sail in response to news of the German deployments that would ultimately lead to the Battle of Jutland. *Erin* departed at 21:45; back at Scapa *Agincourt* had weighed anchor at 20:30, with *Canada* following at 22:15. All were at sea with their squadrons over two hours before the German forces had left Wilhelmshaven.[4]

Jutland
The 1st BS had recently been reinforced by the new *Revenge*, replacing *Vanguard*, which moved to the 4th BS. As a result, the 6th Div, of which *Agincourt* at that time formed part, had as many kinds of big guns as ships: *Agincourt* had 12in/45s, *Hercules* 12in/50s, *Marlborough* 13.5in and *Revenge* 15in. As deployed, the 6th Div was at the rear of the British line, with *Agincourt* the very last ship. She opened fire at 18:24 with her main battery, at what was believed to be a German battlecruiser, but may

actually have been the light cruiser *Wiesbaden* (1915). A hit was claimed, as was another at 18:32, before the target was blocked by the presence of the 12th DF. At 19:08 *Agincourt* altered course to avoid a torpedo that just missed astern, and shortly afterwards she spotted four German battleships. She opened fire, and continued to fire until 19:26. Firing fourteen-gun broadsides – which were reported as visually most spectacular! – she may have hit SMS *Markgraf* at 19:14, and certainly twice hit *Kaiser* at 19:23/26. One of the latter caused little damage, but the other hit created an 8ft x 3ft hole in the upper deck, although this had little effect on the ship's capability. Like most British armour-piercing shell at this time,[5] *Agincourt*'s projectiles broke up rather than penetrating. Her shooting was hampered by the fact that she had not yet been fitted with her director and fire-control table, a failing she shared only with *Erin*. One assumes that their late position in the fitting schedule owed something to the ships' non-standard design. When firing on German destroyers shortly afterwards, seven 6in hits were claimed.

During the night, *Agincourt* spotted a German ship, but refrained from challenging for fear of giving away her division's location. This kind of self-restraint was common during this phase of the battle, and contributed to the German fleet's escape. By the early hours of the morning of 1 June, the 6th Div were lagging a dozen miles astern of the British fleet, owing to torpedo damage to the flagship *Marlborough*. Although the flag was transferred to *Revenge* at 03:00, it would be 16 hours before the new flagship, *Hercules* and *Agincourt* could rejoin the fleet; *Marlborough* was now proceeding independently. During the battle, *Agincourt* fired 144 rounds of 12in and 95 of 6in against enemy ships, plus sixteen 6in and eight 3in against airships.

Hit by two shells from *Agincourt* at the Battle of Jutland, SMS *Kaiser* is here shown off East Fortune in November 1918, en route from the Firth of Forth to internment in Scapa Flow. Compared with her configuration at Jutland, she now sports a heavy tubular foremast. (USNA 165-WW-330B-003)

In contrast to *Agincourt*, which had the second highest (after *Marlborough*) main-battery ammunition expenditure of any British battleship of the main fleet (although greatly exceeded by all of the detached 5th BS, and most of the battlecruisers), *Erin* did not fire her main armament at all during the battle – the only ship in the battle fleet to have this melancholy distinction – and only six rounds of 6in. This was a consequence of the deployed position of her 1st Div at the head of the British line, which had minimal contact with the German forces, and also suffered from being masked by British vessels at a number of points. In *Erin*'s case, it was the presence of *Orion* that prevented her firing on the one occasion that an enemy heavy ship was visible to her. Indeed, *Erin*'s three division-mates together only expended thirty-four rounds of 13.5in ammunition. Two-thirds of these were fired by *Centurion* when she caught a glimpse of the German battlecruiser *Lützow* at 19:16, before having to cease fire when the 2nd Div interposed themselves between her and her opponent.

Canada's position in the 3rd Div placed her in the British centre, and thus in a rather better position to come into action. This she did at 18:40, although only two salvoes were fired, without known result. She resumed firing at 19:20, at an 'indistinct' target to starboard, getting off five salvoes, but again without result. A little before, she had fired her 6in guns at German destroyers, 109 shells of that calibre being expended, as well as a total of 42 14in Armour Piercing Capped (APC) rounds. Her shell outfit differed from standard UK practice in that she carried only APC and High Explosive (HE) shells: there were no Common Pointed Capped (CPC) 14in rounds. *Agincourt*'s outfit was also non-standard, with no HE and a special CPC filled with TNT; all the 12in rounds she fired during the battle were the latter type. These outfits reflected the ships' and their armaments' foreign specification.

After Jutland

The Grand Fleet was back at Scapa around midday on 2 June, and in the wake of the battle a reorganisation of the Grand Fleet saw the 4th BS become an all-12in force, with *Canada*, *Royal Oak*, *Benbow* and *Emperor of India* leaving for the 1st BS, in exchange for *Colossus*, *Neptune*, *Collingwood*, *Hercules* and *St Vincent*. The 1st BS now comprised the 15in-gunned *Royal Oak*, *Revenge* and *Royal Sovereign*, the 13.5in-gunned *Marlborough*, *Emperor of India* and *Benbow*, plus *Canada* and *Agincourt*. The latter was very much the 'odd man out' as far as size of gun was concerned, but her speed was more in keeping with that of the *Revenge*s than the now rather plodding older 12in ships. *Erin* remained with the 2nd BS.

The rounds of exercises continued, both within the Flow and at sea. On 17 June, *Canada* suffered another torpedo-tube problem while carrying out a torpedo exercise. This time the starboard forward tube was affected, leading to the flooding of the forward flat and the need for divers to plug the tube so that the water could be pumped out. *Erin* was at Invergordon from the 9th to the 21st, recording on the 10th that 'Drowned this day by accident. John Munay, Leading Seaman R.N., a native of Ireland aged 25^{yrs} 167 days serving in this ship. The body was recovered.' While there, her main-battery director was finally installed (but not yet her secondary ones), together with a Dreyer Mk I fire-control table. The topmast was shortened, the bridge screened in, and an additional AA gun fitted on the aft superstructure. On her return to Scapa, the new fire-control equipment was the subject of an intensive series of drills and tests in the Flow between 27 June and 4 July.

Since it was known that much of the High Seas Fleet was under repair as a result of Jutland, no British fleet operations took place in June, and only one deployment in July. Involving the whole battle fleet, this began soon after noon on 17 July, and involved exercises to the north and east of the Shetlands. Carried out during the 18th and 19th, these were based around what had been observed of German tactics at Jutland, the ships returning towards their bases on the morning of the 20th, *Erin* arriving at Scapa at 13:18 and *Agincourt* at Cromarty three hours later.

Canada did not take part, having sailed for a refit at Rosyth on the afternoon of 1 July, arriving the next morning and proceeding into No 2 Dry Dock at 16:00 on the 3rd. Alterations included a post-Jutland addition of an inch of armour over the magazine crowns and the coal bunkers, shortening the foretopmast, adding searchlights on platforms abeam legs of the tripod mast, and moving the searchlights from the aft superstructure to the mainmast starfish. There was also a rearrangement

Erin during late 1916, with her main-battery director installed, but her secondary directors not yet complete. *(NMM N16847)*

Canada after her July 1916 refit, with her aft searchlights moved up to the mainmast starfish. *(Author's collection)*

of magazines, shell rooms and transmitting stations, including revisions of their ventilation and refrigeration systems. The ship left dock at 14:40 on 27 July, and secured alongside the North Wall of the basin. Steam trials began at 09:00 on the 29th, and on 2 August *Canada* was at a buoy in the Forth. She put to sea at 17:25 on the 4th, and anchored in Scapa's B6 berth at 09:58 the next morning. Further steam trials were carried out in the Flow on the morning of the 6th.

Agincourt was next to refit, sailing from Scapa at 13:00 on 17 July, and mooring at Invergordon at 16:00 the next day. She would spend a month there, during which time the mainmast was removed and a topmast added to the derrick pole, from which the platforms were also removed. Some 70 tons of extra deck plating was added over the magazines, the ship's missing director installed, the 24in signalling searchlight moved down to the bridge, and a 9ft rangefinder fitted in lieu. The vessel arrived back at Scapa on the morning of 17 August.

The next day, the whole fleet proceeded to sea in reaction to a sortie by the High Seas Fleet to support an abortive bombardment of Sunderland. However, when the German fleet withdrew at 14:35 on the 19th, the Grand Fleet also turned for home, arriving back in Scapa Flow early in the evening of 20 August. Two British light cruisers (*Falmouth* [1910] and *Nottingham* [1913]) had been torpedoed and sunk by German submarines during the operation, and as a result it was agreed that operations should not normally be carried out by larger ships unless an adequate destroyer escort was available.

On the afternoon of the 21st, *Canada* fired two practice torpedoes at *Royal Sovereign* and carried out rangefinder exercises, while *Erin* was

Agincourt in the autumn of 1917; her mainmast had been removed in August 1916, and a pair of searchlight towers added adjacent to the aft funnel in the spring of 1917. HMS *Furious*, in her hybrid form (cf p 191), is visible in the background. (Author's collection)

engaged in torpedo exercises with destroyers. On the 25th, *Erin* sailed for Cromarty. *Canada* continued with rangefinder exercises on the 28th, and undertook a five-minute full-calibre shoot early on the morning of the 29th. During anti-submarine exercises on the afternoon of 1 September, she was hit by two practice torpedoes to starboard and one to port, also reporting a series of heavy underwater blows around 14:00. On her return to her berth, divers began an inspection of the ship's propellers, which continued the next day. On the morning of the 7th, *Canada* exercised paravanes, and later in the day sailed for Rosyth, where she docked in No 1 Dock at 13:15 the next afternoon. She stayed there until the 13th, mooring off the dockyard until she proceeded to sea, en route to Scapa, on the afternoon of the 15th, arriving at 07:59 the next morning.

Erin and the 2nd BS were at Cromarty from 24 August to 18 September. The fleet sailed on 20 September for a sweep that took it between Orkney and the Shetland Islands and the Norwegian coast for tactical exercises. *Erin*, *Canada* and *Agincourt* were all back at Scapa on the morning of the 22nd. *Erin* and *Canada* undertook exercises during the following week, and on the evening of 2 October the 1st BS put to sea, together with some of the 2nd CS and the 12th DF, for a cruise into the North Sea, returning on the morning of the 4th. The 2nd BS, also with elements of the 2nd CS, and destroyers of the 11th and 15th DF, made a similar deployment from the 8th to the 10th.

On the afternoon of 11 October, *Canada* sailed to Rosyth, arriving the next morning; *Agincourt* and the rest of the 1st BS went to Cromarty on the 12th, staying for a month, and being joined there by *Canada* on

Erin in 1917, with the final form of her after superstructure, but before the fitting of searchlight towers. *(Author's collection)*

the 30th. The 2nd BS, with the 4th LCS and the 11th DF, cruised to the east of the Shetlands from 2 to 4 November; the following day, *Erin* sailed to Invergordon for a refit, going into the floating dock at 12:40 on the 11th. She was undocked on the morning of the 21st, returning to Scapa Flow on 9 December.

In the interim, *Agincourt* and *Canada* had gone to sea with the fleet on the afternoon of 22 November, carrying out exercises in northern waters before returning to Scapa Flow on the morning of the 24th. *Canada* was in the process of undertaking a range of exercises and trials, including of her torpedo tubes, on 21, 27 and 29 November. These were presumably linked with the problems suffered previously. The last two of these trials involving full-power runs, another one taking place on 23 December. Captain Nicholson was relieved by Captain James Ley on 1 December, and hosted his flag in *Emperor of India* as Rear Admiral 2nd Div on the 7th, thereby continuing to have *Canada* under his command. The new captain, who had come from commanding *Collingwood*, took *Canada* to sea for a sweep by the Grand Fleet that lasted from 19 to 21 December. The 1st BS was subsequently at sea from 31 December to 2 January 1917, the 2nd BS from the 2nd to the 4th

1917

The whole Grand Fleet was again at sea from 13 to 15 January 1917, after which the 1st BS spent 16 January to 11 February at Cromarty. *Canada* went to Rosyth for docking on 7 February, which was completed on the 24th. However, while attempting to leave the dockyard basin, *Canada*'s port propeller was fouled by a wire in the lock around 15:40, and had to remain there while divers attempted to clear the problem. In the end, the ship had to be taken back into the basin the next morning, and at 13:40 went back into dock for the wire to be removed. *Canada*

left dock at 04:30 on the 26th, and was at Scapa at midday on the 27th.

A further reorganisation came on 19 March, when *Agincourt* was reassigned from the 1st to the 2nd BS, rejoining *Erin*, and diluting that formation's all-13.5in artillery. This was a result of *Iron Duke* being relieved of the fleet flag by *Queen Elizabeth* and joining her sisters in the 1st BS, which was now further reinforced by the new *Resolution*. On the day of her transfer, *Agincourt* sailed from Scapa at 14:00, initially for Rosyth, where she moored at 06:30. The next morning, the ship sailed further south to the Tyne, where she entered dry dock at 14:35. She remained there until 5 April; two searchlight towers were fitted abreast the rear of the aft funnel, along with a shortening of the topmast and removal of the yard from the tripod. She sailed for Rosyth in the early afternoon and arrived that evening. The ship departed for Scapa on the afternoon of the 7th, arriving the next morning at 06:00. While *Agincourt* was away, *Erin* and *Canada* accompanied their squadrons to sea from 23 to 25 March, *Canada* undertaking various gunnery exercises between the end of March and the middle of May. These included a full-calibre 6in night firing on 4 April and a daylight one the next day.

On 11 April, Captain Doughty was appointed to commission the new battleship *Ramillies*, and was relieved in command of *Agincourt* by

Agincourt and *Erin* at sea with the 2nd BS during 1918. (NHHC NH 41763)

Agincourt in her final form in 1918, with a second set of searchlight towers around the aft funnel and a high-angle rangefinder on the roof of the control top. (NHHC NH 89142)

Henry Mawby, formerly captain of *Dominion* in the 3rd BS based on the Thames. Two weeks later, command of *Erin* also changed, with Captain Stanley, now promoted Rear Admiral, replaced by Walter Ellerton, formerly of the cruiser *Cornwall*.

The Grand Fleet undertook a sweep from 19 to 21 May, and on the 28th the 6th Div, including *Agincourt* and *Erin*, undertook full-calibre firings in the Pentland Firth, the former firing 73 rounds of 12in and 144 of 6in. The 1st BS, including *Canada*, did the same on the 30th. Exercises in the Flow continued, *Erin* pairing with her squadron-mate *Centurion* for subcalibre concentration firings on a number of occasions between 9 June and 14 July.

The fleet sailed to Rosyth on the morning of 16 July, arriving the next day, and staying until the middle of September. While there, both *Erin* and *Canada* underwent refits, the former being under dockyard control from 9 August to 7 September. Work on *Erin* included the fitting of a pair of searchlight towers behind the second funnel (with a second pair probably added in December, when secondary-battery directors were fully installed on what had once been searchlight platforms of mast supports).

It was probably during this refit, between 28 August and 15 September (but also possibly in at least part during her next refit in January 1918), that *Canada* underwent a number of modifications. Like *Erin*, she had searchlight towers added behind the aft funnel (replacing the original platforms), while her control top was enlarged, a larger rangefinder added atop the aft conning tower, and the aftermost pair of guns in the forward 6in battery taken out, as they were too close to the muzzles of 'Q' turret when trained on forward bearings.

Erin with her full set of searchlight towers, during 1917–18; she was one of seventeen battleships of the Grand Fleet fitted to operate kite-balloons to extend the ship's vision at sea. *(NHHC NH 89154)*

Back at Scapa Flow on 16/17 September, exercises continued, with *Agincourt*, *Canada* and *Erin* all undertaking full-calibre firings between 24 and 29 September. The 2nd BS, with *Agincourt* and *Erin*, was at sea from 1 to 3 November, after which various exercises continued in and near the Flow. The 1st BS, including *Canada*, was at sea from 15 November to provide distant support for the operation that became the Second Battle of Heligoland Bight, but never came close to being involved in what was essentially a cruiser action. The 2nd BS also went to sea on the 17th, but was back at Scapa on the 19th when the 1st BS moored at Rosyth, where it would remain until 13 December. Shortly before her return to Scapa, on 9 December *Canada*'s Captain Ley, who had been promoted to Rear Admiral, left the ship and was replaced by Captain Adolphus Williamson, another former commanding officer of *Dominion*, in which he had replaced Captain Mawbey on his appointment to *Agincourt*.

Agincourt herself joined these ships at Rosyth on 29 November, and having disembarked ammunition at Rosyth, steamed to the Tyne on 2 December, coming alongside at her builder's yard at Walker at 16:00 for a refit. Alterations, which extended into the New Year, would include the installation of the second pair of searchlight towers around the aft funnel. There were, however, concerns at Armstrong's capacity at this time, as they were not only due to be refitting *Agincourt*, but also to add a landing-on deck to *Furious*, and complete *Gorgon* and *Glatton* (cf pp 42, 191).[6]

Erin remained at Scapa, and was thus the only one of the trio to be present when the US 9th Battleship Division (USS *New York*, *Wyoming*, *Florida* and *Delaware*) arrived at Scapa on 7 December to become the

Grand Fleet's 6th BS. The previous day, *Erin* had undertaken starshell firings in the Pentland Firth, and would carry out exercises in the Flow on the 15th, a full-calibre firing in the Pentland Firth on the 21st, and a 6in firing in the Firth on the 27th. She then sailed on the afternoon of the 31st to take part in a sweep that would last until 2 January. *Canada* also carried out exercises during the last weeks of 1917, culminating in full-calibre firings in the Pentland Firth, 6in on 22 December and 14in on Christmas Eve.

1918

Canada began the year with an overnight voyage to Rosyth for a refit, arriving at 10:05 on 4 January 1918, and entering dry dock at 10:10 on the 6th. She was undocked at 13:20 on the 21st, exiting the basin late the following afternoon. She sailed for Scapa at 16:05 on the 24th, anchoring at Scapa at 11:19 the next day.

Erin undertook subcalibre firings in the Flow the same day, and between 27 and 31 January participated with the rest of the Grand Fleet in large-scale exercises. These included the fleet being divided into 'Blue' (German: 5th BS, 2nd BCS, light cruisers, destroyers and two submarine flotillas) and 'Red' (Allied: rest of Grand Fleet) forces for a set-piece battle. Arriving back at Scapa at 01:26 on 31 January, she and her division left again at 16:44, for more exercises, in this case with ships from Rosyth (including the 5th BS and 2nd BCS, plus destroyers and submarines).[7] *Erin* finally moored at Rosyth at midday on 2 February. Over the next few days, *Canada* was active within Scapa Flow, including subcalibre exercises against destroyer attacks in company with *Resolution* on 5 February. However, she was now about to lose her Captain Williamson: he was placed on the Retired List as physically unfit on 9 February, to die of pneumonia on 14 July, aged only 51. A new commanding officer, Captain Hugh Watson (previously of *Bellerophon*), was appointed on 13 February, and would remain in post until after the end of the war.

From the latter part of 1917, an important aspect of the Grand Fleet's task had become the protection of convoys from Scandinavia, especially since an attack by the light cruiser-minelayers *Brummer* and *Bremse* in October 1917 had annihilated a convoy's destroyer escort and most of its merchantmen. As a result, formations of big ships from the Grand Fleet were now being deployed to escort the regularly-timetabled convoys. On 15 February, the 4th BS was carrying out this duty when signals intelligence suggested that German battlecruisers were at sea. Accordingly, the Grand Fleet put to sea early the next morning, *Canada* from Scapa at 02:50, with the 1st BS, and *Erin* with the 2nd BS from Rosyth at 03:50.

The deployment was undertaken in the teeth of a severe gale, and a number of ships suffered weather damage. No sign was found of German ships, and the fleet turned back, *Canada* mooring back at Scapa at 01:53 on the 17th and *Erin* at Rosyth at 07:30. The latter was at sea with her squadron from 25 February to 1 March, and then returned to Scapa from Rosyth around midday on 6 March. *Canada* was at sea with her own squadron from 4 to 8 March, but also continued to undertake gunnery exercises in and around Scapa Flow.

On the Tyne, work continued on *Agincourt* into March 1918, modifications including the addition of a hooded high-angle rangefinder to her foretop and 3in anti-aircraft guns on the quarterdeck. The ship was placed in the floating dock at Jarrow on the 19th for hull work, remaining in the dock until 17:50 on 1 April; she then sailed immediately for Rosyth, arriving the next morning, and proceeding the next afternoon onwards to Scapa, mooring at 07:42 on the 4th. The previous day, *Erin* and her regular Divisional exercise partner *Centurion* had undertaken full-calibre 13.5in firings in the Pentland Firth, which were repeated on 11 April, before the two ships sailed with the rest of the 4th Div to Rosyth. The latter port had, on 12 April 1918, taken over from Scapa as the main base of the Grand Fleet, although Scapa Flow was still employed as an anchorage, especially for exercises, for which its large area of sheltered waters remained ideal.

In April 1918, the German High Seas Fleet attempted to intercept a Scandinavian convoy, both from the point of view of destroying its merchantmen and their valuable cargoes, but also their escorting detached battle squadron: since the beginning of the war a key part of the German naval strategy had been to eliminate discrete elements of the Grand Fleet.

So, in accordance with what they believed to be the British convoy timetable, on 23 April the German Scouting Force (the battlecruisers and their supporting light cruisers and destroyers) put to sea to intercept, with the High Seas Fleet following-on to deal with any British capital ships. Unfortunately for the British, the German cypher key had been changed on 21 April. As a result, the kind of information hitherto provided from signals intelligence was not available. Fortunately, the Germans had wrongly calculated the convoy schedule, and there was no convoy actually at sea.

The German forces proceeded further from base than ever before in search of the non-existent ships, but it was not until the morning of the 24th that a signal – resulting from a major engine breakdown in the battlecruiser *Moltke* – alerted the British to the sortie. The full Grand

Canada in late 1918, after the fitting of flying-off platforms on 'A' and 'X' turrets. (Author's collection)

Fleet sailed from a fog-bound Rosyth early in the afternoon (*Canada* weighed anchor at 14:15, *Erin* at 14:17; *Agincourt* was currently at Scapa, working-up after her refit). However, by then the Germans had realised their error regarding the presence of a convoy after all, and had turned back just as the Grand Fleet left the Forth estuary. There was thus little possibility of an interception, although the British fleet remained at sea throughout the 25th, with *Agincourt* leaving Scapa at 01:25 that morning, hoping to catch up. The Rosyth ships were back in the Forth on the 26th, and *Agincourt* was back at Scapa the next morning. There was, nevertheless, one British success, in that the crippled *Moltke* was torpedoed and further damaged by HMS/M *E42* on her final approach to home waters. This would be the final sortie by the High Seas Fleet before the end of the war.

Agincourt joined the rest of the fleet at Rosyth on 14 May, having continued her round of exercises and trials at Scapa in the interim. *Canada* and *Erin* also undertook various exercises around the Firth of Forth, often utilising the Burntisland anchorage while so engaged. On the afternoon of 9 June, the whole fleet sailed to Scapa Flow, arriving a day later. There, the ships embarked on various exercises, *Canada* carrying out subcalibre firings and concentration exercises with the fleet flagship *Queen Elizabeth* on 14, 21 and 24 June, and 3 July; she also carried out firings in conjunction with *Erin* on 19 June. *Agincourt* undertook full-calibre firings on 27 June and 4 July, and a torpedo firing on 29 June.

Erin sailed for Invergordon at 22:00 on 30 June, arriving at 05:55 on 1 July, and entering the floating dock at 12:47. She remained in dock for two weeks, leaving Cromarty at 11:00 on the 16th, and arriving at

Rosyth at 22:20 the next day. As part of her refit she was fitted with flying-off platforms on 'B' and 'Q' turrets, and a hooded high-angle rangefinder above the foretop, the latter as recently installed in in *Agincourt*. All three windfalls were present at Rosyth when King George V visited the fleet on 22 July.

The 2nd BS was at sea from 1 to 4 August, while *Canada* towed the target for a 2nd Div firing on the morning of 12 August. The fleet went to sea for exercises on the afternoon of 22 August, with the Scapa-based 4th BS and 2nd BCS acting as the Blue (German) fleet, during which aircraft from the carrier *Furious* were the first to report the 'enemy' ships. The Grand Fleet returned to its bases the next morning, undertaking a further exercise from 23 to 25 September, in this case ending in Scapa Flow.

Exercises then followed in the Flow and in the Pentland Firth, where *Erin*, *Agincourt*, *Orion* and *Conqueror* carried out full-calibre concentration firings on the 28th. The ships returned southwards in the early afternoon of the 30th, mooring at Rosyth 24 hours later. Here, they continued the rounds of exercises in the Forth estuary that had been a fixture since the fleet had moved to Rosyth, the Armistice on 11 November finding *Agincourt* in the process of setting up targets for the following day's exercise.

On 21 November, *Agincourt*, *Canada* and *Erin* were all in the Firth of Forth for the arrival of the German warships to be interned under the terms of the Armistice. The 2nd BS lay on the north of the German line of advance, directly astern of the fleet flagship, *Queen Elizabeth*, with

Erin in floating dock at Invergordon, either in July 1918 or April/May 1919. The ships at the bottom left are the hulks *Mars* (ex-battleship [1896]), *Akbar* and *Algiers* (ex-ironclads *Temeraire* [1876] and *Triumph* [1870]), while the cruiser at the top is either *Isis* (1896) or *Crescent* (1892). (Author's collection)

HM Ships *King George V, Ajax, Centurion, Erin* and *Agincourt* in the Firth of Forth in 1918, with one of the *Iron Duke* class behind *Agincourt*'s stern. *(NHHC NH 89131)*

Erin as fourth ship of the squadron lines, and *Agincourt* eighth, placing her directly in front of the USS *New York*, flagship of the 6th BS. *Canada* lay with the 1st BS on the south side, ninth in the line, after *Iron Duke*.

The 1st BS left for Scapa Flow on 26 November, accompanying the second batch of German vessels moving from the Forth. *Canada* departed Rosyth at 11:25, arriving at the Flow at 10:50 the next morning. During December, she was involved in various exercises, including acting as a target for her squadron-mates' secondary batteries on 10–14 December. At 11:15 on 29 December, she left Scapa for the last time, arriving at Rosyth at 20:00. For the time being she remained part of the 1st BS, but the latter's 13.5in-gunned ships were all transferred to the Mediterranean in March 1919, leaving just *Canada* alongside the five *Revenge* class. The 2nd BS proceeded to Scapa in two parts, *Erin* leaving Rosyth on 28th and *Agincourt* on the 29th, each arriving the following mornings.

1919

On 1 January 1919, Captain Ellerton was relieved in command of *Erin* by Captain Herbert Richmond, swapping posts with him to become Director of Training and Staff Duties at the Admiralty. For the first weeks of the new year, the normal exercise routine was maintained at Scapa for the 2nd BS, *Erin* and *Agincourt* going to sea on the morning of the 13th for full-calibre shoots in the Pentland Firth, returning in the evening. On the 16th, *Erin* undertook subcalibre throw-off firing with *King George V* in the Flow, and the next day towed a target for the 3rd Div; on the 18th, *Agincourt* was used as a target for more firing by *Erin* and *King George V*.

This marked the end of *Agincourt*'s operational service. The next day, *Erin*, along with *King George V, Orion, Conqueror, Monarch* and *Thunderer* were ordered reduced to three-fifths complement. Of the other ships of the 2nd BS, *Ajax* and *Centurion* were detached to

Portsmouth in preparation for deployment to the Mediterranean and Black Sea in a wholly-new 4th BS, while *Agincourt* left Scapa at 12:14 on the 21st, in company with the cruiser *Bellona*, and arrived at Rosyth at 08:40 the following day.

Agincourt received a new commanding officer on 19 February 1919, when Captain Robert Hamilton, the ship's first torpedo officer in August 1914 and her executive officer since 7 January 1917, relieved Captain Mawby. However, his role was to oversee the battleship's reduction to reserve, March and April being taken up with defusing shells and disembarking ammunition. On 21 April, *Agincourt* entered Rosyth's No 3 Dock at 15:00 for what would prove to be her final docking as an intact ship. On 23 June, Captain Hamilton left the ship, Commander Vincent Bowring taking over her skeleton crew.

Following her arrival at Rosyth at the end of December, *Canada* had been docked on 21 January 1919. She was undocked on 12 February, and moored in the dockyard basin, with HMS/M *K7* alongside until 3 March, and then *K15* until the 14th. On 28 February, Captain Watson left the ship, although his relief would not arrive for another month. The ship left the basin at 10:30 on 22 March, and moored at the D9 buoy in the Forth at 11:15, where she coaled and oiled. Her new commanding officer, Captain George Tomlin, came aboard on the 28th; he had been the original Navigating Officer of *Agincourt*, and had now come from the cruiser *Liverpool*.

Erin had left Scapa with her squadron at 13:50 on 21 January, not long after *Agincourt*, arriving at Rosyth the following morning. On 13 March she went to sea with *King George V* and *Thunderer* for subcalibre practice, and shifted berth within the Forth anchorage on the 21st.

On 7 April 1919, the Grand Fleet was disestablished and many of its ships – including *Erin*, but not *Agincourt* and *Canada* – transferred to the new Atlantic and Home Fleets. *Agincourt* and *Canada* now became part of the Rosyth Division of the Reserve Fleet. A major contributor to their reduction to reserve status was their armaments. While *Erin* had an battery essentially uniform with the navy-order 13.5in-gunned ships, *Canada*'s 14in guns were unique, while the writing was already on the wall for all 12in-gunned ships. The 'old' 4th BS had been dispersed by the end of March, while the two 12in-gunned vessels in the Mediterranean (*Superb* and *Temeraire*) were to come home as soon as relieved by *Iron Duke* class ships. The 12in-gunned battlecruisers *Inflexible* and *Indomitable* were also reduced to reserve in March, although *New Zealand* remained active for the time being, carrying now-Viscount Jellicoe on his 1919–20 tour of the British Empire. *Australia* had resumed her role as flagship of the Royal Australian Navy, although this was soon curtailed by cost issues.

The Windfall Battleships

Rio de Janeiro / Sultan Osman I / Agincourt
as built

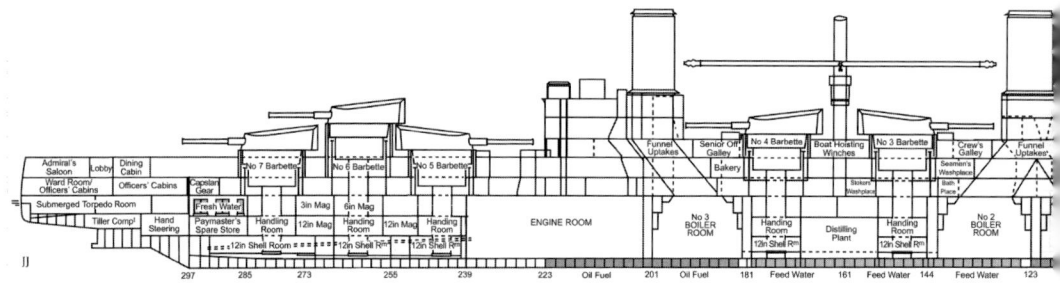

Agincourt
as mobile fleet base

Key
1. Commanding Officer's Cabin
2. Emergency Sleeping Quarters for 10 Officers
3. Offices
4. Mining Workshop
5. Cable Tank
6. Torpedo Workshop
7. Torpedo Head Magazine (Stbd)
   Wet Guncotton Magazine/DC Stowage (Port)
8. Depth Charge Stowage
9. 3in HA Magazine
10. Paymaster's Store
11. Electricians' & W/T Workshop
12. W/T Store
13. Minelaying & Minesweeping Gear
14. Stowage for Mines
15. 5.5in Shell Room
16. Engine Smiths' & Boilermakers' Shop (Stbd)
    Foundry & Coppersmiths' Shop (Port)
17. Boat Deck
18. Pontoon
19. Pier Material
20. W/T Office
21. Garage Workshop
22. Garage
23. Guns & Mountings
24. Central Stores
25. Armourers' Workshop
26. Marines' Camp Equipment
27. Small Arms Magazine (Stbd)
    Field Gun Ammunition (Port)
28. Central Storekeeping Compartment
29. Cable Tank (Stbd)
    Central Storekeeping Compartment
30. Pom-Pom Magazine
31. 5.5in Magazine
32. Victualling Stores
33. Cold Storage

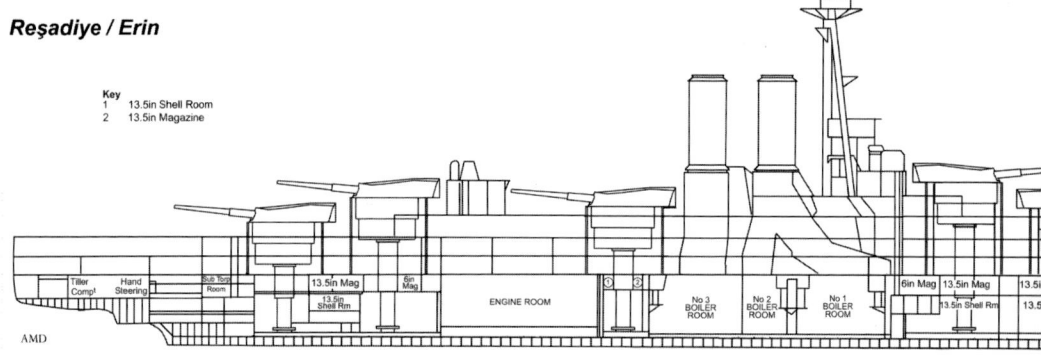

Reşadiye / Erin

Key
1. 13.5in Shell Room
2. 13.5in Magazine

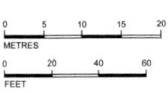

Almirante Latorre as completed as *Canada*

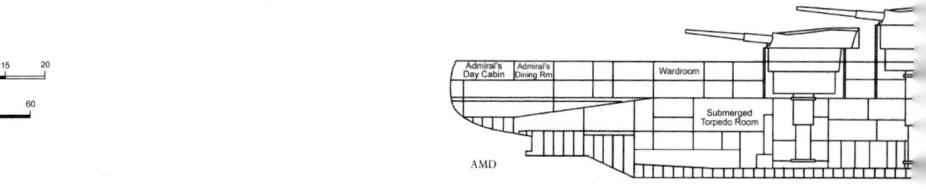

With the Grand Fleet

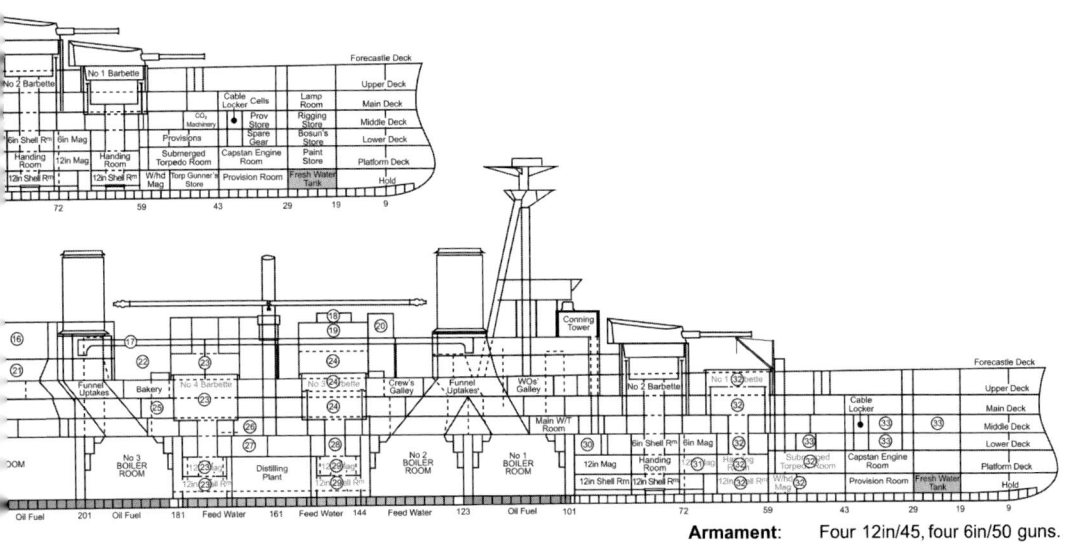

Armament: Four 12in/45, four 6in/50 guns.

Agincourt, 1914

Displacement:	24,792 tons (light), 27,850 tons (load), 30,860 tons (deep).
Dimensions:	632ft (pp), 668ft (wl), 671.5ft (oa) x 89ft x 29.8ft (deep).
Machinery:	Twenty-two Babcock & Wilcox boilers (235psi); four-shaft Parsons turbines; SHP 34,000 = 22kt.
Bunkerage:	1500 (normal), 3200 (max) tons coal; 620 tons oil.
Endurance:	14,000 nautical miles @ 10kt.
Armament:	Fourteen 12in/45 Mk XIII (7 x 2), twenty 6in/50 Mk XIII, ten 3in 23cwt Mk I, four 3pdr guns; three 21in submerged torpedo tubes.
Protection: (see also p 259)	Main belt 4–6–9–6–4in; upper belt & battery 0–6–0in; screen bulkheads 6in; forward bulkhead 3in; after bulkhead 6–3in; stern bulkhead 2.5in; torpedo bulkheads (magazines only) 1–1.5in; forecastle deck (battery only) 1.5in; main deck 1–1.5–0in; middle deck 0–1–1.5–1in; lower deck 1–0–1–0–1.5–2.5in; barbettes 9–3–2in; turrets 12–10–8in; conning tower 12–4in, 8–3in (tube); aft conning tower 9–3in, 6–2in (tube).
Complement:	1109.

Erin, 1914

Displacement:	22,780 tons (load), 25,250 tons (deep), 26,180 tons (extra deep).
Dimensions:	525ft (pp), 553ft (wl), 559.5ft (oa) x 91.6ft x 28.4ft (load), 30.9ft (deep).
Machinery:	Fifteen Babcock & Wilcox boilers (235psi); four-shaft Parsons turbines; SHP 26,500 = 21kt.
Bunkerage:	900/2120 tons coal; 710 tons oil.
Endurance:	6800 nautical miles (coal) @ 10kt; 10,600 nautical miles (coal & oil) @ 10kt.
Armament:	Ten 13.5in/45 Mk VI (5 x 2), sixteen 6in/50 Mk XVI, six 6pdr guns; four 21in submerged torpedo tubes.
Protection: (see also p 259)	Main belt 0–4–6–12–4–0in; middle belt 0–4–6–9–4in; upper belt 0–8–0in; battery 5in; side bulkheads 8–5in; forward & aft bulkheads 4in; torpedo bulkheads 1.5in; forecastle deck (battery only) 1.5in; upper deck 0–1.5–0in; main deck 0–1.5–0in; lower deck 3–1–3in; barbettes 10–9–5–3in; turrets 11–4in; conning tower 12–4in, 6in (tube); aft conning tower 4in, 3in (tube).
Complement:	1070.

Canada, 1915

Displacement:	26,968 tons (light), 28,622 tons (normal), 32,188 tons (deep).
Dimensions:	625ft (pp), 654.8ft (wl), 661ft (oa) x 92ft x 29.5ft (normal), 31.9ft (deep).
Machinery:	Twenty-one Yarrow large-tube boilers (250psi); four-shaft Parsons and Brown-Curtis turbines; SHP 37,000 = 22.75kt.
Bunkerage:	1050/3300 tons coal; 520 tons oil.
Endurance:	8800 nautical miles @ 10kt.
Armament:	Ten 14in//45 Mk I (5 x 2), sixteen 6in/50 Mk XVII, two 3in AA, four 3pdr guns; four 21in submerged torpedo tubes.
Protection: (see also p 259)	Main belt 0–4–6–9–4–0in; middle belt 0–4–6–7–4–0in; upper belt 0–4.5–0in; battery 6in; forward screen bulkheads 3in; aft screen bulkheads 4.5in; forward & aft bulkheads 4in; torpedo bulkheads (magazines only) 2–1.25in; shelter deck 1in; forecastle deck 0–1.5–1in; upper deck 0–1.5–0in; main deck (aft) 1.5–0in; middle deck 0–1–0in; lower deck (forward) 2in; (aft) 4in; barbettes 10–6–4in; turrets 10–4–3in; conning tower 11–3in, 6–3in (tube); aft conning tower 6–2in, 6–3in (tube).
Complement:	1170.

The Grand Fleet Battle Squadrons

Fleet Flagship: *Iron Duke* (Aug 14–Feb 17); *Queen Elizabeth* (Feb 17-Apr 19)

1st BS	2nd BS	3rd BS	4th BS	5th, 6th & 7th BS
August 1914	**August 1914**	**September 1914**	**August 1914**	(Comprised Channel Fleet until first half of 1915)
Collingwood	*Ajax*	*Africa*	*Agincourt*	
Colossus	*Audacious*	*Albemarle*	*Bellerophon*	
Hercules	(† 27 Oct 14)	*Britannia*	*Dreadnought* (F)	
Marlborough (F)	*Centurion*	*Commonwealth*	*Temeraire*	
Neptune	*Conqueror*	*Dominion*		
St Vincent (2F)	*King George V* (F)	*Duncan*	**September 1914**	
Superb	*Orion* (2F)	*Exmouth*	*Agincourt*	
Vanguard	*Thunderer*	*Hibernia* (2F)	*Bellerophon*	
		Hindustan	*Dreadnought* (F)	
December 1914	**December 1914**	*King Edward VII* (F)	*Erin*	
Collingwood	*Ajax*	*Russell* (3F)	*Temeraire*	
Colossus	*Audacious*	*Zealandia*		
Hercules	(† 27 Oct 14)		**December 1914**	
Marlborough (F)	*Centurion*	**December 1914**	*Agincourt*	
Neptune	*Conqueror*	*Africa*	*Bellerophon*	
St Vincent (2F)	*King George V* (F)	*Britannia*	*Benbow* (F)	
Superb	*Orion* (2F)	*Commonwealth*	*Dreadnought*	
Vanguard	*Thunderer*	*Dominion*	*Emperor of India* (2F)	
		Hibernia (2F)		
April 1915	**April 1915**	*Hindustan*	*Erin*	
Collingwood	*Ajax*	*King Edward VII* (F)	*Temeraire*	
Colossus	*Centurion*	*Zealandia*		
Hercules	*Conqueror*		**January 1915**	
Marlborough (F)	*King George V* (F)	**April 1915**	*Agincourt*	
Neptune	*Monarch*	*Africa*	*Bellerophon*	
St Vincent (2F)	*Orion* (2F)	*Albemarle*	*Benbow* (F)	
Superb	*Thunderer*	*Britannia*	*Dreadnought*	
Vanguard	*Warspite*	*Commonwealth*	*Emperor of India* (2F)	
		Dominion	*Erin*	
July 1915	**July 1915**	*Hibernia* (2F)	*Temeraire*	
Collingwood	*Ajax*	*Hindustan*		
Colossus	*Centurion*	*King Edward VII* (F)	**June 1915**	
Hercules	*Conqueror*	*Russell*	*Agincourt*	
Marlborough (F)	*King George V* (F)	*Zealandia*	*Bellerophon*	
Neptune	*Monarch*		*Benbow* (F)	
St Vincent (2F)	*Orion* (2F)	**July 1915**	*Dreadnought*	
Superb	*Thunderer*	*Africa*	*Emperor of India* (2F)	
Vanguard	*Warspite*	*Albemarle*	*Erin*	
		Britannia	*Queen Elizabeth*	
October 1915	**October 1915**	*Commonwealth*	*Temeraire*	
Agincourt	*Ajax*	*Dominion*		
Collingwood	*Centurion*	*Hibernia* (2F)		
Colossus	*Conqueror*	*Hindustan*		
Hercules	*King George V* (F)	*King Edward VII* (F)		
Marlborough (F)	*Monarch*	*Russell*		
Neptune	*Orion* (2F)	*Zealandia*		
St Vincent (2F)	*Thunderer*			
Vanguard				

1st BS
November 1915
Agincourt
Collingwood
Colossus
Hercules
Marlborough (F)
Neptune
St Vincent (2F)
Vanguard

February 1916
Agincourt
Collingwood
Colossus
Hercules
Marlborough (F)
Neptune
St Vincent (2F)
Vanguard

May 1916
5th Div
Collingwood
Colossus
Neptune
St Vincent (2F)
6th Div
Agincourt
Hercules
Revenge
Marlborough (F)

June 1916
1st Div
Marlborough
Revenge
Royal Oak (F)
Royal Sovereign
2nd Div
Agincourt
Benbow
Canada
Emperor of India (2F)

2nd BS
November 1915
Ajax
Centurion
Conqueror
Erin
King George V (F)
Monarch
Orion (2F)
Thunderer

February 1916
Ajax
Centurion
Conqueror
Erin
King George V (F)
Monarch
Orion (2F)
Thunderer

May 1916
1st Div
Ajax
Centurion
Erin
King George V (F)
2nd Div
Conqueror
Monarch
Orion (2F)
Thunderer

June 1916
5th Div
Conqueror
Monarch
Orion (2F)
Thunderer
6th Div
Ajax
Centurion
Erin
King George V (F)

December 1916
Ajax
Centurion
Conqueror
Erin
King George V (F)
Monarch
Orion (2F)
Thunderer

3rd BS
October 1915
Africa
Albemarle
Britannia
Commonwealth
Dominion
Hibernia (2F)
Hindustan
King Edward VII (F)
Russell
Zealandia

December 1915
Africa
Albemarle
Britannia
Commonwealth
Dominion
Hindustan
King Edward VII (F)

February 1916
Africa
Britannia (F)
Commonwealth
Dominion
Hibernia
Hindustan
Zealandia

29 April 1916
Withdrawn from battlefleet

4th BS
September 1915
Agincourt
Bellerophon
Benbow (F)
Canada
Dreadnought
Emperor of India (2F)
Erin
Queen Elizabeth
Temeraire

October 1915
Agincourt
Bellerophon
Benbow (F)
Canada
Dreadnought
Emperor of India (2F)
Erin
Temeraire

November 1915
Bellerophon
Benbow (F)
Canada
Dreadnought
Emperor of India (2F)
Superb
Temeraire

February 1916
Bellerophon
Benbow (F)
Canada
Dreadnought
Emperor of India (2F)
Superb
Temeraire

May 1916
3rd Div
Canada
Emperor of India (2F)
Superb
4th Div
Bellerophon
Benbow (F)
Royal Oak
Temeraire

5th BS
October 1915
Barham (F)
Queen Elizabeth
Warspite

November 1915
Barham (F)
Queen Elizabeth
Warspite

February 1916
Barham (F)
Malaya
Queen Elizabeth
Valiant
Warspite

May 1916
7th Div
Barham (F)
Malaya
Queen Elizabeth
Valiant
Warspite

June 1916
7th Div
Barham
Malaya
Queen Elizabeth (F)
Valiant
Warspite

August 1916
Barham (F)
Malaya
Queen Elizabeth
Valiant
Warspite

October 1916
Barham (F)
Malaya
Queen Elizabeth
Valiant
Warspite

THE WINDFALL BATTLESHIPS

1st BS	2nd BS	4th BS	5th BS	6th BS
September 1916	**March 1917**	**June 1916**	**March 1917**	
Agincourt	*Agincourt*	*3rd Div*	*Barham* (F)	
Benbow	*Ajax*	*Bellerophon*	*Malaya*	
Canada	*Centurion*	*Colossus* (2F)	*Valiant*	
Emperor of India (2F)	*Conqueror*	*Superb*	*Warspite*	
Marlborough	*Erin*	*Temeraire*		
Marlborough (F)	*King George V* (F)	*4th Div*		
Revenge	*Monarch*	*Collingwood*		
Royal Oak	*Orion* (2F)	*Hercules* (F)		
Royal Sovereign	*Thunderer*	*Neptune*		
		Vanguard		
March 1917	**April 1917**	*Spare*		
Benbow	*Agincourt*	*St Vincent*		
Canada	*Ajax*			
Emperor of India	*Centurion*	**December 1916**	**June 1917**	
Iron Duke	*Conqueror*	*Bellerophon*	*Barham* (F)	
Marlborough (2F)	*Erin*	*Collingwood*	*Malaya*	
Resolution	*King George V* (F)	*Colossus* (2F)	*Valiant*	
Revenge (F)	*Monarch*	*Hercules* (F)	*Warspite*	
Royal Oak	*Orion* (2F)	*Neptune*		
Royal Sovereign	*Thunderer*	*St Vincent*		
		Superb		
April 1917	**August 1917**	*Temeraire*		
Benbow	*Agincourt*	*Vanguard*		
Canada	*Ajax*			
Emperor of India (2F)	*Centurion*	**March 1917**		
Iron Duke	*Conqueror*	*Bellerophon*		
Marlborough	*Erin*	*Collingwood*		
Resolution	*King George V* (F)	*Colossus* (2F)		
Revenge (F)	*Monarch*	*Hercules* (F)		
Royal Oak	*Orion* (2F)	*Neptune*	**August 1917**	
Royal Sovereign	*Thunderer*	*St Vincent*	*Barham* (F)	
		Superb	*Malaya*	
August 1917	**November 1917**	*Temeraire*	*Valiant*	
Benbow	*Agincourt*	*Vanguard*	*Warspite*	
Canada	*Ajax*			
Emperor of India (2F)	*Centurion*	**June 1917**		
Iron Duke	*Conqueror*	*Bellerophon* (2F)		
Marlborough	*Erin*	*Collingwood*		
Resolution	*King George V* (F)	*Colossus*		
Revenge (F)	*Monarch*	*Hercules* (F)		
Royal Oak	*Orion* (2F)	*Neptune*		
Royal Sovereign	*Thunderer*	*St Vincent*		
		Superb		
	December 1917	*Temeraire*		
	Agincourt	*Vanguard*		
	Ajax			
	Centurion	**August 1917**	**October 1917**	**December 1917**
	Conqueror	*Bellerophon* (2F)	*Barham* (F)	*Delaware*
	Erin	*Collingwood*	*Malaya*	*Florida*
	King George V (F)	*Colossus*	*Valiant*	*New York* (F)
	Monarch	*Hercules* (F)	*Warspite*	*Wyoming*
	Orion (2F)	*Neptune*		
	Thunderer	*St Vincent*		
		Superb		
		Temeraire		

1st BS	2nd BS	4th BS	5th BS	6th BS
November 1917 *Benbow* *Canada* *Emperor of India* (2F) *Iron Duke* *Marlborough* *Ramillies* *Resolution* *Revenge* (F) *Royal Oak* *Royal Sovereign* **December 1917** *Benbow* *Canada* *Emperor of India* (2F) *Iron Duke* *Marlborough* *Ramillies* *Resolution* *Revenge* (F) *Royal Oak* *Royal Sovereign* **May 1918** *Benbow* *Canada* *Emperor of India* (2F) *Iron Duke* *Marlborough* *Ramillies* *Resolution* *Revenge* (F) *Royal Oak* *Royal Sovereign* **October 1918** *Benbow* *Canada* *Emperor of India* (2F) *Iron Duke* *Marlborough* *Ramillies* *Resolution* *Revenge* (F) *Royal Oak* *Royal Sovereign* **March 1919** *Canada* *Ramillies* *Resolution* (2F) *Revenge* (F) *Royal Oak* *Royal Sovereign*	**May 1918** *Agincourt* *Ajax* *Centurion* *Conqueror* *Erin* *King George V* (F) *Monarch* *Orion* (2F) *Thunderer* **October 1918** *Agincourt* *Ajax* *Centurion* *Conqueror* *Erin* *King George V* (F) *Monarch* *Orion* (2F) *Thunderer* **February 1919** *King George V* (F) *Orion* (2F) *Conqueror* *Erin* *Monarch* *Thunderer*	**October 1917** *Bellerophon* *Collingwood* *Colossus* (2F) *Hercules* (F) *Neptune* *St Vincent* *Superb* *Temeraire* **December 1917** *Bellerophon* *Collingwood* *Colossus* (2F) *Hercules* (F) *Neptune* *St Vincent* *Superb* *Temeraire* **May 1918** *Bellerophon* *Collingwood* *Colossus* (2F) *Dreadnought* *Hercules* (F) *Neptune* *St Vincent* *Superb* *Temeraire* **October 1918** *Bellerophon* *Collingwood* *Colossus* (2F) *Dreadnought* *Hercules* (F) *Neptune* *St Vincent* **January 1919** *Bellerophon* *Collingwood* *Colossus* (2F) *Dreadnought* *Hercules* (F) *Neptune* *St Vincent*	**December 1917** *Barham* (F) *Malaya* *Valiant* *Warspite* **May 1918** *Barham* (F) *Malaya* *Valiant* *Warspite* **October 1918** *Barham* (F) *Malaya* *Valiant* *Warspite* **March 1919** *Barham* (F) *Malaya* *Valiant* *Warspit*	**February 1918** *Delaware* *Florida* *New York* (F) *Texas* *Wyoming* **May 1918** *Delaware* *Florida* *New York* (F) *Texas* *Wyoming* **August 1918** *Arkansas* *Florida* *New York* (F) *Texas* *Wyoming* **October 1918** *Arkansas* *Florida* *New York* (F) *Texas* *Wyoming* **1 December 1918** Left for USA

Commanding Officers of HMS *Agincourt*

7 August 1914–10 January 1916
Captain Douglas Romilly Lothian Nicholson (1867–1946)
Promoted Captain in 1904, he subsequently commanded *Hyacinth*, *Inflexible*, *Lord Nelson*, *St Vincent* and *Conqueror*, before taking over *Victoria and Albert* in December 1913. After leaving *Agincourt* on promotion to Rear Admiral, he became 2FO of the 3rd and then 4th BS, and then FO of the re-formed 3rd BS in 1919. Knighted the same year, he retired as a full Admiral in 1926.

10 January 1916–11 April 1917
Captain Henry Montagu Doughty (1870–1921)
Promoted Captain in 1908, he had commanded *Leviathan*, *Niobe*, *Sutlej*, *King Alfred*, *Melpomene*, *Hermione*, *Sutlej* (again) and *Abercrombie* before joining *Agincourt*. On leaving the ship, he commissioned *Ramillies*, before moving to *Royal Sovereign*; he was promoted Rear Admiral in November 1919.

17 April 1917–19 February 1919
Captain Henry Lancelot Mawbey (1870–1933)
Promoted Captain in 1907, he subsequently commanded *Endymion*, *Dartmouth* and *Dominion*. He was promoted Rear Admiral on 10 February 1919, and became FO Nore Reserve on 17 March. He retired in 1924.

19 February 1919–23 June 1919
Captain Robert Cecil Hamilton (1882–1947)
Appointed to *Agincourt* as torpedo officer in 1914, and her executive officer on 7 January 1917, he was promoted Captain on 31 January 1919. After leaving *Agincourt* he commanded *Conqueror* and then *Centurion*, being promoted Rear Admiral and retiring in 1930.

25 June 1919–1 April 1920
Commander Vincent Lewin Bowring (1875–1951)
Promoted Commander in 1909, he had previously commanded *Violet*. He retired as a Captain in 1921.

Commanding Officers of HMS *Erin*

23 August 1914–26 April 1917
Captain the Hon Victor Albert Stanley (1867–1934)
Promoted Captain in 1905, he subsequently commanded *Essex* and the Royal Naval College Dartmouth, before being appointed to *Erin*. He left her on promotion to Rear Admiral, and went to the Admiralty. He retired as a full Admiral in 1926.

26 April 1917–31 December 1918
Captain Walter Maurice Ellerton (1870–1948)
Promoted Captain in 1910, he had previously commanded *King Alfred*, *Carnarvon* and *Cornwall*. On leaving *Erin* he became Director of Training and Staff Duties at the Admiralty. He retired as a Vice Admiral.

1 January 1919–1 December 1919
Captain Herbert William Richmond (1871–1946)
Promoted Captain in 1908, he commanded *Dreadnought*, *Furious*, *Vindictive*, *Commonwealth* and *Conqueror*, before becoming Director of Training and Staff Duties at the Admiralty, and then going to *Erin*, swapping posts with Ellerton. After leaving the ship he became President of the Royal Naval War College at Greenwich, and then CinC East Indies. Knighted in 1926, he retired as a full Admiral in 1931, and was elected Master of Downing College Cambridge in 1934.

1 December 1919–12 January 1921
Captain Percival Henry Hall Thompson (1874–1950)
Promoted Captain in 1913, he was Naval Advisor to New Zealand and commander of *Philomel* from May 1914 to May 1919. After *Erin*, he commanded *Royal Oak*, retiring as a full Admiral in 1932.

14 January 1921–6 May 1922
Captain William Douglas Paton (1874–1952)
Promoted Captain in 1914, he commanded *Concord* and, after leaving *Erin*, *Calliope* and *Marlborough*. He retired as a Rear Admiral in 1928.

Commanding Officers of HMS *Canada*

30 June 1915–1 December 1916
Captain William Coldingham Masters Nicholson (1863–1932)
Promoted Captain in 1905, he subsequently commanded *Berwick*, *Achilles*, the *Vernon* establishment and *Emperor of India*. Promoted Rear Admiral, he became 2FO of the 1st BS on leaving *Canada*; knighted in 1919, he retired as a full Admiral in 1925.

1 December 1916–December 1917
Captain James Clement Ley (1869–1946)
Promoted Captain in 1906, he commanded *Endymion*, *London*, *Cornwall* and *Collingwood*, before joining *Canada*. Promoted Rear Admiral on 5 October 1917, and retired as a Vice Admiral in 1923.

9 December 1917–February 1918
Captain Adolphus Huddlestone Williamson (1869–1918)
Promoted Captain in 1908, he commanded *King Edward VII*, *Queen*, *Royal Arthur*, *Berwick*, *Vengeance* and *Dominion*, before being appointed to *Canada*. However, his health failed and he was retired in February 1918, dying in July.

13 February 1918–28 February 1919
Captain Hugh Dudley Richards Watson (1872–1954)
Promoted Captain in 1908, he subsequently commanded *Essex* and *Bellerophon*. He retired as a full Admiral in 1930.

28 March 1919–4 October 1920
Captain George Napier Tomlin (1875–1947)
Promoted Captain in 1914, he had been Navigating Officer of *Agincourt* from her commissioning until January 1915. He was then Senior Naval Officer Ramsgate until May 1917, when he took command of *Ceres*, and then *Weymouth* and *Liverpool*. Having handed over *Canada* to Chile, he later commanded *Malaya*, before retiring as a Rear Admiral in 1925.

CHAPTER 5

Alternative Service: *Erin, Canada* and *Agincourt*

THE CREATION OF THE ATLANTIC AND Home Fleets saw a rationalisation and reconfiguration of the battle squadrons. The Atlantic Fleet's 1st BS now comprised the *Revenge* class, the 2nd BS the *Queen Elizabeth*s. The home-based 13.5in vessels, with their reduced crews, were redesignated as the Home Fleet's 3rd BS. The rest of the 13.5in ships became the 4th BS in the Mediterranean Fleet. Under the new arrangements *Erin* now served alongside the *Orion* class, with *King George V* as squadron flagship.

Erin: reserve flagship and turret drillship

Erin steamed from Rosyth en route to Invergordon at 16:00 on 23 April 1919, arriving at 07:25 on the 24th. Having discharged ammunition and propellant, *Erin* entered the floating dock at 08:55 on the 26th, and was high and dry by 02:35 the next morning. Refitting complete, flooding-down of the dock commenced at 11:00 on 15 May, the ship being towed out at 14:10 the next day. Ammunitioning began at 06:10 on the 17th,

Erin at the end of the First World War. *(Author's collection)*

and at 20:58 on the 19th she slipped her moorings, arriving at Rosyth at 19:30 the following evening.

She and her squadron remained there until the morning of 15 July, when the battleships sailed for Lowestoft, anchoring off the town the following evening. On the morning of the 17th they moved down the coast to the Medway, anchoring off Southend-on-Sea late that afternoon. Together with a vast swathe of vessels of the Atlantic, Home and Reserve Fleets, they were there for a review by the King to mark Peace Day (19 July). Like other ships, *Erin* was open to visitors from 11:00 on the 21st.

The fleet dispersed on the morning of 24 July, the 3rd BS sailing for Portland where it remained (apart from a brief exercise on 1 September) until it was disestablished on 1 November. On the same day the Home Fleet became the Reserve Fleet, with *King George V*, which had moved to Portsmouth in October, as its flagship. The *Orion*s and *Erin* all initially remained at Portland, but on 17 November, it was directed that:

> [a] vessel of the "ORION" class is to be detached by the Vice Admiral Commanding, Reserve Fleet, for duty as Turret Drill Ship at the Nore, and is to proceed to the Nore accordingly.
>
> On arrival at the Nore, the vessel is to be paid off and commissioned with a Chatham Reserve Complement. The vessel selected is thus to become a Chatham ship for manning purposes.[1]

In the event, it was *Erin*, rather than one of her squadron-mates, that was selected for this duty, the ship leaving Portland at 15:30 on 11 December and steaming east, mooring to No 1 buoy at Sheerness at 10:44 on the 13th, moving to No 6 on the 17th.

The following day the ship's log records that at 12:00 she:

> Paid off. Discharged Ship's Company to Devonport. Recommissioned with Reserve Complement from Chatham for duty as Turret Drill Ship at the Nore, this being HMS 'Erin's' 2nd Commission.

An hour later, 108 ratings joined from Chatham depot and at 18:30 thirteen marines and one sergeant joined from Chatham barracks. In her turret drill role, *Erin* relieved *Superb*, which would pay-off in March 1920, later becoming a target ship.

Erin also replaced *Inflexible* (p 204) as flagship and parent ship of the Nore Reserve at the end of January 1920, flying the flag of Rear

Admiral Mawby, formerly the Captain of *Agincourt*. He would be relieved six weeks later on 17 March by Vivian Bernard (1868–1934); he was in turn followed on 17 March 1921 by William Alderson (1867–1946), who remained with *Erin* until the end of her service a year later. The Nore appointment was then downgraded to a Captain's command. On 1 December, *Erin* herself welcomed a new commanding officer, Captain Percival Thompson, the former Naval Advisor to New Zealand, relieving Captain Richmond, who had been appointed President of the Royal Naval War College at Greenwich after a year in *Erin*.

With a final complement of 248, *Erin* was also used to accommodate Boys and Youths awaiting drafting. As such, she occupied No 6 buoy at Sheerness for her remaining career, with the exception of two periods away for docking and refit. First, she left Sheerness at 11:26 on 29 June 1920 and arrived at Spithead the following morning, moving into Portsmouth Harbour around midday. On the afternoon of 1 July she passed through 'C' Lock into No 3 basin, where she was dry-docked in No 14 Dock on the morning of 7 July. The ship remained there until the 27th, when she was undocked and placed at No 7 berth. There, painting ship began on 3 August, completing on the 14th. Two days later she passed out of the basin, sailing on the afternoon of the 18th and arriving back in the Thames estuary around midday the following day. She was back at her usual berth a day later.

On 12 January 1921, Captain Thompson left the ship for *Royal Oak*, Captain William Paton becoming *Erin*'s last commanding officer two days later. The ship next departed her mooring on 14 October 1921, when she sailed from the Medway for Rosyth, arriving on the morning of the 16th. The ship entered No 2 dock at 10:00 on the 19th, remaining there until 16 November. She was then in the dockyard basin until 16 December, when she departed for the Nore, being back at her buoy at Sheerness early in the afternoon of the 17th. This was to be *Erin*'s last move under her own power, as in February 1922 the Washington Naval Treaty would be signed, which would doom many ships to a premature demise (see pp 214–15).

Canada: troopship

Although laid up at Rosyth in March 1919, *Canada* would make two substantial voyages during her remaining 16 months under the British flag. A number of major British warships had been deployed to the eastern Mediterranean and Black Sea at the end of 1918,[2] in connection with both the Turkish armistice and the Russian Civil War. The need to demobilise 'hostilities-only' officers and ratings and wider reductions in manning created a requirement for regular exchanges of personnel between the Mediterranean and the UK, and a number of battleships (as well as smaller vessels) were employed in facilitating this.

Some of these trooping activities were carried out during operational deployments to and from theatre, but others made use of ships brought forward from reserve for this specific purpose. *Thunderer* and *Monarch* (reduced to reserve 1 November 1919) would be employed in this role in 1920, and *Monarch* again in 1921, but in 1919 the choice fell on *Canada*. Accordingly, she sailed from Rosyth on the morning of 9 June, arriving at Spithead on the evening of the following day. The next morning she shifted to the North Railway Jetty at Portsmouth, where she took aboard around 1100 men for transport east, made up of some 350 engine-room personnel, 500 seamen, 150 marines and 100 miscellaneous ratings. She departed for Gibraltar on the morning of the 15th, arriving on the 19th. The ship sailed for Malta on the afternoon of the 20th, entering Grand Harbour around midday on the 23rd. *Canada* remained there until the 26th, when she left for Phaleron Bay, stopping there on the 28th, before proceeding on to Mudros the next day. Early on the morning of 2 July she sailed for Constantinople, arriving there that evening.

She remained until the evening of 4 July, when she departed for Mudros, where she arrived at 13:00 the next day. On the 6th, the ship left for Malta (8th to 10th), Gibraltar (13th to 15th) and Devonport,

Canada at Constantinople on 3 or 4 July 1919. *(Author's collection)*

Canada at Malta on one of her trooping voyages, in June/July or November 1919. (Author's collection)

where she moored at 19:00 on the 18th. On the 20th, she left for Portsmouth, where she stayed until the 28th, discharging the men whom she had carried back from eastern waters. She then proceeded back to her Reserve berth at Rosyth, which she reached on the evening of 30 July 1919.

Canada remained at Rosyth until October. At 09:00 on the 21st, a navigating party joined from Portsmouth, with the ship's crew employed on disembarking 14in shells and embarking canteen stores. On the afternoon of the next day, at 16:15, the collier *Hambourn* came alongside, coaling lasting from 07:15 on the morning of the 23rd to 16:20 that afternoon. Further preparations for sea continued the following day, including cleaning the ship and at 14:00 hoisting in her boats.

At 09:00 on 25 October, the battleship slipped her moorings and shaped a course for Plymouth, where she moored at 17:00 on the 27th. At 07:05 the next morning she proceeded up the Hamoaze, to moor at 08:21 to embark ratings for passage to the Mediterranean. The 29th was taken up with coaling from the collier *Hedwig Heidmann*, as was much of the following day. Work was finished at 15:15 and at 20:07 *Canada* put to sea. Cape St Vincent was sighted at 16:41 on 2 November and at 11:15 the ship anchored at Gibraltar. At 14:00 the discharge of baggage began, as did the disembarkation of men destined for the cruiser *Ceres*, the sloop *Clio* and the survey vessel *Merlin*.

On 4 November, *Canada* left Gibraltar at 17:03 en route to Malta, painting ship commencing at sea the next day; cleaning and painting would continue through much of the deployment. She arrived at Malta at 08:00 on the 8th, and at 14:00 began disembarking personnel destined for her old squadron-mates *Emperor of India*, *Benbow* and *Marlborough*, the depot ship *Blenheim*, and the destroyers *Speedy*, *Stuart*, *Sportive* and *Tribune*. At 17:00 personnel disembarked for the depot ships (ex-battleships) *Caesar* and *Hannibal*. The following day, at 13:00, she sent to SS *Porto* officers and ratings destined for Constantinople. Disembarkations continued on the 10th, with personnel for *Ajax* leaving from 10:00, and more for *Benbow* at 14:00.

At 11:00 on 11 November, a two-minute silence was observed for the first anniversary of the Armistice, and the next day personnel came aboard from the Malta depots *Egmont* and *Fareham* for passage to the UK. On the 20th, divers examined *Canada*'s submerged torpedo tubes – perhaps an echo of her problems in 1916? – and on the 24th the embarkation of provisions began at 14:00. Baggage came aboard the following day, when the holystoning of the deck was also undertaken. This was the final phase in the process of beautifying the ship that had begun between Gibraltar and Malta, all aimed towards the ball that was held on the quarterdeck on the 26th. The next afternoon, more officers and ratings joined for passage, and at 16:30 on the 29th the ship left Malta for home.

At 09:30 on 3 December, she made fast alongside the South Mole at Gibraltar, and at 09:30 on the 9th moored to No 2 buoy at Plymouth. Baggage and mails having been landed that afternoon, *Canada* departed at 06:06 on the morning of the 10th, arriving at Spithead at 17:49. The next morning she moved up to the North Ship Jetty at Portsmouth, where personnel heading to the Chatham depot went ashore, followed at 15:00 by those belonging to Portsmouth. At 09:00 on the 12th, she moved down to the North Railway Jetty, where she would remain for a month.

On the afternoon of 13 January 1920, *Canada* moved to a mooring at Spithead. At 18:00, twenty ratings joined for passage to Rosyth, with ten more coming aboard later. Coaling was carried out on the 17th, and at 09:00 on the 19th course was set for Rosyth, which was reached at 09:35 on the 21st; her navigating party disembarked the following afternoon, and returned to Portsmouth. *Canada* would remain at Rosyth until the summer.

Agincourt: mobile naval base depot ship

When considering post-war requirements for the defence of the Empire, the Admiralty set up a Local Defence Division to look into the navy's basing needs in the event of any conflict with Japan, the USA or in Europe.[3] Amongst its recommendations was the concept of the 'mobile naval base' (MNB), which would allow a temporary base to be set up in any chosen location, by men and materiel landed by a specialist MNB depot ship (MNBDS). This ship would be fast enough to accompany the fleet, and would carry everything necessary for the establishment of the MNB, complete with gun and searchlight defences, a Royal Marine garrison, and repair and support facilities. The MNBDS would also act as the base's administrative centre, provide fresh water through a large distilling plant, and support harbour craft and specialist units such as a boom defence vessel and a small mine/cable layer. If converted from a warship, parts of its original armament might allow the MNBDS to contribute directly to the defence of the base.

Although no documentation survives to explain the choice of the vessel for conversion, the decision to rebuild *Agincourt* as the MNBDS probably derived from the fact that she was a modern, very large, fast hull with no future as a battleship. In March 1921, it was finally decided that the 12in gun had no future in the Royal Navy, with all vessels carrying the weapon slated for disposal. In the wake of this, during the summer of 1921 the UK offered to sell *Agincourt* to Brazil for £1 million, to include refitting and conversion to oil fuel. This was declined,[4] and the only sale to Brazil achieved by the UK was of the destroyer *Porpoise* (1913), which was sold to Thornycroft for refurbishment and onward sale to Brazil, becoming *Alexandrino de Alencar* in 1920 and *Maranhão* in 1927.

Agincourt was identified as the future MNBDS in early 1921, with the intention of including £39,000 in the 1921–2 Estimates for the conversion. Work would involve the removal of all armament apart from '2' and '6' turrets and the 6in guns at forecastle level, which could be used in defence of the MNB. The empty barbettes of the other 12in

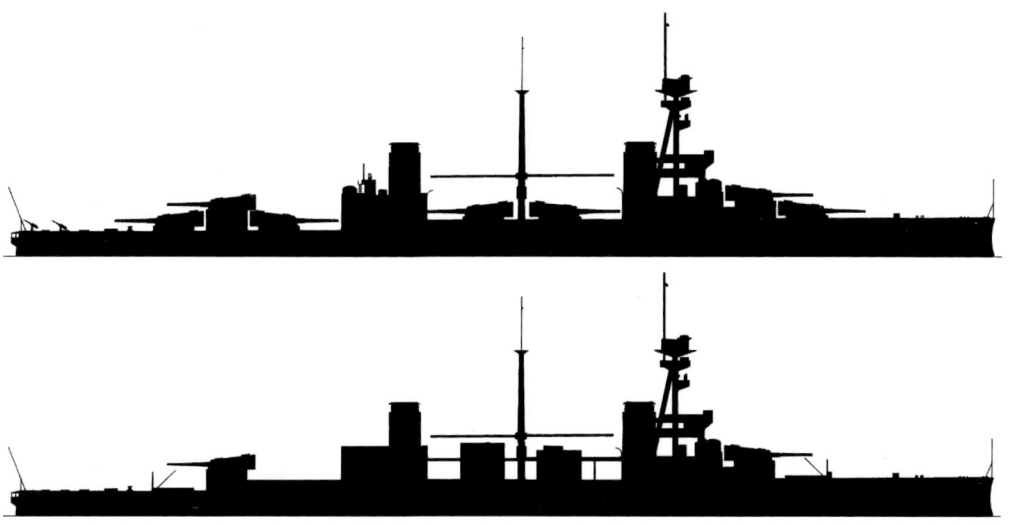

Silhouettes of *Agincourt* in her final battleship form, and as projected as a mobile fleet base depot ship. (Author)

mountings would be employed for a variety of purposes: '1' for victualling stores; '3' as central store; '4' to hold guns and mountings for deployment ashore; '5' as a cable tank; and '7' as a mining workshop, with the actual mines stored in the former shell and handling rooms below. Flying decks on both sides of the ship would join the forward and aft superstructures to support boats. Four large horse boats would be carried on the forecastle deck, allowing material to be carried ashore. The forecastle deck itself was to be extended aft to '6' barbette to provide workshop and storage space, as would an extended after superstructure (for plans, see pp 172–3).

The ship had been paid off and reduced to care & maintenance on 1 April 1920, Commander Bowring being placed on the Retired List with the rank of Captain on 5 May 1921. Since then, she had been moored in the stream off Rosyth Dockyard. Now, on 20 October 1921 it was announced that *Agincourt* would recommission using the reserve crew of *Princess Royal*, also laid up at Rosyth, with the battlecruiser to be manned by volunteers from the crews of *Neptune* and *Hercules*, which were paying-off at Rosyth as part of the cull of 12in-armed capital ships.

As such, *Agincourt* recommissioned on 2 November 1921 as a tender to the parent ship of the Reserve Fleet (at first *New Zealand*, then *Lion* from 6 December). Her crew were tasked with preparing the ship for rebuilding at Portsmouth, removing stores and dismantling fittings that would be no longer required, based on drawings for the work that were completed at Rosyth in early December 1921. It was anticipated that the move south would occur in October 1922, with *Agincourt* ready for service as the MNBDS in 1923. However, in February 1922 her future would, like that of many other ships, be fundamentally changed by the signing of the Washington Treaty.

Chapter 6

Alternative Service: *Eagle*

Designing an Aircraft Carrier

WHEN THE DECISION WAS TAKEN TO acquire *Cochrane* for conversion to a 'seaplane carrier', experience with such vessels was extremely limited.[1] The first launch of an aeroplane from a British warship had been on 10 January 1912, from a platform erected over the forecastle of the battleship *Africa* (1905), with the first underway example from a similar arrangement on her sister *Hibernia* on 2 May the same year.

A proposal for a purpose-built 'parent ship for naval aeroplanes and torpedo boat destroyers' was put forward by the Beardmore company in December 1912, with a superstructure and a funnel on each beam, flanking a through-deck for take-offs and landings. This was not proceeded with, but in May 1913 the cruiser *Hermes* (1898) recommissioned with rudimentary aircraft accommodation fore and aft, including a launching ramp on the forecastle. She then operated aircraft during and after the summer manoeuvres, providing much useful experience in the new skill of maritime aviation.

As a result, in May 1914 a partly-built merchant hull was purchased on the stocks and entirely redesigned as an aircraft carrier. The machinery was moved aft, to make room for a hangar occupying the forward two-thirds of the hull, together with workshops and stores to maintain her aircraft. Cranes were installed to hoist seaplanes on and off the water. She completed as *Ark Royal* in December 1914. She was preceded into service by a recommissioned *Hermes* and three cross-Channel steamers converted to seaplane carriers. The latter trio carried out the world's first carrier strike, against Cuxhaven, on 25 December 1914. Further short-sea steamers were subsequently added to the fleet, and the earlier ones refitted with better aviation facilities. Also converted was the much larger Atlantic liner *Campania* (1892), which operated with the Grand Fleet as the first ship ever referred to as a 'fleet carrier'.

Campania was, however, too old and slow for her role. In July 1917, the new 31.5kt large light cruiser *Furious* joined the fleet with her forward 18in turret replaced by a hanger and flying-off deck; another hangar and what was intended to be a landing-on deck was fitted in lieu of the after gun and mainmast between November 1917 and March

The Windfall Battleships

Ark Royal as built. *(Author's collection)*

Furious in 1918, following the addition of a flying-on deck in lieu of her aft superstructure and turret. *(NHHC NH 60972)*

Argus in 1918.
(NHHC NH 63225)

1918. The ship's bridge, tripod mast and funnel were retained, however, and the disturbed airflow made the aft deck untenable for landings. This failing (shared with another converted cruiser, *Vindictive*, commissioned in September 1918), underlined conclusions emerging from wind-tunnel tests, which indicated that flying decks should be through-decks, without obstructions.

In the meantime, an unfinished Italian liner, *Conte Rosso*, had been selected in September 1916 for completion as the carrier *Argus*. From the outset, it was decided that the funnel gases should be trunked aft to discharge at the stern to keep them from interfering with landing aircraft. The concept of providing superstructures either side of the flight deck was, however, retained, with short islands joined by a navigating bridge that spanned the flight deck. In addition, after a false start in February 1917, a purpose-built carrier (to be *Hermes*) had been ordered from Armstrong in July of that year. She was also to have twin islands, but because she had double the installed power of *Argus*, each island would have a conventional funnel.

The initial plans for *Eagle*'s conversion were along the same lines,[2] featuring a full-length flight deck with twin islands, both carrying a pair of funnels and a tripod mast. The masts' relative positions were to be staggered to hinder estimates of the ship's direction of travel by an enemy. As in the current plans for *Argus* and *Hermes*, a bridge would carried between the islands, 20ft above the flight deck. A crane abaft each island would be used for seaplane-recovery. The hangar was to be 400ft long, with lifts amidships and aft; aircraft fuel (petrol) stowage would be principally in tins on the forecastle deck, protected by ~1in plating. The ship was intended to serve as a flagship.

Early thoughts regarding both *Eagle* and *Hermes* included a catapult at the forward end of the flight deck, to make it easier to launch aircraft in poor weather.[3] Although there had been hopes that this might be

Hermes as completed. Although ordered before *Cochrane* was acquired to become *Eagle*, her construction at Armstrong ran in parallel with *Eagle*'s conversion, and they shared a number of features. Construction was suspended pending the outcome of the trials carried out on the semi-complete *Eagle*, and the two ships commissioned within a week of each other, both having suffered major issues with the installation of their lifts. Like *Eagle*, she was lost in action in 1942, in *Hermes*' case to Japanese bombs. *(NHHC NH 60468)*

installed in such a way as not affect the usability of the deck, this proved not to be possible, and the idea was not taken forward.

The armament planned for the conversion was intended to allow the ship to stand up to an enemy light cruiser, and thus featured nine single 6in guns (of the Pattern TT/Mk XVII type already ordered for *Cochrane*), modified to give 20-degree elevation (the best technically possible). One was on the centreline at the stern and the rest on the beam. Two 4in/45 Mk V AA guns were to be sited forward of the island, two atop the island and one aft of it. Late additions to the design were six, soon reduced to four, fixed triple sets of above-water torpedo tubes,

two on each side, at a cost of 11 tons of coal; no spare torpedoes were to be included.

Vertical armour was also based on protection from cruisers and smaller vessels. Accordingly, the 9in armour manufactured for *Cochrane*'s main belt was diverted to the re-armouring of the battlecruiser *Repulse*, which was carried out at Portsmouth from the end of 1918 until the end of 1920.[4] Instead, *Eagle* had the 4.5in plate intended for the uppermost strake of her side protection installed as the main belt. The fore and aft 4in closing bulkheads were retained, while no change was made to the horizontal protection, leaving the main (now hangar) deck 1.5in thick, the middle deck 1in over the belt and the lower deck 4in over the steering gear. One-inch plate was applied to the hull side above the belt, and 1in to the flight deck over the hangar. Barbettes and other structures above upper deck level (except for the forecastle forward of the former 'B' barbette) were dismantled. The upper deck, with its 1.5in armour, was to be the hangar floor.

Oil capacity was increased from 500 tons to 1750 tons by adapting the former forward and aft 14in magazines and shell rooms for the storage of oil. They were also employed for the stowage of heavy bombs and as auxiliary machinery spaces. The midships magazines and shell-rooms were used to house aircraft ordnance. The 3200 tons of coal was retained in part for its protective value. A 100kW (later 175kW) diesel generator was added alongside the original turbo-generators.

Evolving thinking regarding carrier superstructures impacted the topside design of *Eagle*. The problems caused by the centreline superstructure of *Furious* led in early April 1918 to demands that the in-hand vessels be made flush-decked, with no superstructures at all. While this was fairly straightforward in the case of *Argus*, with her aft-trunked funnels, it was clear that this could not be done in *Hermes* and *Eagle*, and as a compromise it was agreed that just the port islands would be deleted in these ships. In the case of *Eagle*, the formal decision was made on 10 May. This was the origin of the arrangement of carrier superstructures that would be applicable to the vast majority of such vessels down to the present day.[5] All boiler uptakes were accordingly re-routed to starboard, with the now-obsolete openings in the port side of the upper deck plated over.

The surviving island was remodelled to minimise air turbulence, and accommodate all boiler uptakes, the bridge, and its tripod mast remodelled to carry all the 6in gun directors. The importance of these was reflected by pressure from the fleet to increase the number of 6in weapons from the original nine. All this resulted in a decision, on 5 May 1918, to replace the 4in guns fore and aft of the island and the aftermost island-top one, with 6in weapons, to give a seven-gun broadside, leaving just one 4in AA gun between the funnels. This reflected CinC Grand Fleet's perception that the ship's own aircraft would be the most effective defence against aerial threats. This view was reversed when *Furious* was bombed later in 1918, and *Eagle* would ultimately revert to her originally-planned gun outfit. On 29 May, the term 'aircraft carrier' was formally adopted for all aviation vessels other than kite-balloon ships.

Once her conversion was approved, work on *Eagle* was pushed forward (with priority over *Hermes*). She was launched on 8 June 1918 by Willa Page, wife of the US Ambassador, and towed down-river to High Walker ten days later. It had been decided in March that all further work, including fitting the engines, would be done there. In June it was also decided that the mast be moved forward 14ft, as part of baselining the revised design. Work continued steadily into the autumn, with various meetings to discuss minor modifications, for example to the bridge arrangements in October 1918; in November, *Eagle* was some nine months from completion. One change to the design was initiated by a paper dated 8 February 1919, on improving accommodation for crews by reducing the number of ships fitted as flagships. While the focus was on removing flag accommodation from the battlecruisers *Lion* and *Princess Royal*, the wider implementation of the policy led to a decision on 6 August to delete all flag facilities from *Eagle*.

Also in February 1919, on the 13th, it was proposed that work on *Eagle* be accelerated. This would be to allow flying trials to be carried out during the summer, in order to inform future carrier developments. Planning was now underway regarding the future carrier fleet, and experiments were urgently needed, especially regarding landing-on and the viability of island superstructures, before decisions were taken on such things as the reconstruction of *Furious*. However, by March it was clear that there was no possibility of bringing the ship to full completion in time.

Given the priority of the trials, in early March it was discussed whether, by omitting anything not specifically required for their conduct, *Eagle* could be made fit for sea in time. As a result, the Admiralty wrote to Armstrong on 11 March querying whether the ship might be ready in time 'if the vessel is completed as a big steam barge, without any gun or torpedo armament, and with a very small complement, except for machinery which should be complete, and with the minimum of fittings such as ventilators, pumping, etc., to take the ship through the trials'.

Back to a Battleship?

However, carrying through these proposals was derailed when the Chilean government gave notice that they were interested in invoking their rights set out in the October 1914 Memorandum that governed the purchase of *Latorre* (which they were then negotiating to reacquire [pp 226–7]) with reference to her sister as well. These were that '[i]f the war is over before the ship in completed she shall be delivered on completion to Chile if the Chilean Government so desire on the basis of the original contract, and so that the Chilean Government shall have not lost or gained by the ship having been taken over'. On 23 October 1919, it was reported to the Admiralty Board that

> the Chilean Government have enquired whether the Admiralty would be willing to return the "CANADA" ("ALMIRANTE LATORRE") to the Chilean Government at a fair price, as contemplated by the agreement under which she was taken over by the Admiralty in 1914. They also asked whether the Admiralty would allow Chile to repurchase the "EAGLE" ("ALMIRANTE COCHRANE") in her present state, with a view to her reconstruction as a Battleship.
>
> The Chilean representative has stated unofficially that his Government attach great importance to getting two ships of a class, and if the "EAGLE" cannot be returned, it is possible that the application for the "CANADA" may be withdrawn.
>
> It had been agreed by the Naval Staff and the Controller that it is desirable to accede to the request for the return of the "CANADA", particularly as under the agreement of 1914 the Admiralty, should they refuse to return the "CANADA", would be under an obligation to pay the difference between her cost and that of a new Battleship to replace her.
>
> As regards the "EAGLE", the Treasury have enquired specifically whether the vessel cannot be re-transferred to the Chilean Government, and it is understood that her re-transfer would be a great relief to Vote 8, the further expenditure necessary to complete her as an Aeroplane Carrier being estimated at £450,000.
>
> It had also been suggested that if re-transferred it might be possible to arrange for her reconstruction as a Battleship to be carried out in one of the Royal Dockyards, thus reducing the number of discharges necessary in the immediate future.
>
> The First Sea Lord, on behalf of the Naval Staff, stated that, while they would have preferred to retain the "EAGLE" and considered her a highly desirable addition to the Fleet, they felt that the reasons for her return on ground of economy were so strong that this course should be accepted. It was accordingly agreed to, subject to the proviso that she should be reconditioned

in a Royal Dockyard, owing to the desirability of not employing private yards on anything but merchant shipping.

Two days previously, on 21 October 1919, Armstrong had been instructed that '[a]ll work on "EAGLE" is to cease except such as will require to be done whether ship reverts to Battleship or completes as Airplane carrier. This order is to take effect forthwith but no objection to work continuing to expiration of usual notice for such men as cannot be diverted to other work.' On the 23rd, Armstrong were further informed that the '[s]hip is to be rendered seaworthy for proceeding to a Southern Yard and such men as are necessary for this work may be kept on stock [?*sic*]'.

At a meeting on the 24th, the Admiralty asked the firm for time-estimates for:

- removing the hangar structure preparing the vessel to steam away;
- preparing the vessel to steam, only removing such structure as can be removed in that period;
- preparing the vessel for towing by tugs, removing such structure as can be removed within that period and complete machinery work, as far as possible, in that period which would be necessary for a battleship;
- time it would take to put all auxiliary machinery, stores, spare gear and fittings on board at the Armstrong Naval Yard.

In response, Armstrong calculated that these tasks would, respectively, require: 18 weeks/£82,000; 12 weeks/£76,080; 16 weeks/Admiralty cost; 16 weeks.

However, the meeting was also informed that Armstrong would require some two years to provide the ship's complete battleship armament. There could accordingly be no question of having the ship ready for delivery before the beginning of 1922. This was in contrast to the six months needed to finish her as an aircraft carrier. On the basis of this, it was suggested that the flying trials – which were still urgently needed – could be carried out in the near future, leaving ample time for reconstruction as a battleship before the necessary guns and mountings would be ready for installation. Thus, rather than being stripped of her aircraft carrier features before transfer to the south, she would be brought to the state contemplated earlier in the year, steamed south, employed in the trials (with any necessary modifications carried out at Portsmouth Dockyard), and then taken in hand for completion – whether as a battleship or as a carrier.

This way ahead was rapidly endorsed, and in November 1919 Armstrong were given detailed instructions regarding the necessary work, which was begun on 11 November. This included getting 'C' and 'D' boiler rooms (the after pair) in working order (to burn oil only: the ash ejectors could be left unfinished), with their uptakes and the after funnel completed in full, as well as the engine rooms and steering gear. A hope by CinC Atlantic Fleet that 'A' and 'B' boiler rooms might also be made operational to allow full-speed steaming was frustrated by the need to keep costs to a minimum.

The flight deck was to be fully riveted, with arrester gear installed, and the aft lift opening plated over; the forward one was to be given a removable cover. Lifts would not be fitted and their machinery wells on the hangar deck planked over. The island was to be completed, including the bridge, but with the fore-funnel opening closed off and a simple pole mast only. Accommodation was to be provided for 400 men and 30 officers, many of the latter to be visitors during the trials. All available materials and fittings that had not been yet installed were to be loaded aboard for transit to Portsmouth (including all remaining armour procured for the ship as a battleship). No armament would be installed, and the ports for the torpedo tubes plated over.

On 8 December 1919, it was formally announced that '[i]t has been approved that H.M.S. "Eagle" should be completed to steam away from the Tyne at as early a date as possible and that a series of flying trials should be carried out for obtaining data for future similar ships'. The following day there was added the rider that '[t]here is only to be essential expenditure and only such fittings as to permit of flying on and off trials', to emphasise that, as had been confirmed to CinC Atlantic Fleet on 20 November, that the intention was still that the ship should subsequently be reconverted to a battleship for Chile.

The removal of *Eagle* from the Armstrong yard was not simply owing to the question of her reconversion or/and use for flying trials. With the end of the war there was a need to both cut back on contract expenditure, and to maximise utilisation of the resources of the Royal Dockyards. As a result, most ships lying incomplete in private shipyards were to be towed to a Dockyard for completion (or in some cases disposal). Accordingly, *Hermes* was also scheduled for a tow south, in her case to Devonport, where she would arrive in January 1920. The cruiser *Dunedin* had been towed from High Walker to Devonport at the beginning of 1919, and *Emerald* would be towed from there to Chatham following her launch at High Walker in May 1920. Her sister *Enterprise* had been taken from John Brown's at Clydebank to Devonport a few months earlier, and *Dunedin*'s sisters *Durban*, *Despatch* and *Diomede* had been taken respectively from Scotts at Greenock, Fairfield at Govan and

Eagle as she was rigged for her 1921 flying trials; she had steamed from the Tyne to Portsmouth in this form, carrying her forefunnel and its uptake lashed to the aft end of the flight deck. *(NHHC NH 61022)*

Vickers at Barrow, to Devonport, Chatham and Portsmouth Dockyards. The completion of a number of 'Admiralty S' and 'Modified W' class destroyers was also dealt with in the same way.

Work on *Eagle* continued at High Walker into the New Year, and on 10 January 1920 it was directed that the ship was to be docked before leaving the Tyne. Steam was raised for the first time on 3 March, and basin trials begun on the 16th. It had been planned that *Eagle* would leave for Portsmouth on 9 April, but this was delayed by a breakdown in oil suction. It was not until the 23rd that she ran her first sea trial over the St Abbs measured mile, making 18.5kt on 15,440 shp, while displacing 21,630 tons. Departing for Portsmouth the next day, she maintained over 16kt on a 4-hour trial on the 25th, generating an average of 15,501 shp.

The ship arrived at Portsmouth on 26 April, where her arresting gear was installed, with the first trials with aircraft beginning on 10 May, while *Eagle* was still alongside. The trials programme,[6] which eventually included 143 landings, ran until the end of October, finishing with bad-weather trials in the Pentland Firth on the 27th. *Eagle* paid off at Devonport on 16 November 1920, and transferred to Portsmouth on 21 February 1921 for completion.

Even before the trials had begun, doubts were being raised over the wisdom of the decision to reconvert and sell the ship back to Chile. In

April, the Chilean naval attaché had enquired after the acceptability of an offer of £1.4 million for the ship, since Admiral Gomez needed a figure to use in gaining the necessary approvals back in Chile. In the subsequent Admiralty discussions, the key issues were on one hand the operational desirability of keeping the ship, and on the other, the employment benefits to the Dockyards of the reconversion work, and the fact that the receipts from the sale had already been assumed in the current Naval Estimates.

It was, however, unclear what the actual costs of reconditioning as a battleship would be. Thus, during June 1920 estimates were put together as to the costs of not only reconverting *Eagle* to a battleship, but also plugging the capability gap caused by her sale by building a replacement aircraft carrier.

As far as the reconversion was concerned, the scope of the work was very considerable, as is made clear by this review of the changes made during the conversion from battleship to carrier:

> The upper deck was stripped clean from aft up to about station 60, and on this space was built the hangar with the flying deck over...
>
> The old funnel uptakes which of course came up at the centre line, were cut away and new uptakes built and led to the

extreme starboard side of the vessel. This alteration necessitated the patching of the middle deck in wake of the old uptake openings, and the cutting of very large holes in the protective deck to accommodate the new uptakes.

The boiler room uptakes were also altered considerably, being transferred from the middle line to the port and starboard sides of the ship, necessitating further large holes being cut in the middle deck.

The engine room ventilation was also diverted to the sides, but the holes in the middle deck were not altered.

It will thus be seen that the middle deck in wake of the boiler room has been extensively cut about, and at present is of little value as a protective deck.

The forward and after shell room and magazine compartments have been converted into deep fuel tanks, and where necessary wash bulkheads fitted. The midship magazines and shell room have been fitted out as bomb stores for Aircraft.

The submerged torpedo tubes have all been removed and

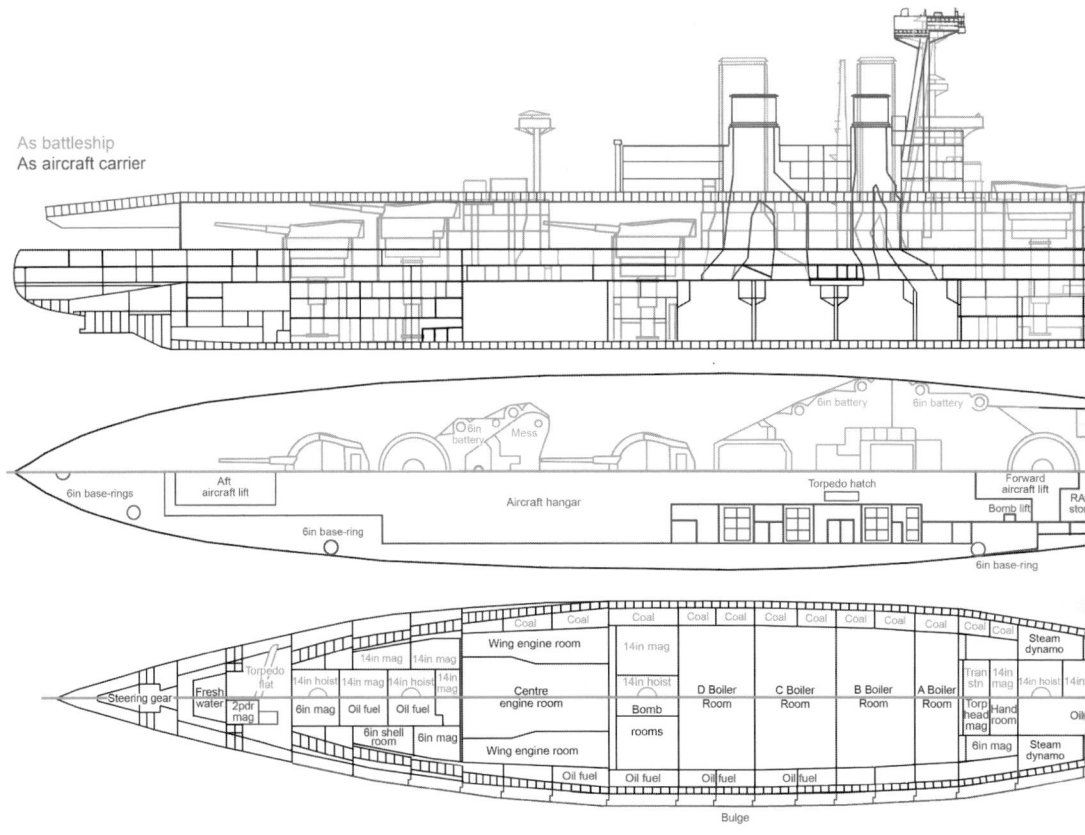

Internal arrangements of *Eagle* and *Canada* compared, showing the major changes made in the aircraft-carrier conversion. (Author)

the sides plated up, and six triple above-water tubes fitted in lieu. The tubes are all on the main deck.

The side armour as originally arranged, consisted of 9" and 4½", but the 9" armour was not fitted, and some of this armour is now under treatment for fitting on the "REPULSE", whereas, the 4½" armour which formed the upper strake was lowered to form the main belt of the ship. This necessitated several of the 4½" plates at the ends of the vessel being re-treated to fit the contour of the vessel in the new positions.

All the original guns (both primary and secondary) and barbettes, I believe, have been utilised for other services and the armament of the vessel now consists of twelve 6" and four 4" high angle guns.[7]

All the cabin accommodation and messing arrangements were re-arranged to suit British practice, also the large number of Officers carried in this ship.[8]

As a result, reconversion costs estimated at £1.856 million had to be added to *Eagle*'s sunk costs of £3 million, giving a total cost of just under £5 million. As it was clear that Chile would be unlikely to pay much more than £1.4 million for the ship, selling *Eagle* to Chile even without replacing her capability would present the UK with a loss of £3.6 million, of which the reconversion costs would be new money. Building a new carrier to replace *Eagle* was estimated to add between a further £3.25 million and £4.25 million, depending on the speed required. This meant that the true comparison was between the £0.3 million needed to complete *Eagle*, and a figure of over £8 million if she were to be sold and replaced.

The 'savings' that underpinned the Board decision of October 1919 had thus proved wholly illusory. In addition, a report by *Eagle*'s captain in July made it clear that the ship was indeed a valuable addition to the UK's capability. It accordingly seemed inevitable that *Eagle* should be retained and completed by the Royal Navy. This view was endorsed by an Admiralty meeting on 25 July 1920, which admitted that the financial case was overwhelming.

There was now a need to break the bad news to the Treasury. It was hoped to sweeten the pill by at the same time requesting approval to sell other ships to Chile instead. With *Eagle* no longer a viable option, Chile was offered a package-deal of the battlecruisers *Inflexible* and *Indomitable*, both of which had paid off at the end of March 1920, and six 'M' class destroyers. The provision of the battlecruisers would essentially fulfil the paragraph of the October 1914 Memorandum that '[i]f the ship should be sunk or irreparably damaged in the war Great

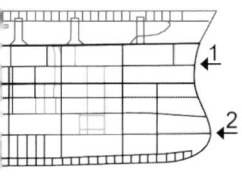

1 Upper/hangar deck

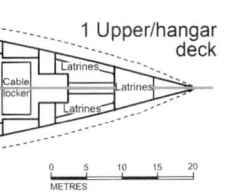

2 Platform deck

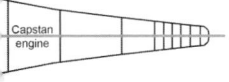

Erin's predecessor as flagship of the Nore Reserve, *Inflexible*, at Sheerness in 1919, with the ex-Greek *Chester* alongside. The battlecruiser would later be offered for sale to Chile as part-compensation for the retention of *Eagle*. (Author's collection)

Britain would, if the Chilean Government so desire, cede to Chile a battleship of approximately equal power at an agreed price, provided that the safety of Great Britain and her naval superiority were not endangered thereby' (implying that the carrier conversion had irreparably damaged the ship as a battleship). Negotiations proceeded through into September, but before the end of August, the Admiralty was forced to minute the Treasury that

> [i]t was originally contemplated to transfer the "EAGLE" (late "ALMIRANTE COCHRANE") to Chile but the Admiralty consider it essential to retain her. If she were not retained a new Aircraft Carrier would have to be laid down next year even if only for peace requirements. If "EAGLE" is retained the construction of a new Aircraft Carrier can, so far as peace training is concerned, be deferred probably until a general programme of construction for war purposes is recommended. Chile therefore now asks for "INFLEXIBLE" and "INDOMITABLE" in lieu of "EAGLE" and 6 M. Class T.B.Ds in addition.[9]

On 24 September 1920, it was announced that '[i]t has been approved by the Board that H.M.S. "EAGLE" should now be completed as an Aircraft Carrier, and the necessary adjustments made in the Estimates'.

Alternative Service: *Eagle*

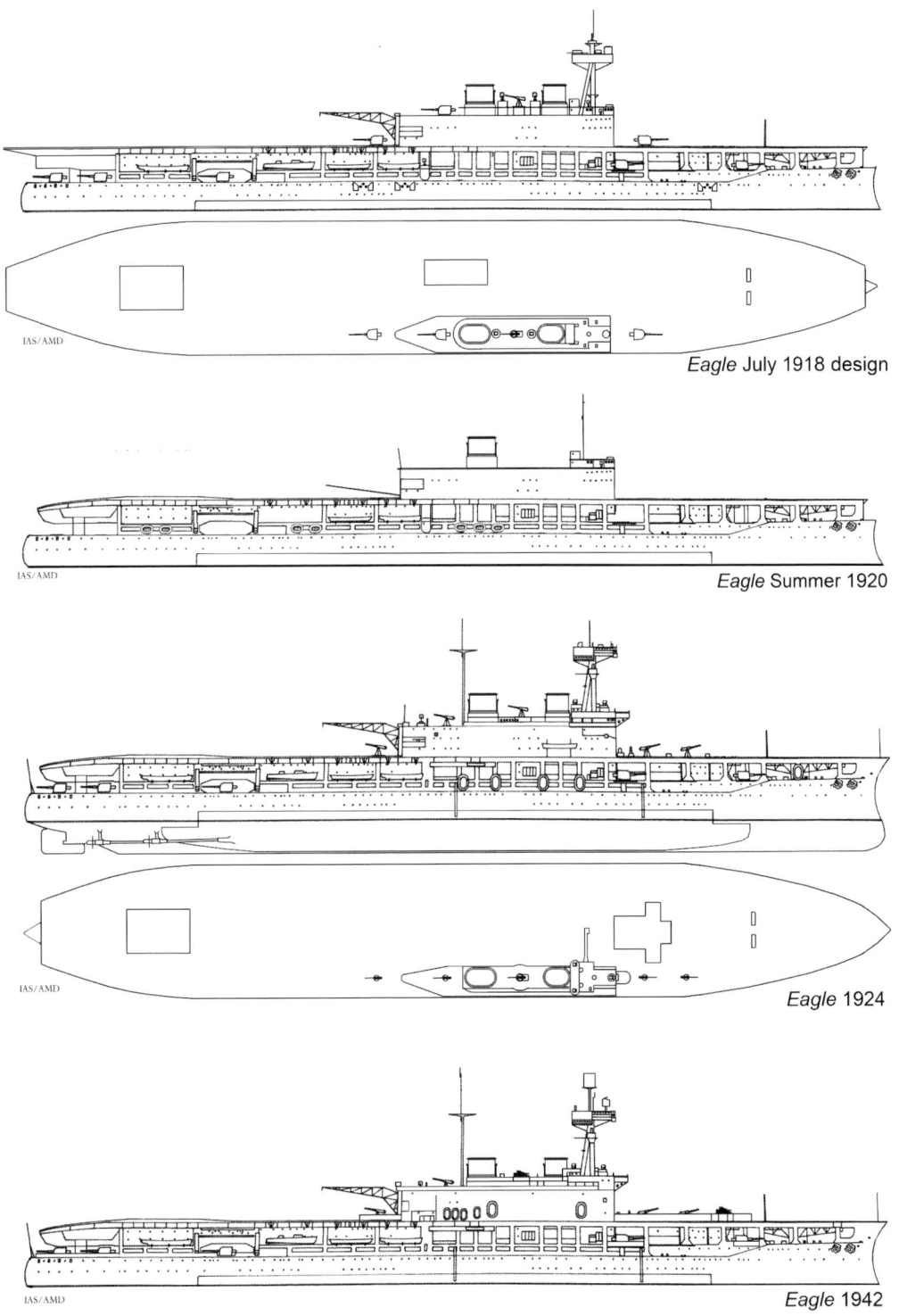

Eagle July 1918 design

Eagle Summer 1920

Eagle 1924

Eagle 1942

Onward and Upward

Her captain's July review of *Eagle*'s capabilities was endorsed by CinC Atlantic Fleet, including strong recommendations for changes to be implemented during her final completion. These included: oil-firing only (on grounds of deck-space limiting coaling to 50 tons-per-hour, coal smoke reducing visibility for pilots landing-on, and damage to aircraft by coal dust; *Argus* was oil-only); an anti-aircraft-only armament (delete torpedo tubes and 6in guns omitted or reduced to five); improve island airflow; omit tripod mast (for airflow reasons); and move the forward lift ahead of the hangar (as current location interfered with arresting gear).

These recommendations were considered by DNC, and largely accepted, except for the issue of armament, where responsibility lay elsewhere. He noted, however, that if 6in guns were retained, the tripod mast was necessary to carry the directors, and in any case it was not likely to materially contribute to air turbulence. Nevertheless, wind-tunnel testing at the National Physical Laboratory, Teddington, resulted in modifications to the form of the island (including the cutting-back of its upper platform where this overhung the flight deck) and fairing of the front end of the flight deck into the ship's bow. Various other changes were made to the control top and the upperworks, bulletproof plating added to the bridge, and the searchlight fit was now fixed at two 36in, two 24in and four 10in units.

As far as armament was concerned, the decision at the end of December 1920 was to fit nine 6in, six 4in and two of the new multi-barrelled pom-poms, and omit the torpedo tubes. In practice, only five of the 4in guns were installed, and the delays in the development of the multiple pom-pom meant that *Eagle* would not receive her first one until 1933, her second following in 1937.

Already on 23 July 1920 the completion of *Eagle* was being assumed in a wide-ranging review of future carrier requirements.[10] Both she and *Hermes* were to be completed, *Furious* was to be reconstructed with double hangars, as was either *Courageous* or *Glorious*, and *Argus* altered 'as necessary'. The carriers were to deliver to the fleet at least '45 Artillery Observation Planes, which would allow 18 Planes being in the air simultaneously', together with '22 Reconnaissance Planes, allowing 6 to be in the air simultaneously', and '1 flight of 12 Torpedo Planes or Bombers'. *Eagle* would carry '25 artillery Machines for five divisions [of the fleet]'. *Argus* and *Furious* would carry ten such aircraft each, those from *Furious* supporting the two battlecruiser divisions. The latter ship would also carry torpedo bombers and fighters, but at this stage *Hermes* was to carry fighters only, and *Courageous/Glorious* just reconnaissance machines.

Work on final completion of *Eagle* began at Portsmouth on 24 March 1921, in accordance with a specification issued on 14 February. This incorporated the various modifications noted above into the design, with the final completion specification issued to the Dockyard on 5 May. However, on 16 February it had been decided to add anti-torpedo bulges of the type already being fitted in the *Revenge* class, with confirmation given to the Dockyard on 13 July. Plans were supplied in August, which also included details of changes to fuel stowage, as the bulges incorporated additional oil-fuel bunkerage, giving *Eagle* a total capacity of 3750 tons. Of this, 500 tons would only be available in emergencies, owing to their contribution to underwater protection. The addition of bulges made *Eagle* unable to pass through the Panama Canal – the only UK warship at the time so handicapped. The planned tinned petrol storage had already been replaced by bulk storage for 8100 gallons. Work on adding the bulges (estimated to take six months) could not, however, begin until the necessary dry dock was vacated by *Royal Sovereign*, due to leave in January/February 1922.

Completion would be further delayed by a number of factors, including shortages of manpower in the constructive department and problems with the hoists for the 4in guns. Most important was the

Eagle as completed. (NHHC NH 61020)

procurement of the lifts. Invitations to tender had been issued in August 1921, but no practicable designs were forthcoming, and as a result Armstrong were asked to tender an Admiralty design of lift that had been given to them 'unofficially'. However, the firm were unwilling to take responsibility for delivering the novel technology proposed. Eventually, on 30 May 1922, tenders from Armstrong were accepted for the lifts of both *Eagle* and *Hermes*, with the delivery of those for *Eagle* agreed in July as being by 1 March 1923 – three months after the latest estimate for the completion of the ship herself. In the event, the lifts (the forward an electric one, the aft one electro-hydraulic) had still not been delivered in December 1923.

The ship being otherwise all but complete, she ran sea trials on 9–10 September 1923. In light of the experience with *Canada*, adjustments were made to allow the turbines to make full use of the available steam, and thus reach the 50,000–55,000 shp desired to give the ship adequate speed for her role as an aircraft carrier. In particular, the pressure in the 1st stage of the HP turbines was limited to 100psi. Even then, slight leakage of turbine joints was observed when *Eagle* made 24.37kt on 52,100 shp during the trials, resulting in her authorised full power being henceforth limited to 50,000 shp, giving a maximum speed of ~23.5kt. Endurance was of 4800nm at 16kt. The first post-completion landing-on trial took place on 5 October.

Installation of the lifts was finally completed during February 1924, allowing *Eagle* to recommission on 26 February and join the Mediterranean Fleet on 7 June, carrying twenty-four aircraft. A short Devonport refit at the end of 1925 removed the longitudinal arresting gear and two single 2pdr pom-poms added forward of the 4in guns in

Aerial view of *Eagle*, off Copacabana, Rio de Janeiro, in April 1931, showing her deck layout. At this stage, she did not carry arrester gear, the original longitudinal ones having been removed in 1926, and new transverse ones not installed until 1936. The Blackburn Ripon being launched is carrying HRH the Prince of Wales, who had opened the British Industries Exhibition at Buenos Aires on 14 March. (*NHHC NH 60944*)

Eagle at Hong Kong between 1932 and 1935; the submarine depot ship *Medway* (1928) is in the background. (NHHC NH 72556)

front of the island; the ship's petrol capacity was also increased. Returning to the Mediterranean, in 1928 she was joined by the newly-converted *Courageous*. *Eagle* was refitted again in early 1929, before returning to the Mediterranean.

A major Devonport refit ran from August 1931 to 28 November 1932, which included replacement of the 4in gun between the funnels with an octuple pom-pom. A quadruple 0.5in MG was added aft and high-angle director fitted to the control top. She then departed for the Far East in the spring of 1933, receiving an additional quadruple 0.5in in 1936. She remained on the China Station until the beginning of 1935, when she moved back to the Mediterranean, going to Devonport to pay off in June.

She began a refit early the next year, receiving transverse arrester gear; a second octuple pom-pom replaced the 2pdrs forward of the island. Two more quadruple 0.5in MGs were installed in sponsons at the bow. Back on the China Station in 1937, she had just completed an August–September 1939 refit at Singapore when the Second World War began. She remained in the Far East and Indian Ocean until May 1940, including repairs in Singapore during March–May following an accidental explosion. She sailed for the Mediterranean, via Colombo, on 9 May, arriving on 26 May.

Eagle remained in the Mediterranean until April 1941, when she sailed via the Red Sea to the South Atlantic, where she remained until she went into refit at Liverpool on 1 November. The 0.5in MGs were superseded by a dozen 20mm Oerlikons and radar added to the HA director, an air warning set also being fitted. She had now swapped 750

Eagle

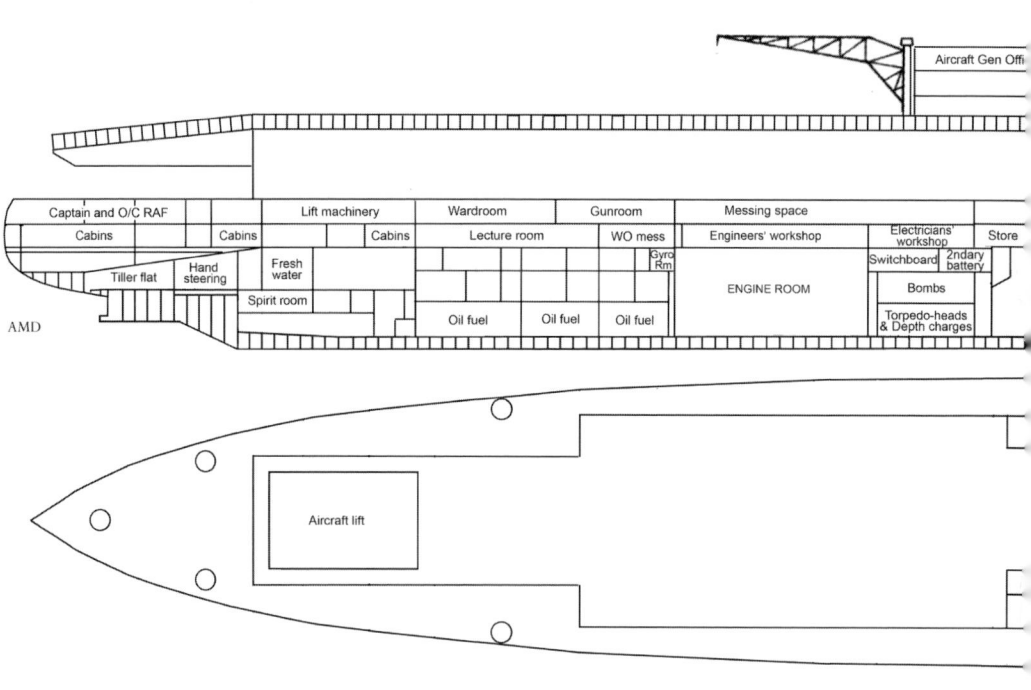

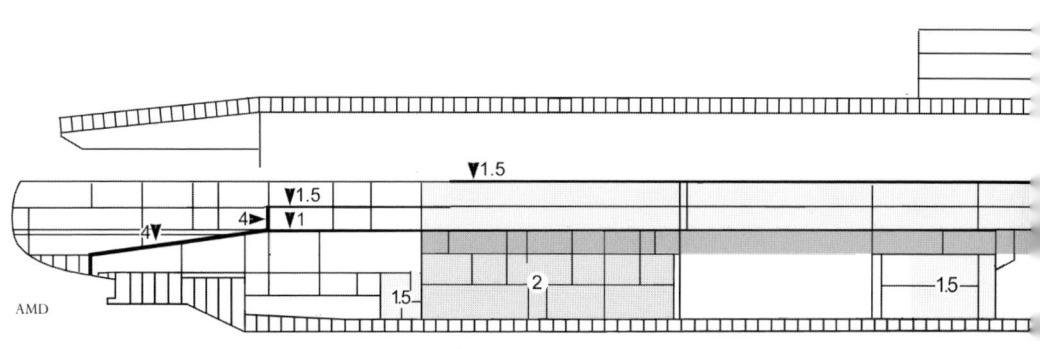

Alternative Service: *Eagle*

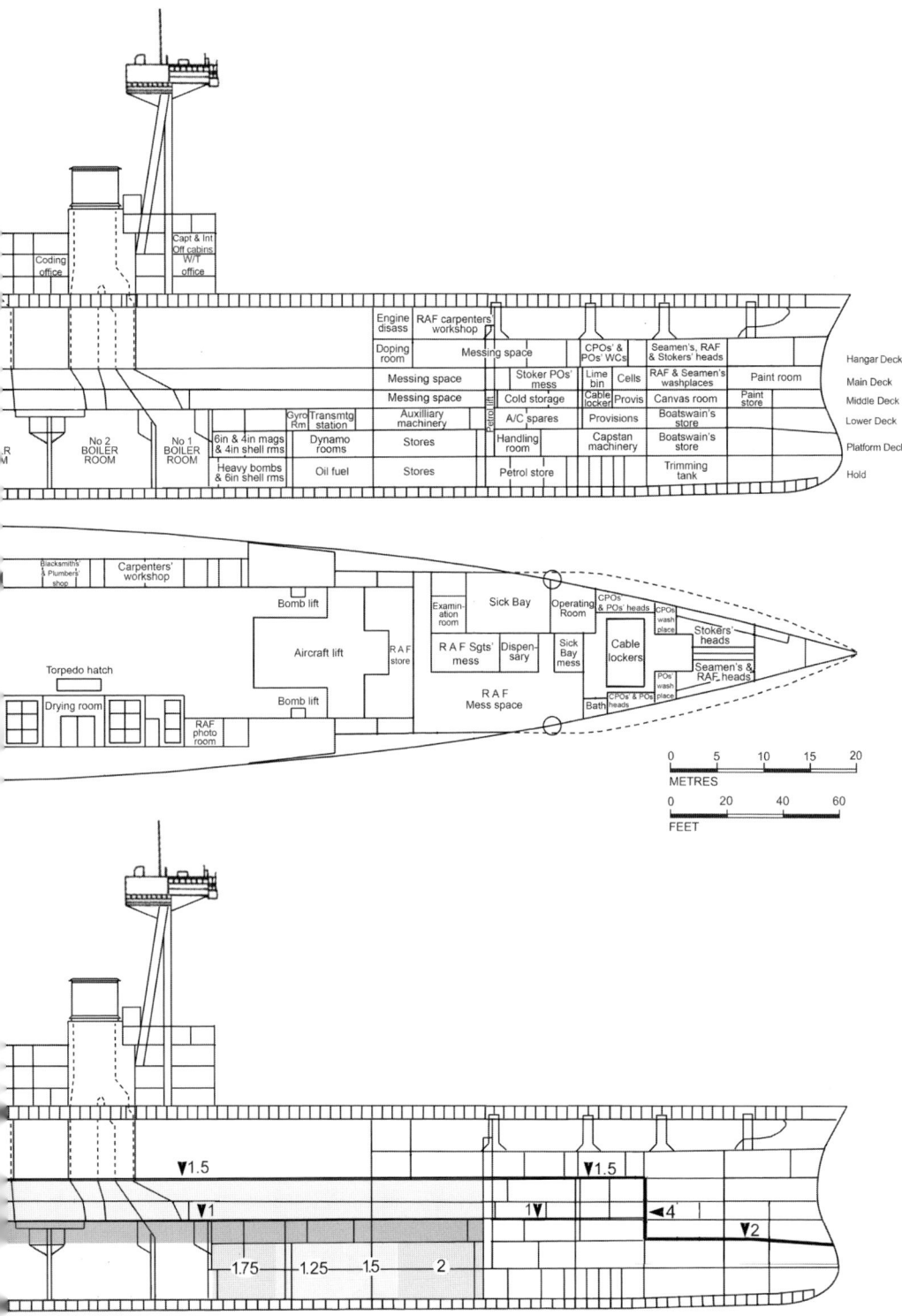

211

The Windfall Battleships

Eagle sinking after being torpedoed by *U73* on 11 August 1942.

tons of oil fuel for 3000 gallons of petrol, cutting the ship's endurance to 2780nm at 17.5kt. Work having been completed on 9 January 1942 the carrier sailed for Gibraltar on 16 February, arriving on 23 February to join Force H. By now, her best speed was down to around 20kt.

The remainder of *Eagle*'s career was spent in aiding in the resupply of Malta. This included ten voyages between February and July 1942 to fly-off Spitfires to reinforce the island's defences, punctuated by periods of repair. Finally, while covering the 'Pedestal' convoy on 11 August she was hit by four torpedoes from the German submarine *U73*, and sank within four minutes, 70nm south of Cape Salinas, with the loss of 131 men, although 929 were rescued.

Eagle, 1924

Displacement:	21,850 tons (standard), 24,550 tons (load).
Dimensions:	627ft (pp), 667.5ft (oa) x 105ft x 24.7ft (load); flight deck 652ft x 96ft.
Machinery:	Twenty-one Yarrow large-tube boilers (250psi); four-shaft Parsons and Brown-Curtis turbines; SHP 50,000 = 24 knots.
Bunkerage:	3750 tons oil; 8300 gallons aviation spirit.
Endurance:	3790 nautical miles @ 19kt.
Armament:	Nine 6in/50 Mk XVII, five 4in Mk V AA, four 3pdr, four 0.303in (2 x 2) guns; 24 aircraft.
Protection:	Main belt 0–4.5–0in; upper belt 0–1–0in; forward & aft bulkheads 4in; torpedo bulkheads (former battleship magazines only) 2–1.25in; flight deck (over hangar only) 1in; hangar deck 1.5in; main deck (aft) 1.5–0in; middle deck 0–1–0in; lower deck (forward) 2in; (aft) 4in; shields 3–1.5in.
Complement:	791.

CHAPTER 7

Ends and New Beginnings

For Disposal

OF THE SMALLER 'WINDFALLS', ATTEMPTS TO sell *Gorgon* back to Norway were rejected. A key issue was that she had been extensively bulged for her inshore bombardment role, and was now too wide to fit in the dry dock at the Horten naval base. Enquiries from Argentina and Peru came to nothing, but in 1920 it seemed that she might be going to Romania along with six 'M' class destroyers. This also fell through, and *Gorgon* ended her career as an explosives trials hulk, finally being sold for scrap in 1928.

There was also no success in selling the ex-Greek cruisers and destroyers (less the lost *Medusa*) back to their original owner. *Chester* thus paid off on 31 March 1920, followed by *Birkenhead* on 25 May, with all of the ex-Greek ships sold for scrap during 1921.[1] There was of course no possibility of the ex-Turkish destroyers being returned, and all were sold (as were two of the ex-Greek destroyers) to T W Ward for scrap on 9 May 1921, as part of a mass sale (at £2-4-0 [£2.20] per ton).[2]

Gorgon as an ordnance test hulk between 1922 and 1928. (Author's collection)

The Doom of Washington

Concern at the political and economic consequences of the large naval programmes in progress or planned during the immediate post-war years led, in November 1921, to the opening in Washington DC of a conference between the UK, the USA, Japan, France and Italy on the limitation of naval strength.

In the final Washington agreement, which was signed on 6 February 1922, the UK was reduced to twenty-two capital ships, comprising *Thunderer* and all later extant Royal Navy-ordered battleships and battlecruisers.[3] Everything else (both completed and building) was to be destroyed within 18 months of the ratification of the Treaty, either by sinking in deep water, or scrapped to exacting standards laid down in the Treaty.[4] The ships for scrapping were explicitly listed, and included *Agincourt* and *Erin*.

Agincourt

It is not impossible that *Agincourt* might have been saved if the MNBDS conversion had actually been carried through by the time of the Treaty, as *Courageous* and *Glorious*, vessels with big guns but not of true capital rank, were not mentioned for disposal.[5] However, as still an intact battleship at the end of the 1921 she was doomed under Article XIII that stated that, apart from aircraft-carrier conversions 'as provided in Article IX, no ship designated in the present Treaty to be scrapped may be reconverted into a vessel of war'. On 17 February 1922 this was formally acknowledged and instructions for *Agincourt*'s disposal requested.[6]

Erin

A possible escape-route for *Erin* had been considered in December 1921, prior to the signature of the Treaty, but by which time its shape was clear. Given her 6in secondary battery, she was of similar capability to the *Iron Duke*s, which were scheduled for retention under the Treaty. The suggestion was that *Erin* might be retained in lieu of *Thunderer* which, along with the *King George V*s, was only to kept in the short term. This was pending the completion of the new battleships *Nelson* and *Rodney*, allowed to the UK to balance the 16in-gunned ships being retained by the USA and Japan.

In assessing the option of swapping *Erin* for *Thunderer*, it was noted that while *Erin* had a better secondary battery, she was otherwise of equivalent capability to the older ship, but suffered from the fact that, as already noted (p 22), she was too broad to dock at Devonport, Malta or Gibraltar. Most importantly, *Thunderer* had been extensively refitted between February and May 1921 as a cadet training ship to replace the battleship *Temeraire* and the cruiser *Carnarvon* that had been jointly fulfilling the role since September 1919. *Erin*'s endurance was 20 per cent lower than that of the older ship (cf p 23), a negative factor where the long cruises inherent in the cadet training role were concerned. But the deciding factor was that if *Thunderer* were to be scrapped instead of *Erin*, additional expenditure would be required to convert *Erin* (or another vessel) to undertake her cadet training role. Accordingly, it was decided that it should be *Erin* that would be disposed of, and on 13 March 1922 she began to discharge ammunition & stores (cf below); at 09:00 on 6 May 1922 the battleship paid off for disposal.

In any case, any reprieve for *Erin* would have lasted for only four years. With the completion of *Nelson* and *Rodney* looming, *Thunderer*, *King George V* and *Ajax* were all sold for scrap in December 1926, while *Centurion* replaced *Agamemnon* as the radio-controlled target ship allowed to the UK by the Washington Treaty.

The scrapheap

The Washington Treaty became effective on 17 August 1923, starting a countdown to the 'destruction' of the ships to be disposed of that would run out in January 1925. However, the process of disposal had long since begun: indeed, some ships listed in the Treaty had been slated for scrapping before the Washington conference had even convened, following the Admiralty decision in March 1921 to dispose of all 12in-gunned ships. Accordingly, by the end of 1921, all such ships had either been sold, hulked (*Colossus* and *Collingwood*), placed on the disposal list or scheduled for conversion to another role (*Agincourt*).

Agincourt's conversion was formally cancelled on 23 February 1922 (17 days after the signature of the Washington Treaty). The de-storing of ships scheduled for disposal under the Treaty was a significant task, since the process lay on the critical path to the ships' availability for sale.[7] Owing to the work towards preparing her for reconstruction, *Agincourt* was ahead of the game in this, and had completed de-storing by the middle of March; she paid off on 7 April 1922.

As well as *Agincourt*, five of the ships required to be scrapped under the Treaty were at Rosyth in February 1922. *Neptune* and *Hercules* had already been paid off for disposal during 1921; indeed, the latter had already been sold. *New Zealand* had almost finished disembarking her stores, and paid off on 19 April, but *Lion* and *Princess Royal* still required complete de-storing before they could be paid off and placed on the disposal list.

Originally it was intended that all the 'Washington' ships, except *Agincourt* and *New Zealand*, should de-store at Devonport (*Erin*, *Orion*, *Lion* and *Princess Royal*) or Portsmouth (*Conqueror*, *Monarch* and *Collingwood*). However, the need to get the process underway before impending naval redundancies bit, and difficulties in bringing *Lion* and *Princess Royal* down from their current berths at Rosyth, meant that it was announced on 11 March that the process should be carried out where the ships currently lay. Accordingly, the crew of *Agincourt* were assigned to aid the removal of stores from the two battlecruisers as soon as she herself had paid off.[8] As a result, it proved possible to pay off *Princess Royal* on 1 May 1922, and *Lion* on the 30th of that month. *Erin* was to de-store in the Medway, and successfully paid off on 6 May. In June 1922 forty men are recorded as working on the dismantling of fittings aboard the battleship, now moored in the stream off Chatham.

Formal authority to sell *Erin* and *Agincourt*, together with *New Zealand*, *Princess Royal* and *Orion*, was given on 16 December 1922, the contracts for demolition explicitly requiring work to be complete by '18 months from date of ratification of [the Washington] Treaty'. The ships were sold in two batches. *Erin* and *Orion* went to Cox & Danks on 16 January 1923 (for £20,100 each), to be broken up alongside the former South-Eastern & Chatham Railway pier at Queenborough, only 2 miles from *Erin*'s former berth at the Nore. *Erin* arrived on 3 February, after a 25-mile tow from Chatham by four tugs, and was berthed at high tide. Work was begun immediately, beginning with the foretop. *Orion* was handed over to the breakers at Devonport on the 12th, and joined *Erin* at Queenborough later the same month.

The Admiralty Sales Ledger page including sales dictated by the Washington Treaty. (Author)

Ends and New Beginnings

Orion and *Erin* being broken up at Queenborough, viewed from the bridge-wing of *Orion*. (Author's collection).

Erin's forward turrets being dismantled. (Author's collection)

217

Top: *Princess Royal*, *Agincourt* and *New Zealand* berthed along the south wall of the Main Basin at Rosyth Dockyard in late 1923. They had been handed over to the shipbreakers on 25 January that year. *New Zealand*'s demolition is well advanced, with *Agincourt* shorn of all superstructure apart from barbettes and turrets, but *Princess Royal* is still superficially intact. Bottom: detail of the hulk of *Agincourt*, stripped of all superstructure, except for her barbettes and turrets, with severed guns still present in '6' turret. (*Archives New Zealand*)

Top: the after part of *Agincourt*, viewed from the bridgework of *Princess Royal*, showing the severed guns in '6' turret. The vessel at top left is the storeship *Imperieuse*, originally the ironclad *Audacious* (1869). Bottom: forecastle of *Agincourt*, with the cut-down hulk of *New Zealand* behind; beyond, anchored in the Forth, is the armoured cruiser *Sutlej*, which had been sold to T W Ward as long ago as 9 May 1921. However, owing to the congestion of many shipbreaking yards with surplus British and surrendered German tonnage, *Sutlej* would not be towed from Rosyth to Preston for breaking-up until 26 February 1924; her demolition had been completed there by 30 June 1925. (*Archives New Zealand*)

Cutting through the 1.5in armoured upper deck of *Agincourt* adjacent to '4' turret, with the forward funnels of the still superficially-intact *Princess Royal* looming behind. (Archives New Zealand)

ENDS AND NEW BEGINNINGS

View from the top of the 30-ton crane (visible in the bottom image on p 219), showing the state of *Agincourt* in late 1924. The circular bulkhead towards the bottom of the image is the base of the midships derrick, with the cleared '4' magazine and aft boiler rooms beyond. The aft part of the ship has been cut down to well below the in-service waterline, but she was still insufficiently mutilated to meet the terms of the Washington Treaty. *(Archives New Zealand)*

The Windfall Battleships

Top: the hulk of *Agincourt* in dry dock to be cut in half. Bottom: the stern of *Agincourt* in drydock, showing her four screws still in place. The docking was used as an opportunity for removing them. *(Archives New Zealand)*

ENDS AND NEW BEGINNINGS

Agincourt's hulk is cut through between two watertight bulkheads. Note the gas cylinders at the bottom left for the oxyacetylene cutting-torches. *(Archives New Zealand)*

a. The forward half of *Agincourt* alongside after being removed from drydock.
b. The stern half of the ship; the ships in the background are 1916-launched Admiralty 'Leaf' class oilers.
c. The point at which the aft part of the ship was cut from the rest; the ship visible on the left is the light cruiser *Centaur*, under refit.
d. The forward half of the hulk is eased through the lock at Rosyth, heading for the beaching ground. *(Archives New Zealand)*

Ends and New Beginnings

Agincourt's bow section arrives at the beaching-ground. (Archives New Zealand)

Agincourt, *New Zealand* and *Princess Royal* were purchased by the Exeter-based firm of electrical engineers J & W Purves on 22 January 1923 (*New Zealand* for £21,000 and the other two for £25,000 each), although the contract was immediately transferred to the newly-established Rosyth Shipbreaking Company. The ships were taken over 'as lying' against the south wall of the main basin at Rosyth Dockyard on 25 January. Demolition work began with *New Zealand*, and once she was well advanced, *Agincourt* was begun, work continuing until she was shorn of all superstructures except her disarmed turrets. Attention then shifted to *Princess Royal*. By March 1923 *New Zealand* was ready for transfer to the beaching-ground outside the north-west dockyard wall. *Princess Royal* and *Agincourt* had by now both been stripped to upper-deck level, other than the remains of their heavy gun-mountings. As soon as *New Zealand* had been moved out of the basin and around to the beaching ground, her place against the dockyard wall was taken by the *Princess Royal*, whose stripping was then given priority, with the result that as soon as *New Zealand* had been reduced to the last few scraps, *Princess Royal* was able to take her place on the beaching-ground at the end of September 1924.

However, as the Washington Treaty's January 1925 deadline approached, *Agincourt*, although now well cut-down, was judged not yet sufficiently mutilated to meet contractual commitments.[9] Discussions with the Admiralty concluded with an agreement that cutting the hull in two on the beaching-ground would discharge the company's obligations, but bad weather prevented the hulk from passing through the Dockyard locks on the only day prior to the deadline that would allow its beaching on the highest spring tide. As the next such tide was after the deadline, it was ultimately agreed the hulk would be taken into one of the Dockyard's dry docks and cut in half there. This proved successful and within 48 hours of entering the dock both halves had been floated out, to be taken to the beaching-ground for final breaking up on the next convenient tide. Within a short while the last traces of the 'great battleship' had gone.

And So To Chile

In contrast to the demise of her erstwhile comrades *Agincourt* and *Erin*, *Canada* was about to begin a new phase of her career – one that would last nearly four decades. Under the October 1914 agreements (pp 29–30), Chile had the option to repurchase the ship 'at a price based upon the original contract, either in good repair or with an allowance for the cost of repair'. These terms also applied to the other ships taken over by the UK, although of the destroyers *Almirante Riveros* was no longer available, having been sunk as HMS *Tipperary* at Jutland in 1916.

Approaches were made by Chile to the UK soon after the end of the war, not only about repurchases, but also about the possibility of new-build vessels. Although the latter were decidedly ephemeral, things went sufficiently far as to lead to the Coventry Syndicate to produce proposals for 660–670ft, 28kt battlecruisers in October 1919.[10] But it was by no means certain that the Chileans would even repurchase, with significant opposition from the Chilean Navy and Finance Ministries, and concerns at the worn nature of the ships, following their hard war service.

However, from November 1919, the Chilean Minister in London, Don Agustín Edwards, supported by Rear Admiral Luis Gomez Carreño, negotiated an agreement under which *Canada*, the surviving three destroyers and the tug (*Sibbald*) would be acquired for £1.4 million (already on deposit in the UK from the 1914 reimbursement of instalments paid for *Latorre*). This was around a third of the original price of *Latorre*, but reflected 'wear and tear' and the outstanding full repairs to *Canada*'s strained engines (p 32). The deal, which was accepted by the Chilean President, also included training and consultancy services to aid in the integration of the ships into the Chilean navy, and the whole Royal Navy stock of 14in shells for the battleship's unique main guns.[11] There were reports that the 'V' class destroyer *Vampire* might also be sold to replace the lost *Tipperary*, but this did not happen.

As described on pp 196–204, the question of the reacquisition of what was now HMS *Eagle* was also discussed. However, given the issues regarding her reconversion to a battleship, the British government offered the battlecruiser *Inflexible* instead, with her sister *Indomitable* available as an enhancement, for £200,000 each, plus £600,000 for modernisation.[12] Six destroyers were also available. However, a press leak led to a furious debate on the utility of ageing battlecruisers against using the funds for submarines and aircraft. In the end, neither battlecruisers, submarines nor aircraft were purchased.[13]

The deal was finally done on 24 April 1920, and on 31 May the formal announcement was made that

> Canada (at Rosyth), Botha (at Chatham), Faulknor (at Devonport), tug Stoic (at Chatham) have been purchased by the Chilean Government & arrts are being made for the vessels not now at Devonport to be navigated to that port as soon as practicable, the necessary navigation parties being provided from Devonport Depot.
>
> On arrival at Devonport the vessels are to be reduced to Reserve Complement pending further instructions.

Canada departed Rosyth at 10:00 on 27 June 1920, mooring at Devonport's No 9 buoy at 16:30 on the 29th. She was preceded by *Botha*, *Broke* and *Stoic* (ex-Chilean *Piloto Sibbald*). *Faulknor* was already at Devonport.

On the morning of 30 June, a conference took place between the Dockyard authorities, a Chilean commission, led by Admiral Gomes, and FO Devonport Reserve to plan the handover process. A first instalment of the Chilean crews, comprising 500 men, arrived soon afterwards. Work began to prepare the battleship for a brief refit prior to her transfer, including beginning the disembarkation of 14in shells on 19 July. On 26 July a Chilean working party arrived alongside in SS *Angamos*, and on the 31st the last of the British crew left for their depots in Devonport and Portsmouth. On 1 August the battleship ceased to be HMS *Canada*, hoisting the Chilean ensign and the flag of Rear Admiral Gomez. As once

Almirante Latorre on 24 December 1921. (Underwood & Underwood via LoC)

again *Almirante Latorre*, she remained in UK waters until November, with Captain Tomlin remaining assigned to her until 18 October to facilitate the transition to full Chilean control. He received a letter of commendation from the Chilean government for his efforts. Tomlin later commanded *Malaya* during 1924–5.

The three surviving Chilean destroyers were also handed over on 1 August 1920, having been overhauled by their builder on the Isle of Wight. Although HMS *Botha* reverted to her original name of *Almirante Williams*, HMS *Broke* became *Almirante Uribe* (rather than *Almirante Goñi*) and HMS *Faulknor* (ex-*Almirante Simpson*) became *Almirante Riveros* (ii), taking the original name of the sunken *Tipperary*.

By 16 November 1920, *Latorre*'s full Chilean complement of 1175 men had come aboard, and undertook her first trials under the Chilean flag. She sailed for the Pacific on the 27th, accompanied by *Almirante Uribe* and *Almirante Williams*; *Almirante Riveros* followed later. En-route, on 14 January 1921, the battleship stopped for dry-docking at Balboa, at the Pacific end of the Panama Canal, since the 800ft x 116ft x 36ft dock being built for her at Talcahuano had been delayed and would not complete until July 1924. She finally arrived at Valparaiso on 20 February 1921, a decade after her order had been placed with Armstrong.

CHAPTER 8

The Aging Queens of Latin America

WITH THE ARRIVAL OF *ALMIRANTE LATORRE* IN her home waters, each of the South American 'great powers' finally had dreadnoughts. Although Chile would never get a second ship, she could still claim the most powerful single vessel in the region – and eventually its very last battleship. In her White-built destroyers, she also had its most powerful flotilla craft, and in her 'H' class submarines the most modern sub-surface vessels.

Argentina, Brazil and Chile had signed a Treaty of Non-Aggression, Consultation and Arbitration in May 1915, although this did not include an Argentine-Chilean proposal, dating back to 1907, that there should be a 'discreet equivalence' of the three powers' naval forces. With the end of the First World War, the overseas major powers' interest in South American naval procurement prospects had been revived. This began with a US mission to Peru to reorganise the navy and establish a submarine base for four new boats, ordered from the Electric Boat company of Groton CT (two in April 1924, two in October 1926). The Peruvian navy's existing two French-built boats (p 94) were discarded for lack of batteries and spares.

As previously described, the British had attempted to sell vessels over and above the Chilean ships taken over during the war. They would ultimately establish a naval mission in Chile in 1925. This followed the setting-up of a US naval mission in Brazil in 1923, which recommended a major ten-year naval programme, comprising some 150,000 tons of ships. However, the threat of a fresh bout of Latin American naval rivalry resulted in a suggestion at the third meeting of the League of Nations in 1922 that the Washington Treaty regime be extended to Latin American naval powers. Brazil objected on the grounds that she had older and less capable ships than Argentina or Chile, and the matter was taken forward to the Fifth Pan-American Conference in Santiago in March 1923.[1]

At Santiago, Chile proposed a general principle that would provide for parity between the three powers for five years. Brazil replied with a suggestion of a capital-ship limit of 80,000 tons for each navy (Argentina currently had 55,880 tons, Brazil 38,562 tons and Chile 28,000 tons). Argentina argued for a capital-ship allocation of 55,000 tons, plus 60,000 tons of cruisers and destroyers, 25,000 tons of aircraft carriers, and

15,000 tons of submarines. In response, Chile drafted an agreement that would give each of the three countries 66,000 tons of capital ships (increasing to 90,000 tons after five years), 85,000 tons of other surface warships and 15,000 tons of submarines (both also with a one-third uplift after five years).

Brazil objected to any limits on vessels other than capital ships, and it was clear that all the national proposals were based on local advantage, the Brazilian one giving themselves the scope for a new 35,000-ton 'Washington' battleship, but limiting any new Argentine ship to 24,120 tons. The Argentine proposal kept the status quo between Argentina and Brazil (with Argentina having more powerful ships), but allowed Chile to acquire one additional ship to give numerical parity between the powers. Although potentially leaving Chile in a stronger position through larger, newer and more powerful vessels, it was clearly recognised by the Argentines that a second Chilean battleship was unlikely in the short to medium term, given the Washington Treaty's ban on its signatories building battleships within their territories or selling old ones for further service abroad.

Accordingly, no substantive agreement was reached, and the final act of the Conference merely included a resolution calling on all parties to recognise the Washington Treaty capital-ship size and gun-calibre limits.

Almirante Latorre

The day after *Latorre* and her accompanying destroyers arrived in Chile, the ship was reviewed by the President of the Republic, Arturo Alessandri Palma, and joined the Chilean navy's operational squadron, still flying the flag of Admiral Gomez and under the command of Captain Braulio Bahamonde.[2] In April 1922, *Latorre* was detached to Balboa for a further docking. On her return she rejoined the fleet for training off Coquimbo and Puerto Aldea. On 15 November, she carried President Alessandri on a visit to the provinces of Coquimbo and Atacama in the wake of the earthquake in these areas five days earlier, joining the cruiser *Chacabuco* and destroyer *Almirante Uribe*, which were already there providing aid.

Experience was now showing that the use of Chilean bituminous coal, rather than the Welsh steam coal she had used in British service, reduced *Latorre*'s endurance by a quarter. As a result, a stock of Welsh coal was kept at Talcahuano for emergency use. There are no records of the ship using her oil-firing capability during the 1920s.

From April 1923 to April 1924, the ship wore the flag of Rear Admiral Luis Langlois, who was followed by Rear Admiral Luis

Guillermo Soffia. On 15 July 1924, with the President aboard, she was the first ship to dock in the new big dry dock at Talcahuano, marking the end of a dozen years of delayed work by French contractors. In 1925 Rear Admiral Arturo Swett hoisted his flag, and in September the same year *Latorre* was the venue when the President hosted a reception for the British Prince of Wales, who was touring Latin America aboard the battlecruiser HMS *Repulse*. Less happily, in January she had taken aim at the Valparaiso–Santiago railway line during the tenure of the military regime that interrupted President Alessandri's term between January and March 1925.

The following year, she wore the flag of Rear Admiral Braulio Bahamonde, her former Captain, by which time she had steamed less than 9,000 miles since 1923, having spent only 39 days at sea. Bahamonde was replaced in January 1927 by Rear Admiral Alfredo Searle, who in turn, on 10 February, ceded leadership of the operational fleet to *Latorre*'s own Captain José Manuel Montalva. Commodore Hippolytus Marchant then took over on 26 April. These rapid changes were the result of events leading up to the resignation of President Emiliano Figueroa in May 1927, which was followed by the authoritarian presidency of Carlos Ibáñez.

By the late 1920s, Chile's relations with Peru were deteriorating over territorial aspects of the Treaty of Ancon which had ended the War of the Pacific in 1883, while between 1926 and 1928 the Peruvian navy had commissioned their new four US-built submarines and their base. It was also recognised that even Chile's newest warships were already a decade old. As a result, and aided by the newly-arrived British naval mission, planning went ahead for a renewal of the Chilean navy, beginning with 1927 orders for the six *Serrano* class destroyers from Thornycroft and three *Capitan O'Brien* class submarines (plus the

Almirante Latorre during the 1920s, essentially unchanged from her time in British service, including the presence of flying-off platforms on 'B' and 'X' turrets. *(Author's collection)*

submarine depot ship *Araucano*) from Vickers-Armstrong; all commissioned during 1928–9. Two heavy cruisers were also planned, but were never funded.

As part of the renewal process, on 19 November 1928, a commission was set up to consider *Latorre*'s material condition and necessary modifications. She was suffering both from her long-term engine problems (dating back to her trials in 1915), as well as the obsolescence common to all battleships of pre-Jutland vintage. As a result, the following month the Chilean government invited the British Admiralty to bid to undertake an extensive refit at Devonport; a £1.4 million contract was placed in early June 1929. The choice of the dockyard was in part owing to its long experience of battleship refits, including that of *Latorre* before her return to Chile. On 15 May 1929, she sailed from Valparaiso to Plymouth under the command of Captain Calixto Rogers. She called at Balboa before transiting the Panama Canal on the 24th, and then proceeding to Port of Spain, Trinidad, to coal on the 28th. From here, she proceeded to Plymouth via the Azores Islands, sailed from there on 19 June, arriving on the 24th. She was moved to Devonport Dockyard the following day.

Modernisation

Largely carried out in the floating dock *AFD4*,[3] and lasting until March 1931, *Latorre*'s refit was one of the most comprehensive of its kind to date. Her boilers were reduced in number from twenty-one to eighteen, converted to oil firing and updated, while the battleship's old engines were replaced by Parsons geared turbines. These were ordered from Vickers-Armstrong on 15 June 1929 (as Barrow Job 657) at a cost of £162,000, running shop trials during May–June 1930, and being delivered to Devonport in two batches, the outer machinery on 1 June and the inner on the 30th. The new engines were installed on 10 July (port engine room), 12 July (starboard) and 21 July (centre). New generators were also installed. Basin trials were run on 10 November, and the engines were fully capable of taking all the steam produced by the renewed boilers during her sea trials between 1 and 10 December, reaching 24kt at 56,803 shp during her 8-hour trial on 8 December 1930. This result was despite the addition of anti-torpedo bulges, and a post-refit displacement 2,000 tons higher than before. Additional weights included an additional 2in of armour over the magazines, designed to keep them safe from 12in shells. Searchlights were removed from the bridge.

The bulges, of the kind being installed in the British *Queen Elizabeth* and *Revenge* classes, not only greatly enhanced the ship's protection from underwater weapons, but resolved most of her problems

Almirante Latorre in dry dock, showing her anti-torpedo bulges. *(Author's collection)*

Almirante Latorre after her reconstruction; see also drawing on p 152. *(Author's collection)*

with trim, which went back to the decision to fit 6in, rather than 4.7in, secondary guns during the original building phase. As a result she became much less wet forward than hitherto.

The main battery was overhauled and the guns re-lined, although no attempt was made to increase elevation, since *Latorre* was still able to outrange the Brazilian and Argentine battleships; the considerable extra costs of modifying mountings was thus not felt justifiable. Stocks of new-design armour-piercing shells were acquired and transported direct to Chile. The directors for the secondary battery were replaced by new ones on the upper bridge, but it did not prove possible to increase the elevation of the 6in guns themselves. Four single 4in/45 Mk V anti-aircraft mountings were installed on the after superstructure, controlled by the British HACS I system, and the submerged torpedo tubes were removed.

A base for a catapult was fitted on the quarterdeck, following the current pattern in both UK and US battleships. The actual catapult was built in Italy, and sent direct to Chile for installation there. However, while *Latorre* was under refit, the Chilean navy had lost its air arm to the air force in 1930, complicating the allocation and operation of any aircraft from the battleship. As a result, although trials were carried out in 1932, only five launches are recorded between 1935 and the catapult's removal in late 1942.

The battleship ran her acceptance trials on 11 February 1931, followed by post-refit and gunnery trials the following day, and then began to complete with stores. On the 17th, the Mayor of Plymouth presented the ship with a silver salver acknowledging 'the employment for two years given to 2,000 British workers and for the splendid behaviour observed by the ship's crew' during her refit. At this time, the

Great Depression had pushed unemployment in the UK to some 20 per cent.

With work completed, *Latorre* sailed for home on 5 March 1931 under the command of Captain Abel Campos, proceeding again via the Azores, Port of Spain and the Panama Canal. She arrived back in Chile on 12 April 1931, with the 33-ton tugs *Intrepido* and *Moctezuma* as deck loads. However, within a few months of her return to Chile, *Latorre* became involved in a major mutiny.[4]

In reaction to the Great Depression now raging, the Chilean government imposed pay cuts on government employees (including sailors). This resulted in a lower-deck meeting aboard the battleship at Coquimbo on 31 August 1931, which decided on mutiny. In the early hours of the next morning, junior members of her crew, and of those of the armoured cruiser *O'Higgins*, seven destroyers and some submarines took over their vessels. That afternoon (1 September), the mutineers radioed the Navy Minister underlining that their demonstration was not linked with any political movement, and was solely aimed at the restoration of pay levels and the punishment of those mismanaging the state; they also rejected any use of force. These demands were elaborated in a longer message that night.

Meanwhile, personnel at the Talcahuano naval base joined the mutiny, some ships, led by the cruiser *Blanco Encalada*, sailing to join the vessels at Coquimbo, leaving two old cruisers and a few smaller vessels behind. Other bases also joined the rebellion, including part of the naval air arm on the 4th. The latter surrendered when attacked on the 5th, as did Talcahuano on the 6th, the destroyer *Riveros* being badly damaged by shore artillery. However, the ships at Coquimbo, now joined by the *Blanco Encalada* group, continued the mutiny.

On the 6th, the US ambassador to Chile was asked whether the US would provide Chile immediately with two submarines, tear gas and armour-piercing bombs to confront the mutineers. This was on the grounds that the mutiny had 'continental' significance. The provision of submarines was rejected as contrary to the Washington Treaty and the other desiderata as unachievable in the desired timescale.

The Chilean authorities had attempted negotiations by Admiral Edgardo von Schroeders, a former executive officer of *Latorre*, but it was clear that no settlement would be possible before the arrival of the ships from Talcahuano. However, by the time the latter had reached the anchorage, the mutineers had been reduced to just those on the ships now at Coquimbo. On the 6th, an air strike was launched against the mutinous fleet, comprising two Junkers R-42 trimotor and two Vickers Vixen bombers, two Vickers-Wibault 121 fighters, nine Curtis Falcon observation aircraft and two Ford 5-AT-C transports. The submarine

Guale (ex-*H4*) surrendered after being strafed, and while no other damage was done to the fleet, the attack resulted in the destroyers *Hyatt* and *Riquelme* defecting and steaming to Valparaiso to surrender.

Offers to negotiate were rejected by the government. In reaction to a threat by the leaders of the mutiny to bombard coastal towns, the destroyers *Videla*, *Orella*, *Aldea* and *Serrano* also defected. On 7 September, *Latorre* notified the authorities that her mutineers had surrendered and that *Blanco Encalada* was under the control of the battleship's officers. Finally, *O'Higgins* and the depot ship *Araucano* gave up later that same day.

The fallout from the mutiny, together with the ongoing economic crisis, and continued political instability, had a major impact on the Chilean navy. Many officers and men were dismissed or forced into retirement, and swingeing cuts were imposed on the organisation itself, the operational fleet being reduced to *O'Higgins*, a single flotilla of destroyers and a single flotilla of submarines. The selection of ships to remain operational was heavily influenced by a shortage of oil, so that only two of the new *Serrano* class destroyers were available at any one time, with the brunt of operations falling on the five coal-fired ships of the *Almirante Lynch* class.

Around the same time, there was conflict to the north of Chile, when Colombia and Peru clashed during the 'Leticia Incident' of September 1932–May 1933, regarding a territorial dispute in the Amazon rainforest. This led to Peru purchasing from Estonia two ex-Russian destroyers (*Almirante Guise* [ex-*Lennuk*, ex-*Avtroil*] and *Almirante Villar* [ex-*Vambola*, ex-*Spartak*, ex-*Mikula*]), both of which had been launched in 1915.

The rest of the Chilean navy, including *Latorre*, was laid up at Talcahuano. The economic and political situation even led to questions being raised as to whether the battleship had a future in the Chilean navy. Press rumours suggested that she might be sold to Japan, although this seems to have been based on reports that Brazil and Argentina were thinking of disposing of their own battleships in advance of the World Disarmament Conference, held in Geneva during 1932–4. In reality, no such moves were being made, and Chile had no plans to sell *Latorre*.

The battleship remained at Talcahuano with a skeleton crew until February 1935, when funds were found to provide fuel for her and other oil-fired vessels. Over the next few months *Latorre* undertook three cruises, one to the far south of Chile. These included exercises that featured rare launches of aircraft from her catapult. A light anti-aircraft battery was added during the late 1930s in the form of ten single 0.5in Hotchkiss machine guns on the turret roofs. Operations continued over the following years, including rendering assistance following the Chillán earthquake of 24 January 1939, alongside the British and French cruisers *Exeter*, *Ajax* and *Jeanne d'Arc*.

Chile remained neutral at the outbreak of the Second World War, but broke off relations with the Axis powers in January 1943, and declared war on Japan in April 1945. Its naval activities were accordingly primarily matters of protecting the country's neutral status, *Latorre* and the *Serrano* class destroyers being given camouflage during 1943. Reports that the USA made approaches to Chile over the purchase of *Latorre*, the modern destroyers and the submarine flotilla in the wake of the attack on Pearl Harbor in December 1941 appear to have no basis in fact: only a few merchantmen were actually acquired. Nevertheless, Chile's break of diplomatic relations in 1943 gave her access to Lend-Lease material from the Allies, which included eighteen 20mm Oerlikon AA weapons for installation in *Latorre*, and a quadruple 0.5in mount to be fitted in place of the former catapult.

Latorre remained active throughout, exercising with the destroyer flotilla off Valparaiso, and periodically in more distant waters. In 1940, she sank the destroyer *Almirante Riveros* (stricken 1933) as a target, and between 1942 and 1945 she steamed some 28,000 miles, over three times further than during any earlier comparable period.

On board *Almirante Latorre* in 1950. *(Author's collection)*

Soon after the end of the war, the battleship was fitted with her first radar set (a war-surplus item originally fitted in a US landing craft), with Type SG, SO and SU sets later added, their consoles being placed in the transmitting station. However, if *Latorre* were to retain any effectiveness – regarded as necessary for as long as Brazil and Argentina retained battleships and cruisers – much more needed to be done. In 1950 studies were undertaken regarding the updating of both the battleship and four ex-Canadian 'River' class frigates acquired in 1946. This included a visit by a team from Vickers-Armstrong during May and June 1950. The decision to modernise *Latorre* was seemingly not affected by Chile's commissioning of two ex-US cruisers (*O'Higgins* [ex-*Brooklyn*] and *Capitán Prat* [ex-*Nashville*]) on 9 January 1951. They had been acquired as part of a three-way sale by the USA, which had also provided similar pairs to Brazil and Argentina.

The first phase of the proposed work was the overhaul of the machinery and the installation a new anti-aircraft battery, and a contract was signed with Vickers-Armstrong to that effect on 17 October 1951. As authorised by the government on 23 August 1950, the work would be carried at Talcahuano, but with materials and supervision provided by the British company at a cost of £1.2 million.[5]

Structurally, the shelter deck was to be extended out to the sides abreast the second funnel, requiring the deletion of a further pair of 6in guns and removing any possibility of training 'Q' turret forward of the beam; the mainmast was to be replaced by a short, light tripod. Six twin 4in HA/LA countersunk turrets (Mk 16* guns in Mk 19C RP 52 mountings), would be installed, four abreast and just forward of the second funnel, and two on top of the after superstructure, the control gear including Types 262 and 291M radar. 12,100 rounds of live HE

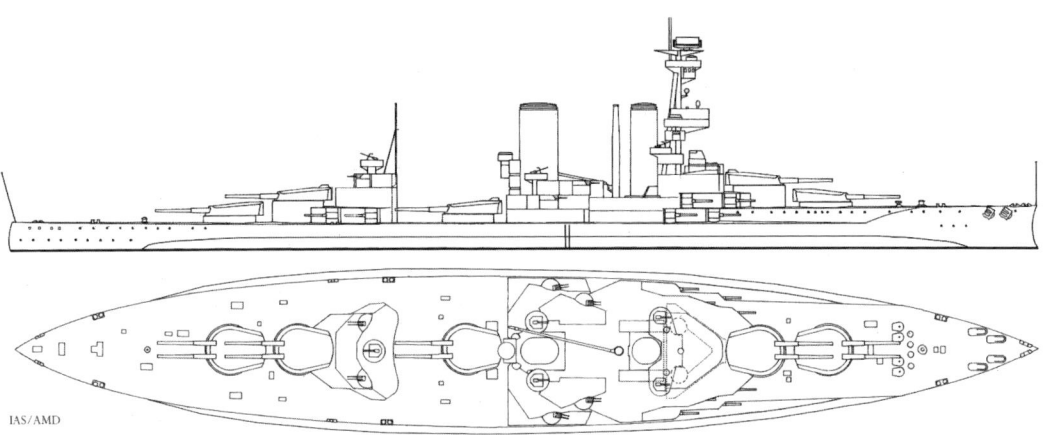

Almirante Latorre planned refit authorised in 1950

and 78 of practice ammunition were included in the package. Five twin 40mm Bofors L/70 mountings were also planned, abreast the bridge, abreast the second funnel, and one on the centreline atop the after superstructure. Updates of the main-battery fire control were also to be carried out, including Type 275 gunnery radar, and a large search set atop the foremast, replacing the old spotting top, which was to be moved to below the main-battery director platform. New run-in and out cylinders for the 14in guns were also required. Internal orders were raised by Vickers-Armstrong on 20 March 1953 for the 4in mountings and associated fuze setters, to be manufactured at Scotswood.

In the meantime, the limited arcs of the 'Q' turret following these changes had led the Chilean authorities to decide the previous month that this mounting should be removed altogether to allow a better layout of the new AA guns; Vickers-Armstrong accordingly began work on amended drawings. In the meantime, the ship had remained active, the British Naval Attaché reporting that 'the battleship *Almirante Latorre*, flagship of the squadron, has done a considerable amount of sea time during [1951] and carried out a very successful full calibre 14in shoot which was witnessed by the Minister of Defence and high-ranking officers of the Navy, Army and Air Force'.[6]

However, on 11 March 1951 an explosion during the commissioning of a generator on board had killed four men, and by early 1953 it had become clear some of the required work could not after all be carried out in Chile. *Latorre* would therefore need to be taken to the UK if all required work was to be carried out. By September, Vickers-

Almirante Latorre on arrival at Yokohama for scrapping, in August 1959. (Author's collection)

THE AGING QUEENS OF LATIN AMERICA

Armstrong were aware that the costs of doing so were 'causing the authorities great concern and doubts have been expressed as to whether the large expenditure is justified and whether it would not be wiser to cancel the existing commitments for the new secondary armament etc for the Latorre and incorporate as many of the items as possible in new construction or possibly in the 3 Corvettes purchased from Canada'.[7]

In November 1953, Vickers-Armstrong were endeavouring to avoid any new commitments under the contract as 'it is anticipated we shall receive instructions in the near future to cancel this work'.[8] While half the design work was now done, no material had yet been ordered, and the few components were capable of reassignment. The inevitable decision to cancel was made in January 1954, it being decided to divert the funds to the building of two new destroyers by Vickers-Armstrong, although a public fiction was at first maintained that *Latorre* would still be modernised. The new contract was signed on 17 May 1955, the resulting *Almirante Williams* and *Almirante Riveros* being launched in 1958 and completed in 1960.

Accordingly, *Latorre* was formally placed in reserve on 11 March 1954, and moored in the approach channel to No 2 Dock at Talcahuano. There, she provided tender, workshop, accommodation and oil storage facilities for ships under refit. She continued to be maintained to a level giving a degree of combat ability, including regular dry-docking until 1958, when her naval career finally came to an end.

Legislation for the decommissioning of *Latorre* (plus two destroyers, three submarines and various other small vessels) and her sale for scrap

Latorre being scrapped at the beginning of the 1960s. *(Author's collection)*

was passed on 14 February 1958, and work began on de-storing and the removal of reusable equipment. She decommissioned on 1 August, ending a 43-year career – six years in the British navy and 37 in that of Chile. *Latorre* was sold for scrap to Mitsubishi Heavy Industries in February 1959 for $881,110 (£308,350). Towed away from Talcahuano by the tug *Cambrian Salvos* on 29 May 1959, she arrived at Yokohama, Japan, on 28/29 August to be broken up. A considerable number of components were used in the restoration of the Vickers-built Japanese battleship *Mikasa*,[9] which was completed in 1961. So passed the very last of the dreadnoughts that had loomed so large in naval circles in the run-up to the First World War.

Minas Geraes and *São Paulo*

In contrast to *Latorre*, which had remained in the eyes of her navy an effective unit into the 1950s – and might have remained so into the 1960s had finances been less critical – the Brazilian vessels that had started the whole South American dreadnought race had passed from active service before the end of the 1940s. They, did, however, like the Chilean ship, serve in a belligerent fleet during the First World War.

Brazil had declared neutrality at the beginning of the First World War, which was revoked on 28 June 1917 in the wake of the torpedoing of various of her merchantmen under Germany's unrestricted submarine warfare campaign. War was finally declared on 24 October 1917, making Brazil the only Latin-American state to be a belligerent during the war. A Naval Division in War Operations, comprising the cruisers *Bahia* and *Rio Grande do Sul*, and the destroyers *Parahyha*, *Rio Grande do Norte*, *Piauhy* and *Santa Catharina*, was activated in January 1918, and operated off the West African coast.

There was an aspiration that *Minas Geraes* and *São Paulo* be sent to join the Grand Fleet, but their condition was too poor, the ships having not been refitted since first arriving in Brazilian waters. They were accordingly sent in turn to New York for refit. *São Paulo* departed first on 17 June 1918, suffering major boiler problems on passage, being forced into Bahia by the failure of all but four boilers. Temporary repairs were made by engineers from the battleship USS *Nebraska*, which happened to be in the port, and which then escorted the Brazilian ship to New York.

São Paulo's refit took place between August 1918 and January 1920, work on her sister lasting from August 1920 to October 1921. The bridgework was modified, with Sperry fire-control equipment fitted and rangefinders atop the superfiring turrets. Each turret had its guns separated by an armour screen and the 3pdrs atop them were removed.

The Aging Queens of Latin America

Two 3in/50 AA guns were added abreast the after funnel, and a new searchlight platform was placed above the aft conning tower; the 47mm guns were removed from turret roofs, and a number of 37mm weapons fitted adjacent to each turret.

After her refit was completed, *São Paulo* sailed across the Atlantic to pick up ammunition in Gravesend, and then back to the Americas, carrying out firing trials off Cuba, in the Gulf of Guacanayabo on the south-east coast. The battleship returned to Brazil in early 1920, departing in August for Belgium, to bring King Albert I and Queen Elisabeth to Brazil for a state visit. Sailing on 1 September 1920, they arrived at Rio de Janeiro on the 19th, re-embarking in *São Paulo* on 16 October to return to Europe. Having deposited her royal passengers back in Belgium, the ship steamed to Portugal to embark the remains of the Brazilian Emperor Pedro II (deposed in 1889, died 1891) and Empress Teresa Cristina for reburial in Brazil.

São Paulo under refit at New York Navy Yard during 1918–20. *(NHHC NH 77322)*

Minas Geraes leaving New York in October 1921 after completion of her refit; the new rangefinders atop her superimposed turrets are clearly visible. (Author's collection)

On 5 July 1922, mutinous soldiers seized Fort Copacabana in Rio de Janeiro, and the next morning *São Paulo* bombarded the fort, scoring two hits from five salvos, encouraging its surrender. A mutiny occurred aboard *São Paulo* herself on 4 November 1924, the mutineers attempting to encourage the crews of other ships, including *Minas Geraes*, to join them. Unsuccessful except in the case of a torpedo boat, a 6pdr was fired at *Minas Geraes*, wounding one member of the crew.

São Paulo was then sailed out of harbour, the ship being fired on by Forts Santa Cruz and Copacabana, damaging her fire-control system and forefunnel. The battleship returned fire and proceeded to Rio Grande do Sul, where rebel forces were active, pursued by *Minas Geraes*. When the rebels could not be found, *São Paulo* moved on to Montevideo, arriving on 10 November, where the mutineers disembarked and were granted asylum. *Minas Geraes* then escorted her sister back to Rio de Janeiro, arriving on the 21st.

São Paulo at Buenos Aires in 1935, having carried Brazilian President Getúlio Vargas to a summit with the leaders of Argentine and Uruguay. Also present are *Rivadavia* and *Moreno* (left), one of the *Independencia* class and an Argentine *Rosario* class gunboat (1908, right), and, in the background, the Argentine destroyers *Catamarca* and *Jujuy*. (Author's collection)

The Aging Queens of Latin America

During the Constitutionalist Revolution of June–October 1932, *São Paulo* acted as the flagship of the naval blockade of Santos (actually enforced by the cruiser *Rio Grande do Sul* and the destroyers *Mato Grosso*, *Pará* and *Sergipe*). After refits in 1934 and 1935, *São Paulo* led three naval training exercises, and in 1935 the battleship carried the Brazilian President to Buenos Aires to meet with his Argentine and Uruguayan opposite numbers, escorted by the cruisers *Bahia* and *Rio Grande do Sul* and much of the Argentine fleet, including *Rivadavia* and *Moreno*.

Ten of the main-deck 4.7in weapons had been removed from *Minas Geraes* and *São Paulo* by 1931, reducing their secondary batteries to twelve guns. Major modernisation was scheduled for the 1930s, and *Minas Geraes* was reconstructed at Rio de Janeiro Dockyard between June 1931 and the spring of 1938. She recommissioned on 10 June 1938, but further work was carried out piecemeal between 1939 and 1943.

Modifications included reboilering with six oil-fired Thornycroft units, the lower part of the former forward boiler room and the twelve side coal bunkers being converted to hold fuel oil, giving two per stokehold. The upper bunkers were removed and the upper part of the ex-boiler space used for a distilling plant. The new boilers, which allowed maximum power to be increased to 30,000ihp (for 22kt), exhausted through a new broad funnel abaft the tripod mast, the forefunnel being suppressed. New turbogenerators replaced the former dynamos. The maximum elevation of the 12in guns was increased from 15 to 18 degrees, and two further 4.7in guns installed abreast the bridge. The existing 3in AA guns were moved to a sponsored platform between the

Aerial view of *Minas Geraes* as rebuilt, with a *Carioca* class minelayer (1938–9) lying alongside. The new platforms for the 3in AA guns are clearly visible abreast the aft conning tower; see also drawing on p 62. *(Author's collection)*

Minas Geraes in 1942. *(Author's collection)*

funnel and the after conning tower, where they were joined by a further pair. Six Danish 20mm Madsen AA guns were also installed, pairs being fitted atop the superimposed turrets. The fire-control system was updated with new Zeiss rangefinders, and the searchlights moved from aft (where they were replaced by a rangefinder) to a platform halfway up the tripod mast.

Despite her modernisation, *Minas Geraes* saw little further active service, being employed during the Second World War (which Brazil joined in August 1942) as harbour defence ship at Salvador. While it had been intended to rebuild *São Paulo* as well, she was judged to be in too poor a condition and ended her career as a floating battery at Recife. Stricken on 2 July 1947, she remained temporarily in service as a training hulk, being dry-docked for the last time in November 1948. She was sold to the British Iron and Steel Corporation (Salvage) on 24 August 1951, for scrapping by Metal Industries at Faslane.[10] The ship was then prepared for the tow to the UK at Rio de Janeiro, some 4000 hours being expended, in particular on the blocking and shoring of the former 4.7in main-deck gunports.

A 'runner' crew was engaged to man the old battleship, while two British tugs, *Bustler* and *Dextrous*, were contracted for the voyage, which began at Rio on 20 September 1951, at an average speed of 4kt. 'A' turret shifted at one point, but was secured, but on 4 November the convoy was forced to heave-to by a north-westerly gale some 15nm north of the Azores, tow-lines snapping at 17:30. *São Paulo* was soon lost from view

Minas Geraes around 1942.
(NHHC NH 59893)

The Windfall Battleships

and was never seen again. A formal UK Board of Trade investigation was held in October 1954, but in the absence of any direct evidence could not determine the exact cause of the sinking, although there were suspicions that some of the gunport closures could have given way.

Minas Geraes was decommissioned on 16 May 1952, but remained a stationary headquarters ship for the Naval CinC until 17 December. Stricken on 31 December 1952, she was sold to the Italian SA Cantiere Navale de Santa Maria and departed in tow for Genoa on 1 March 1954. She arrived there on 22 April for breaking-up. Like Chile and Argentina, Brazil had acquired in 1951 two cruisers from the USA, in this case *Barosso* (ex-*Philadelphia*) and *Tamandare* (ex-*St Louis*). These gave the Brazilian navy a pair of large modern vessels, far more useful than the two old battleships, although, as already noted, Chile had seen such cruisers as a supplement to their battleship, not a replacement.

Rivadavia and *Moreno*

Argentina did not actively participate in either world war (joining the Second only in March 1945), although the conflicts kept her naval forces active in support of her neutrality. In a 1917 reorganisation, *Rivadavia* and *Moreno* became the 1st Div, the former being sent during the year to Comodoro Rivadavia to help put down one of a series of strikes by oil workers there.[11] On 17 May, *Moreno* became the first ship to use the new dry dock at Puerto Belgrano. In November she went to Rio de

Moreno and *Rivadavia* alongside early in the ships' careers. (Author's collection)

A Brazilian and an Argentine dreadnought off Rio de Janeiro, possibly in November 1917 or October 1922. (NHHC NH 50068)

Janeiro to join in celebrations for Brazil's national day. Operations became increasingly constrained, however, by a coal shortage, including the cancellation of the year's firing practice.

However, in 1918 it proved possible for *Rivadavia* to carry the President on a visit to the southern part of the country. The ship was also able to carry a new ambassador to New York, touching at Rio de Janeiro and Hampton Roads en route. She returned with a load of gold bullion, arriving at Puerto Belgrano on 23 September. In the meantime, *Moreno* carried out her scheduled training regime, including exercises in the South Atlantic. In 1920, *Moreno* became the top-firing ship of the navy, beating the armoured cruiser *Belgrano*. A continuing interest in adding a third battleship led to some suggestions that Argentina might try and buy the incomplete Italian battleship *Francesco Caracciolo*, launched in 1920 with no prospect of completion in its original role for the Italian navy.[12]

In 1922 *Rivadavia* reduced to reserve at Puerto Belgrano, *Moreno* replacing her as flagship of the 1st Div, visiting Rio de Janeiro in September and returning to Puerto Belgrano in October. In 1923 she joined her sister in reserve at Puerto Belgrano, while plans were finalised for the modernisation of the ships. These had been initiated in November 1918, with discussions between the US and Argentine authorities over having the work carried out in the USA by *Rivadavia*'s original builder, Fore River. A bill was passed the following year allocating funds for refits, and *Rivadavia* departed Puerto Belgrano on 6 August 1924, arriving at Boston on 30 August.

While work was starting on her sister's refurbishment, *Moreno*

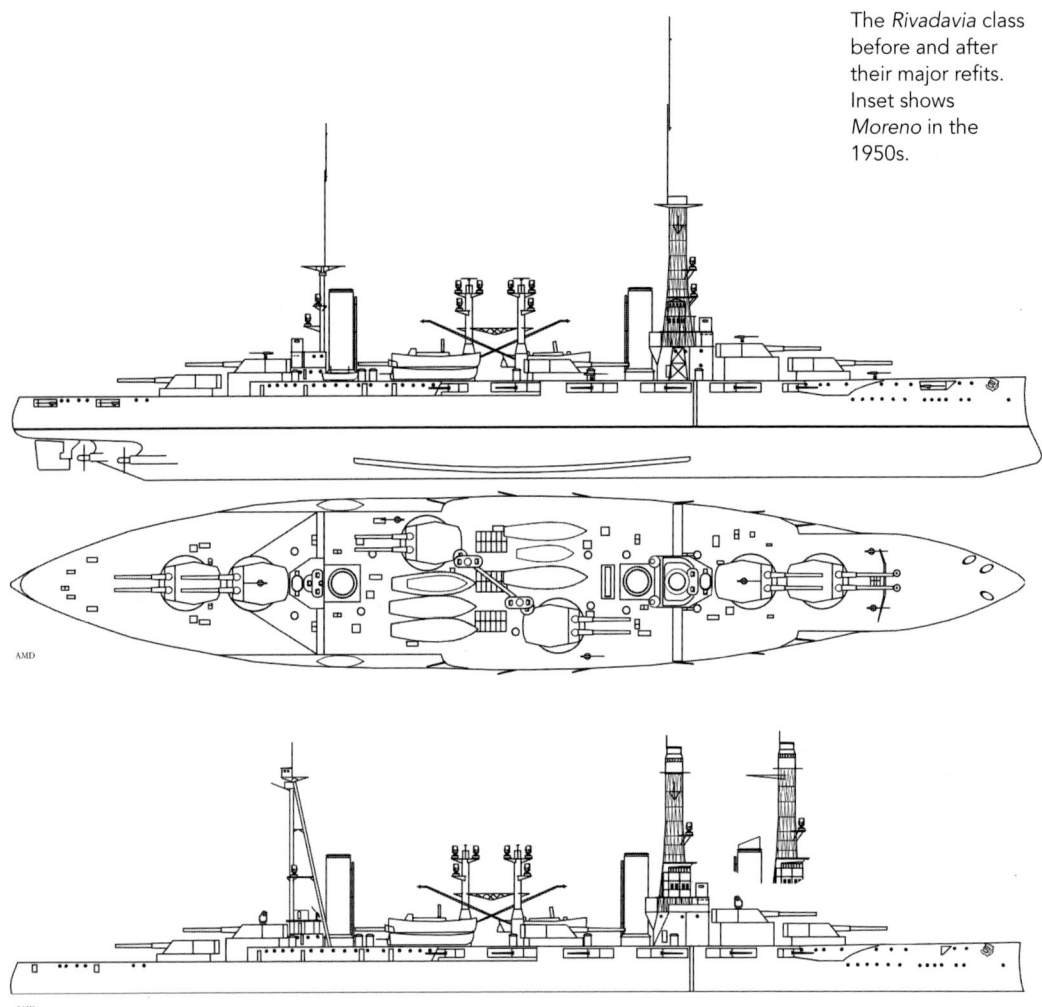

The *Rivadavia* class before and after their major refits. Inset shows *Moreno* in the 1950s.

returned to service on 24 November 1924, sailing for the Pacific via the Panama Canal for a commemoration of the centenary of the Battle of Ayacucho during the Peruvian War of Independence from Spain. She then visited Valparaiso and Callao, before transiting the Canal again and sailing for Philadelphia, whence she sailed to Quincy to join her sister at the Fore River yard.

Modifications to the sisters included changing the firing of the boilers from coal to oil (with a maximum of 5500 tons of the latter now carried) and an overhaul of the turbines and shafts. A new fire-control system was fitted, with rangefinders on 'B' and 'X' turrets, and a tripod replaced the existing mainmast. The 4in guns were deleted, and four 3in AA weapons and four 3pdrs added; the torpedo tubes were also overhauled. The ships gaining some 1000 tons during the work, but oil

Rivadavia (front) and *Moreno* refitting at the Fore River shipyard during 1925–6. (Author's collection)

firing allowed a 14 per cent increase of maximum power to 45,000 shp, trials yielding up to 23.2kt.

Work on *Rivadavia* was completed in early 1926, the ship returning home in April. *Moreno* sailed from Boston in June, arriving at Puerto Belgrano in August. The latter part of the year was occupied in both ships by working-up, trials and exercises. In 1927 both ships joined the Training Division (with *Rivadavia* as flagship), alongside the cruisers *Garibaldi* and *Buenos Aires* and the tug *Azopardo*. *Moreno* was detached in February to carry the President from Mar del Plata to Comodoro Rivadavia. *Rivadavia* conducted exercises off Mar del Plata during June and July, off San Antonio and Golfo Nuevo in September, off San Matias in early October, and off Mar del Plata again in December.

In January 1928 the Training Division was dissolved, and the ships transferred to the main fleet but *Rivadavia* and *Moreno* remained moored at Puerto Belgrano all year. The new year, however, saw the ships active once more, with *Moreno* flagship of the 1st Div, which also comprised her sister and the new destroyers *Cervantes* and *Juan de Garay*. The division exercised in the Atlantic, and visited Buenos Aires in December. In addition, *Moreno* acted as a seagoing cadet training ship for a voyage that began in mid-February and reached the latitude of the southern tip of the continent.

The two destroyers had joined the fleet in late 1927, having been bought while under construction in Spain for the Spanish navy.[13] They represented the first tranche of the 1926 Naval Procurement Act, which provided for two cruisers, five destroyers and three submarines, as well an infrastructure improvements.[14] Three similar vessels to the ex-Spanish destroyers (*Mendoza*, *La Rioja* and *Tucumán*) would be built in the UK to a direct Argentine order during 1928–9, with the cruisers *Almirante Brown* (ii) and *Veinticinco de Mayo* constructed in Italy during 1927–31. Also procured from Italy were the submarines *Santa Fé*, *Santiago del Estero* and *Salta* (commissioned 1932–3).

The battleships remained with the 1st Div into 1930, carrying out exercises in the Atlantic until the formation was dissolved on 19 September, when *Rivadavia* went into reserve. The division was re-established in 1931, with *Rivadavia* flagship of both the 1st Div and the active fleet. Both battleships carried out exercises in the Golfo Nuevo. The year 1931 saw a further step in the updating of the navy, with the commissioning of two Italian-built 7.5in-armed cruisers, *Almirante Brown* and *25 de Mayo*.

The year of 1932 saw *Rivadavia* in reduced readiness at Puerto Belgrano. *Moreno*, however, remained operational. She returned to full commission the next year, joining *Moreno* in the Armoured Division of the operational fleet. In August 1933, *Moreno* acted as flagship of a division that also included the destroyers *Tucumán*, *Mendoza* and *La Rioja*, carrying the President to Montevideo and Rio de Janeiro, returning to Puerto Belgrano on 22 October.

The years 1934–6 saw the ships serving as the Armoured Division, undertaking exercises at sea, and forming part of the Argentine-Brazilian assembly of warships that escorted the Brazilian president, embarked in *São Paulo*, to Buenos Aires (see p 242, above). In January 1937, *Rivadavia* and *Moreno* visited Valparaiso and Callao along with other units of the fleet. On 6 April, the battleships sailed for Europe, *Moreno* representing Argentina at the naval review at Spithead to mark the coronation of King George VI on 20 May, while *Rivadavia* made a visit to Brest, where she was then joined by her sister. The two battleships then proceeded to Wilhelmshaven, before returning to Puerto Belgrano on 29 June. Back with the fleet, they undertook exercises over the following two years, which saw the addition of further new ships to the navy, in particular the training cruiser *La Argentina*, commissioned in January 1939, and the seven *Buenos Aires* class destroyers. The cruiser and three destroyers (*Buenos Aires*, *Corrientes* and *Entre Rios*) had all been built at Barrow by Vickers-Armstrong, two destroyers (*Misiones* and *Santa Cruz*) coming from Cammell Laird, and two more (*San Luis* and *San Juan*) from John Brown. All were variations on contemporary Royal Navy designs.

In September 1939, *Rivadavia* and *Moreno* visited Rio de Janeiro, carrying cadets, returning to Puerto Belgrano on the 14th, escorted by

The Aging Queens of Latin America

Moreno at Wilhelmshaven in June 1937. *(Author's collection)*

the destroyers *Buenos Aires*, *Corrientes*, *Misiones* and *Santa Cruz* in view of potential risks arising from the recent outbreak of the Second World War. As Argentina remained neutral until 27 March 1945, routine remained largely unchanged, with exercises and port visits undertaken by the Armoured Division down to 1946.

That year, both ships were involved in diplomatic missions, *Rivadavia* carrying a delegation, ordered by the new President Juan Perón and led by a national senator, that left Puerto Belgrano on 29 October 1946, calling at Port of Spain, Veracruz, Havana, Puerto Principe, Ciudad Trujillo (Santo Domingo), La Guayra, Puerto Cabello, Cristóbal Colón, Cartagena and Port of Spain (again), before returning on 22 December. *Moreno* carried the Argentine Vice-President Hortensio Quijano to the inauguration of President Gabriel González Videla of Chile in November.

The ships' active careers were, however, nearing their end. Both remained active during 1947, but *Rivadavia* spent 1948 moored in Puerto Belgrano, joined by *Moreno* the following year, which now became harbour headquarters ship for the fleet, wearing the flag of the CinC in 1950. She was also used to accommodate a number of training groups. While *Moreno* continued in these roles down to 1955 (acquiring a clinker screen around her forefunnel during her very last years), *Rivadavia*'s status was steadily downgraded, until by the end of 1952 she no longer had her own crew, being under the care of that of *Moreno*. She was also now gradually being stripped of fittings, which continued into 1956. By now the Argentine navy had, like those of Brazil and Chile, acquired cruisers from the USA in 1951 (*General Belgrano* [ex-*Phoenix*] and *Neuve de Julio* [ex-*Boise*]), which provided much more

Rivadavia soon after arrival in Italy for scrapping in May 1957, and during the early stages of the breaking-up process. *(Author's collection)*

The Aging Queens of Latin America

Moreno leaving Puerto Belgrano on 12 May 1957, at the beginning of her long tow to Japan for scrapping. *(Author's collection)*

253

economical 'big ships' for Argentine high-sea service than the aging battleships.

Moreno was used to hold army personnel arrested during the September 1955 coup against President Perón, by which time she was manned by a one-third crew. She was stricken on 8 October 1956, *Rivadavia* following on the 13th, and tenders invited for the sale of the battleships for scrap.

The flag was ceremonially lowered on *Rivadavia* on 1 February 1957, and on *Moreno* on the 19th. *Rivadavia* was sold on 8 February to the Italian Azienda Ricupieri e molizione Marittimi SpA (ARDEM) for $2.28 million. She was towed to Vado Ligure, Savona (40km west of Genoa), where she arrived on 25 May; scrapping lasted into 1960–1.

Moreno was also sold on 8 February 1957, to Boston Metals (Baltimore) for $2,469,660; she was then re-sold to a Japanese breaker, Yawata Iron and Steel. On 12 May 1957, she was towed out of Puerto Belgrano by the tugs *Clyde* and *Ocean*, proceeding via the Panama Canal and Honolulu, and arriving in Japan on 16 August, after one of the longest tows to date. Lloyd's certified her total scrapping in July 1959. The funds raised by the sale of the two battleships, and that of the armoured cruiser *Pueyrredón*,[15] contributed to the purchase of the aircraft carrier HMS *Warrior* in July 1958, which became the Argentine *Independencia* in January 1959.

CHAPTER 9

Retrospect

HM Ships *Agincourt*, *Erin*, *Canada* and *Eagle* provide an interesting set of lenses for the study of the naval history of the earlier twentieth century. First, they are examples of the 'export dreadnought', something rather different from the kind of ship produced by designers employed by the major navies. Such ships were built to specifications issued by the customer navy, but the designs were very much those of the shipyards, with widely differing vessels offered against the same requirement. In doing so, they usually strove to impress through providing extra guns or speed, the most impressive of all being perhaps *Rio de Janeiro/Sultan Osman I/Agincourt* with her fourteen main guns, the largest number of big guns ever fielded on the centreline (pipping the Italian *Conte di Cavour/Caio Duilio* classes [1911, 1913] by one barrel). But while such ships seemed on the surface to show that private industry could do 'better' than the official designers (a fiction maintained to this day), the former had almost always to cut some corners on protection, habitability and operability, as became clear when taken into service by a major navy.

On the other hand, the four ships in question showed something of the sheer versatility of their designers, in the way that designs could be produced and modified in quick time, and tailored almost 'on the hoof' to emerging and changing requirements. All were ultimately the products of Josiah Perrett and Eustace Tennyson D'Eyncourt's skills as naval architects and designers, and while looking rather different, they all shared a basic DNA, seen most clearly in the elegant plough stems that separated them from their Admiralty-designed contemporaries.

Second, the ships' very existence illuminated the national rivalries of Latin America and the Balkans, whose resulting naval races absorbed huge amounts of national treasure, as well as saddling nations with increasing amounts of international debt, as foreign loans became a key part of the financing of these expensive behemoths. In these competitions, the ultimate aim of defence spending – the protection of national interests and security – became rather lost in a desire to build big, impressive ships, rather than to produce the kind of balanced force of cruisers and torpedo craft that might have been more suitable. Questions of actually operating and supporting the resulting ships were also often not properly considered, although the excessive boilering of

Almirante Latorre and *Almirante Cochrane* indicated realism on the part of the Chilean authorities as to matters of maintenance.

Third, the means by which they became parts of the Royal Navy demonstrate the difference between how a nation about to go to war deals with the assets belonging to a potential near-term enemy, and those of a confirmed neutral with whom important trade links exist. Thus, the future *Agincourt* and *Erin* were taken over without notice. Although the plan had been to reimburse their Turkish owners, the latter's rapid slide towards the Central Powers nullified this intent, contributing to long-running post-war wrangling. That the act actually made any difference to the Ottoman decision to throw in their lot with Germany, as is often alleged, seems unlikely. But it certainly provided Turkey with a useful propaganda grievance in justifying her joining hostilities against the UK. In contrast, dealings with Chile over *Canada*-to-be were utterly courteous, and the agreement reached over the battleship, and some destroyers also being built in the UK, was a generous one. When applied to the purchase of *Eagle*-to-be, such terms were rather *too* generous, since they failed to take into account the implications of trying to convert an aircraft carrier back to a battleship, with major embarrassments for the Admiralty.

Fourth, the careers of the three that served with the Grand Fleet provide case-studies on how most capital ships spent their lives during the First World War. Much of it was taken up with simply 'being' – lying at anchor in Scapa Flow, Cromarty Firth or the Firth of Forth until needed. This was, however, regularly punctuated by exercises, often within the protected confines of the anchorages, or close offshore, but sometimes comprising more extensive forays into the North Sea or the Atlantic. On occasion, these might have been prompted by actual or potential movements by the German High Seas Fleet, when contact with the Germans was conceivable. Yet it was on only one occasion that the fleets actually met in combat at Jutland, when the contrasts in the experiences of capital ships at the battle are brought into sharp relief by those of *Agincourt* and *Erin*, for significant parts of the war squadron- and division-mates (albeit not at Jutland). Firing fourteen-gun broadsides, *Agincourt* had the second-highest ammunition expenditure of any battleship in the main fleet, and hit one, if not two, German battleships. At the other end of the spectrum *Erin* was the one British capital ship of the battle not to fire a single round of main-battery ammunition.

After the war, *Erin*, as the most 'British-standard' of the trio, remained in active service for a full year after the Armistice, before taking up what was intended to be a long-term reserve role. In contrast, the other two were rapidly reduced to reserve, although *Canada* would

Retrospect

From admiral to bird of prey: HMS *Eagle*, the gift horse that underwent the greatest of all transformations. (Author's collection)

emerge twice during 1919 to act as a troopship to the Mediterranean. While her future was already becoming secure through Anglo-Chilean negotiations for her re-purchase, that of *Agincourt* was much more problematic. She was not only non-standard in design, but the 12in gun she carried was now being withdrawn from the navy along with all the remaining original dreadnoughts and battlecruisers. But she still had size and modernity, which held out the prospect of a long-term future as depot ship for the new mobile naval base concept.

Then came the Washington Naval Treaty, dooming both *Agincourt* and *Erin* to the scrapheap only a decade after launch. In contrast, the Chilean ships were about to embark on new and distinguished long-term careers. Once again *Almirante Latorre*, the former *Canada* would serve her original owners for almost four full decades, and with slightly more luck could have remained an operational warship into the 1960s. As it was, she outlived all the other South American dreadnoughts. All but one of them had also remained on the national naval lists into the 1950s, the final manifestations of the great naval races of the pre-First World War era. *Latorre*'s sister would, as HMS *Eagle*, be a pioneer of naval aviation. The first fully-effective fleet aircraft carrier in the world, she would serve the Royal Navy for two decades until sunk in action protecting Operation 'Pedesta' in 1942, the convoy that guaranteed the survival of Malta against the Axis onslaught.

Looking back from over a century after they were built, the 'windfalls' remain ships of great interest. The utterly unique and (in her final form) elegant *Agincourt* is one of the most instantly recognisable ships of the past, while the towering funnels of *Canada* and the tightly spaced funnels and 'back-to-front' mast of *Erin* also make them stand out from the uniformity of the rest of the Grand Fleet. For her whole career, *Eagle* was the only two-funnelled carrier in the world (if one disallows the horizontal ducts of Japanese vessels of the type), and again instantly distinguishable from her peers. It is hoped that this book helps fix their place in both the naval and political history of the first half of the twentieth century.

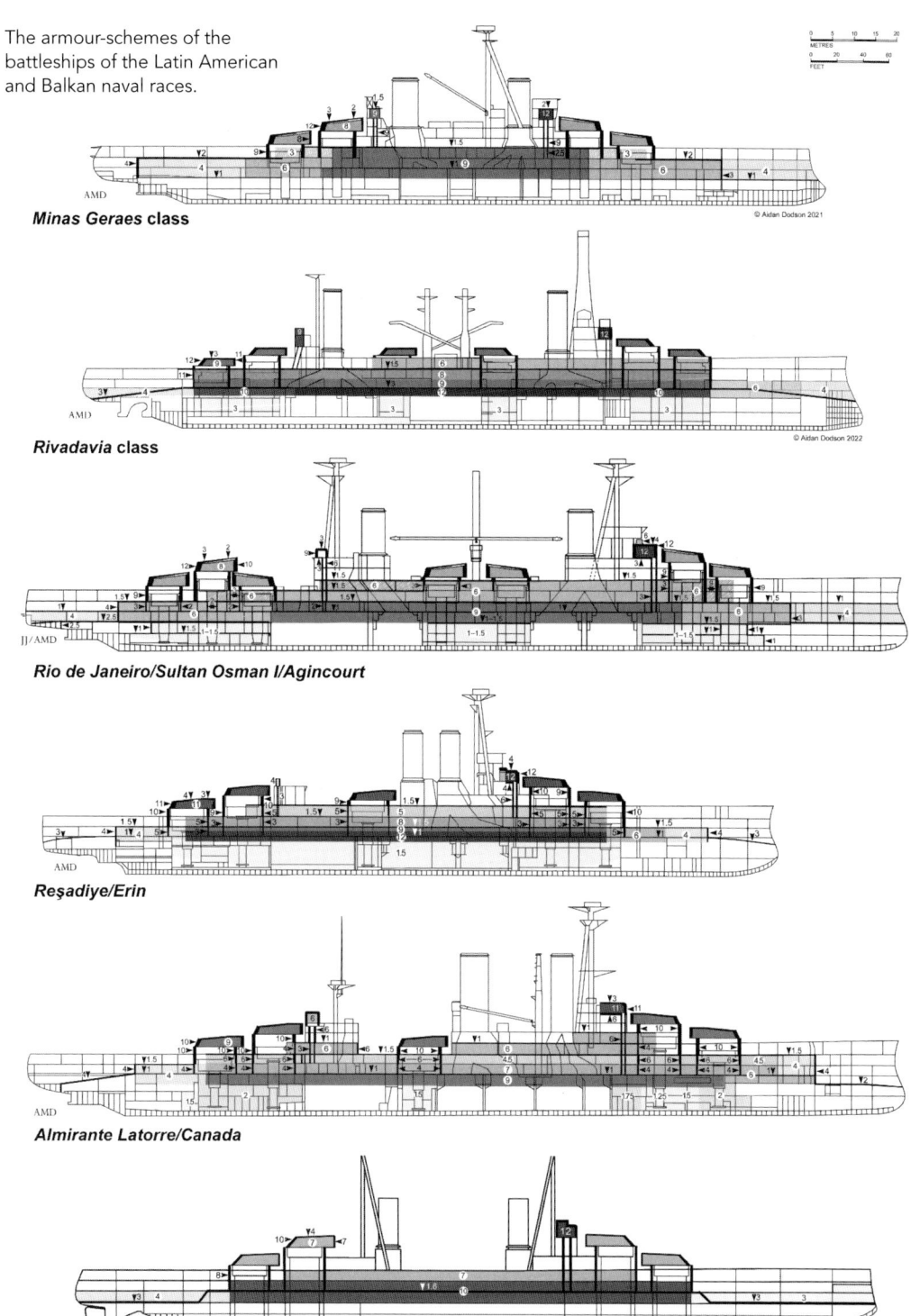

The armour-schemes of the battleships of the Latin American and Balkan naval races.

Minas Geraes class

Rivadavia class

Rio de Janeiro/Sultan Osman I/Agincourt

Reşadiye/Erin

Almirante Latorre/Canada

Salamis/Vasilèfs Giorgios

Appendix 1

Warships Under Construction for Foreign Customers in August 1914 – by Builder

Loc	Type	Cust	Yard	Name
FRA	BB	GRC	Penhoët	*Vasilèfs Konstantinos*
	DD	ARG	Dyle et Bacalan	*Rioja* = *Opinâtre* (11 Aug 14)
	DD	ARG	Dyle et Bacalan	*Mendoza* = *Aventurier* (11 Aug 14)
	DD	ARG	At & Ch Bretagne	*San Juan* = *Téméraire* (11 Aug 14)
	DD	ARG	At & Ch Bretagne	*Salta* = *Intrépide* (11 Aug 14)
	DD	TUR	Normand	Unnamed
	DD	TUR	Normand	Unnamed
	DD	TUR	Normand	Unnamed
	DD	TUR	Normand	Unnamed
	DD	TUR	Normand	Unnamed
	DD	TUR	Normand	Unnamed
	SS	GRC	Schneider	Unnamed = *Amazone* (14 Aug 15)
	SS	GRC	Schneider	Unnamed = *Antigone* (14 Aug 15)

APPENDIX 1

Disp (normal)	Laid down	Launch	Comp	Fate
23,250	9 Jul 14	–	–	Cancelled 1916.
930	1910	1911	16 Sep 14	FRA 9 Aug 14; sold 25 Apr 35; BU Toulon.
930	1910	18 Feb 11	17 Sep 14	FRA 10 Aug 14; sold 1940; BU Toulon.
930	1910	8 Dec 11	2 Nov 14	FRA 9 Aug 14; sold 26 May 37; BU.
930	1910	25 Sep 11	29 Sep 14	FRA 10 Aug 14; sold 1938; BU Toulon.
1040	–	–	–	Never begun.
1040	–	–	–	Never begun.
1040	–	–	–	Never begun.
1040	–	–	–	Never begun.
1040	–	–	–	Never begun.
1040	–	–	–	Never begun.
457/670	1913	Aug 16	18 Jun 17	FRA 3 Aug 15; sold 14 Feb 36 at Bizerte.
457/670	1912	Oct 16	18 Jun 17	FRA 3 Aug 15; sold 2 May 29 at Bizerte.

The Windfall Battleships

Loc	Type	Cust	Yard	Name
	SS	JPN	Schneider	*No 14* = *Armide* (Aug 15)
	SS	JPN	Schneider	*No 15* = *Ha10* (1923)
	SS	TUR	Schneider	Unnamed
	SS	TUR	Schneider	Unnamed
GER	BB	GRC	Vulcan	*Salamis* = *Vasilèfs Georgios* (1914)
	CL	RUS	Schichau	*Muravev-Amurskiy* = *Pillau* (1914) = *U* (1920) = *Bari* (1920)
	CL	RUS	Schichau	*Admiral Nevelskoi* = *Elbing* (9 Jan 15)
	DD	ARG	Germania	*Santiago* = *G101* (6 Aug 14)
	DD	ARG	Germania	*San Luis* = *G102* (6 Aug 14)
	DD	ARG	Germania	*Santa Fé* = *G103* (6 Aug 14)
	DD	ARG	Germania	*Tucuman* = *G104* (6 Aug 14)
	TB	NLD	Vulcan	*Z1* = *V105* (10 Aug 14) = *Mazur* (1920)

APPENDIX 1

Disp (normal)	Laid down	Launch	Comp	Fate
457/670	1912	11 Nov 13	25 Jun 16	FRA 3 Aug 15; sold 15 Feb 36.
457/670	1912	7 Apr 14	20 Jul 17	Stricken 1 Nov 28.
?	–	–	–	Never begun.
?	–	–	–	Never begun.
19,500	23 Jul 13	11 Nov 14	–	BU Bremen 1932.
4390	21 May 13	11 Apr 14	14 Dec 14	GER Aug 14; surrendered Cherbourg 20 Jul 20; to ITA Sep 20; IT commission 23 Jan 24; bombed Livorno 28 Sep 43; BU 1944–8.
4390	21 May 13	21 Nov 14	4 Sep 15	Scuttled 1 Jun 16 North Sea, after collision SMS *Posen*.
1116	1914	12 Aug 14	4 Mar 15	GER 6 Aug 14; scuttled Scapa Flow 21 Jun 19; sold 12 Sep 24; salved 13 Apr 26; re-sold & BU Jun 26–Mar 29.
1116	1914	16 Sep 14	8 Apr 15	GER 6 Aug 14; scuttled Scapa Flow 21 Jun 19; salved Jul/Aug 19; to US; bombing target off Cape Henry VA 13 Jul 21.
1116	1914	14 Nov 14	11 May 15	GER 6 Aug 14; scuttled Scapa Flow 21 Jun 19; sold 12 Sep 24; salved 30 Sep 25; re-sold; stranded in tow off Rosehearty 25 Nov 25; BU.
1116	1914	28 Nov 14	5 Jun 15	GER 6 Aug 14; scuttled Scapa Flow 21 Jun 19; sold 12 Sep 24; salved 30 Apr 26; re-sold & BU Aug 26–Mar 29.
421	1914	26 Aug 14	5 Jan 15	GER 10 Aug 14; surrendered Rosyth 19 Aug 20; to BRA; POL 1920; bombed GER aircraft Oksywie 1 Sep 39.

Loc	Type	Cust	Yard	Name
	TB	NLD	Vulcan	Z2 = *V106* (10 Aug 14)
	TB	NLD	Vulcan	Z3 = *V107* (10 Aug 14)
	TB	NLD	Vulcan	Z4 = *V108* (10 Aug 14) = *Kaszub* (1920)
	SS	A-H	Germania	U7 = *U66* (28 Nov 14)
	SS	A-H	Germania	U8 = *U67* (28 Nov 14)
	SS	A-H	Germania	U9 = *U68* (28 Nov 14)
	SS	A-H	Germania	U10 = *U69* (28 Nov 14)
	SS	A-H	Germania	U11 = *U70* (28 Nov 14)
	SS	NOR	Germania	A5 = *U0* (14 Aug 14) = *UA* (28 Aug 14)
ITA	DD	ROM	Pattison	*Vijelie* = *Sparviero* (Jun 15) = *Mărăști* (Jul 20) = *Lovkyi* (Oct 44) = *D1* (1948) = *D11* (1952) = *D3* (1956)
	DD	ROM	Pattison	*Vârtej* = *Nibbio* (Jun 15) = *Mărăști* (Jul 20) = *Legkyi* (Oct 44) = *D2* (1948) = *D12* (1952) = *D4* (1956)

APPENDIX 1

Disp (normal)	Laid down	Launch	Comp	Fate
421	1914	26 Aug 15	25 Jan 15	GER 10 Aug 14; surrendered Rosyth 19 Aug 20; sold 13 Jun 21; BU.
421	1914	12 Dec 14	3 Mar 15	GER 10 Aug 14; mined off Libau 8 May 15.
421	1914	12 Dec 14	23 Mar 15	GER 10 Aug 14; surrendered Rosyth 5 Aug 20; to POL 1920; internal explosion Danzig 20 Jul 25; salved 29 Jul 25 & BU.
791/933	1913	22 Apr 15	23 Jul 15	GER 28 Nov 14; missing North Sea after 3 Sep 17.
791/933	1913	15 May 15	4 Aug 15	GER 28 Nov 14; surrendered Harwich 20 Nov 18; sold 17 Jun 20; BU Fareham.
791/933	1913	1 Jun 15	17 Aug 15	GER 28 Nov 14; gunfire HMS *Farnborough* off Dunmore Head 22 Mar 16.
791/933	1913	24 Jun 15	4 Sep 15	GER 28 Nov 14; missing Irish Sea after 24 Jul 17.
791/933	1913	20 Jul 15	22 Sep 15	GER 28 Nov 14; surrendered Harwich 20 Nov 18; sold 3 Mar 19; BU Bo'ness 1922.
270/335	1912	9 May 14	14 Aug 14	GER 5 Aug 14; surrendered Harwich 24 Nov 18; foundered in tow off Folkstone Apr 19.
1600	29 Jan 14	26 Mar 17	15 Jul 17	ITA 5 Jun 15; ROM 1 Jul 1920; USSR 20 Oct 44; ROM 12 Oct 45; stricken Apr 61.
1600	15 Jul 14	30 Jan 18	15 May 18	ITA 5 Jun 15; ROM 1 Jul 1920; USSR 20 Oct 44; ROM 12 Oct 45; stricken Apr 61.

Loc	Type	Cust	Yard	Name
	DD	ROM	Pattison	*Vifor* = *Aquila* (Jun 15) = *Melilla* (Jan 39)
	DD	ROM	Pattison	*Viscol* = *Falco* (Jun 15) = *Ceuta* (Jan 39)
	DD	PRT	Ansaldo	*Liz* = *Arno* (Mar 15)
	DD	TUR	Orlando	Unnamed
	DD	TUR	Orlando	Unnamed
	DD	TUR	Orlando	Unnamed
	DD	TUR	Orlando	Unnamed
	SS	GER	San Giorgio	*U42* = *Balilla* (Jun 15)
	SS	RUS	San Georgio	*Svyatoy Georgiy* = *Argonauta* (Jun 15)
UK	BB	TUR	Armstrong	*Sultan Osman I* (ex-*Rio de Janeiro*) = *Agincourt* (2 Aug 14)
	BB	TUR	Vickers	*Reşadiye* (ex-*Mehmed Reşad V*) = *Erin* (2 Aug 14)
	BB	CHL	Armstrong	*Almirante Latorre* (ex-*Valparaiso*) = *Canada* (9 Sep 14) = *Almirante Latorre* (1 Aug 20)
	BB	CHL	Armstrong	*Almirante Cochrane* (ex-*Santiago*) = *Eagle* (Mar 18)
	BB	BRA	Armstrong	*Riachuelo*
	BB	TUR	Vickers	*Fatih Sultan Mehmed*

Appendix 1

Disp (normal)	Laid down	Launch	Comp	Fate
1600	11 Mar 14	26 Jul 16	8 Feb 17	ITA 5 Jun 15; SPA 5 Jan 39; BU 1950.
1600	19 Aug 16	16 Aug 19	20 Jan 20	ITA 5 Jun 15; SPA 5 Jan 39; BU 1948.
600	1914	22 Dec 14	Jun 15	UK Mar 15; collision HMS *Hope* off Dardanelles 23 Mar 18.
672	–	–	–	Never begun.
672	–	–	–	Never begun.
672	–	–	–	Never begun.
672	–	–	–	Never begun.
728/875	18 Aug 13	4 Aug 15	8 Aug 15	ITA Jun 15; gunfire A-H TBs Adriatic 14 Jul 16.
255/306	11 Mar 13	5 Jul 14	1 Feb 15	ITA Jun 15; stricken 1928.
27,528	14 Sep 11	22 Jan 13	25 Aug 14	UK 2 Aug 14; sold 22 Jan 23; BU Rosyth Jan 23–Mar 25.
22,750	1 Aug 11	3 Sep 13	Aug 14	UK 2 Aug 14; sold 16 Jan 23; BU Queenborough.
28,000	1 May 12	27 Nov 13	13 Sep 15	UK 9 Sep 14; CHL 1 Aug 20; sold Feb 59; BU Japan.
28,000	24 Feb 13	8 Jun 18	Feb 24	UK 28 Feb 18; torpedoed GER *U73* Mediterranean 11 Aug 42.
30,500	–	–	–	Work stopped 13 May 15.
22,750	Jun 14	–	–	Cleared from slip Sep 14.

Loc	Type	Cust	Yard	Name
	CDS	NOR	Armstrong	*Bjørgvin* = *Glatton* (Apr 15)
	CDS	NOR	Armstrong	*Nidaros* = *Gorgon* (Apr 15)
	CL	GRC	Cammell Laird	*Antinavarchos Kountouriotis* = *Birkenhead* (1915)
	CL	GRC	Cammell Laird	*Lambros Katsonis* = *Chester* (1915)
	CL	TUR	Armstrong	Unnamed [Job 877]
	CL	TUR	Armstrong	Unnamed [Job 878]
	DD	TUR	Hawthorn Leslie	Unnamed = *Napier* (Nov 14) = *Talisman* (15 Feb 15)
	DD	TUR	Hawthorn Leslie	Unnamed = *Narbrough* (Nov 14) = *Termagant* (15 Feb 15)
	DD	TUR	Hawthorn Leslie	Unnamed = *Offa* (Nov 14) = *Trident* (15 Feb 15)
	DD	TUR	Hawthorn Leslie	Unnamed = *Ogre* (Nov 14) = *Turbulent* (15 Feb 15)
	DD	GRC	J Brown	*Kriti* = *Medea* (Aug 14)
	DD	GRC	J Brown	*Lesvos* = *Medusa* (Aug 14)
	DD	GRC	Fairfield	*Chios* = *Melampus* (Aug 14)
	DD	GRC	Fairfield	*Samos* = *Melpomene* (Aug 14)

APPENDIX 1

Disp (normal)	Laid down	Launch	Comp	Fate
4900	26 May 13	9 Jun 14	8 Sep 18	UK Nov 14; scuttled DD torpedoes after internal explosion Dover 16 Sep 18; salved May 25–Mar 26 & BU.
4900	11 Jun 13	8 Aug 14	25 May 18	UK Nov 14; sold 28 Aug 28; BU Pembroke Dock.
5185	27 Apr 14	18 Jan 15	May 15	UK c Feb 15; sold 26 Oct 21; BU Newport.
5235	7 Oct 14	8 Dec 15	May 16	UK c Feb 15; sold 9 Nov 21; BU Llanelli.
3550	–	–	–	UK 2 Aug 14; work stopped Jan 15.
3550	–	–	–	UK 2 Aug 14; work stopped Jan 15.
1098	7 Dec 14	15 Jul 15	1 Jan 16	UK 2 Aug 14; sold 9 May 21; BU Greys.
1098	17 Dec 14	26 Aug 15	18 Mar 16	UK 2 Aug 14; sold 9 May 21; BU Briton Ferry 25 Jan 23.
1098	1 Jul 15	20 Nov 15	24 Mar 16	UK 2 Aug 14; sold 9 May 21; BU Greys.
1098	1915	5 Jan 16	May 16	UK 2 Aug 14; collision GER BB *Westfalen* North Sea 1 Jun 16.
1007	8 Apr 14	30 Jan 15	May 15	UK Aug 14; sold 9 May 21; BU Milford Haven Oct 22.
1007	1914	27 Mar 15	1915	UK Aug 14; collision UK DD *Laverock* off Schleswig 25 Mar 16.
1040	1914	16 Dec 14	29 Jun 15	UK Aug 14; sold 22 Sep 21; BU Germany.
1040	1914	1 Feb 15	16 Aug 15	UK Aug 14; sold 9 May 21; BU New Holland.

269

The Windfall Battleships

Loc	Type	Cust	Yard	Name
	DD	JPN	Yarrow	*Urakaze*
	DD	JPN	Yarrow	*Kawakaze* = *Intrepido* (5 Jul 16) = *Audace* (25 Sep 16) = *TA20* (21 Oct 43)
	DD	CHL	White	*Almirante Simpson* = *Faulknor* (Aug 14) = *Almirante Riveros* (ii) (May 20)
	DD	CHL	White	*Almirante Goñi* = *Broke* (Aug 14) = *Almirante Uribe* (May 20)
	DD	CHL	White	*Almirante Williams* = *Botha* (Aug 14) = *Almirante Williams* (May 20)
	DD	CHL	White	*Almirante Riveros* = *Tipperary* (Aug 14)
	SS	TUR	Beardmore	Unnamed
	SS	TUR	Beardmore	Unnamed
USA	BB	ARG	Fore River	*Rivadavia*
	BB	ARG	NY Sbg	*Moreno*
	SS	CHL	Seattle C & DD	*Iquique* = *CC1* (Aug 14)
	SS	CHL	Seattle C & DD	*Antofagasta* = *CC2* (Aug 14)

Appendix 1

Disp (normal)	Laid down	Launch	Comp	Fate
907	1 Oct 13	16 Feb 15	14 Oct 15	Delivered 1919; hulked 1936; bombed US aircraft Yokosuka 18 Jul 45; BU 1948.
922	1 Oct 13	27 Sep 15	23 Dec 16	ITA 3 Jul 16; captured GER 12 Sep 43; gunfire UK DE *Avon Vale* and *Wheatland* off Zadar 1 Nov 44.
1694	1913	26 Feb 14	25 Aug 14	UK Aug 14; to CHL May 20; stricken 1933; expended as target by *Latorre* 1940.
1704	1913	25 May 14	1914	UK Aug 14; to CHL May 20; stricken 1933.
1742	1913	2 Dec 14	1915	UK Aug 14; to CHL May 20; stricken 1933.
1737	1913	5 Mar 15	Jun 15	UK Aug 14; gunfire GER BB North Sea 31 May 16.
665/800	–	–	–	Material used for UK *E25*.
665/800	–	–	–	Material used for UK *E26*.
27,940	25 May 10	26 Aug 11	Dec 14	Sold 8 Feb 57; BU Savona 1957–61.
27,940	9 Jul 10	23 Sep 11	25 Feb 15	Sold 11 Jan 57; BU Japan from Aug 57.
313/373	1911	3 Jun 13	1914	CAN 6 Aug 14; discarded 1925.
313/373	1911	31 Dec 13	1914	CAN 6 Aug 14; discarded 1925.

Appendix 2

Warships Under Construction for Foreign Customers in August 1914 – by Customer

Customer	Type	Name	Builder	Ordered/Purchased
Austria-Hungary	SS	*U7*	Germania, GER	1913
	SS	*U8*	Germania, GER	1913
	SS	*U9*	Germania, GER	1913
	SS	*U10*	Germania, GER	1913
	SS	*U11*	Germania, GER	1913
Argentina	BB	*Rivadavia*	Fore River, USA	1910
	BB	*Moreno*	NY Sbg, USA	1910
	DD	*Rioja*	Ch Bretagne, FRA	1910
	DD	*Mendoza*	Ch Bretagne, FRA	1910
	DD	*San Juan*	Ch Bretagne, FRA	1910
	DD	*Salta*	Ch Bretagne, FRA	1910
	DD	*Santiago*	Germania, GER	1914
	DD	*San Luis*	Germania, GER	1914
	DD	*Santa Fé*	Germania, GER	1914
	DD	*Tucuman*	Germania, GER	1914
Brazil	BB	*Riachuelo*	Armstrong, UK	–
Chile	BB	*Almirante Latorre*	Armstrong, UK	1911
	BB	*Almirante Cochrane*	Armstrong, UK	1912
	DD	*Almirante Simpson*	White, UK	1913
	DD	*Almirante Goñi*	White, UK	1913
	DD	*Almirante Williams*	White, UK	1913
	DD	*Almirante Riveros*	White, UK	1913
	SS	*Iquique*	Seattle C & DD, USA	1911
	SS	*Antofagasta*	Seattle C & DD, USA	1911
Germany	SS	*U42*	San Georgio, ITA	1913
Greece	BB	*Salamis*	Vulcan, GER	1912
	BB	*Vasilèfs Konstantinos*	Penhoët, FRA	1914
	CL	*Antinavarchos Kountouriotis*	Cammell Laird, UK	1914
	CL	*Lambros Katsonis*	Cammell Laird, UK	1914
	DD	*Kriti*	J Brown, UK	1914
	DD	*Lesvos*	J Brown, UK	1914
	DD	*Chios*	Fairfield, UK	1914
	DD	*Samos*	Fairfield, UK	1914
	SS	Unnamed	F Ch Gironde, FRA	1913
	SS	Unnamed	F Ch Gironde, FRA	1912

Appendix 2

Customer	Type	Name	Builder	Ordered/Purchased
Japan	DD	*Urakaze*	Yarrow, UK	1913
	DD	*Kawakaze*	Yarrow, UK	1913
	SS	*No 14*	Schneider, FRA	1912
Netherlands	TB	*Z1*	Vulcan, GER	1914
	TB	*Z2*	Vulcan, GER	1914
	TB	*Z3*	Vulcan, GER	1914
	TB	*Z4*	Vulcan, GER	1914
Norway	CDS	*Bjørgvin*	Armstrong, UK	1913
	CDS	*Nidaros*	Armstrong, UK	1913
	SS	*A5*	Germania, GER	1912
Portugal	DD	*Liz*	Ansaldo, ITA	1913
Romania	DD	*Vijelie*	Pattison, ITA	1913
	DD	*Vârtej*	Pattison, ITA	1913
	DD	*Vifor*	Pattison, ITA	1913
	DD	*Viscol*	Pattison, ITA	1913
Russia	CL	*Muravev-Amurskiy*	Schichau, GER	1913
	CL	*Admiral Nevelskoi*	Schichau, GER	1913
	SS	*Svyatoy Georgiy*	San Giorgio, ITA	1913
Turkey	BB	*Sultan Osman I*	Armstrong, UK	1913
	BB	*Reşadiye*	Vickers, UK	1911
	BB	*Fatih Sultan Mehmed*	Vickers, UK	1914
	CL	Unnamed [Job 877]	Armstrong, UK	1914
	CL	Unnamed [Job 878]	Armstrong, UK	1914
	DD	Unnamed	Hawthorn Leslie, UK	1914
	DD	Unnamed	Hawthorn Leslie, UK	1914
	DD	Unnamed	Hawthorn Leslie, UK	1914
	DD	Unnamed	Hawthorn Leslie, UK	1914
	DD	Unnamed	Normand, FRA	1914
	DD	Unnamed	Normand, FRA	1914
	DD	Unnamed	Normand, FRA	1914
	DD	Unnamed	Normand, FRA	1914
	DD	Unnamed	Normand, FRA	1914
	DD	Unnamed	Normand, FRA	1914
	DD	Unnamed	Orlando, ITA	1914
	DD	Unnamed	Orlando, ITA	1914
	DD	Unnamed	Orlando, ITA	1914
	DD	Unnamed	Orlando, ITA	1914
	DD	Unnamed	Orlando, ITA	1914
	SS	Unnamed	Beardmore, UK	1914
	SS	Unnamed	Beardmore, UK	1914
	SS	Unnamed	Schneider, FRA	1914
	SS	Unnamed	Schneider, FRA	1914

Notes

Preface

1 R Hough, *The Big Battleship: or The Curious Career of H.M.S. Agincourt* (London: Michael Joseph, 1966), p 164.
2 Ibid., pp 163–4.
3 S Breyer, *Battleships and Battle Cruisers 1905–1970* (London: Macdonald, 1973), p 136.
4 D Murfin, 'The Mobile Naval Base', *Warship* [XLII] (2020), pp 188–92.
5 Published in the USA as *The Great Dreadnought: The strange story of H.M.S. Agincourt, the mightiest battleship of World War I* (New York: Harper & Row, 1967).
6 D Topliss, 'The Brazilian Dreadnoughts 1904–1914', *Warship International* XXV/3 (1988), pp 240–89.

Chapter 1: August 1914 and Beyond

1 For a comprehensive study of capital ship-building in the UK, see I Johnston and I Buxton, *The Battleship Builders: constructing and arming British capital ships* (Barnsley: Seaforth, 2013). For a detailed account of Armstrong's shipbuilding, see P Brook, *Warships for Export: Armstrong warships 1867–1927* (Gravesend: World Ships Society, 1999).
2 For histories of Vickers down to 1914, see J D Scott, *Vickers: a history* (London: Weidenfeld and Nicolson, 1962), pp 3–94, and C Trebilcock, *The Vickers Brothers* (London: Europa Publications, 1977).
3 See Johnston and Buxton, *Battleship Builders*, pp 228–9.
4 Presumably because the standard system ('A' and 'B' for forward turrets, 'P' and 'Q' for midships mountings, and 'X' and 'Y' aft) could not handle more than six turrets.
5 The frequent statement that they were designated by the days of the week has no official basis, although it is possible that the crew may have so-referred to them colloquially.
6 Gunnery practice for gun, turret and fire-control personnel, using small (~1in calibre) rifles attached to the barrels of the big guns to simulate the actual firing.
7 The Divisional structure varied over time; the Divisions just before and just after Jutland are noted on p 177.
8 D'Eyncourt Papers, National Maritime Museum, DEY/16, dated 9 September 1914.
9 J Conlin, '"Our Dear Reşadiye": The Legend and the Loans behind Ottoman Naval Rearmament, 1908–1914', *The International History Review* 43 (2021), pp 243–62. DOI: 10.1080/07075332.2021.1938634.
10 TNA T 1/12061/22405.
11 Not as early as September 1914, as is generally stated, as Vickers maintained the hope that they might complete the ship for the Turks right up to the outbreak of war with them on 5 November, and were enquiring whether the Admiralty wished to take over the contract for the ship after this date.
12 While the *Centaur*s were the latest iteration of the ongoing 'C' class design, the Turkish pair had been essentially developments of the basic type established by *Hamidiye* (iii) and *Mecidiye* (both 1903) and perpetuated in the *Drama* (1912): see pp 102, 104. Machinery for both British and Turkish ships was to be supplied by Vickers, but was of totally different designs and built under different works numbers.
13 I Johnston, *Beardmore Built: the rise and fall of a Clydeside shipyard* (Clydebank: Clydebank District Libraries & Museums Department, 1993), p 77.
14 And (apart from US guns [Mk II] bought to be used in monitors: see pp 138–9) would not be used again until the Mk VII in the *King George V* class of the late 1930s. It had, however, been supplied by Vickers to the Japanese (for the *Kongo* class battlecruiser and *Fuso* class battleships), and the Russians (for the *Ismail* class battlecruisers), and was now the standard US calibre.
15 TNA ADM 116/1629, fol. 25–27.
16 As was also the contemporary intent in other navies, to keep the senior officers safe during combat. In the USA this was taken to the extent of providing only the most rudimentary bridgework to

make it impossible to run the ship other than from the conning tower. However, experience showed that it was often impossible to efficiently con the ship from the tower, and proper/enlarged bridgework had to be fitted in all combatant navies during and after the First World War.

[17] *Malaya*'s outturn was £3.1 million.

[18] Published statements that her big guns had been diverted to monitors are incorrect, as the only 14in guns so-employed were weapons made in the USA for the Greek battleship *Salamis* (see further pp 138–9, below).

[19] N Friedman, *Naval Weapons of World War One. Guns, torpedoes, mines and ASW weapons of all nations: an illustrated directory* (Barnsley: Seaforth, 2011), p 47.

[20] NMM ADM/SC/407, fol 16.

[21] ADM 116/1629, which holds the papers related to the purchase of *Cochrane*.

[22] TNA CAB 24/42/7.

[23] TNA CAB 23/5/42.

[24] TNA ADM 116/1629, fol 70.

[25] TNA ADM 116/1629, dated 10 May 1918.

[26] TNA ADM 116/1629, fol 69.

[27] See A Dodson, 'HMS Eagle and the Chilean Connection', *The Aviation Historian* 42 (2023), pp 36–44. J M Bruce, *The Bristol M.1* (Leatherhead: Profile Publications, 1967) – the principal publication on the type – erroneously gives (p 8) the number of M.1s as six, and places the delivery as in 1917.

[28] TNA AIR 1/39/15/2.

[29] J M Andrae, *Latin-American Military Aviation* (Leicester: Midland Counties Publications, 1982), p 95; http://ivansiminic.blogspot.com/2012/04/sucesos-de-1920.html.

[30] 'The Chilean Air Service', *Flight* XI/2 (1919), p 55.

[31] For the fates of the Babies, see http://ivansiminic.blogspot.com/2017/05/normal-0-microsoftinternetexplorer4.html.

[32] http://ivansiminic.blogspot.com/2012/04/sucesos-de-1920.html.

[33] For these, see A Dodson and D Nottelmann, *The Kaiser's Cruisers, 1871–1918* (Barnsley: Seaforth, 2021), pp 152–4.

[34] I Buxton, *Big Gun Monitors: design, construction and operations 1914–1945*, 2nd edition (Barnsley: Seaforth, 2008), pp 106–13.

[35] G Smith, *Britain's Clandestine Submarines, 1914-1915* (New Haven CT: Yale University Press, 1964); E C Fisher, 'The subterfuge submarines', *Warship International* XIV (1977), pp 200–26; J D Perkins, 'Canadian Vickers-built H class submarines of the Royal Navy', *Warship* XII (1988), pp 130–7, 203–5.

[36] The boats were all given names in 1924: *Guacolda* (*H1*); *Tegualda* (*H2*); *Rucumilla* (*H3*); *Guale* (*H4*); *Quidora* (*H5*); *Fresia* (*H6*).

[37] Dodson and Nottelmann, *Kaiser's Cruisers*, pp 181–3, 195–7.

[38] See ibid, pp 190–3.

[39] Attempts were made by the Russian authorities to continue building the four ships that had actually been laid down as fleet minesweepers, but by February 1917 they were only 18 per cent complete, and were then cancelled.

Chapter 2. The Latin-American Connection

[1] See W H Bille, 'Launch of the British Ironclad NEPTUNE', *Warship International* IV/3 (1967), pp 227–8.

[2] For the naval side of the revolution, see R L Scheina, *Latin America: a naval history 1810–1987* (Annapolis MD: Naval Institute Press, 1993), pp 59–66; this book remains the fundamental source for the naval history of South America. For the South American naval race in general, and on US perspectives on it in particular, see S W Livermore, 'Battleship diplomacy in South America: 1905-1925', *Journal of Modern History* 16 (1944), pp 341–8. See also https://reportedebatalla.wordpress.com/2019/07/12/sud-acorazados-argentina-vs-brasil-vs-chile/.

[3] It is unclear how far the various Argentine and Chilean acquisitions were direct reactions to each other, or simply parallel tracks of escalation (see Scheina, *Latin America*, p 48).

[4] https://www.secretprojects.co.uk/threads/argentinian-never-were-warship-designs-and-proposals.32632/#19.

[5] For an overview of the history of the Brazilian navy during its battleship era, see J R Martins Filho, 'The Battleship *Minas Geraes* (1908)', in B Taylor (ed), *The World of the Battleship: the lives and careers of twenty-one capital ships from the world's navies, 1880–1990* (Barnsley: Seaforth, 2018), pp 129–52.

[6] Acquired from Armstrong in October 1893; she had been purchased 'off the peg', along with five torpedo boats from Schichau and a former yacht, to give the government some kind of naval force to oppose the rebellious navy.

[7] H Lengerer, 'The Genesis of the Six-Six Fleet', *Warship* [XLI] (2019), pp 46–57.

8 As the name of the Brazilian city was then spelled; it was later changed to 'Gerais', but the ship's name was never officially altered.

9 The contract had originally stated that the machinery would be built by Humphreys & Tennant, but this firm closed down in 1907, having struggled in making the turbines for HMS *Invincible*, built by Armstrong.

10 K P Kozyurenok, 'Sankt-Peterburg - «Rio de Janeiro»', *Gangut* 38 (2006), p 81.

11 I Buxton, *Big Gun Monitors*, pp 93–105.

12 Kozyurenok, 'Sankt-Peterburg - «Rio de Janeiro»', p 82.

13 Ibid, pp 88–90.

14 Ibid, p 85.

15 My thanks go to Ian Buxton for information on the history of this dock section; see also <https://www.clydemaritime.co.uk/troon_shipbreaking/floating-dock/>

16 Topliss, 'The Brazilian Dreadnoughts 1904–1914', p 284.

17 Kozyurenok, 'Sankt-Peterburg - «Rio de Janeiro»', p 95.

18 P G Halpern, *The Mediterranean Naval Situation 1908–1914* (Cambridge MA: Harvard University Press, 1971), p 340 n104; there would have been no armament-compatibility issues, as the Italian fleet was already armed with British-pattern guns (cf n 24 below).

19 For details, see Norman Friedman, *The British Battleship 1906-1946* (Barnsley: Seaforth Publishing, 2015).

20 Ibid, pp 151, 381 nn40–42.

21 https://www.secretprojects.co.uk/threads/argentinian-never-were-warship-designs-and-proposals.32632/#322, #324.

22 S McLoughlin, *Russian and Soviet Battleships* (Annapolis MD: Naval Institute Press, 2003), pp 213–15.

23 The layout went back to the *Duilio* class laid down in 1873, and used in the first Italian dreadnought, *Dante Alighieri*, laid down in 1909. The arrangement was familiar to the Argentines though their *Garibaldi* class armoured cruisers.

24 Who part-owned both the main Italian ordnance plants, designed the guns and mountings and provided technical advice. Capacity constraints would mean that the guns and mountings for the Italian battleship *Leonardo da Vinci* (laid down in 1910) had to be built by Vickers in the UK, and both they and Italian-made systems were all badly delayed, impacting on the Italian dreadnought programme (see E Bagnasco and A de Toro, *Italian Battleships: Conte di Cavour and Duilio Classes 1911–1956* [Barnsley: Seaforth, 2021], pp 24–5, 27, 36–8; Johnston and Buxton, *Battleship Builders*, pp 200–1).

25 Scheina, *Latin America*, pp 83–4.

26 Lattice masting was also a feature of contemporary German and Russian designs, contrasting with the tripod favoured by the UK to support aloft fire-control positions. However, the only non-US ships to actually carry them were the Russian *Andrei Pervozannyi* class (1906–7).

27 For an extensive contemporary account of the Argentine ships, see 'The Argentine Battleships Moreno and Rivadavia', *Engineering* 81 (1911), pp 555–7.

28 N Friedman, *U.S. Battleships: an illustrated design history* (Annapolis MD: Naval Institute Press, 1985), pp 68–9; this design had fourteen 12in guns, but was unbalanced, and an in-house Bureau of Construction & Repair ten-gun design was chosen for what became the *Delaware* class.

29 Aidan Dodson, *The Kaiser's Battlefleet: German capital ships 1871–1918* (Barnsley: Seaforth, 2016), p 34.

30 For these see Friedman, *British Battleship*, p 384 n67.

31 An undated drawing exists of an Elswick 14in/50 gun for a 'Chilean battlecruiser', but nothing more is known about it (Friedman, *Naval Weapons*, p 49).

32 J Brooks, 'The Mast and Funnel Question: fire-control positions in British dreadnoughts 1905-1915', *Warship* XIX (1995), pp 40–60.

33 Although *Dupuy de Lôme* was indeed refitted on schedule, her actual handover to Peru did not occur until September 1912. By then, the Peruvians were having second thoughts about the utility of the old ship, especially as one of the spurs to her acquisition in the first place (the sale of the Italian cruiser *Umbria* to Ecuador) had fallen through. As a result, payments to France were stopped after only a third of the purchase price had been made, and the ship remained in the French port of Lorient while negotiations stalemated. A deal under which the ship was returned to French ownership was agreed in January 1917, the ex-*Dupuy de Lôme* being briefly used as a mooring hulk in mid-1918. She was sold for conversion to a merchant ship in October 1918, and although completed in December 1919, her career as a cargo ship was brief: after a disastrous maiden voyage, *Peruvier* (as she had been renamed)

was laid up and finally broken up in 1923. For full details of the ship's career, see L Feron, 'The cruiser *Dupuy-de-Lôme*', *Warship* XXXIII (2011), pp 32–47.

[34] Modern sources state that she (as HMS *Eagle*) differed in having thirty-two boilers, rather than *Latorre*'s twenty-one. However, the original plans show an identical machinery arrangement in both ships. The error would seem to be traceable to early 1920s editions of *Jane's Fighting Ships*, which appears to have been followed slavishly in all later sources.

Chapter 3: The Balkan Connection

[1] For a comprehensive study of naval power in the Mediterranean up to the outbreak of the First World War, see Halpern, *The Mediterranean Naval Situation 1908–1914*.

[2] For a history of the ships of the Ottoman navy, see B Langensiepen and A Güleryüz, *The Ottoman Steam Navy 1828–1923* (London: Conway Maritime Press, 1995); see also I A Sturton, 'Through British Eyes: Constantinople Dockyard, the Ottoman Navy, and the Last Ironclad. 1876–1909', *Warship International* LVII/2 (2020), pp 132–66, which corrects a number of errors in Langensiepen and Güleryüz's volume.

[3] Described in detail in 'The Reconstruction of the Turkish Battleship "Mesoudie"', *Engineering* 71 (1901), pp 529–30.

[4] For this, and the immediately following, see Langensiepen and Güleryüz, *Ottoman Steam Navy*, pp 16–18, and D. Nottelmann, *Die Brandenburg-Klasse: Höhepunkt des deutschen Panzerschiffbaus* (Hamburg: E S Mittler, 2002), pp 80–7.

[5] Brook, *Warships for Export*, pp 143–4; Friedman, *British Battleship*, pp 384–5 nn78–80.

[6] Brook, *Warships for Export*, pp 143–4.

[7] Friedman, *British Battleship*, p 385 n81.

[8] See Conlin, '"Our Dear Reşadiye"'.

[9] Kozyurenok, 'Sankt-Peterburg - «Rio de Janeiro»', p 95.

[10] On Turko-Russian relations during the lead-up to the First World War see R P Bobroff, *Roads to Glory: Late Imperial Russia and the Turkish Straits* (London: I B Tauris, 2006); for Russian planning and negotiations at this time, see also Halpern, *The Mediterranean Naval Situation 1908–1914*, pp 308–11.

[11] While the first two vessels did indeed commission on schedule, delays in the delivery of her British-built machinery meant that *Aleksandr III* was not ready until 1917.

[12] McLoughlin, *Russian and Soviet Battleships*, p 283.

[13] Conlin, '"Our Dear Reşadiye"'.

[14] McLoughlin, *Russian and Soviet Battleships*, p 284.

[15] Discussions for which had been ongoing since early 1913, probably with the same Vickers/Armstrong/Brown work-sharing as with *Reşadiye* (cf Johnston and Buxton, *Battleship Builders*, pp 286–7).

[16] To be delivered in 24 and 26 months, respectively.

[17] To be delivered in 21, 22, 23 and 24 months, respectively.

[18] Written by James Stewart (ADM 137/881, fol. 257–71).

[19] Having been worn out during the Balkan wars, they had been removed and sent to the UK for re-lining.

[20] It appears that they had been laid down as 'speculations' with the connivance of the Italian navy to get round a lack of funds in the relevant years of the navy's budget (Dodson, *Before the Battlecruiser*, p 101).

[21] Orlando seem to have been fairly confident of the market, as they ordered the guns for a further ship of the class that was never built (ibid).

[22] Differing from her Italian sisters, which had 10in and 8in weapons.

[23] P Brook, 'Armstrong's unbuilt warships', *Warship* XXI (1997–1998), pp 32–3.

[24] For British bids in general, see Friedman, *British Battleship*, pp 158, 384–5.

[25] Johnston and Buxton, *Battleship Builders*, p 285.

[26] Thanks go to Dirk Nottelmann for providing copies of the Greek telegram and the Tirpitz minute from the German archives.

[27] Brook, 'Armstrong's unbuilt warships', p 33.

[28] Johnston and Buxton, *Battleship Builders*, pp 288–9.

[29] A report (in H W Underwood, 'Professional Notes', *Proceedings of the United States Naval Institute* 46/9 (1920), p 1501) that she was taken to Kiel and used as an accommodation ship finds no support in either wartime aerial photographs of Kiel (information courtesy of Dirk Nottelmann), the records of the Naval Inter-Allied Control Commission, or the documentation relating to the ship in TNA.

[30] For the history of these weapons, see Buxton, *Big Gun Monitors*, pp 11, 16–17, 21, 229–30.

[31] Friedman, *Naval Weapons*, p 47.

[32] The following account is based on papers held on TNA ADM 116/2461, together with Z Fotakis, *Greek naval strategy and policy, 1910-1919* (London: Routledge, 2005).

[33] On the execution of this part of the Treaty, see A Dodson and S Cant, *Spoils of War: the fate of enemy fleets after the two world wars* (Barnsley: Seaforth, 2020), pp 33, 75–80, 88–91.
[34] For the relationships between the two powers and their 1930 Naval Protocol, see D Chessum, 'The Greece-Turkey Naval Protocol of 1930', *Warship International* LVIII/3 (2021), pp 193–8.

Chapter 4: With the Grand Fleet
[1] TNA ADM 137/995, dated 19 November 1914.
[2] Respectively then comprising: *Sutlej, Doris, Juno, Isis, Venus* and *Pelorus*; *Amphitrite, Argonaut, Europa, Highflyer, Vindictive* and *Challenger*; and *Bacchante, Charybdis, Diana, Eclipse* and *Talbot*.
[3] TNA ADM 137/995, dated 19 Dec 14.
[4] For the battle, see J Campbell, *Jutland: an analysis of the fighting* (London: Conway Maritime Press, 1986).
[5] I McCallum, 'The Riddle of the Shells, 1914-1918', *Warship* XXV (2002–3), pp 3–25; XXVI (2004), pp 9–20; XXVII (2005), pp 9–24.
[6] NMM ADM/SC/336A.
[7] While leaving the Forth on the evening of the 31st, the submarines *K4* and *K17* were sunk in collisions, and *K6, K7, K14* and *K22*, and the cruiser *Fearless* all damaged, in what was dubbed 'the Battle of May Island'.

Chapter 5: Alternative Service: *Erin*, *Canada* and *Agincourt*
[1] NMM ADM/SC/336B.
[2] D Snook, 'British naval operations in the Black Sea, 1918-1920, Part I', *Warship International* XXVI/1 (1989), pp 44–50.
[3] On this and the immediately following, see Murfin, 'The Mobile Naval Base'.
[4] Scheina, *Latin America*, p 354 n8.

Chapter 6: Alternative Service: *Eagle*
[1] For a history of British early aircraft-carrying vessels, see N Friedman, *British Carrier Aviation: the evolution of the ships and their aircraft* (London: Conway Maritime Press, 1988), pp 22–89, and R D Layman, *Before the Aircraft Carrier: the development of aviation vessels 1849–1922* (London: Conway Maritime Press, 1989) pp 31–81.
[2] For overviews of the ship's development and career, see D Brown, *HMS Eagle*, Warship Profile 35 (Windsor: Profile Publications, 1973); Friedman, *British Carrier Aviation*, pp 73–87. These have been supplemented and corrected by material from *Eagle*'s ship's covers, TNA ADM/SC/406A–C.
[3] ADM/SC/407, fol 3–10.
[4] It replaced *Repulse*'s original 6in main belt, the latter being shifted to form the battlecruiser's new upper belt.
[5] The only exceptions were the small number of true flush-deck carriers, with no islands at all, and the Japanese *Akagi* and *Hiryu*, which had theirs to port. For the latter, see H Lengerer, 'The aircraft carriers of the *Shôkaku* class', *Warship* XXXVII (2015), pp 90–1.
[6] See Friedman, *British Carrier Aviation*, pp 79–81.
[7] This paragraph is not wholly correct: the 6in guns were actually those originally ordered for *Cochrane* (p 194), while the main mountings, and most of the guns, were still incomplete (p 33).
[8] NMM ADM/SC406A, fol. 59.
[9] NMM ADM/SC406A, fol. 76.
[10] NMM ADM/SC/336B.

Chapter 7. Ends and New Beginnings.
[1] *Medea* and *Melpomene* to Ward on 9 May, *Melampus* to Cohen on 22 September, *Birkenhead* to Cashmore on 26 October, and *Chester* to Rees on 9 November.
[2] This sale comprised some quarter of a million tons of warships, including five battleships (one of which was *Dreadnought*), six big cruisers, six light cruisers, three flotilla leaders and a swathe of destroyers. Owing to the sheer number of ships involved, and yard capacity, some would not actually be broken up for some time, the cruiser *Sutlej* as late as 1924 (cf p 219).
[3] *Collingwood* and *Colossus*, which at the time of the conference formed a boys' training establishment at Portland, could also be retained in their roles as hulks. However, *Collingwood* was paid off at the end of March 1922 and sold for scrap in December, and the establishment closed on 11 May 1922. *Colossus* then transferred to Devonport to become an accommodation ship for the boys' training establishment *Impregnable*, in commission from 3 January 1924 until paid off on 3 January 1928; she was sold for scrap in August.
[4] It was also permitted that one vessel could be retained at a time as a disarmed mobile target ship; at the time of the conference this was *Agamemnon*.
[5] While they were both soon converted to aircraft carriers, planning for which reconstruction was already under way, this was *not* under Article IX of

the Washington Treaty (under which *Lexington*, *Saratoga*, *Akagi* and *Kaga* were converted by the USA and Japan), as neither *Courageous* nor *Glorious* had been listed for disposal in the Treaty's Section II.
6 TNA ADM1/8620/35.
7 For the following see TNA ADM1/8620/35.
8 TNA ADM 1/8620/35.
9 The Washington Treaty required that breaking up 'shall always involve the destruction or removal of all machinery, boilers and armour, and all deck, side and bottom plating'.
10 Johnston and Buxton, *Battleship Builders*, p 291.
11 Friedman, *British Battleship*, p 384 n70.
12 Some published sources state that *Princess Royal* was offered to Chile, but this finds no support in the archives.
13 P Somervell, 'Naval Affairs in Chilean Politics, 1910–1932', *Journal of Latin American Studies* 16 (1984), pp 389–90.

Chapter 8: The Aging Queens of Latin America

1 On this and the following, see D Chessum, 'A Naval History of Interwar Naval Arms Control' (PhD Dissertation, University of New South Wales, 2017), §4.3; see also G J Montenegro, 'An Argentinian naval buildup in the disarmament era: the Naval Procurement Act of 1926', *Warship* XXV (2002–3), p 119.
2 For a detailed account of *Latorre*'s Chilean career, see C Tromben Corbalán and F Wilson Lazo, 'Almirante Latorre', in Taylor (ed), *The World of the Battleship*, pp 247–67.
3 Completed in 1915, sold out of Admiralty service in 1948, and foundered in Norwegian waters in 2018.
4 For this, see W F Sater, 'The Abortive Kronstadt: The Chilean Naval Mutiny of 1931', *Hispanic American Historical Review* 60 (1980), pp 239–68.
5 I A Sturton, 'Battleship End-Notes: *Almirante Latorre*,' *Warship* XXVIII (2006), pp 124–5.
6 TNA ADM 1/25807, dated 14 February 1952.
7 T&WA DS.VA/6/38/4, dated 14 September 1953.
8 T&WA DS.VA/6/38/4, dated 4 November 1953.
9 *Mikasa* had been stripped of many components in the wake of the Japanese defeat in the Second World War.
10 For this and the following, see C Baker, *What Happened to the Battleship: 1945 to the present* (Barnsley: Seaforth, 2022), pp 261–2.
11 For the ships' careers, see http://www.histarmar.com.ar/Armada%20Argentina/HistoriaAcorazadosArgentinos.htm, http://www.histarmar.com.ar/Armada%20Argentina/Buques1900a1970/AcARARivadavia-Historia.htm, http://www.histarmar.com.ar/Armada%20Argentina/Buques1900a1970/AcARAMoreno-Historia.htm.
12 The Italian navy had planned to complete the ship as an aircraft carrier, along similar lines to HMS *Argus* (cf p 193), but funds were never available, and the hull was sold for conversion to a merchantman, which in turn did not happen; although the hull remained laid up for some time, the ongoing costs of preservation resulted in it being sold for scrap in the autumn of 1926 (E Cernuschi and V P O'Hara, 'Search for a Flattop: the Italian navy and the aircraft carrier 1907–2007', *Warship* XXIX [2007], pp 63–7).
13 *Cervantes* was ex-*Churruca* and *Juan de Garay* was ex-*Alcala Galiano*; replacements with the same names were built for Spain. They were modified versions of the British *Scott* class.
14 Montenegro, 'An Argentinian naval buildup in the disarmament era', pp 120–3.
15 Also originally sold to Boston Metals, but in her case re-sold to ARDEM and broken up near *Rivadavia* from July 1957.

Bibliography

Andrae, J M, *Latin-American Military Aviation* (Leicester: Midland Counties Publications, 1982).

Anon, 'The Argentine Battleships Moreno and Rivadavia', *Engineering* 81 (1911), pp 555–7.

——, 'The Reconstruction of the Turkish Battleship "Mesoudie"', *Engineering* 71 (1901), pp 529–30.

Bagnasco E, and A de Toro, *Italian Battleships: Conte di Cavour and Duilio Classes 1911–1956* (Barnsley: Seaforth, 2021).

Baker, C, *What Happened to the Battleship: 1945 to the present* (Barnsley: Seaforth, 2022).

Bille, W H, 'Launch of the British Ironclad NEPTUNE', *Warship International* IV/3 (1967), pp 227–8.

Bobroff, R P, *Roads to Glory: Late Imperial Russia and the Turkish Straits* (London: I B Tauris, 2006).

Breyer, S, *Battleships and Battle Cruisers 1905–1970* (London: Macdonald, 1973).

Brook, P, 'Armstrong's unbuilt warships', *Warship* XXI (1997–1998), pp 26–35.

——, *Warships for Export: Armstrong warships 1867–1927* (Gravesend: World Ships Society, 1999).

Brooks, J, 'The Mast and Funnel Question: fire-control positions in British dreadnoughts 1905-1915', *Warship* XIX (1995), pp 40–60.

Brown, D, *HMS Eagle*, Warship Profile 35 (Windsor: Profile Publications, 1973).

Bruce, J M, *The Bristol M.1* (Leatherhead: Profile Publications, 1967).

Buxton, I, *Big Gun Monitors: design, construction and operations 1914–1945*, 2nd edition (Barnsley: Seaforth, 2008).

Campbell, J, *Jutland: an analysis of the fighting* (London: Conway Maritime Press, 1986).

Cernuschi, E, and V P O'Hara, 'Search for a Flattop: the Italian navy and the aircraft carrier 1907–2007', *Warship* XXIX (2007), pp 61–80.

Chessum, D, 'A Naval History of Interwar Naval Arms Control' (PhD Dissertation, University of New South Wales, 2017).

——, 'The Greece-Turkey Naval Protocol of 1930', *Warship International* LVIII/3 (2021), pp 193-8.

Conlin, J, '"Our Dear Reşadiye": The Legend and the Loans behind Ottoman Naval Rearmament, 1908–1914', *International History Review* 43 (2021), pp 243–62. DOI: 10.1080/07075332.2021.1938634.

Dodson, A, *The Kaiser's Battlefleet: German capital ships 1871–1918* (Barnsley: Seaforth, 2016).

————, 'HMS Eagle and the Chilean Connection', *The Aviation Historian* 42 (2023), pp 36–44.

————, and S Cant, *Spoils of War: the fate of enemy fleets after the two world wars* (Barnsley: Seaforth, 2020).

————, and D Nottelmann, *The Kaiser's Cruisers, 1871–1918* (Barnsley: Seaforth, 2021).

Feron, L, 'The cruiser *Dupuy-de-Lôme*', *Warship* XXXIII (2011), pp 32–47.

Fisher, E C, 'The subterfuge submarines', *Warship International* XIV/3 (1977), pp 200–26.

Fotakis, Z, *Greek naval strategy and policy, 1910-1919* (London: Routledge, 2005).

Friedman, N, *British Carrier Aviation: the evolution of the ships and their aircraft* (London: Conway Maritime Press, 1988).

————, *Naval Weapons of World War One. Guns, torpedoes, mines and ASW weapons of all nations: an illustrated directory* (Barnsley: Seaforth, 2011).

————, *The British Battleship 1906-1946* (Barnsley: Seaforth Publishing, 2015).

————, *U.S. Battleships: an illustrated design history* (Annapolis MD: Naval Institute Press, 1985).

Gratz, G A, 'Re: The Brazilian Dreadnoughts 1904–1914', *Warship International* XXXI/3 (1994), pp 221–5.

Halpern, P G, *The Mediterranean Naval Situation 1908–1914* (Cambridge MA: Harvard University Press, 1971).

Hough, R, *The Big Battleship: or The Curious Career of H.M.S. Agincourt* (London: Michael Joseph, 1966)/*The Great Dreadnought: The strange story of H.M.S. Agincourt, the mightiest battleship of World War I* (New York: Harper & Row, 1967).

Jellicoe, J R, *The Grand Fleet 1914–1916: its creation, development and work* (London: Cassell).

Johnston, I, *Beardmore Built: the rise and fall of a Clydeside shipyard* (Clydebank: Clydebank District Libraries & Museums Department, 1993).

Johnston, I, and I Buxton, *The Battleship Builders: constructing and arming British capital ships* (Barnsley: Seaforth, 2013).
Kozyurenok, K P, 'Sankt-Peterburg - «Rio de Janeiro»', *Gangut* 38 (2006), pp 80–101.
Langensiepen, B, and A Güleryüz, *The Ottoman Steam Navy 1828–1923* (London: Conway Maritime Press, 1995).
Layman, R D, *Before the Aircraft Carrier: the development of aviation vessels 1849–1922* (London: Conway Maritime Press, 1989).
Lengerer, H, 'The aircraft carriers of the *Shôkaku* class', *Warship* XXXVII (2015), pp 90–109.
_____ , 'The Genesis of the Six-Six Fleet', *Warship* [XLI] (2019), pp 46–57.
Livermore, S W, 'Battleship diplomacy in South America: 1905-1925', *Journal of Modern History* 16 (1944), pp 341–8.
Martins Filho, J R, 'The Battleship *Minas Geraes* (1908)', in B Taylor (ed), *The World of the Battleship: the lives and careers of twenty-one capital ships from the world's navies, 1880–1990* (Barnsley: Seaforth, 2018), pp 129–52.
McCallum, I, 'The Riddle of the Shells, 1914-1918', *Warship* XXV (2002–3), pp 3–25; XXVI (2004), pp 9–20; XXVII (2005), pp 9–24.
McLoughlin, S, *Russian and Soviet Battleships* (Annapolis MD: Naval Institute Press, 2003).
Montenegro, G J, 'An Argentinian naval buildup in the disarmament era: the Naval Procurement Act of 1926', *Warship* XXV (2002–3), pp 116–25.
Murfin, D, 'The Mobile Naval Base', *Warship* [XLII] (2020), pp 188–92.
Nottelmann, D, *Die Brandenburg-Klasse: Höhepunkt des deutschen Panzerschiffbaus* (Hamburg: E S Mittler, 2002),
Perkins, J D, 'Canadian Vickers-built H class submarines of the Royal Navy', *Warship* XII (1988), pp 130–37, 203–5.
Sater, W F, 'The Abortive Kronstadt: The Chilean Naval Mutiny of 1931', *Hispanic American Historical Review* 60 (1980), pp 239–68.
Scheina, R L, *Latin America: a naval history 1810–1987* (Annapolis MD: Naval Institute Press, 1993).
Scott, J D, *Vickers: a history* (London: Weidenfeld and Nicolson, 1962).
Smith, G, *Britain's Clandestine Submarines, 1914-1915* (New Haven CT: Yale University Press, 1964).
Snook, D, 'British naval operations in the Black Sea, 1918-1920, Part I', *Warship International* XXVI/1 (1989), pp 36–50.
Somervell, P, 'Naval Affairs in Chilean Politics, 1910–1932', *Journal of Latin American Studies* 16 (1984), pp 381–402.
Sturton, I A, 'Battleship End-Notes: *Almirante Latorre*,' *Warship* XXVIII (2006), pp 124–5.
_____ , 'Through British Eyes: Constantinople Dockyard, the Ottoman Navy, and the Last Ironclad. 1876–1909', *Warship International* LVII/2 (2020), pp 132–66.
Topliss, D, 'The Brazilian Dreadnoughts 1904–1914', *Warship International* XXV/3 (1988), pp 240–89.
Trebilcock, C, *The Vickers Brothers* (London: Europa Publications, 1977).
Tromben Corbalán, C, and F Wilson Lazo, '*Almirante Latorre*', in B Taylor (ed), *The World of the Battleship: the lives and careers of twenty-one capital ships from the world's navies, 1880–1990* (Barnsley: Seaforth, 2018), pp 247–67.
Underwood, H W, 'Professional Notes', *Proceedings of the United States Naval Institute* 46/9 (1920), pp 1493–539).

Web-pages

<http://dreadnoughtproject.org/tfs/index.php/H.M.S._Agincourt_(1913)>
<http://dreadnoughtproject.org/tfs/index.php/H.M.S._Canada_(1913)>
<http://dreadnoughtproject.org/tfs/index.php/H.M.S._Erin_(1913)>
<http://dreadnoughtproject.org/tfs/index.php/Herbert_William_Richmond>
<http://dreadnoughtproject.org/tfs/index.php/Percival_Henry_Hall_Thompson>
<http://dreadnoughtproject.org/tfs/index.php/Victor_Albert_Stanley>
<http://dreadnoughtproject.org/tfs/index.php/Walter_Maurice_Ellerton>
<http://dreadnoughtproject.org/tfs/index.php/William_Douglas_Paton>
<http://www.dreadnoughtproject.org/tfs/index.php/Adolphus_Huddlestone_Williamson>
<http://www.dreadnoughtproject.org/tfs/index.php/Douglas_Romilly_Lothian_Nicholson>
<http://www.dreadnoughtproject.org/tfs/index.php/George_Napier_Tomlin>
<http://www.dreadnoughtproject.org/tfs/index.php/Henry_Lancelot_Mawbey>
<http://www.dreadnoughtproject.org/tfs/index.php/Henry_Montagu_Doughty>
<http://www.dreadnoughtproject.org/tfs/index.php/Hugh_Dudley_Richards_Watson>
<http://www.dreadnoughtproject.org/tfs/index.php/James_Clement_Ley>
<http://www.dreadnoughtproject.org/tfs/index.php/Robert_Cecil_Hamilton>

<http://www.dreadnoughtproject.org/tfs/index.php/Vincent_Lewin_Bowring>
<http://www.dreadnoughtproject.org/tfs/index.php/William_Coldingham_Masters_Nicholson>
<https://www.clydemaritime.co.uk/troon_shipbreaking/floating-dock/>
<http://www.histarmar.com.ar/Armada%20Argentina/Buques1900a1970/AcARARivadavia-Historia.htm>
<http://www.histarmar.com.ar/Armada%20Argentina/Buques1900a1970/AcARAMoreno-Historia.htm>
<http://www.histarmar.com.ar/Armada%20Argentina/HistoriaAcorazadosArgentinos.htm>
<http://ivansiminic.blogspot.com/2012/04/sucesos-de-1920.html>
<http://ivansiminic.blogspot.com/2017/05/normal-0-microsoftinternetexplorer4.html>
<https://reportedebatalla.wordpress.com/2019/07/12/sud-acorazados-argentina-vs-brasil-vs-chile/>
<https://www.secretprojects.co.uk/threads/argentinian-never-were-warship-designs-and-proposals.32632/#19>
<https://www.secretprojects.co.uk/threads/argentinian-never-were-warship-designs-and-proposals.32632/>

Archival material

UK National Archives
ADM 1/8599/18
ADM 1/8620/35
ADM 53/32973
ADM 53/32974
ADM 53/32975
ADM 53/32976
ADM 53/32977
ADM 53/32978
ADM 53/32979
ADM 53/32980
ADM 53/32981
ADM 53/36910
ADM 53/36911
ADM 53/36912
ADM 53/36913
ADM 53/36914
ADM 53/36915
ADM 53/36916
ADM 53/36917
ADM 53/36918
ADM 53/40989
ADM 53/40990
ADM 53/40991
ADM 53/40992
ADM 53/40993
ADM 53/40994
ADM 53/40995
ADM 53/40996
ADM 53/40997
ADM 53/40998
ADM 53/40999
ADM 53/41000
ADM 53/41001
ADM 53/41002
ADM 53/41003
ADM 53/41004
ADM 53/69499
ADM 53/69500
ADM 53/69501
ADM 53/69502
ADM 53/69503
ADM 53/77048
ADM 53/77049
ADM 53/77050
ADM 116/1629
ADM 137/881/2
ADM 137/995
AIR 1/39/15/4
AIR 1/642/17/122/243
CAB 24/42/7
T 1/12061/22405

Cambridge University Library
GBR/0012/MS Vickers Doc 26
GBR/0012/MS Vickers Doc 27
GBR/0012/MS Vickers Doc 28
GBR/0012/MS Vickers Doc 31
GBR/0012/MS Vickers Doc 52
GBR/0012/MS Vickers Doc 52
GBR/0012/MS Vickers Doc 589
GBR/0012/MS Vickers Doc 589
GBR/0012/MS Vickers Doc 705
GBR/0012/MS Vickers Doc 811
GBR/0012/MS Vickers Doc 1106
GBR/0012/MS Vickers Doc 1106
GBR/0012/MS Vickers Doc 1107
GBR/0012/MS Vickers Doc 1107
GBR/0012/MS Vickers Doc 1108
GBR/0012/MS Vickers Doc 1109
GBR/0012/MS Vickers Doc 1115
GBR/0012/MS Vickers Doc 1368
GBR/0012/MS Vickers Doc 2283
GBR/0012/MS Vickers Doc 2336
GBR/0012/MS Vickers Doc 2455

National Maritime Museum
ADM/SC/332
ADM/SC/334
ADM/SC/336A
ADM/SC/336B
ADM/SC/406A–C
DEY/16

Tyne & Wear Archives
DS.VA/6/38/4

Index

Dates are of the launch of the vessel(s)

A5 (NOR, 1914) see *UA*
Abdül Hamid (TUR, 1903) see *Hamidiye*
Abdul Hamid II, Ottoman Sultan 96, 107, 109
Abdul Kadir (TUR, nl) 100, 101
Abdül Mecidiye (TUR, 1903) see *Mecidiye*
Abdulaziz, Ottoman Sultan 96
Abercrombie (UK, 1915) 138, 154, 180
Abukir (UK, 1900) 148
Achilles (UK, 1905) 148, 182
Actée (FRA, 1909) 89
Admiral Nevelskoi (RUS, 1914) see *Elbing*
AFD4 (UK, 1912) 32, 232
AFD5 (UK, 1912) 144
Affonso Penna (BRA, 1910) 65, 74
Africa (UK, 1905) 176, 177, 191
Agamemnon (UK, 1906) 216, 281 n4
Agincourt (UK, 1913) 6–7, 8–9, 17–20, 21, 22, 23, 27, 28, 29, 33, 59, 142, 143, 144, 145, 147, 148, 149–71, 172–3, 174, 176–9, 180, 182, 185, 188–90, 214, 215–26, 255; see also *Sultan Osman I*, *Rio de Janeiro*
Agincourt (UK, nl), 27
Aguirre (PER, 1890) see *Dupuy de Lôme*
Aigli class (GRC, 1913) 128
Airco DH9 37
Ajax (UK, 1911) 170, 176–9, 188, 215
Ajax (UK, 1934) 236
Akagi (JAP, 1925) 281 n5, 282 n5
Akbar, ex-*Temeraire* (UK, 1876) 169
Akhisar class (TUR, 1904) 103
Albany (US, 1899) 57
Albemarle (UK, 1901) 176–7
Alcala Galiano (SPA, 1925) see *Juan de Garay*
Aldea (CHL, 1928) 235
Alencar, Alexandrino Faria de (Brazilian naval officer) 60, 61, 74
Alessandri Palma, Arturo (President of Chile) 230–1
Alexandrino de Alencar (BRA, 1913) see *Porpoise*
Algiers, ex-*Triumph* (UK, 1870) 169
Almirante Abreu (BRA, 1899) see *Albany*
Almirante Brown (ARG, 1880) 49
Almirante Brown (ARG, 1929) 250
Almirante Cochrane (CHL, 1874) 49
Almirante Cochrane (CHL, 1918) 15, 28, 29, 30, 33–8, 91–2, 94, 119, 120, 191, 194–5, 197, 204, 256, 266, 272, 278 n21, 281 n7; see also *Eagle*
Almirante Condell (CHL, 1890) 51
Almirante Condell (CHL, 1913) 95
Almirante Goñi (CHL, 1914) 39–40, 95, 228, 270, 272; see also *Broke*, *Almirante Uribe*

Almirante Grau (PER, 1906) 89
Almirante Guise (PER, 1915) 235
Almirante Latorre (CHL, 1913) 4, 27–32, 35, 36, 39, 75, 91–2, 93–4, 132, 133, 152, 172–3, 197, 227–8, 229, 230–40, 256, 257, 258, 266, 271, 272, 259; see also *Canada*
Almirante Lynch (CHL, 1890) 51–2
Almirante Lynch (CHL, 1912) 95, 235
Almirante Riveros (CHL, 1914) 228, 234, 236, 270; see also *Faulknor*, *Almirante Simpson*
Almirante Riveros (CHL, 1915) 39, 45, 226, 270, 272; see also *Tipperary*
Almirante Riveros (CHL, 1958) 239
Almirante Simpson (CHL, 1914) 39, 95, 228, 270, 272; see also *Faulknor*, *Almirante Riveros*
Almirante Tamandaré (BRA, 1890) 57, 58
Almirante Uribe (CHL, 1914) 40, 228, 230, 270; see also *Broke*, *Almirante Goñi*
Almirante Villar (PER, 1915) 235
Almirante Williams (CHL, 1914) 39, 95, 228, 270, 272; see also *Botha*
Almirante Williams (CHL, 1958) 239
Amazonas (BRA, 1896) 57
Amazonas (BRA, 1908) 68
Amazone (FRA, 1916) 45, 260
Amphitrite (UK, 1898) 281 n2
Anáhuac (MEX, 1898) see *Marshal Deodoro*
Andrei Pervozannyi class (RUS, 1906–7) 279 n26
Ansaldo, Gio & Co 53, 79, 80, 81, 83, 101, 102–05, 266, 273
Antalya (TUR, 1904) see *Nikopolis*
Antigone (FRA, 1916) 45, 260
Antinavarhos Kountouriotis (GRC, 1915) 38, 133, 268, 272; see also *Birkenhead*
Antofagasta (CHL, 1913) 42–3, 94, 270, 272; see also *CC2*
Aquidabã (BRA, 1885) 50, 51, 57, 60
Aquila (ITA, 1916) 141, 266
Aquitania (UK, 1913) 22
Araucano (CHL, 1929) 232, 236
Arethusa class (UK, 1913–14) 25
Argentina 9, 10, 38, 44, 45, 47, 48, 49, 50, 52–5, 57, 64, 69, 74, 77–89, 90, 94, 95, 116, 117, 118, 128–9, 133–4, 213, 229, 230, 233, 235, 237, 242, 243, 246–54, 260, 262, 270, 272, 282 n1
Argonaut (UK, 1898) 281 n2
Argonauta (ITA, 1914) 266
Argus (UK, 1917) 33, 193, 195, 206, 282 n12
Ark Royal (UK, 1914) 191, 192

Arkansas (US, 1911) 85, 179
Armide (FRA, 1913) 45, 262
Armstrong, Sir W G, Whitworth & Co (Elswick; Walker) 6, 8, 12, 13, 14, 17, 18, 29–31, 33, 38, 41–2, 51, 52, 53, 57, 59, 63, 65, 69, 73–7, 79, 80, 82, 83, 89, 91, 94, 102, 103, 104, 110–12, 116, 117, 118–19, 120, 124–5, 127, 128, 129, 130, 133, 137, 139, 165, 193, 194, 196, 198, 199, 208, 228, 266, 268, 272, 273, 278 n6, 279 n9, 280 n15
Armstrong Designs: 352 58; 354 58; 364 58; 365 58; 405 58; 406 58; 439A 59, 62; 494A 61; 640 71, 73, 76; 641 73; 643 69, 71, 73; 644 71, 73; 645 69, 71, 73; 653 69, 71, 73; 666 73, 89, 90; 669 90, 91; 670 73, 76, 77, 90, 91; 671 76, 77; 672 76, 77; 682 71, 73; 683 73; 684 73; 684A 73; 685 72, 73; 685A 73; 686 72, 73; 687 73; 688 72, 73; 689 72, 73, 74; 689C 111; 690 73, 74; 690A 73; 691 119; 695 89–90, 91; 696 90, 91; 698A 110, 111, 146; 698B 111; 699 110; 700 76, 110; 735 127; 737 127; 738 127; 741 127, 130, 133; 743 127; 781 76, 77; 782 76, 77; 783 76, 77; 784 76, 77; 785 76, 77; 786 76, 77; 787 76, 77; 788 76, 77
Arno (UK, 1914) 266
Asar-i Tevfik (TUR, 1868) 98, 101, 104, 105, 106, 113
Audace (ITA, 1915) 41, 270
Audacious (UK, 1912) 143, 151, 176
Australia (AUS, 1911) 156, 171
Austria-Hungary 44, 48, 96, 264, 272
Aventurier (FRA, 1911) see *Mendoza*
Averof (GRC, 1911) 107, 109, 114, 116, 126, 127
Avnillah (TUR, 1869) 98, 101, 103, 106, 113
Avro 504 36, 37
Aziziye (TUR, 1864) 98, 99

B97 (GER, 1914) 48
B98 (GER, 1915) 48
B109 (GER, 1915) 48
B110 (GER, 1915) 48
B111 (GER, 1915) 48
B112 (GER, 1915) 48
Bacchante (UK, 1901) 281 n2
Bacellar Pinto Guedes, Duarte Huet de (Brazilian Naval Officer) 69, 73, 74
Baggs, Albert G (UK Chief Gunner) 143
Bahamonde, Braulio (Chilean naval officer) 230, 231
Bahia (BRA, 1909) 63, 64, 67, 240, 243
Balilla (ITA, 1915) 266

283

Barbaros Hayreddin (TUR, 1891) 109–10, 120–1, 133
Barham (UK, 1914) 151, 153, 177–9
Bari (ITA, 1914) see *Pillau*
Barosso (BRA, 1896) 57
Barosso (BRA, 1936) 246
Barrow-in-Furness 12–13, 15, 55, 59, 61, 65–6, 67, 74, 112, 114, 115, 200, 232, 250
Bayern class (GER, 1915) 74
Beardmore, William, & Co (Dalmuir) 12, 27, 118, 128, 140, 191, 270, 273, 274
Belleisle (UK, 1876) see *Peyk-i Şeref*
Bellerophon class (UK, 1907) 19, 151
Bellerophon (UK, 1907) 20, 33, 142, 166, 176–9, 182
Benbow (UK, 1913) 33, 143, 147, 158, 176–9, 187, 188
Berkefşan (TUR, 1894) 123
Bernardino Rivadavia (ARG, 1902) 54
Berwick (UK, 1902) 182
Bethlehem Steel Corp 43, 89, 94, 128, 132, 138, 139
Birkenhead 12, 22, 129
Birkenhead (UK, 1915) 38, 39, 213, 268, 281 n1
Birmingham class (UK, 1913–18) 39, 133
Birmingham (UK, 1913) 75
Bjørgvin (NOR, 1914) see *Glatton*
Blanco Encalada (CHL, 1875) 49, 52
Blanco Encalada (CHL, 1893) 234, 235
Blenheim (UK, 1894) 188
Blohm und Voss (Hamburg) 48, 79, 83, 108–09
Blucher (GER, 1908) 107–08
Boise (US, 1936) see *Neuve de Julio*
Boston 44, 88, 247, 249
Botha (UK, 1914) 39, 227, 228, 270; see also *Almirante Williams*
Bowring, Vincent Lewin (UK naval officer) 171, 180, 190
Brazil 6, 8, 9, 12, 15, 49, 50, 51, 52, 57–77, 78, 79, 80, 84, 85, 89, 90, 96, 110, 115, 117, 118, 125, 132, 189, 229, 230, 233, 235, 237, 240–6, 247, 250, 251, 263, 266, 272
Bremse (GER, 1916) 46, 166
Breslau (GER, 1911) 23, 24
Bretagne class (FRA, 1913) 132, 133
Bretagne, Ateliers et Chantiers de (Nantes) 85, 260, 272
Bristol M.1C 37
Britannia (UK, 1904) 176–7
British Columbia 42–3
Broke (UK, 1914) 39, 227, 228, 270; see also *Almirante Goñi*, *Almirante Uribe*
Brooklyn (US, 1936) see *O'Higgins*
Brummer (GER, 1915) 46, 166
Buenos Aries class (ARG, 1937) 250–1
Buenos Aries (ARG, 1895) 52, 249
Buenos Aires (ARG, 1937) 251
Büruç-u Zafer (TUR, 1878) 96

Caesar (UK, 1996) 188
Caio Duilio class (ITA, 1913) 255
Calliope (UK, 1914) 181
Cammell Laird (Birkenhead) 12, 13, 38, 85, 128, 129, 133, 250, 268, 272; see also Laird Brothers
Campania (UK, 1892) 38, 191
Canada (UK, 1913) 7, 8, 9, 30–3, 35, 59, 151–71, 173, 175, 177–9, 182, 186, 187, 188, 197, 202, 208, 226, 255, 256, 257, 258, 259, 266; see also *Almirante Latorre*
Canadian (UK Merc, 1900) 22
Canadian Vickers (Montreal) 43
Capitan O'Brien class (CHL, 1928–9) 231
Capitan Prat (CHL, 1890) 51, 54, 92, 94
Capitán Prat (CHL, 1937) 237
Carioca class (BRA, 1938–9) 243
Carnarvon (UK, 1903) 181, 215
Caroline (UK, 1914) 9
Catamarca (ARG, 1911) 84, 89, 242
CC1 (CAN, 1913) 43, 95, 270; see also *Iquique*
CC2 (CAN, 1913) 43, 95, 270; see also *Antofagasta*
Ceara (BRA, nl) 63
Ceara (BRA, 1915) 67
Centaur class (UK, 1916) 25, 26, 224, 277 n12
Centurion (UK, 1911) 158, 164, 167, 170, 176–9, 180, 215
Ceres (UK, 1917) 182, 187
Cervantes (ARG, 1925) 249, 282 n13
Ceuta (SPA, 1919) see *Falco*
Chacabuco (ARG, nl) 53
Chacabuco (CHL, 1898) 44, 53, 230
Challenger (UK, 1902) 281 n2
Chao Ho (CHN, 1911) 129, 137
Charles Mitchell & Co (Low Walker) 12
Charybdis (UK, 1893) 281 n2
Chatham class (UK, 1911–15) 133
Chatham Dockyard 22, 38, 55, 184, 188, 199, 200, 216, 227
Chester (UK, 1915) 38, 39, 204, 213, 268, 281 n1; see also *Lambros Katsonis*
CH14 (CAN, 1915) 43
CH15 (CAN, 1915) 43
Chile 7, 9, 12, 13, 15, 19, 27, 28, 29–30, 33, 35–8, 39–40, 42, 43, 44, 49, 50, 51, 52, 53, 54, 55, 57, 58, 59, 74, 78, 89, 90, 91, 92–3, 94–5, 107, 117, 118, 120, 132, 133, 182, 196–8, 199, 200–01, 203–04, 226–40, 246, 251, 256, 258, 272
Chios (GRC, 1914) 40, 133, 268, 272; see also *Melampus*
Churchill, Winston 17, 22, 134
Churruca (SPA, 1925) see *Cervantes*
Cochrane (UK, 1905) 143
Collingwood (UK, 1908) 158, 162, 176–9, 182, 215, 281 n3
Colossus class (UK, 1910) 61, 92
Colossus (UK, 1910) 158, 176–9, 215, 281 n3
Commonwealth (UK, 1903) 176–7, 181
Connecticut class (US, 1904–6) 134
Conqueror (UK, 1911) 147, 169, 170, 176–7, 180, 181, 215
Constantinople (Istanbul) 96, 98, 99, 100, 101, 103, 105, 106, 109, 110, 113, 118, 124, 186, 188
Constitucion (CHL, 1903) see *Swiftsure*
Conte de Cavour class (ITA, 1911) 255
Córdoba (ARG, 1912) 85, 89
Cornwall (UK, 1902) 164, 181, 182
Coronel Bolognesi (PER, 1906) 89
Corrientes (ARG, 1937) 250, 251
Courageous (UK, 1916) 42, 206, 209, 214, 282 n5
Coventry Ordnance Works 13, 128, 133, 226

Cramp, William & Sons (Philadelphia) 79, 102, 128
Crescent (UK, 1892) 169
Cressy (UK, 1899) 148
Cromarty Firth 144, 148, 149, 150, 153, 154, 155, 156, 159, 161, 162, 168, 256
Curtis Falcon 234

D1 (ROM, 1917) see *Sparviero*
D2 (ROM, 1918) see *Nibbio*
D3 (ROM, 1917) see *Sparviero*
D4 (ROM, 1918) see *Nibbio*
D11 (ROM, 1917) see *Sparviero*
D12 (ROM, 1918) see *Nibbio*
Dante Alighieri (ITA, 1910) 279 n23
Dartmouth (UK, 1910) 180
Delaware (US, 1909) 89, 165, 178–9, 279 n28
Delfin (GRC, 1911) 127
Demirhisar class (TUR, 1907) 107
Deodoro (BRA, 1898) see *Marshal Deodoro*
Derfflinger (GER, 1913) 143
Despatch (UK, 1919) 199
Devonport Dockyard 16, 22, 40, 184, 186, 199, 200, 208, 209, 214, 215, 216, 227, 232, 281
Diana (UK, 1895) 281 n2
Dimirhisar (TUR, 1907) 123
Diomede (UK, 1919) 199
Dogger Bank, Battle of 147
Dominion (UK, 1903) 30, 164, 165, 176–7, 180, 182
Doris (UK, 1896) 281 n2
Doughty, Henry Montagu (UK naval officer) 154, 163, 180
Drama (TUR, 1912) see *Libia*
Dreadnought (UK, 1906) 8, 19, 20, 33, 60, 63, 90, 143, 151, 176–9, 181
Dresden class (GER, 1907–8) 70
Dreyer fire control table 31, 159
Drski (BUL, 1907) 141
Duff, Alexander (UK naval officer) 148
Duilio class (ITA, 1876–8) 279 n23
Duilio class (ITA, 1913) see *Caio Duilio*
Duncan (UK, 1901) 176
Dunedin (UK, 1918) 199
Dupuy de Lôme (FRA, 1890) 89, 94
Durban (UK, 1919) 199
Dyle et Bacalan, Société Anonyme de Travaux (Bordeaux) 85, 260

E25 (UK, 1915) 27, 271
E26 (UK, 1915) 27, 271
E42 (UK, 1915) 168
Eagle (UK, 1918) 7, 9, 38, 59, 191–212, 227, 255, 256–8, 266; see also *Almirante Cochrane*
Eastern Construction Committee 118
Eclipse (UK, 1894) 281 n2
Edwards, Don Agustín (Chilean diplomat) 94, 226
Eidsvold class (NOR, 1900) 58
Elbing (GER, 1914) 46, 262
Elli, Battle of 114
Ellerton, Walter Maurice (UK naval officer) 164, 170, 181
Elswick 28, 35, 59, 63, 69, 75, 90, 94, 119
Elswick Ordnance Company 12, 13, 15, 19, 23, 120, 279
Emerald (UK, 1920) 199
Emperor of India (UK, 1913) 33, 143, 147, 158, 162, 176–9, 182, 187

Endymion (UK, 1891) 180, 182
Enterprise (UK, 1919) 199
Entre Rios (ARG, 1937) 250
Enver Pasha (Turkish politician) 24
Erin (UK, 1913) 7, 8, 9, 14, 20–3, 28, 31, 32, 33, 59, 142–74, 176–9, 181, 183–5, 214–15, 216, 217, 226, 255–8, 266; see also *Reşadiye*
Esmeralda (CHL, 1883) 12, 51, 92
Esmeralda (CHL, 1896) 52
Essex (UK, 1901) 181, 182
Europa (UK, 1897) 281 n2
Exeter (UK, 1929) 236
Exmouth (UK, 1901) 176

F1 (BRA, 1914) 67
F3 (BRA, 1914) 67
F5 (BRA, 1914) 67
Fairfield Shipbuilding & Engineering Co (Govan) 12, 13, 40, 58, 128, 133, 199, 268, 272
Falco (ITA, 1919) 141, 266
Falmouth (UK, 1910) 160
Fatih (TUR, 1868) see *König Wilhelm*
Fatih Sultan Mehmed (TUR, nl) 15, 26, 44, 118, 119, 120, 124, 266, 273
Faulknor (UK, 1914) 39, 227, 228, 270; see also *Almirante Simpson*, *Almirante Riveros*
Fearless (UK, 1912) 281 n7
Fei Hung (CHN, 1912) see *Helle*
Felixstowe F2A 38
Ferre (PER, 1912)
Feth-i Bülend (TUR, 1869) 98, 101, 103, 106
Feyza-i Bahri (TUR, nl) 100
Fiat-San Giorgio (La Spezia) 67
First Balkan War 113–14, 128, 129
floating dock 12, 26, 32, 65, 74, 118, 124, 127, 140, 144, 155, 162, 167, 168, 169, 183, 232; see also *AFD4*, *AFD5*
Florida (US, 1910) 165, 178–9
Ford 5-AT-C 234
Fore River Ship and Engine Company (Quincy MA) 43, 44, 79, 80, 83, 84, 85, 86, 89, 94, 247, 248, 249, 270, 272
Forges et Chantiers de la Méditerranée (La Seyne) 44, 51, 57, 58, 79, 83, 118
Forth, Forth of 16, 144, 157, 160, 168, 169, 170, 171, 219, 256, 281 n7
France 33, 37, 39, 41, 44, 45, 47, 65, 75, 77, 79, 80, 81, 83, 84, 85, 89, 94, 96, 106, 113, 116, 117, 118, 125, 127, 128, 132, 133, 136, 137, 141, 214, 229, 231, 236, 247, 260–1, 263, 272, 279
Francesco Caracciolo (ITA, 1920) 247
Franz Ferdinand, Archduke 16
Fresia (CHL, 1915) see *H6*
Furious (UK, 1896) 181
Furious (UK, 1916) 39, 42, 161, 165, 191, 192, 196, 206
Fuso class (JAP, 1914–15) 277 n14

G37 class (GER, 1915) 47
G101 (GER, 1914) 47, 262
G102 (GER, 1914) 47, 262
G103 (GER, 1914) 47, 262
G104 (GER, 1914) 47, 262
Garibaldi (ARG, 1895) 52, 53, 88, 249
Gavriil (RUS, 1915) 47
Gayret-i Vetaniye (TUR, 1909) 110, 123

General Belgrano (ARG, 1897) 52, 89
General Belgrano (ARG, 1938) 251
General O'Higgins (CHL, 1897) 52, 53, 234, 235
General Wolfe (UK, 1915) 26
George V, King 17, 137, 149, 169
Germania, Schiff-und Maschinenbau-AG (Kiel) 47, 48, 58, 79, 80, 84, 85, 101, 104, 122, 128, 137, 262, 264, 272, 273
Germany 8, 17, 19, 23, 24, 40, 41, 44, 45–8, 70, 71, 75, 79, 81, 83, 84, 88, 89, 96, 98, 107, 108, 109–10, 112, 113, 114, 123, 125, 128, 131, 133, 134, 137, 138, 139–40, 142, 147, 148, 154, 155, 156, 158, 160, 166, 167, 169, 170, 212, 219, 240, 256, 262–9, 272–3
Giuseppe Garibaldi (ITA, 1895) see *Garibaldi* (ARG)
Giuseppe Garibaldi (ITA, 1898) see *Pueyrredón*
Giuseppe Garibaldi (ITA, 1899) 113
Glatton (UK, 1914) 41–2, 165, 268
Glorious (UK, 1916) 206, 214, 282 n5
Goeben (GER, 1911) 23, 24, 108, 140; see also *Yavuz Sultan Selim*
Gogland class (RUS, nl) 47
Gomez Carreño, Luis (Chilean naval officer) 226
González Videla, Gabriel (President of Chile) 251
Gorgon (UK, 1914) 41–2, 165, 213, 268
Greece 12, 38, 39, 40, 44, 45, 75, 85, 96, 107, 109, 112, 113, 114, 116, 120, 125–41, 204, 213, 260, 262, 268, 272
Guacolda (CHL, 1915) see *H1*
Guale (CHL, 1915) see *H4*

'H' class (UK, 1915–20) 43, 138, 229
H1–H10 (UK, 1915) 43
H1 (CHL, 1915) 44, 278 n36
H2 (CHL, 1915) 44, 278 n36
H3 (CHL, 1915) 44, 278 n36
H4 (CHL, 1915) 44, 235, 278 n36
H5 (CHL, 1915) 44, 278 n36
H6 (CHL, 1915) 44, 278 n36
H11–H20 (UK, 1915) 43
H13 (UK, 1915) see *H1* (CHL)
H14 (UK, 1915) see *CH14*
H15 (UK, 1915) see *CH15*
H16 (UK, 1915) see *H2* (CHL)
H17 (UK, 1915) see *H3* (CHL)
H18 (UK, 1915) see *H4* (CHL)
H19 (UK, 1915) see *H5* (CHL)
H20 (UK, 1915) see *H6* (CHL)
Hamidabad (TUR, 1907) 123
Hamidiye (TUR, 1875) 96
Hamidiye (TUR, 1885) 96, 98, 100
Hamidiye (TUR, 1903) 25, 104, 113, 114, 121–2, 277 n12
Hamilton, Robert Cecil (UK naval officer) 171, 180
Hannibal (UK, 1896) 188
Haruna (JPN, 1913) 41
Hawke (UK, 1891) 148
Hawthorn, Leslie, R & W & Co (Hebburn) 12, 26, 118, 268, 273
Helle (GRC, 1912) 136, 137
Hercules (UK, 1910) 156, 157, 158, 176–9, 190, 215
Hermes (UK, 1898) 191
Hermes (UK, 1919) 33, 35, 39, 193, 194, 195, 196, 199, 206, 208

Hermione (UK, 1893) 180
Hibernia (UK, 1905) 176–7, 191
Hiei (JPN, 1912) 40
Hifz-ur Rahman (TUR, 1869) 100
Highflyer (UK, 1898) 281 n2
Hindustan (UK, 1903) 176–7
Hogue (UK, 1900) 148
Hrabri (BUL, 1907) 141
Huáscar (PER, CHL, 1865) 51
Hüdavendiagar (TUR, nl) 100
Humaytá (BRA, 1927) 58
Humber (UK, 1913) 67
Humphreys, Tennant & Co (Deptford) 13, 279 n9
Hyacinth (UK, 1898) 180
Hyatt (CHL, 1928) 235
Hydra (GRC, 1889) 125, 126, 128

Ibáñez, Carlos (President of Chile) 231
İclaliye (TUR, 1869) 96, 98
Idaho (US, 1905) see *Lemnos*
Idaho (US, 1917) 136
Imperator Aleksandr III (RUS, 1914) 116, 280 n11
Imperatritsa Ekaterina Velekaya (RUS, 1914) 116
Imperatritsa Mariya (RUS, 1913), 116
Imperial Ottoman Docks, Arsenals and Naval Construction Company 116, 124
Imperieuse (UK, 1869) 219
Impregnable (UK establishment) 281 n3
Indefatigable class (UK, 1909–11) 19
Indefatigable (UK, 1909) 92
Independencia class (ARG, 1890–1) 242
Independencia (ARG, 1890) 52
Independencia (ARG, 1944) 254
Independencia (BRA, 1874) 49–50, 96
Indiana class (US, 1893) 53
Indomitable (UK, 1907) 171, 203, 204, 227
Indomito class (ITA, 1912–13) 118
Inflexible (UK, 1907) 143, 171, 180, 184, 203–04, 227
Intrépide (FRA, 1911) 45, 260
Intrepido (ITA, 1915) see *Audace*
Invincible class (UK, 1907) 19, 107
Invincible (UK, 1907) 143, 279 n9
Ioann Zlatoust (RUS, 1906) 116
Iquique (CHL, 1913) 42–3, 94, 270, 272; see also *CC1*
Iron Duke class (UK, 1912–13) 19, 23, 33, 90, 151
Iron Duke (UK, 1912) 28, 142, 147, 153, 163, 170, 176, 178–9
Isis (UK, 1896) 169, 281 n2
Izyaslav class (RUS, 1915) 118

Japan 12, 13, 19, 23, 40, 41, 44, 45, 52, 55, 57, 59, 87, 134, 188, 194, 214, 235, 236, 240, 253, 254, 258, 267, 271, 273, 277, 281 n5, 282 n5
Javary (BRA, 1913) see *Severn*
Jeanne d'Arc (FRA, 1930) 236
Jellicoe, John 22, 143, 171, 274
John Brown Shipbuilding & Engineering Co (Clydebank) 12, 13, 40, 58, 77, 79, 93, 112, 120, 133, 199, 250
Juan de Garay (ARG, 1925) 249, 282 n13
Jujuy (ARG, 1912) 89, 242
Juno (UK, 1895) 281 n2
Jutland, Battle of 9, 26, 39, 156–8, 159, 226, 232, 256

K4 (UK, 1916) 281 n7
K6 (UK, 1916) 281 n7
K7 (UK, 1916) 171, 281 n7
K14 (UK, 1917) 281 n7
K17 (UK, 1917) 281 n7
K22 (UK, 1916) 281 n7
Kaga (JPN, 1921) 282 n5
Kaiser class (GER, 1911–12) 61
Kaiser (GER, 1911) 157
Kapitan Konon-Zotov (RUS, 1915) 47
Kashima class (JPN, 1905) 13, 59
Kasuga (JPN, 1903) see *Berndardino Rivadavia*
Kaszub (POL, 1915) see *V108*
Kawakaze (JPN, 1915) see also *Audace*
Kervanos (GRC, 1912) 128, 129
Kilkis (GRC, 1905) 136, 140
King Alfred (UK, 1901) 180, 181
King Edward VII class (UK, 1903–5) 19, 31, 59
King Edward VII (UK, 1903) 176–7, 182
King George V class (UK, 1911–12) 20, 22, 23, 28, 33, 92, 151, 214
King George V (UK, 1911) 20, 23, 28, 33, 92, 170, 171, 176–9, 183, 184, 215, 277 n14
Kirishima (JPN, 1913) 41
Knox, Philander (US politician) 94
Kolberg class (GER, 1908–9) 70
Kongo (JPN, 1912) 40, 124, 277 n14
König class (GER, 1913–14) 134
König Wilhelm (GER, 1868) 96
Konstantinos I, King of Greece 131, 132
Kriti (GRC, 1915) 40, 133, 268, 272; see also *Medea*
Kronprinz (GER, 1914) 134
Kurfürst Friedrich Wilhelm (GER, 1891) see *Barbaros Hayreddin*

La Argentina (ARG, 1937) 250
La Plata (ARG, 1874) 89
La Plata (ARG, 1911) 85
La Rioja (ARG, 1929) 250
La Seyne see Forges et Chantiers de la Méditerranée
Laird Brothers (Birkenhead) 51, 52; see also Cammell Laird
Lambros Katsonis (GRC, 1915) 38, 39, 133, 268, 272; see also *Chester*
Lemnos (GRC, 1905) 136, 140
Lemnos, Battle of 114
Langlois, Luis (Chilian naval officer) 230
Leao, Margues (Brazilian naval officer) 70
Legkyi (RUS, 1918) see *Nibbio*
Lesvos (GRC, 1915) 40, 133, 268, 272; see also *Medusa*
Letyashti (BUL, 1908) 141
Leviathan (UK, 1901) 180
Lexington (US, 1925) 282 n5
Ley, James Clement (UK naval officer) 162, 165, 182
Libertad (ARG, 1890) 52, 89
Libertad (CHL, 1903) see *Triumph*
Libertad (CHL, 1914) see *Almirante Latorre*
Libia (ITA, 1912) 104, 116
Lieutenant Ilin (RUS, 1914) 47
Lion (UK, 1910) 20, 92, 190, 196, 215, 216
Liverpool (UK, 1909) 171, 182
Liz (PRT, 1914) see *Arno*

Loch Ewe 20, 22, 142
London (UK, 1899) 182
Lord Nelson class (UK, 1906) 19, 77
Lord Nelson (UK, 1906) 180
Lovkyi (RUS, 1917) see *Sparviero*

'M' class (UK, 1914–16) 40, 203, 213
Mackensen class (GER, 1917–20) 74
Madiera (BRA, 1913) see *Mersey*
Mahmoudiye (TUR, 1864) see *Hamidiye*
Maine (US, 1890) 50
Maine (US, 1901) 136
Maipu (ARG, nl) 53
Malaya (UK, 1915) 155, 177–9, 182, 228, 278 n17
Maranhão see *Porpoise*
Mărășești (ROM, 1918) see *Nibbio*
Mărăști (ROM, 1917) see *Sparviero*
Marchant, Hippolytus 231
Mariano Moreno (ARG, 1903) 54
Markgraf (GER, 1913) 131, 134, 157
Marksman (UK, 1915) 26
Marlborough (UK, 1912) 151, 156, 157, 158, 176–9, 181, 187
Mars (UK, 1896) 169
Marshal Deodoro (BRA, 1898) 57, 58, 60
Marshal Floriano (BRA, 1899) 57, 60
Mawbey, Henry Lancelot (UK naval officer) 165, 180
Mazur (POL, 1914) see *V105*
McBride, Sir Richard (Prime Minister of British Columbia) 42–3
Mecediye (TUR, 1903) 102, 122
Medea (UK, 1915) 40, 268, 281 n1; see also *Kriti*
Medusa (UK, 1915) 40, 213, 268; see also *Lesvos*
Medway (UK, 1928) 209
Melampus (UK, 1914) 40, 268, 281 n1; see also *Chios*
Melilla (SPA, 1916) see *Aquila*
Melpomene (UK, 1891) 180
Melpomene (UK, 1915) 40, 268, 281 n1; see also *Samos*
Mendoza class (ARG, 1911) 85
Mendoza (ARG, 1911) see *Aventurier*
Menoza (ARG, 1928) 250
Mersey (UK, 1913) 67
Mesudiye (TUR, 1874) 96, 98, 100, 101, 102, 103, 104, 113, 120
Mikasa (JPN, 1900) 13, 240, 282 n9
Mikhail (RUS, 1916) 47
Minas Geraes (BRA, 1908) 59, 62, 63, 65, 66, 68, 69, 70, 74, 75, 77, 78, 79, 81, 83, 110, 240–6, 259
Ministro Zenteno (CHL, 1896) 52
Misiones (ARG, 1937) 250–1
Mississippi (US, 1905) see *Kilkis*
Mississippi (US, 1917) 135
Mitra (ARG, 1902) see *Bernardino Rivadavia*
mobile fleet base depot ship 6, 172, 188–90
Moltke (GER, 1910) 108–09, 167–8
Monarch (UK, 1911) 147, 170, 176–9, 186, 215
Montalva, José Manuel (Chilean naval officer) 231
Montt, Jorge (Chilean naval officer & politician) 52
Moreno (ARG, 1903) see *Mariano Moreno*
Moreno (ARG, 1911) 87–9, 116, 133,

242, 243, 246–54, 270, 272, 274, 279 n27, 282 n11
Muavenet-i Millye (TUR, 1909) 110, 123
Mühlgraben Shipyard (Riga) 47
Muin-i Zafer (TUR, 1869) 96, 98, 101, 103, 106, 122
Mukaddeme-i Hayir (TUR, 1872) 98, 101
Munay, John (Irish seaman) 159
Murad V, Ottoman Sultan 96
Muravev-Amurskiy (RUS, 1914) see *Pillau*

Nashville (US, 1937) see *Capitán Prat*
Nassau class (GER, 1908) 80
Natal (UK, 1905) 143, 154
Naval Construction & Armaments Co (Barrow-in-Furness) see Vickers
Navarchos Miaoulis (GRC, 1877) 125
Nea Genea (GRC, 1912) 128, 129
Necm-i Şevket (TUR, 1868) 100
Nelson (UK, 1925) 214, 215
Neptune (UK, 1874) see *Independencia* (BRA)
Neptune (UK, 1909) 61, 90, 156, 158, 176–9, 190, 215
Neshid Pasha (TUR Merc) 17
Neuve de Julio (ARG, 1936) 251
New Mexico (US, 1917) 135
New Orleans (US, 1896) 57
New York (US, 1912) 74, 129, 165, 170, 178–9
New York Navy Yard 88, 241
New York Shipbuilding (Camden NJ) 79, 85, 132, 137
New Zealand (UK, 1911) 156, 171, 190, 215, 216, 218–19, 225, 226
Newport News Shipbuilding & Dry Dock Co 79
Nibbio (ITA, 1918) 141, 264
Nicholson, Douglas Romilly Lothian (UK naval officer) 18, 154, 180
Nicholson, William Coldingham Masters (UK naval officer) 32, 162, 182
Nidaros (NOR, 1914) see *Gorgon*
Niki class (GRC, 1906–7) 125, 128
Nikopolis (GRC, 1904) 12
Niobe (UK, 1897) 180
Nisshin (JPN, 1903) see *Mariano Moreno*
No 14 (JPN, 1913) see *Armide*
No 15 (JPN, 1914) 45, 262
Noble, Sir Andrew (Director of Armstrong) 74
Nore, The 27, 39, 40, 180, 184, 185, 204, 216
Normand, Chantiers et Ateliers (Le Havre) 260, 273
Noronha, Juilio César de (Brazilian naval officer) 57, 59
North Dakota (US, 1908) 79
Nottingham (UK, 1913) 160
Nueve de Julio (ARG, 1892) 52, 88
Nümune-Hamiyet (TUR, 1909) 110, 123
Nüsretiye (TUR, 1885) see *Hamidiye*

O'Higgins (CHL, 1897) see *General O'Higgins*
O'Higgins (CHL, 1936) 237
Opinâtre (FRA, 1911) 45, 260
Orbay, Hüseyin Rauf (Turkish naval officer) 16

Orella (CHL, 1928) 235
Orfey class (RUS, 1914–16) 47
Orhaniye (TUR, 1865) 99, 100, 101
Orion class (UK, 1910–11) 28, 33, 69, 92, 151, 183, 184
Orion (UK, 1878) see *Bürüç-u Zafer*
Orion (UK, 1910) 158, 169, 170, 176–9, 215, 216, 217
Orlando, Cantiere navale Fratelli (Livorno) 125, 128, 266, 273, 280 n21
Osmaniye class (TUR, 1864–5) 100
Osmaniye (TUR, 1864) 98, 99, 101
Ottoman Empire see Turkey
Ottoman Navy League (Donanma Cemiyeti) 24, 109, 110, 112, 117

Pacts of May 54
Palmers Shipbuilding and Iron Co (Jarrow) 128
Panama Canal 43, 89, 207, 228, 232, 234, 248, 254
Panthir (GRC, 1911) 128, 129
Pará class (BRA, 1908–10) 64, 67
Pará class (BRA, 1908), 243
Paton, William Douglas (UK naval officer) 181, 185
Pattison, Societa (Naples) 141, 264, 266, 273
Pedro II, Emperor of Brazil 240
Pedro de Aragon (SPA, nl) 54
Peleng-i Derya (TUR, 1890) 123
Pelorus (UK, 1896) 281 n2
Penhoët, Ateliers et Chantiers de Saint-Nazaire 44, 128, 133, 260, 272
Perkins (US, 1909) 79
Perón, Juan 251, 254
Perrett, Josiah (Armstrong naval architect) 59, 61, 89, 110, 112, 255
Peyk-i Şeref (TUR, 1876) 96
Peyk-i Şevket (TUR, 1906) 104, 105, 122
Philadelphia (US, 1936) see *Barosso*
Philomel (NZ, 1890) 181
Phoenix (US, 1938) see *General Belgrano*
Pillau (GER, 1914) 46, 262
Piloto Sibbald (CHL, 1915) 226, 227
Pisa class (ITA, 1907–8) 58, 116, 117, 125
Porpoise (UK, 1913) see *Alexandrino de Alencar*
Portsmouth Dockyard 17, 26, 39, 40, 144, 149, 171, 184, 185, 186, 187, 188, 190, 195, 198, 199, 200, 207, 215, 277
Posen (GER, 1908) 263
Presidente Errazuriz (CHL, 1890) 51
Presidente Pinto (CHL, 1890) 51, 69
Princess Royal (UK, 1911) 20, 92, 143, 190, 196, 216, 219–20, 225–6, 282 n12
Psara (GRC, 1890) 126
Pueyrredón (ARG, 1898) 52, 54, 254

Queen (UK, 1902) 182
Queen Elizabeth class (UK, 1913–15) 19, 23, 27, 28, 31, 74, 77, 183, 232
Queen Elizabeth (UK, 1913) 33, 151, 163, 168, 169, 176–7
Queen Mary (UK, 1912) 20
Quidora (CHL, 1915) see *H5*
Quijano, Hortensio (Vice-President of Argentina) 251

Ramillies (UK, 1916) 163, 178–9

Regina Margherita class (ITA, 1901) 54, 55
Renown (UK, nl) 27, 31
Repulse (UK, nl) 27, 31
Repulse (UK, 1915) 195, 205, 231, 281 n4
Reşadiye (TUR, 1913) 14, 15, 17, 19, 20–4, 31, 42, 92, 111, 112, 114–16, 117, 118, 119–20, 124, 127, 129, 131, 132, 133, 266, 273, 259; see also *Erin*
Reshad-i-Hamiss (TUR, non-existent) 112
Resistance (UK, nl) 27, 31
Resolution (UK, 1915) 163, 166, 178–9
Revenge class (UK, 1914–16) 19, 27, 31, 77, 120, 154, 170, 183, 207, 232
Revenge (UK, 1915) 154, 156, 158, 177–9
Revolta da Armada 57
Revolta da Chibata (Revolt of the Lash) 67–8, 69, 85
Riachuelo (BRA, 1883) 50, 60, 67
Riachuelo (BRA, nl) 15, 27, 76, 77, 87, 266, 272
Richmond, Herbert William (UK naval officer) 170, 181, 185
Rio de Janeiro (BRA, 1913) 8, 59, 63, 67, 65, 69–77, 79, 85, 94, 110, 116, 118, 132, 172–3, 255, 259, 266; see also *Sultan Osman I*, *Agincourt*
Rio Grande do Sul (BRA, 1909) 63, 67, 68, 240, 242, 243
Rioja (ARG, 1911) see *Opinâtre*
Rioja (ARG, 1929) see *La Rioja*
Riquelme (CHL, 1928) 235
Ricadavia (ARG, nl) see *Pedro de Aragon*
Rivadavia (ARG, 1902) see *Bernardino Rivadavia*
Rivadavia (ARG, 1911) 84, 86–8, 116, 242, 243, 246–54, 259, 270, 272
Roca (ARG, 1903) see *Mariano Moreno*
Roca (ARG, nl) 85
Rodney (UK, 1925) 214, 215
Rogers, Calixto (Chilian naval officer) 232
Romania 44, 97, 141, 213, 264–6, 273
Rosario (ARG, 1908) 242
Rosyth 32, 144, 147, 148, 155, 156, 159, 161–2, 163, 164, 165, 166, 167, 168, 169, 170, 171, 183, 184, 185–6, 188, 190, 215, 216, 218–25, 227, 263, 265, 267
Rothschild (bankers) 75
Royal Aircraft Factory SE5A 37
Royal Arthur (UK, 1891) 182
Royal Naval College, Dartmouth 21, 180, 181
Royal Oak (UK, 1914) 151, 158, 177–9, 181, 185
Royal Sovereign class (UK, 1891–2) 107
Royal Sovereign class (UK, 1914–16) see *Revenge* class
Royal Sovereign (UK, 1915) 158, 160, 177–9, 180, 207
Rucumilla (CHL, 1915) see *H3*
Russell (UK, 1901) 176–7
Russia 24, 44, 45, 46, 47, 50, 55, 69–70, 75, 80, 94, 116, 117–18, 141, 155, 185, 235, 273
Russo-Baltic Shipyard (Reval) 46

'S' class (UK, 1918–19) 200
S49 class (GER, 1915) 47

S165 (GER, 1909) see *Muavenet-i Millye*
S166 (GER, 1909) see *Yadigar-i Millet*
S167 (GER, 1909) see *Nümune-Hamiyet*
S168 (GER, 1909) see *Gayret-i Vetaniye*
St Louis (BRA, 1938) see *Tamandare*
St Vincent class (UK, 1908–9) 90, 151
St Vincent (UK, 1908) 176–9, 180
Şaiye (TUR, nl) 100
Salamis (GRC, 1913) 45, 127, 129–31, 132, 133, 137–41, 259, 262, 272, 278 n18
Salta (ARG, 1911) see *Intrépide*
Salta (ARG, 1932) 250
Samos (GRC, 1915) 40, 133, 258, 272; see also *Melpomene*
Samsun class (TUR, 1907) 107
Samsun (TUR, 1907) 123
San Francisco (US, 1889) 57
San Luis class (ARG, 1911) 85
San Juan (ARG, 1911) see *Téméraire*
San Luis (ARG, 1914) see *G102*
San Juan (ARG, 1937) 250
San Martin (ARG, 1896) 52
Santa Cruz (ARG, 1937) 250, 251
Santa Fé (ARG, 1914) see *G103*
Santa Fé (ARG, 1931) 250
Santiago (ARG, 1914) see *G101*
Santiago del Estero (ARG, 1911) see *Panthir*
Santiago del Estero (ARG, 1932) 250
São Paulo (BRA, 1909) 59, 61, 63, 66–7, 75, 83, 115, 240–6, 250
Saratoga (US, 1925) 282 n5
Schichau, Friedrich (Danzig) 45, 47, 84, 107, 123, 137, 273, 278
Schneider, Forges et Chantiers de la Gironde (Chalon-sur-Saône) 45, 127, 128, 141, 260, 262, 273
Schroeders, Edgardo von (Chilean naval officer) 234
Schwab, Charles M (Director of Bethlehem Steel) 43, 138
Scotts Shipbuilding & Engineering Co (Greenock) 199
Searle, Alfredo (Chilean naval officer) 231
Seattle Construction and Drydock Company 95, 270, 272
Selimiye (TUR, nl) 100
Serrano (CHL, 1928) 231, 235, 236
Sevastopol class (RUS, 1911) 70, 80
Severn (UK, 1913) 67
Shannon (UK, 1906) 143
Sheerness 27, 156, 184, 185, 204
Short 184 37
Shumni (BUL, 1908) 141
Şivrihisar (TUR, 1907) 123
Škoda Works (Plzeň) 128
Smeli (BUL, 1907) 141
Soffia, Luis Guillermo (Chilean naval officer) 231
Solimões (BRA, 1913) see *Humber*
Sopwith Baby 37
Sopwith Camel 37
Sparviero (ITA, 1917) 141, 264
Speedy (UK, 1918) 188
Spetsai (GRC, 1889) 126
Sportive (UK, 1918) 188
Stanley, The Hon Victor Albert (UK naval officer) 21, 164, 181
Sterett (US, 1910) 79
Stoic (UK, 1915) see *Piloto Sibbald*

Strogi (BUL, 1908) 141
Stuart (UK, 1918) 188
Sturdee, Doveton (UK naval officer) 148
Sultan Osman I (TUR, 1913) 15, 16–18, 21, 24, 27, 42, 75, 116, 117, 118, 119, 120, 124, 132, 133, 134, 172, 255, 257, 266, 273; see also *Rio de Janeiro*, *Agincourt*
Sultan Reshad V (TUR, 1913) see *Reşadiye*, *Erin*
Sultanhisar (TUR, 1906) 123
Superb (UK, 1875) see *Hamidiye*
Superb (UK, 1907) 69, 151, 171, 176–9, 184
Sutlej (UK, 1899) 180, 219, 281 n2
Svetlana (RUS, 1915) 46
Sviatoi Evstafi (RUS, 1906) 116
Svyatoy Georgiy (RUS, 1914) see *Argonauta*
Swett, Arturo (Chilean naval officer) 231
Swiftsure (UK, 1903) 54–5, 58, 59, 107

Taft, William (US President) 79
Talbot (UK, 1895) 281 n2
Talisman (UK, 1915) 26–7, 268
Tamandaré (BRA, 1890) see *Almirante Tamandaré*
Tamandare (BRA, 1938) 246
Taşköprü class (TUR, 1907–8) 107
Tegualda (CHL, 1915) see *H2*
Temeraire (UK, 1907) 20, 33, 142, 151, 169, 171, 176–9, 215
Téméraire (FRA, 1911) 45, 260
Tennyson d'Eyncourt, Eustace (Armstrong designer) 73, 74, 255
Termagant (UK, 1915) 26, 268
Tevfik Pasha, Ahmet (Turkish statesman) 115
Texas (US, 1892) 50
Texas (US, 1912) 74, 85, 178–9
Thames Iron Works & Shipbuilding Co (Blackwall) 128
Thompson, Percival Henry Hall (UK naval officer) 181, 185
Thunderer (UK, 1911) 170, 171, 176–9, 186, 214, 215
Thyella class (GRC, 1906–7) 125, 128
Tiger (UK, 1913) 20, 90, 143
Tipperary (UK, 1915) 39, 226, 227, 228, 270; see also *Almirante Riveros*
Tirpitz, Alfred von 47, 107, 109, 131
Tokad (TUR, 1904) see *Totoi*
Tomlin, George Napier (UK naval officer) 171, 182, 228
Tordenskjold class (NOR, 1897) 58
Totoi (GRC, 1904) 129
Tribune (UK, 1918) 188
Trident (UK, 1915) 26–7, 268
Triumph (UK, 1903) 54–5, 59, 107
trooping voyages 185–8
Tucuman (ARG, 1914) see *G104*
Tucumán (ARG, 1928) 129, 250
Turbulent (UK, 1916) 26, 268
Turgut Reis (TUR, 1891) 109–10, 121, 133

Turkey 6, 7, 12, 15, 16–27, 31, 38, 65, 68, 69, 74, 75, 77, 92, 96–125, 127, 128, 129, 132, 133, 134, 140, 142, 185, 213, 256, 273

U7 (A-H, 1915) see *U66*
U8 (A-H, 1915) see *U66*
U9 (A-H, 1915) see *U66*
U9 (GER, 1910) 148
U10 (A-H, 1915) see *U66*
U11 (A-H, 1915) see *U66*
U29 (GER, 1913) 148
U42 (GER, 1915) see *Balilla*
U66 (GER, 1915) 48, 264
U67 (GER, 1915) 48, 264
U68 (GER, 1915) 48, 264
U69 (GER, 1915) 48, 264
U70 (GER, 1915) 48, 264
U73 (GER, 1940) 212, 267
UA (GE, 1914) 48, 264
Umikaze class (JPN, 1910) 41
Union Iron Works (San Francisco) 43
Urakaze (JPN, 1915) 41, 270, 273
Uruguay 49, 79, 242, 243

V5 (GER, 1912) see *Nea Genea*
V6 (GER, 1912) see *Kervanos*
V49 class (GER, 1915) 47
V99 (GER, 1915) 48
V100 (GER, 1915) 48
V105 (GER, 1914) 47, 262
V106 (GER, 1915) 47, 264
V107 (GER, 1915) 47, 264
V108 (GER, 1915) 48, 264
Valiant (UK, 1914) 155, 177–9
Valparaiso (CHL, 1913) see *Almirante Latorre*
Vampire (UK, 1917) 227
Vanguard (UK, 1909) 61, 156, 176–8
Varese (ITA, 1896) see *San Martin*
Varese (ITA, 1897) see *General Belgrano*
Vargas, Getúlio (President of Brazil) 242
Vârtej (ROM, 1918) see *Nibbio*
Vasilèfs Georgios (GRC, 1867) 125
Vasilèfs Georgios (GRC, 1914) see *Salamis*
Vasilèfs Konstantinos (GRC, nl) 44, 133, 137, 272
Vasilissa Olga (GRC, 1869) 125
Veinticinto de Mayo (ARG, 1890) 52
Veinticinco de Mayo (ARG, 1929) 250
Vengeance (UK, 1902) 13, 182
Venizelos, Eleftherios 127, 128, 129
Venus (UK, 1895) 281 n2
Vickers, Sons & Maxim/Vickers Ltd (Barrow-in-Furness) 8, 12, 13, 14, 21, 22, 23, 24, 36, 37, 41, 43, 59, 65, 66, 67, 74, 79, 80, 83, 89, 101, 110, 111, 112, 118, 119, 120, 124, 125, 127, 128, 133, 137, 200, 266, 273
Vickers Designs: 172A 59; 192 77; 211 77; 214 77; 428 81; 509 127; 512 110; 514 110; 519 110; 670 77; 671 77; 672 77; 677 76–7; 688 76–7; 689 76–7; Job 447 74
Vickers Vixen 234

Vickers-Armstrong 232, 237–9, 240, 250
Vickers-Wibault 121 234
Victoria (UK, 1887) 12
Victoria and Albert (UK, 1899) 17, 180
Videla (CHL, 1928) 235, 251
Vifor (ROM, 1916) see *Aquila*
Vijelie (ROM, 1917) see *Sparviero*
Vindictive (UK, 1897) 181, 281 n2
Vindictive (UK, 1918) 193
Vinte Quatro de Maio (BRA, 1885) see *Aquidabã*
Violet (UK, 1897) 180
Virginia class (US, 1904) 134
Viscol (ROM, 1919) see *Falco*
Von der Tann (GER, 1909) 89
Vulcan, AG (Bremen/Hamburg) 45, 46, 47–8, 60, 125, 128, 129, 130, 139–41, 262, 264, 272, 273

Wallsend Slipway 69, 93
Warrior (UK, 1944) see *Independencia*
Warspite (UK, 1913) 151, 176–9
Washington Naval Treaty 9, 185, 190, 214–15, 216, 221, 226, 229, 230, 234, 258, 282 n5
Watson, Hugh Dudley Richards (UK naval officer) 166, 171, 182
Watts, Alfred (UK naval officer) 31, 59
Weddigen, Otto (German naval officer) 148
Weißenburg (GER, 1891) see *Turgut Reis*
Westfalen (GER, 1908) 26, 269
Weymouth (UK, 1910) 182
White, J Samuel (Cowes) 12, 39, 95, 229, 270, 272
Wiesbaden (GER, 1915) 157
Wilhelm II, Kaiser 71, 108, 128, 131
Williamson, Adolphus Huddlestone (UK naval officer) 165, 166, 182
Wilson, Woodrow (US President) 134
Wyoming (US, 1911) 165, 179
'W' class (UK, 1919) 200

Xifias (GRC, 1912) 127

Yadigar-i Millet (TUR, 1909) 110, 123
Yarrow Shipbuilders (Scotstoun) 12, 25, 41, 64, 125, 133, 270
Yavuz Sultan Selim (TUR, 1911) 140
Ying Swei (CHN, 1911) 137
Yunus (TUR, 1901) 123

Z1 (NLD, 1914) see *V105*
Z2 (NLD, 1915) see *V106*
Z3 (NLD, 1915) see *V107*
Z4 (NLD, 1915) see *V108*
Zealandia (UK, 1904) 176–7
Zeballos, Estanislao (Argentine politician) 79